THE WORLD OF YESTERDAY

An Autobiography by Stefan Zweig

"And meet the time as it seeks us."
SHAKESPEARE: *Cymbeline*

THE WORLD
OF
YESTERDAY

An Autobiography by

STEFAN ZWEIG

Introduction by Harry Zohn

UNIVERSITY OF NEBRASKA PRESS · Lincoln and London

Introduction to the Bison Book Edition

HARRY ZOHN

Brandeis University

"THREE LIVES" was Stefan Zweig's working title for his autobiography in which he took one last, long, nostalgic look at
the world of yesterday to whose culture he had made a significant contribution. At the age of sixty the distinguished
Austrian man of letters felt that he had lived three lives in
three different ages: the golden "world of security" before the
First World War, the turbulent yet fruitful decade and a half
that followed in its wake, and the Hitler era up to the outbreak
of the Second World War, when Zweig's story ends. Too
exhausted to start a fourth, Zweig took his life in Brazil soon
after completing his autobiography, at a time when the prospects for the realization of all he had ever striven for looked
particularly bleak. "Three Lives" would have been thoroughly
in keeping with the master psychologist's penchant for writing
biographical triptychs: the stories of three masters of prose,
three adepts at self-portraiture, three demon-driven poets and
philosophers, three mental healers. But with characteristic self-
abnegation Zweig eventually decided to shift the emphasis from
his lives to his times, to memorialize the world of yesterday,
subtitling his book in the original German "memoirs of a
European."

The World of Yesterday was not intended as Zweig's literary
testament, although today we may read it as a skillful summa-
tion of an era as seen through the eyes of one of its outstanding
citizens. Even in happier years Zweig had often mentioned his
plans for such a book, originally envisaged as a chronicle of the
cultural currents of his age, with the First World War as a

focal point. He intended this book as a bridge between the
generations, one that would tell young people about a world
which had already become historical, legendary, largely incomprehensible to them. In a letter to his British friend Joseph
Leftwich, Zweig expressed his intention of writing "the history
of our Vienna, our culture, our freedom." "Our youth has
already become history, never to return," he wrote; "the next
years will be full of confusion, hatred, bitterness; for us the
best is over, and our only task is to testify truthfully for the day
that will come." He was convinced—so he told Robert van
Gelder, who interviewed him in 1940—that no other times
could equal the changes that the generation then of middle
age had seen. Zweig felt duty-bound to bear witness; he knew
that he had an urgent and incredible tale to tell, and he hastened
to get this memento of an age down on paper while he was
still able to do so. For he felt that in the turbulence of a war-
torn world a writer lacked peace of mind and concentration,
that writing was the only therapy vouchsafed him.

The World of Yesterday is not a conventional autobiography,
for it is a mirror of an age rather than of a life. The real
reason for this is not the fact that Zweig wrote the book under
unfavorable conditions, in an elegiac mood, at a time of homeless wandering when he lacked the books, notes, diaries, letters,
and other aids to recollection that most autobiographers take
for granted. Zweig was far too shy and modest a man to want
to write the story of his life, although he often encouraged
others to do so, particularly in times when truth was truly
stranger than fiction.

The international renown which his books brought him—
his works appeared in thirty languages, and at one time he
was the most translated writer in the world—made Zweig a
public figure, but he yearned for personal anonymity and had
an almost pathological aversion to lecture tours on which he had
to "sing," as he put it. Although he was charmed by the power
of the written word and regarded its worldwide dissemination as

a boon, he strove to keep his own personality inviolate amidst the multifarious temptations and obligations besetting an international celebrity. Thus *The World of Yesterday* is as self-effacing a document as one is likely to find in modern literature. Those looking for the full story of Zweig the man and writer will not find it in this book; that must be obtained from other sources: the book by Friderike Maria Zweig, the writer's first wife, whom he was able to consult for details of the life they shared for twenty-five years; their correspondence extending over three decades; the volume of tributes and reminiscences edited by Hanns Arens—to mention but a few works available in English. Not without justification did Virgilia Sapieha call *The World of Yesterday* "a glass-encased record of a mind," complaining that "in no part of the book does Zweig allow the bones and marrow of daily life and personal relations to show through." Apart from a few anecdotes, Zweig's autobiography is indeed devoid of personal material, for he was loath to expose himself, his esteemed contemporaries, and persons close to him to the glare of a public spotlight. Besides, he had already written warmly and personally about such beloved *compagnons de route* as Verhaeren, Rolland, Masereel, Freud, and Toscanini. What gives this vibrant record of an age its tragic effectiveness is the fact that it was written by an erstwhile cosmopolitan and citizen of the world who was now subjected to all the harassments of an enemy alien, at a time when personal acquaintance with an unimportant secretary in some passport office was infinitely more valuable than the friendship of a Romain Rolland, Arturo Toscanini, or Sigmund Freud. With the world thus out of joint, personal considerations seemed utterly trivial to Stefan Zweig.

In a time fraught with peril and bereft of grace, Zweig intoned a long lament for his expulsion from the paradise of the "world of security," the Austro-Hungarian empire, although he was realist enough to see that the world in which he grew up was in many ways a fool's paradise, that the "world of security was naught but a castle of dreams." By "security" Zweig meant those political, economic, and social circumstances that guaranteed a writer personal freedom, mobility, and concentration. Zweig tells the story of a generation that seemed fated to experience at first hand a dictum of the nineteenth-century Austrian dramatist Franz Grillparzer: "The road of modern culture leads from humanitarianism via nationalism to bestiality." Despite his highly favorable account of Austro-Hungarian culture, Zweig gives a sober portrait of his fascinating native city and sweeps away many of the misconceptions about *Altwien*. With becoming candor he describes the absurd and hypocritical customs and mores of his youth. He speaks for a whole generation—and more—when he criticizes the authoritarian school system which produced stifling learning-mills so full of paralyzing pressures and so conducive to psychological scars. In *Eros Matutinus,* a daringly frank chapter written in the liberating atmosphere of Brazil, Zweig the Freudian moralist (if that is not a contradiction in terms) advocates a natural, relaxed relationship between the sexes and a realistic and helpful sex education. In the almost classic pattern of talented young Viennese Jews of his generation, Zweig disdained the business interests of his father and chose a "flight into the intellectual." Like his sober, conservative, unostentatiously wealthy father, Zweig declined all outward trappings of fame, such as prizes, offices in associations, and decorations. Vienna, that "wonderfully orchestrated city," was good soil for nurturing the "good European" in Zweig. He found it easy and pleasant to secure a firm foothold in literature, and early in life a characteristic trait of his personality and creativity asserted itself: his desire to inspire, arouse enthusiasm, mediate across national, literary, and personal boundaries, to "translate" in a wider and higher sense. Realizing early in his career that his talents as an interpretive, recreative artist were greater and more important than his original creative gifts, he admiringly and self-effacingly served others: the Flemish poet Emile Verhaeren, the French man of letters Romain Rolland. Zweig put his literary talent, his taste for travel, and his great capacity for friendship and empathy in the service of the idea of international brotherhood and cultural cooperation among the nations. Zweig was a truly non-political man who had no use for ideologies or extremes of any sort; he distrusted politics and hated everything that was designed to disunite people and draw boundaries between nations. Yet he was to learn soon enough that the ivory tower of the esthete is not bomb proof. In retrospect those men of his youth who held his attention to literature seemed "far less important than those who drew it away towards reality." A case in point is Walther Rathenau, later Germany's ill-starred foreign minister in the early years of the Weimar Republic. Zweig gives him credit for broadening his horizon from the purely literary to a contemporary historical outlook and encouraging him to see the world—which Zweig visited not as an arrogant European, but as a youthfully zestful, appreciative, sympathetic guest.

Zweig's golden age of security was shattered forever by the outbreak of the First World War which he viewed, with rather one-dimensional oversimplification, as "a war of brothers brought about by clumsy diplomats and brutal munitions-manufacturers." Quite apart from the suffering produced by the war and the revolution, inflation, unemployment, and stark social and political problems that followed in its wake, Zweig was aghast at the war's power to break ties and corrode loyalties. Unlike many of his fellow men of letters, Zweig was not bedazzled by the lures of chauvinism and did not jump on the pan-German bandwagon. Unaffected by the raptures of patri-otism, he strove—from both Austria and Switzerland, where Rolland was working for the Red Cross, the "heart of Europe"—to restore the community of European intellectuals by means of personal appeals and especially by his pacifist drama *Jeremiah* (1917). Even though the pacifism and humanitarianism preached and practised by Zweig and other like-minded men proved largely ineffectual, Zweig's attitude was thoroughly consistent with his *weltanschauung* and significantly shaped his later literary output. For if there is one theme running through Zweig's many biographies, essays, and works of fiction, it is that of the spiritual superiority of the vanquished. In entitling his collected biographical essays *Baumeister der Welt* (1935), Master Builders of the World, Zweig was not concerned with the titans of action who moved empires, but with the unheroic moral leaders of mankind who have furnished us with enduring examples, even though they may themselves have been crushed by force and iniquity.

Returning to a truncated, scarcely viable Austria at the end of the war, Zweig settled down in Salzburg, a uniquely central and esthetically satisfying location. He found that city "the right springboard to Europe," and from inflation-ridden, politically unstable Austria he was able to emerge into the world again, to live "the life of a European", and to work on the central idea of his life, "the intellectual unification of Europe." His impressive home became a shrine of that idea and the mecca of Europe's and the world's cultural elite, many of whom Zweig numbered among his friends: Rolland, H. G. Wells, Werfel, Emil Ludwig, Shalom Asch, Paul Valéry, Frans Masereel, Jane Addams, Feruccio Busoni, Ravel, Bartok, Bruno Walter, Toscanini. *The World of Yesterday* contains loving pen portraits of many of these as well as others who deserve to be rescued from obscurity and oblivion. Stefan Zweig became accustomed to moving in "a magic circle of exalted figures" consisting of distinguished visitors and friends as well as the great figures of the past with whom he communed via his famous collection of manuscripts and autographs; as the "temporary custodian" of these treasures Zweig derived literary inspiration as well as esthetic delights.

The decade from 1924 to 1933 was a relatively peaceful and extremely productive period for Zweig—"until that one man confused our world," for on the nearby Berchtesgaden mountain "sat the one man who was to destroy all this." With the emergence of Hitlerism, which meant the destruction of everything Zweig had worked for, an almost hypochondriacal uneasiness took hold of him. A world increasingly inured to brutality and bestiality, technical progress coupled with moral regression, the burning of his books in Germany—all these were anathema to his sensitive soul. The indignity of having his Salzburg house searched early in 1934 made him decide to live abroad permanently. Zweig was singularly ill-suited to the role of emigrant— although, truth to tell, he was far better off than most literary exiles, knowing no material want and ultimately acquiring the coveted British citizenship. In the words of a fellow Austrian, Ernst Lothar, "Emigration is for a young man with no memories." Zweig sadly learned a new art, "that of parting from all that once had been our pride and our love," giving up his home, his friends, his books and manuscripts, even his faithful wife. He remembered Grillparzer's words about the sadness of witnessing one's own death and then following one's own corpse in the funeral procession. In his youth Zweig had been insulated by affluence, culture, and a sure sense of style against remote conflicts and conflagrations; now he found himself buffeted about by global clashes and cataclysms. He was surfeited with history, afraid of the upheavals all around him: "As an Austrian, a Jew, an author, a humanist, and a pacifist I have always stood at the exact point where these earthquakes were the most violent." While Zweig never renounced his Jewish faith or repudiated his Jewish background and associations—he repeatedly wrote on Jewish themes and in his autobiography gives a sympathetic account of the Jewish contribution to Austrian and European culture—he was not able to derive spiritual sustenance from Judaism or Jewish martyrdom through the ages. His religion was Europe, and he impotently watched his spiritual homeland commit suicide for the second time within his lifetime. In 1934 he wrote one of his most personal and most self-revealing, therapeutic books, a biography of Erasmus which he described as a "spiritual portrait of the humanist who, though he understood the madness of the time more clearly than the professional world-reformers, for all his sound reason was, tragically enough, unable to oppose unreason." Zweig's tragic final action after a period of tortured traveling about the world may have been the result of a fit of depression, but it is amply foreshadowed in the pages of his autobiography.

The World of Yesterday is more than a distinguished Austrian book of memoirs or a skillfully written, poignant, wonderfully evocative portrait of an era. "Our greatest debt of gratitude," wrote Zweig in his unfinished last work, a study of Montaigne, "is to those who in these inhuman times confirm the human in us, who encourage us not to abandon our unique and imperishable possession: our innermost self." For his life work in general and this autobiography in particular, we have reason to be grateful to Stefan Zweig in this sense. In the words of Walt Whitman, one of Zweig's favorite writers: "This is no book; who touches this touches a man."

STEFAN ZWEIG AT OSSINING, N. Y., SUMMER 1941

CONTENTS

LIST OF ILLUSTRATIONS   xv

PREFACE   xvii

I. THE WORLD OF SECURITY   1

II. SCHOOL IN THE LAST CENTURY   28

III. *EROS MATUTINUS*   67

IV. *UNIVERSITAS VITAE*   92

V. PARIS, THE CITY OF ETERNAL YOUTH   126

VI. BYPATHS ON THE WAY TO MYSELF   160

VII. BEYOND EUROPE   178

VIII. LIGHT AND SHADOW OVER EUROPE   192

IX. THE FIRST HOURS OF THE WAR OF 1914   214

X. THE STRUGGLE FOR INTELLECTUAL
   BROTHERHOOD   238

XI. IN THE HEART OF EUROPE   255

XII. HOMECOMING TO AUSTRIA   281

XIII. INTO THE WORLD AGAIN   304

XIV. SUNSET   326

XV. *INCIPIT* HITLER   358

XVI. THE AGONY OF PEACE   390

PUBLISHER'S POSTSCRIPT   437

BIBLIOGRAPHY OF ORIGINAL WORKS
  OF STEFAN ZWEIG   443

INDEX   447

ILLUSTRATIONS

	FACING PAGE
Stefan Zweig at Ossining, N. Y., Summer 1941	XII
Stefan Zweig as a child, with his brother	26
Stefan Zweig as a young man	98
Stefan Zweig on his last journey to Brazil, August 1941	436

	PAGE
Facsimile of Stefan Zweig's parting message	438

Preface

I HAVE never attached so much importance to my own person that I would have been tempted to tell others the story of my life. Much had to occur, infinitely more events, catastrophes, and trials than are usually allotted to a single generation had to come to pass, before I found the courage to begin a book in which I was the principal person or, better still, the pivotal point. Nothing is further from my thought than to take so prominent a place unless it be in the role of a narrator at an illustrated lecture. Time gives the pictures; I merely speak the words which accompany them. Actually, it is not so much the course of my own destiny that I relate, but that of an entire generation, the generation of our time, which was loaded down with a burden of fate as was hardly any other in the course of history. Each one of us, even the smallest and the most insignificant, has been shaken in the depths of his being by the almost unceasing volcanic eruptions of our European earth. I know of no pre-eminence that I can claim, in the midst of the multitude, except this: that as an Austrian, a Jew, an author, a humanist, and a pacifist, I have always stood at the exact point where these earthquakes were the most violent. Three times they have overthrown my house and my existence, severed me from the past and all that was, and hurled me with dramatic force into the void, into the "I know not whither" which I know so well. But I do not regret this. The homeless man becomes free in a new sense; and only he who has lost all ties need have no *arrière-*

pensée. And so I hope at least to be able to fulfill one of the chief conditions of any fair portrayal of an era; namely, honesty and impartiality.

For truly I have been detached, as rarely anyone has in the past, from all roots and from the very earth which nurtures them. I was born in 1881 in a great and mighty empire, in the monarchy of the Habsburgs. But do not look for it on the map; it has been swept away without trace. I grew up in Vienna, the two-thousand-year-old supernational metropolis, and was forced to leave it like a criminal before it was degraded to a German provincial city. My literary work, in the language in which I wrote it, was burned to ashes in the same land where my books made friends of millions of readers. And so I belong nowhere, and everywhere am a stranger, a guest at best. Europe, the homeland of my heart's choice, is lost to me, since it has torn itself apart suicidally a second time in a war of brother against brother. Against my will I have witnessed the most terrible defeat of reason and the wildest triumph of brutality in the chronicle of the ages. Never—and I say this without pride, but rather with shame—has any generation experienced such a moral retrogression from such a spiritual height as our generation has. In the short interval between the time when my beard began to sprout and now, when it is beginning to turn gray, in this half-century more radical changes and transformations have taken place than in ten generations of mankind; and each of us feels: it is almost too much! My today and each of my yesterdays, my rises and falls, are so diverse that I sometimes feel as if I had lived not one, but several existences, each one different from the others. For it often happens that when I carelessly speak of "my life," I am forced to ask, "which life?"—the one before the World War, the one between the first and the second, or the life of today? Or I find myself saying "my house," and at first I do not know which of my former homes I mean, the one in Bath or the one in Salzburg, or my parental home in Vienna. Or I say "among our people," and then I must acknowledge with dismay that for a long time past I have not belonged to the people of my country any more than I belong to the English or the Americans. To the former I am no longer organically bound; to the latter I have never become wholly linked. My feeling is that the world in which I grew up, and the world of today, and the world between the two, are entirely separate worlds. Whenever, in conversation with younger friends, I relate some episode of the time before the first war, I notice from their astonished questions how much that is still obvious reality to me has already become historical and incomprehensible to them. And some secret instinct tells me that they are right. All the bridges between our today and our yesterday and our yesteryears have been burnt.

I myself cannot help but wonder at the profusion and variety which we have compressed into a single, though highly uncomfortable and dangerous, existence, and the more when I compare it with the manner of living of my ancestors. My father, my grandfather, what did they see? Each of them lived his life in uniformity. A single life from beginning to end, without ascent, without decline, without disturbance or danger, a life of slight anxieties, hardly noticeable transitions. In even rhythm, leisurely and quietly, the wave of time bore them from the cradle to the grave. They lived in the same country, in the same city, and nearly always in the same house. What took place out in the world only occurred in the newspapers and never knocked at their door. In their time some war happened somewhere but, measured by the dimensions of today, it was only a little war. It took place far beyond the border, one did not hear the cannon, and after six months it died down, forgotten, a dry page of history, and the old accustomed life began anew. But in our lives there was no repetition; nothing of the past survived, nothing came back. It was reserved for us to participate to the full in that which history formerly distributed, sparingly and from time to time, to a single country, to a single century. At most, one generation had gone through a revolution, another experienced a putsch, the third a war, the fourth a famine, the fifth national bankruptcy; and many blessed countries, blessed generations, bore none of these. But we, who are sixty today and who, *de jure,* still have a space of time before us, what have we *not* seen, *not* suffered, *not* lived through? We have plowed through the catalogue of every conceivable catastrophe back and forth, and we have not yet come to the last page. I myself was a contemporary of the two greatest wars of mankind, and even passed through each one of them on a different front, the one on the German, the other on the anti-German. Before the war I knew the highest degree and form of individual freedom, and later its lowest level in hundreds of years; I have been celebrated and despised, free and unfree, rich and poor. All the livid steeds of the Apocalypse have stormed through my life—revolution and famine, inflation and terror, epidemics and emigration. I have seen the great mass ideologies grow and spread before my eyes—Fascism in Italy, National Socialism in Germany, Bolshevism in Russia, and above all else that arch-plague nationalism which has poisoned the flower of our European culture. I was forced to be a defenseless, helpless witness of the most inconceivable decline of humanity into a barbarism which we had believed long since forgotten, with its deliberate and programmatic dogma of anti-humanitarianism. It was reserved for us, after centuries, again to see wars without declarations of war, concentration camps, persecution, mass robbery, bombing attacks on helpless cities, all bestialities unknown to the last fifty generations, and which future generations, it is hoped, will not allow to happen. But paradoxically, in the same era when our world fell back morally a thousand years, I have seen that same mankind lift itself, in technical and intellectual matters, to unheard-of deeds, surpassing the achievement of a million years with a single beat of its wings. It has accomplished the conquest of the air by the airplane, the transmission of the human word in a second around the globe, and with it the conquest of space, the splitting of the atom, the conquest of the most insidious diseases, the almost daily realization of the impossible of yesterday. Not until our time has mankind as a whole behaved so infernally, and never before has it accomplished so much that is godlike.

To give witness of this tense, dramatic life of ours, filled with the unexpected, seems to me a duty; for, I repeat, everyone was a witness of this gigantic transformation, everyone was forced to be a witness. There was no escape for our generation, no standing aside as in times past. Thanks to our new organization of simultaneity we were constantly drawn into our time. When bombs laid waste the houses of Shanghai, we knew of it in our rooms in Europe before the wounded were carried out of their homes. What occurred thousands of miles over the sea leaped bodily before our eyes in pictures. There was no protection, no security against being constantly made aware of things and being drawn into them. There was no country to which one could flee, no quiet which one could purchase;

always and everywhere the hand of fate seized us and dragged us back into its insatiable play. Constantly men had to subordinate themselves to the demands of the State, to become the prey of the most stupid politics, to adapt themselves to the most fantastic changes. Always the individual was chained to the common lot, no matter how bitterly he objected; he was carried along irresistibly. Whoever went through this period or, rather, was hunted and driven through it—we knew but few breathing spells—experienced more history than any of his ancestors. And today we again stand at a turning point, an end and a new beginning. It is not without deliberation that I make this retrospect of my life end with a definite date. For that day of September 1939 wrote the final flourish to the epoch which formed and educated us who are in our sixties. But if we with our evidence can transmit out of the decaying structure only one grain of truth to the next generation, we shall not have labored entirely in vain.

I am aware of the unfavorable circumstances, characteristic though they are of our time, in which I am trying to shape my reminiscences. I write them in the midst of war, in a foreign country, and without the least aids to my memory. None of my books, none of my notes, no friends' letters are at hand in my hotel room. Nowhere can I seek information, for in the whole world the mails from country to country have been disrupted or hampered by censorship. We live cut off from one another as we did a hundred years ago, before steamships, railroads, planes, and mails were invented. I have nothing more of my past with me than what I have retained in my mind. All else at this moment is unobtainable or lost. But the good art of not pining over that which is lost has been thoroughly learned by our generation, and it is quite possible that the loss of documentation and detail may actually be an advantage for my book. For I look upon our memory not as an element which accidentally retains or forgets, but rather as a consciously organizing and wisely exclusionary power. All that one forgets of one's life was long since predestined by an inner instinct to be forgotten. Only that which wills to preserve itself has the right to be preserved for others. So choose and speak for me, ye memories, and at least give some reflection of my life before it sinks into the dark!

THE WORLD OF YESTERDAY

I

The World of Security

Still und eng und ruhig auferzogen
Wirft man uns auf einmal in die Welt;
Uns umspülen hunderttausend Wogen
Alles reizt uns, mancherlei gefällt,
Mancherlei verdriesst uns und von
Stund' zu Stunden
Schwankt das leichtunruhige Gefühl;
Wir empfinden, und was wir empfunden
Spült hinweg das bunte Weltgewühl.

GOETHE: *An Lottchen*

WHEN I attempt to find a simple formula for the period in which I grew up, prior to the First World War, I hope that I convey its fullness by calling it the Golden Age of Security. Everything in our almost thousand-year-old Austrian monarchy seemed based on permanency, and the State itself was the chief guarantor of this stability. The rights which it granted to its citizens were duly confirmed by parliament, the freely elected representative of the people, and every duty was exactly prescribed. Our currency, the Austrian crown, circulated in bright gold pieces, an assurance of its immutability. Everyone knew how much he possessed or what he was entitled to, what was permitted and what forbidden. Everything had its norm, its definite measure and weight. He who had a fortune could accurately compute his annual interest. An official or an officer, for example, could confidently look up in the calendar the year when he would be advanced in grade, or when he would be pensioned. Each family had its fixed budget, and knew how much could be spent for rent and food, for

1

vacations and entertainment; and what is more, invariably a small sum was carefully laid aside for sickness and the doctor's bills, for the unexpected. Whoever owned a house looked upon it as a secure domicile for his children and grandchildren; estates and businesses were handed down from generation to generation. When the babe was still in its cradle, its first mite was put in its little bank, or deposited in the savings bank, as a "reserve" for the future. In this vast empire everything stood firmly and immovably in its appointed place, and at its head was the aged emperor; and were he to die, one knew (or believed) another would come to take his place, and nothing would change in the well-regulated order. No one thought of wars, of revolutions, or revolts. All that was radical, all violence, seemed impossible in an age of reason.

This feeling of security was the most eagerly sought-after possession of millions, the common ideal of life. Only the possession of this security made life seem worth while, and constantly widening circles desired their share of this costly treasure. At first it was only the prosperous who enjoyed this advantage, but gradually the great masses forced their way toward it. The century of security became the golden age of insurance. One's house was insured against fire and theft, one's field against hail and storm, one's person against accident and sickness. Annuities were purchased for one's old age, and a policy was laid in a girl's cradle for her future dowry. Finally even the workers organized, and won standard wages and workmen's compensation. Servants saved up for old-age insurance and paid in advance into a burial fund for their own interment. Only the man who could look into the future without worry could thoroughly enjoy the present.

Despite the propriety and the modesty of this view of life, there was a grave and dangerous arrogance in this touching confidence that we had barricaded ourselves to the last loophole against any possible invasion of fate. In its liberal idealism, the nineteenth century was honestly convinced that it was on the straight and unfailing path toward being the best of all worlds. Earlier eras, with their wars, famines, and revolts, were deprecated as times when mankind was still immature and unenlightened. But now it was merely a matter of decades until the last vestige of evil and violence would finally be conquered, and this faith in an uninterrupted and irresistible "progress" truly had the force of a religion for that generation. One began to believe more in this "progress" than in the Bible, and its gospel appeared ultimate because of the daily new wonders of science and technology. In fact, at the end of this peaceful century, a general advance became more marked, more rapid, more varied. At night the dim street lights of former times were replaced by electric lights, the shops spread their tempting glow from the main streets out to the city limits. Thanks to the telephone one could talk at a distance from person to person. People moved about in horseless carriages with a new rapidity; they soared aloft, and the dream of Icarus was fulfilled. Comfort made its way from the houses of the fashionable to those of the middle class. It was no longer necessary to fetch water from the pump or the hallway, or to take the trouble to build a fire in the fireplace. Hygiene spread and filth disappeared. People became handsomer, stronger, healthier, as sport steeled their bodies. Fewer cripples and maimed and persons with goiters were seen on the streets, and all of these miracles were accomplished by science, the archangel of progress. Progress was also made in social matters; year after year new rights were accorded to the individual, justice was administered more benignly and humanely, and even the problem of problems, the poverty of the great masses, no longer seemed insurmountable. The right to vote was being accorded to wider circles, and with it the possibility of legally protecting their interests. Sociologists and professors competed with one another to create healthier and happier living conditions for the proletariat. Small wonder then that this century sunned itself in its own accomplishments and looked upon each completed decade as the prelude to a better one. There was as little belief in the possibility of such barbaric declines as wars between the peoples of Europe as there was in witches and ghosts. Our fathers were comfortably saturated with confidence in the unfailing and binding power of tolerance and conciliation. They honestly believed that the divergencies and the boundaries between nations and sects would gradually melt away into a common humanity and that peace and security, the highest of treasures, would be shared by all mankind.

It is reasonable that we, who have long since struck the word "security" from our vocabulary as a myth, should smile at the optimistic delusion of that idealistically blinded generation, that the technical progress of mankind must connote an unqualified and equally rapid moral ascent. We of the new generation who have learned not to be surprised by any outbreak of bestiality, we who each new day expect things worse than the day before, are markedly more skeptical about a possible moral improvement of mankind. We must agree with Freud, to whom our culture and civilization were merely a thin layer liable at any moment to be pierced by the destructive forces of the "underworld." We have had to accustom ourselves gradually to living without the ground beneath our feet, without justice, without freedom, without security. Long since, as far as our existence is concerned, we have denied the religion of our fathers, their faith in a rapid and continuous rise of humanity. To us, gruesomely taught, witnesses of a catastrophe which, at

a swoop, hurled us back a thousand years of humane
endeavor, that rash optimism seems banal. But even though
it was a delusion our fathers served, it was a wonderful and
noble delusion, more humane and more fruitful than
our watchwords of today; and in spite of my later knowledge
and disillusionment, there is still something in me which
inwardly prevents me from abandoning it entirely. That
which, in his childhood, a man has drawn into his blood
out of the air of time cannot be taken from him. And in
spite of all that is daily blasted into my ears, and all that
I myself and countless other sharers of my destiny have
experienced in trials and tribulations, I cannot completely
deny the faith of my youth, that some day things will rise
again—in spite of all. Even in the abyss of despair in which
today, half-blinded, we grope about with distorted and
broken souls, I look up again and again to those old star-
patterns that shone over my childhood, and comfort myself
with the inherited confidence that this collapse will appear,
in days to come, as a mere interval in the eternal rhythm of
the onward and onward.

Today, now that the great storm has long since smashed
it, we finally know that that world of security was naught
but a castle of dreams; my parents lived in it as if it had
been a house of stone. Not once did a storm, or even a
sharp wind, break in upon their warm, comfortable existence. True, they had a special protection against the winds
of time: they were wealthy people, who had become rich
gradually, even very rich, and that filled the crevices of
wall and window in those times. Their way of life seems
to me to be so typical of the so-called "good Jewish bourgeoisie," which gave such marked value to Viennese culture,
and which was requited by being completely uprooted,

that in telling of their quiet and comfortable existence I am actually being quite impersonal: ten or twenty thousand families like my parents lived in Vienna in that last century of assured values.

My father's family came from Moravia. There the Jewish communities lived in small country villages on friendly terms with the peasants and the petty bourgeoisie. They were entirely free both of the sense of inferiority and of the smooth pushing impatience of the Galician or Eastern Jews. Strong and powerful, owing to their life in the country, they went their way quietly and surely, as the peasants of their homeland strode over the fields. Early emancipated from their orthodox religion, they were passionate followers of the religion of the time, "progress," and in the political era of liberalism they supported the most esteemed representatives in parliament. When they moved from their home to Vienna, they adapted themselves to the higher cultural sphere with phenomenal rapidity, and their personal rise was organically bound up with the general rise of the times. In this form of transition, too, our family was typical. My grandfather on my father's side was a dry goods dealer. In the second half of the century the industrial turn of the tide began in Austria. The mechanical weaving looms and spinning machines imported from England brought, through rationalization, a tremendous lowering of prices as compared with the accustomed hand weaving; and with their gift of commercial insight and their international view, it was the Jewish merchants who were the first in Austria to see the necessity and the advantage of a changeover to industrial production. Usually with but limited capital, they founded the quickly improvised factories, at first run only by water power, which gradually grew into the mighty Bohemian textile industry that dominated all of Austria and the Balkans. Whereas my grandfather, as a typical representative of the earlier era, was engaged in the trade in finished goods, my father determinedly went over into the new era, and in his thirtieth year founded a small weaving mill in Northern Bohemia, which, in the course of the years, slowly and methodically developed into a considerable undertaking.

So careful a manner of expansion in spite of the tempting turn of affairs was entirely in keeping with the times. Furthermore, it was indicative of my father's moderate and entirely ungreedy nature. He was imbued with the credo of his epoch, "safety first." It seemed important to him to own a "solid" (another favorite word of the period) undertaking maintained by his own capital, rather than to create a huge enterprise with the help of bank credits and mortgages. His greatest pride during his lifetime was that no one had ever seen his name on a promissory note or on a draft, and that his accounts were always on the credit side of the ledger in the Rothschild bank, the Kreditanstalt—needless to say, the safest of banks. Any profit that entailed even the shadow of a risk was against his principles, and throughout the years he never participated in anyone else's business. If, none the less, he gradually grew rich and richer, it was not due to incautious speculation or particularly far-seeing operations, but rather thanks to his adapting himself to the general methods of that careful period, namely, to consume only a modest portion of one's income, and consequently to be able to add an appreciably larger sum to one's capital from year to year. Like most of his generation, he would have regarded a man who carelessly ate up half his income without "thinking of the future"—this is another phrase of the age of security—as a doubtful wastrel. Thanks to the constant accumulation of profits, in an era of increasing prosperity in which the State never thought of nibbling off more than a few percent of the income of even the richest,

and in which, on the other hand, State and industrial bonds
bore high rates of interest, to grow richer was nothing more
than a passive activity for the wealthy. And it was worth
while. Not yet, as later at the time of the inflation, were
the thrifty robbed, and the solid business men swindled;
and the patient and the non-speculating made the best
profit. Owing to his observance of the prevailing system of
his time, my father, at fifty, was counted among the very
wealthy, even by international standards. But the living
conditions of my family kept pace only haltingly with the
always rapidly increasing fortune. We gradually acquired
small comforts, we moved from a smaller to a larger
house, in the spring we rented a carriage for the afternoons,
traveled second-class in a sleeping car. But it was not until
he was fifty that my father allowed himself the luxury of
spending a month in the winter with my mother in Nice.
The principle of enjoying wealth, in having it and not
showing it, remained completely unchanged. Though he
was a millionaire, my father never smoked an imported
cigar but, like Emperor Franz Josef, he smoked the cheap
"Virginia," the government-monopoly "Trabuco," popular
cheroots. When he played cards it was always for small
stakes. Unbendingly, he held fast to his comfortable, discreet, and restrained manner of living. Although he was
better educated and socially more presentable than most of
his colleagues—he played the piano excellently, wrote well
and clearly, spoke both French and English—he persistently
refused every honor and office; throughout his life he neither
sought nor accepted any title or dignity, though in his position as a large industrialist these were often offered to him.
That he never asked anything of anyone, that he was never
obliged to say "please" or "thanks" to anyone, was his secret
pride and meant more to him than any external recognition.

   Inevitably there comes into the life of each one of us the

time when, face to face with our own being, one re-encounters his father. That trait of clinging to a private, anonymous mode of life now begins to develop more strongly in me from year to year, even though it stands in marked contrast to my profession, which, to some extent, forces both name and person before the public eye. And it is out of the same secret pride that I have always declined every external honor; I have never accepted a decoration, a title, the presidency of any association, have never belonged to any academy, any committee, any jury. Merely to sit at a banquet table is torture for me; and the thought of asking someone for something—even if it is on behalf of a third person—dries my lips before the first word is spoken. I know how outmoded such inhibitions are in a world where one can remain free only through trickery and flight and where, as Father Goethe so wisely says, "decorations and titles ward off many a shove in the crowd." But it is my father in me, and it is his secret pride that forces me back, and I may not offer opposition; for I thank him for what may well be my only definite possession—the feeling of inner freedom.

~~

My mother, whose maiden name was Brettauer, was of a different, more international origin. She was born in Ancona, in the south of Italy, and spoke Italian as well as German as a child; whenever she discussed anything with my grandmother or with her sister that was not destined for the servants' ears, she reverted to Italian. From my earliest youth I was familiar with risotto and artichokes, then still quite rare, as well as other specialties of the Mediterranean kitchen; and later whenever I went to Italy, I always felt at home from the first moment of my arrival. But my mother's family was by no means Italian, rather it was consciously international. The Brettauers, who originally owned a banking business, had—after the example of the great Jewish banking families, though on a much smaller scale—early distributed themselves over the world from Hohenems, a small place near the Swiss border. Some went to St. Gall, others to Vienna and Paris, my grandmother to Italy, my uncle to New York; and this international contact gave them a better polish, wider vision, and a certain family pride. There were no longer any small merchants or commission brokers in this family, but only bankers, directors, professors, lawyers, and doctors. Each one spoke several languages, and I can recall how natural it was to change from one language to another at table in my aunt's house in Paris. They were a family who made much of solidarity, and when a young girl from among the poorer relatives had reached the marrying age, the entire family collected a considerable dowry to prevent her from marrying "beneath her." My father was respected because he was an industrialist, but my mother, although she was most happily married to him, would never have allowed his relatives to consider themselves on the same plane with her own. This pride in coming from a "good" family was ineradicable in all the Brettauers, and when in later years one of them wished to show me his particular good will, he would say condescendingly, "You really are a regular Brettauer," as if to say, "You fell out on the right side."

This sort of nobility, which many Jewish families arrogated to themselves, sometimes amused and sometimes annoyed my brother and me, even when we were children. We were always being told that these were "fine" people, that others were "not fine." Every friend's pedigree was examined back to the earliest generation, to see whether or not he came from a "good" family, and all his relatives, as well as his wealth, were checked. This constant categorization, which actually was the main topic of every familiar

and social conversation, at that time seemed to be most
ridiculous and snobbish, because for all Jewish families it
was merely a matter of fifty or a hundred years earlier or
later that they had come from the same ghetto. It was not
until much later that I realized that this conception of
"good" family, which appeared to us boys to be a parody of
an artificial pseudo-aristocracy, was one of the most profound and secret tendencies of Jewish life. It is generally
accepted that getting rich is the only and typical goal of
the Jew. Nothing could be further from the truth. Riches
are to him merely a stepping stone, a means to the true
end, and in no sense the real goal. The real determination
of the Jew is to rise to a higher cultural plane in the intellectual world. Even in the case of Eastern orthodox Jewry,
where the weaknesses as well as the merits of the whole
race are more intensely manifested, this supremacy of the
will to the spiritual over the mere material finds plastic
expression. The holy man, the Bible student is a thousand
times more esteemed within the community than the rich
man; even the wealthiest man will prefer to give his daughter in marriage to the poorest intellectual than to a
merchant. This elevation of the intellectual to the highest
rank is common to all classes; the poorest beggar who drags
his pack through wind and rain will try to single out at
least one son to study, no matter at how great a sacrifice,
and it is counted a title of honor for the entire family to have
someone in their midst, a professor, a savant, or a musician,
who plays a role in the intellectual world, as if through his
achievements he ennobled them all. Subconsciously something in the Jew seeks to escape the morally dubious, the
distasteful, the petty, the unspiritual, which is attached to
all trade, and all that is purely business, and to lift himself up to the moneyless sphere of the intellectual, as if—in
the Wagnerian sense—he wished to redeem himself and his

entire race from the curse of money. And that is why among Jews the impulse to wealth is exhausted in two, or at most three, generations within one family, and the mightiest dynasties find their sons unwilling to take over the banks, the factories, the established and secure businesses of their fathers. It is not chance that a Lord Rothschild became an ornithologist, a Warburg an art historian, a Cassirer a philosopher, a Sassoon a poet. They all obey the same subconscious impulse, to free themselves of cold money making, that thing that confines Jewry; and perhaps it expresses a secret longing to resolve the merely Jewish—through flight into the intellectual—into humanity at large. A "good" family therefore means more than the purely social aspect which it assigns to itself with this classification; it means a Jewry that has freed itself of all defects and limitations and pettiness which the ghetto has forced upon it, by means of adaptation to a different culture and even possibly a universal culture. That this flight into the intellectual has become as disastrous for the Jew, because of a disproportionate crowding of the professions, as formerly his confinement in the purely material, simply belongs to the eternal paradoxes of Jewish destiny.

~~

There is hardly a city in Europe where the drive towards cultural ideals was as passionate as it was in Vienna. Precisely because the monarchy, because Austria itself for centuries had been neither politically ambitious nor particularly successful in its military actions, the native pride had turned more strongly toward a desire for artistic supremacy. The most important and the most valuable provinces, German and Italian, Flemish and Walloon, had long since fallen away from the old Habsburg empire that had once ruled Europe; unsullied in its old glory, the capital had remained, the treasure of the court, the preserver of a thousand-year-old tradition. The Romans had laid the first stones of this city, as a *castrum,* a fortress, an advance outpost to protect Latin civilization against the barbarians; and more than a thousand years later the attack of the Ottomans against the West shattered against these walls. Here rode the Nibelungs, here the immortal Pleiades of music shone out over the world, Gluck, Haydn, Mozart, Beethoven, Schubert, Brahms, and Johann Strauss, here all the streams of European culture converged. At court, among the nobility, and among the people, the German was related in blood to the Slavic, the Hungarian, the Spanish, the Italian, the French, the Flemish; and it was the particular genius of this city of music that dissolved all the contrasts harmoniously into a new and unique thing, the Austrian, the Viennese. Hospitable and endowed with a particular talent for receptivity, the city drew the most diverse forces to it, loosened, propitiated, and pacified them. It was sweet to live here, in this atmosphere of spiritual conciliation, and subconsciously every citizen became supernational, cosmopolitan, a citizen of the world.

This talent for assimilation, for delicate and musical transitions, was already apparent in the external visage of the city. Growing slowly through the centuries, organically developing outward from inner circles, it was sufficiently populous, with its two millions, to yield all the luxury and all the diversity of a metropolis, and yet it was not so oversized as to be cut off from nature, like London or New York. The last houses of the city mirrored themselves in the mighty Danube or looked out over the wide plains, or dissolved themselves in gardens and fields, or climbed in gradual rises the last green wooded foothills of the Alps. One hardly sensed where nature began and where the city: one melted into the other without opposition, without contradiction. Within, however, one felt that the city had grown like a tree that adds ring upon ring, and instead of the old fortification walls the Ringstrasse encircled the treasured core with its splendid houses. Within, the old palaces of the court and the nobility spoke history in stone. Here Beethoven had played at the Lichnowskys', at the Esterhazys' Haydn had been a guest; there in the old University Haydn's *Creation* had resounded for the first time, the Hofburg had seen generations of emperors, and Schönbrunn had seen Napoleon. In the Stefansdom the united lords of Christianity had knelt in prayers of thanksgiving for the salvation of Europe from the Turks; countless great lights of science had been within the walls of the University. In the midst of all this, the new architecture reared itself proudly and grandly with glittering avenues and sparkling shops. But the old quarreled as little with the new as the chiseled stone with untouched nature. It was wonderful to live here, in this city which hospitably took up everything foreign and gave itself so gladly; and in its light air, as in Paris, it was a simple matter to enjoy life. Vienna was, we know, an epicurean city; but what is culture, if not to wheedle from the coarse material of life, by art and love, its finest, its most delicate, its most subtle qualities? Gourmets in culinary matters, much occupied with a good wine, a dry fresh beer, sumptuous pastries and cakes, in this city people were also demanding with regard to more subtle delights. Making music, dancing, the theater, conversation, proper and urbane deportment, these were cultivated here as particular arts. It was not the military, nor the political, nor the commercial, that was predominant in the life of the individual and of the masses. The first glance of the average Viennese into his morning paper was not at the events in parliament, or world affairs, but at the repertoire of the theater, which assumed so important a role in public life as hardly was pos-

sible in any other city. For the Imperial theater, the Burgtheater, was for the Viennese and for the Austrian more than
a stage upon which actors enacted parts; it was the microcosm
that mirrored the macrocosm, the brightly colored reflection
in which the city saw itself, the only true *cortigiano* of good
taste. In the court actor the spectator saw an excellent example of how one ought to dress, how to walk into a room, how
to converse, which words one might employ as a man of
good taste and which to avoid. The stage, instead of being
merely a place of entertainment, was a spoken and plastic
guide of good behavior and correct pronunciation, and a
nimbus of respect encircled like a halo everything that had
even the faintest connection with the Imperial theater. The
Minister-President or the richest magnate could walk the
streets of Vienna without anyone's turning around, but a
court actor or an opera singer was recognized by every sales-
girl and every cabdriver. Proudly we boys told one another
when we had seen one of them pass by (everyone collected
their pictures and autographs); and this almost religious
cult went so far that it even attached itself to the world
around them. Sonnenthal's barber, Josef Kainz's cabdriver
were persons to be respected and secretly envied, and elegant youths were proud to have their clothes made by an
actor's tailor. Every jubilee and every funeral of a great
actor was turned into an event that overshadowed all political occurrences. To have one's play given at the Burgtheater was the greatest dream of every Viennese writer,
because it meant a sort of lifelong nobility and brought with
it a series of honors such as complimentary tickets for life
and invitations to all official functions. One virtually
became a guest in the Imperial household. I can still recall
the imposing way in which my own introduction took place.
In the morning, the director of the Burgtheater had asked
me to come to his office, to tell me—after having congratu-

lated me—that my drama had been accepted by the Burg-theater; when I came home at night, his visiting card was in my room. He had paid me, a twenty-six-year-old, a formal return visit, for I, merely by being accepted as an author of the Imperial stage, had become a "gentleman," whom the director of the institution had to treat as a peer. And what-ever happened in the theater indirectly touched everyone, even those who had no direct connection with it. I can remember, for example, that once when I was very young our cook ran into the room with tears in her eyes. She had just been told that Charlotte Wolter—the most prominent actress of the Burgtheater—had died. The grotesque thing about her wild mourning was obviously the fact that this old, semi-illiterate cook had never once been in the fashion-able Burgtheater, and that she had never seen Wolter either on the stage or elsewhere; but a great national actress was the collective property of the entire city of Vienna, and even an outsider could feel that her death was a catastrophe. Every loss, for instance the departure of a beloved singer or artist, was immediately transformed into national mourn-ing. When the "old" Burgtheater, in which Mozart's *Mar-riage of Figaro* was first given, was torn down, all of Vienna's society was formally and sorrowfully assembled there; the curtain had hardly fallen when everybody leapt upon the stage, to bring home at least a splinter as a relic of the boards which the beloved artists had trod; and for decades after, in dozens of bourgeois homes, these insignificant splinters could be seen preserved in costly caskets, as fragments of the Holy Cross are kept in churches. We ourselves did not act much more sensibly when the so-called Bösendorfer Saal was torn down. In itself this little concert hall, which was used solely for chamber music, was a quite unimposing, unartistic piece of architecture, the former riding academy of Count Liechtenstein, unpretentiously remodeled for

musical use with wooden paneling. But it had the resonance
of an old violin, it was a sanctuary for lovers of music,
because Chopin and Brahms, Liszt and Rubinstein had
given concerts there, and because many of the famous quar-
tets had made their first appearance there; and now it was
to make way for a functional building. It was incomprehensible to us who had experienced such unforgettable
hours there. When the last measure of Beethoven, played
more beautifully than ever by the Rosé Quartet, had died
away, no one left his seat. We called and applauded, several
women sobbed with emotion, no one wished to believe
that this was a farewell. The lights were put out in the
hall in order to make us leave. Not one of the four or
five hundred enthusiasts moved from his place. A half hour,
a full hour, we remained as if by our presence we could save
the old hallowed place. And when we were students, how
we fought with petitions, with demonstrations, and with
essays to keep the house where Beethoven died from being
demolished! Every one of these historic buildings in Vienna
was a bit of our soul that was being torn out of our body.

This fanaticism for art, and for the art of the theater in
particular, touched all classes in Vienna. Vienna, through
its century-old tradition, was itself a clearly ordered, and—
as I once wrote—a wonderfully orchestrated city. The
Imperial house still set the tempo. The palace was the
center not only in a spatial sense, but also in a cultural
sense of the supernationality of the monarchy. The palaces
of the Austrian, the Polish, the Czech, and the Hungarian
nobility formed as it were a second enclosure around the
Imperial palace. Then came "good society," consisting of the
lesser nobility, the higher officials, industry, and the "old
families," then the petty bourgeoisie and the proletariat.
Each of these social strata lived in its own circle, and even
in its own district, the nobility in their palaces in the heart

of the city, the diplomats in the third district, industry and the merchants in the vicinity of the Ringstrasse, the petty bourgeoisie in the inner districts—the second to the ninth—· and the proletariat in the outer circle. But everyone met in the theater and at the great festivities such as the Flower Parade in the Prater, where three hundred thousand people enthusiastically proclaimed the "upper ten thousand" in their beautifully decorated carriages. In Vienna everything— religious processions such as the one on the feast of Corpus Christi, the military parades, the "Burg" music—was made the occasion for celebration, as far as color and music were concerned. Even funerals found enthusiastic audiences and it was the ambition of every true Viennese to have a "lovely corpse," with a majestic procession and many followers; even his death converted the genuine Viennese into a spectacle for others. In this receptivity for all that was colorful, festive and resounding, in this pleasure in the theatrical, whether it was on the stage or in reality, both as theater and as a mirror of life, the whole city was at one.

It was not difficult to mock this "theatromania" of the Viennese, and their following up to the most minute details of the lives of their darlings often was more than grotesque. Our Austrian indolence in political matters, and our backwardness in economics as compared with our resolute German neighbor, may actually be ascribed in part to our epicurean excesses. But culturally this exaggeration of artistic events brought something unique to maturity—first of all, an uncommon respect for every artistic presentation, then, through centuries of practice, a connoisseurship without equal, and finally, thanks to that connoisseurship, a predominant high level in all cultural fields. The artist always feels at his best and at the same time most inspired where he is esteemed or even over-estimated. Art always reaches its peak where it becomes the life interest of a people. And just as

Florence and Rome in the Renaissance drew the artists and educated them to greatness, each one feeling that he was in constant competition and had to outdo the others and himself in the eyes of the people, so the musicians and the actors of Vienna were conscious of their importance in the city. In the Vienna Opera and in the Burgtheater, nothing was overlooked; every flat note was remarked, every incorrect intonation and every cut were censured; and this control was exercised at premières not by the professional critics alone, but day after day by the entire audience, whose attentive ears had been sharpened by constant comparison. Whereas in politics, in administration, or in morals, everything went on rather comfortably and one was affably tolerant of all that was slovenly, and overlooked many an infringement, in artistic matters there was no pardon; here the honor of the city was at stake. Every singer, actor, and musician had constantly to give his best or he was lost. It was wonderful to be the darling of Vienna, but it was not easy to remain so; no letdown was forgiven. And this knowledge and the constant pitiless supervision forced each artist in Vienna to give his best, and gave to the whole its marvelous level. Every one of us has, from his youthful years, brought a strict and inexorable standard of musical performance into his life. He who in the opera knew Gustav Mahler's iron discipline, which extended to the minutest detail, or realized the Philharmonic's matter-of-fact energetic exactitude, today is rarely satisfied by any musical or theatrical performance. But with it we also learned to be strict with ourselves at every artistic presentation; a certain level was and remained exemplary, and there are few cities in the world where it was so inculcated into the developing artist. But this knowledge of rhythm and energy went deep into the people, for even the little bourgeois seated at his *Heurigen* demanded good music from the band as he did good wine from the innkeeper. Again, in the Prater the crowds knew exactly which military band had the best "swing," whether it was the *Deutschmeister* or the Hungarians; whoever lived in Vienna caught a feeling of rhythm from the air. And just as this musicality was expressed by us writers in carefully wrought prose, the sense of rhythm entered into others in their social deportment and their daily life. A Viennese who had no sense of art or who found no enjoyment in form was unthinkable in "good society." Even in the lower circles, the poorest drew a certain instinct for beauty out of the landscape and out of the merry human sphere into his life; one was not a real Viennese without this love for culture, without this sense, aesthetic and critical at once, of the holiest exuberance of life.

~~

Adapting themselves to the milieu of the people or country where they live is not only an external protective measure for Jews, but a deep internal desire. Their longing for a homeland, for rest, for security, for friendliness, urges them to attach themselves passionately to the culture of the world around them. And never was such an attachment more effective—except in Spain in the fifteenth century—or happier and more fruitful than in Austria. Having resided for more than two hundred years in the Imperial city, the Jews encountered there an easygoing people, inclined to conciliation, and under whose apparent laxity of form lay buried the identical deep instinct for cultural and aesthetic values which was so important to the Jews themselves. And they met with more in Vienna: they found there a personal task. In the last century the pursuit of art in Austria had lost its old traditional defenders and protectors, the Imperial house and the aristocracy. Whereas in the eighteenth century Maria Theresa had Gluck instruct her daughters in

music, Josef II ably discussed his operas with Mozart, and
Leopold III himself composed music, the later emperors,
Franz II and Ferdinand, had no interest whatever in artistic
things; and our Emperor Franz Josef, who in his eighty
years had never read a book other than the Army Register,
or even taken one in his hand, evidenced moreover a definite
antipathy to music. The nobility as well had relinquished
its erstwhile protector's role; gone were the glorious days
when the Esterhazys harbored a Haydn, the Lobkowitzes
and the Kinskys and Waldsteins competed to have a première of Beethoven in their palaces, where a Countess Thun
threw herself on her knees before the great demigod, begging him not to withdraw *Fidelio* from the Opera. But now
Wagner, Brahms, Johann Strauss, and Hugo Wolf had not
received the slightest support from them. To maintain the
Philharmonic on its accustomed level, to enable the painters
and sculptors to make a living, it was necessary for the people to jump into the breach, and it was the pride and ambition of the Jewish people to co-operate in the front ranks to
carry on the former glory of the fame of Viennese culture.
They had always loved this city and had entered into its life
wholeheartedly, but it was first of all by their love for Viennese art that they felt entitled to full citizenship, and that
they had actually become true Viennese. In public life they
exerted only a meager influence; the glory of the Imperial
house overshadowed every private fortune, the leading positions in the administration of the State were held by inheritance, diplomacy was reserved for the aristocracy, the army
and higher officialdom for the old families, and the Jews did
not even attempt ambitiously to enter into these privileged
circles. They tactfully respected these traditional rights as
being quite matter-of-course. I remember, for example, that
throughout his entire life my father avoided dining at
Sacher's, and not for reasons of economy—the difference in

price between it and the other large hotels was insignificant —but because of a natural feeling of distance; it would have been distressing or unbecoming to him to sit at a table next to a Prince Schwarzenberg or a Lobkowitz. It was only in regard to art that all felt an equal right, because love of art was a communal duty in Vienna, and immeasurable is the part in Viennese culture the Jewish bourgeoisie took, by their co-operation and promotion. They were the real audience, they filled the theaters and the concerts, they bought the books and the pictures, they visited the exhibitions, and with their more mobile understanding, little hampered by tradition, they were the exponents and champions of all that was new. Practically all the great art collections of the nineteenth century were formed by them, nearly all the artistic attempts were made possible only by them; without the ceaseless stimulating interest of the Jewish bourgeoisie, Vienna, thanks to the indolence of the court, the aristocracy, and the Christian millionaires, who preferred to maintain racing stables and hunts to fostering art, would have remained behind Berlin in the realm of art as Austria remained behind the German Reich in political matters. Whoever wished to put through something in Vienna, or came to Vienna as a guest from abroad and sought appreciation as well as an audience, was dependent on the Jewish bourgeoisie. When a single attempt was made in the anti-semitic period to create a so-called "national" theater, neither authors, nor actors, nor a public was forthcoming; after a few months the "national" theater collapsed miserably, and it was by this example that it became apparent for the first time that nine-tenths of what the world celebrated as Viennese culture in the nineteenth century was promoted, nourished, or even created by Viennese Jewry.

For it was precisely in the last years—as it was in Spain

before the equally tragic decline—that the Viennese Jews had become artistically productive although not in a specifically Jewish way; rather, through a miracle of understanding, they gave to what was Austrian, and Viennese, its most intensive expression. Goldmark, Gustav Mahler, and Schönberg became international figures in creative music, Oscar Strauss, Leo Fall, and Kalman brought the tradition of the waltz and the operetta to a new flowering, Hofmannsthal, Arthur Schnitzler, Beer-Hofmann, and Peter Altenberg gave Viennese literature European standing such as it had not possessed under Grillparzer and Stifter; Sonnenthal and Max Reinhardt renewed the city's universal fame as a home of the theater, Freud and others great in science drew attention to the long famous University—everywhere, as scholars, as virtuosi, as painters, as theatrical directors and architects, as journalists, they maintained unchallenged high positions in the intellectual life of Vienna. Because of their passionate love for the city, through their desire for assimilation, they had adapted themselves fully, and were happy to serve the glory of Vienna. They felt that their being Austrian was a mission to the world; and—for honesty's sake it must be repeated—much, if not the most of all that Europe and America admire today as an expression of a new, rejuvenated Austrian culture, in literature, the theater, in the arts and crafts, was created by the Viennese Jews who, in turn, by this manifestation achieved the highest artistic performance of their millennial spiritual activity. Centuries of intellectual energy joined here with a somewhat effete tradition and nurtured, revived, increased, and renewed it with fresh strength and by tireless attention. Only the coming decades will show the crime that Hitler perpetrated against Vienna when he sought to nationalize and provincialize this city whose meaning and culture were founded in the meeting of the most heterogeneous elements, and in her spiritual supernationality. For the genius of Vienna—a specifically musical one—was always that it harmonized all the national and lingual contrasts. Its culture was a synthesis of all Western cultures. Whoever lived there and worked there felt himself free of all confinement and prejudice. Nowhere was it easier to be a European, and I know that to a great extent I must thank this city, which already in the time of Marcus Aurelius defended the Roman —the universal—spirit, that at an early age I learned to love the idea of comradeship as the highest of my heart.

~~

One lived well and easily and without cares in that old Vienna, and the Germans in the North looked with some annoyance and scorn upon their neighbors on the Danube who, instead of being "proficient" and maintaining rigid order, permitted themselves to enjoy life, ate well, took pleasure in feasts and theaters and, besides, made excellent music. Instead of German "proficiency," which after all has embittered and disturbed the existence of all other peoples, and the forward chase and the greedy desire to get ahead of all others, in Vienna one loved to chat, cultivated a harmonious association, and lightheartedly and perhaps with lax conciliation permitted each one his share without envy. "Live and let live" was the famous Viennese motto, which today still seems to me to be more humane than all the categorical imperatives, and it maintained itself throughout all classes. Rich and poor, Czechs and Germans, Jews and Christians, lived peaceably together in spite of occasional chafing, and even the political and social movements were free of the terrible hatred which has penetrated the arteries of our time as a poisonous residue of the First World War. In the old Austria they still strove chivalrously, they abused each other in the news and in the parliament, but at the conclusion of their ciceronian tirades the selfsame representatives sat down together in friendship with a glass of beer or a cup of coffee, and called each other *Du*. Even when Lueger, the leader of the anti-semitic party, became burgomaster of the city, no change occurred in private affairs, and I personally must confess that neither in school nor at the University, nor in the world of literature, have I ever experienced the slightest suppression or indignity as a Jew. The hatred of country for country, of nation for nation, of one table for another, did not yet jump at one daily from the newspaper, it did not divide people from people and nations from nations; not yet had every herd and mass feeling become so disgustingly powerful in public life as today. Freedom in one's private affairs, which is no longer considered comprehensible, was taken for granted. One did not look down upon tolerance as one does today as weakness and softness, but rather praised it as an ethical force.

For it was not a century of suffering in which I was born and educated. It was an ordered world with definite classes and calm transitions, a world without haste. The rhythm of the new speed had not yet carried over from the machines, the automobile, the telephone, the radio, and the airplane, to mankind; time and age had another measure. One lived more comfortably, and when I try to recall to mind the figures of the grown-ups who stood about my childhood, I am struck with the fact that many of them were corpulent at an early age. My father, my uncle, my teacher, the salesmen in the shops, the members of the Philharmonic at their music stands were already, at forty, portly and "worthy" men. They walked slowly, they spoke with measured accent, and, in their conversation, stroked their well-kept beards which often had already turned gray. But gray hair was merely a new sign of dignity, and a "sedate" man consciously avoided the gestures and

high spirits of youth as being unseemly. Even in my earliest
childhood, when my father was not yet forty, I cannot recall
ever having seen him run up or down the stairs, or ever
doing anything in a visibly hasty fashion. Speed was not
only thought to be unrefined, but indeed was considered
unnecessary, for in that stabilized bourgeois world with its
countless little securities, well palisaded on all sides, nothing
unexpected ever occurred. Such catastrophes as took place
outside on the world's periphery never made their way
through the well-padded walls of "secure" living. The Boer
War, the Russo-Japanese War, the Balkan War itself did
not penetrate the existence of my parents. They passed
over all reports of war in the newspapers just as they did
the sporting page. And truly, what did it matter to them
what took place outside of Austria, what did it change in
their lives? In their Austria in that tranquil epoch there
were no State revolutions, no crass destruction of values;
if stocks sank four or five points on the exchange, it was
called a "crash" and they talked earnestly, with furrowed
brows, about the "catastrophe." One complained more as
a habit than because of actual conviction about the "high"
taxes, which *de facto,* in comparison with those of the post-
war period, were nothing other than small tips to the State.
Exact stipulations were set down in testaments, to guard
grandchildren and great-grandchildren against the loss of
their fortunes, as if security were guaranteed by some sort
of invisible promissory note by the eternal powers. Meanwhile one lived comfortably and stroked one's petty cares
as if they were faithful, obedient pets of whom one was not
in the least afraid. That is why when chance places an old
newspaper of those days in my hands and I read the excited
articles about some little community election, when I try
to recall the plays in the Burgtheater with their tiny problems, or the disproportionate excitement of our youthful

STEFAN ZWEIG AS A CHILD
(WITH HIS BROTHER, right)

discussions about things that were so terribly unimportant, I am forced to smile. How Lilliputian were all these cares, how wind-still the time! It had better luck, the generation of my parents and my grandparents, it lived quietly, straight and clearly from one end of its life to the other. But even so, I do not know if I envy them. How they remained blissfully unaware of all the bitter realities, of the tricks and forces of fate, how they lived apart from all those crises and problems that crush the heart but at the same time marvelously uplift it! How little they knew, as they muddled through in security and comfort and possessions, that life can also be tension and profusion, a continuous state of being surprised, and being lifted up from all sides; little did they think in their touching liberalism and optimism that each succeeding day that dawns outside our window can smash our life. Not even in their darkest nights was it possible for them to dream how dangerous man can be, or how much power he has to withstand dangers and overcome trials. We, who have been hounded through all the rapids of life, we who have been torn loose from all roots that held us, we, always beginning anew when we have been driven to the end, we, victims and yet willing servants of unknown, mystic forces, we, for whom comfort has become a saga and security a childhood dream, we have felt the tension from pole to pole and the eternal dread of the eternal new in every fiber of our being. Every hour of our years was bound up with the world's destiny. Suffering and joyful we have lived time and history far beyond our own little existence, while they, the older generation, were confined within themselves. Therefore each one of us, even the smallest of our generation, today knows a thousand times more about reality than the wisest of our ancestors. But nothing was given to us: we paid the price, fully and validly, for everything.

II

School in the Last Century

As a matter of course I was sent to a *Gymnasium* when I had finished attending elementary school. Every well-to-do family took great care to have its sons "educated," if only for purely social reasons. They were taught French and English, they were made familiar with music, and were given governesses at first and then tutors to teach them good manners. But only the so-called "academic" education, which led to the University, carried full value in those days of enlightened liberalism; and that is why it was the ambition of every "good" family to have some sort of doctor's title prefixed to the name of at least one of its sons. The path to the University, however, was fairly long and by no means rosy. Five years of elementary school and eight years of *Gymnasium* were spent on wooden benches; five to six hours were thus taken up each day, and homework was to be mastered in the time that was left. What is more, a "general education" required French, English, Italian—the "living" languages—together with classical Greek and Latin in addition to the regular school work—that is, five languages plus geometry, physics, and the other subjects. It was more than too much, and scarcely left any time for physical development, sport and walks, to say nothing of recreation and gaiety. I can vaguely remember that when we were seven, we had to memorize a song about "joyous and blissful childhood," and sing it in chorus. The melody of that simple, artless little song is still in my ears, but even then the words passed my lips only with difficulty and made an even less

28

convincing impression upon my heart. For, if I am to be honest, the entire period of my schooling was nothing other than a constant and wearisome boredom, accompanied year after year by an increased impatience to escape from this treadmill. I cannot recall ever having been either "joyous" or "blissful" during that monotonous, heartless, and lifeless schooling which thoroughly spoiled the best and freest period of our existence. I must admit that even today I cannot help experiencing a certain feeling of envy when I see with how much more freedom, happiness, and independence children are permitted to develop in the present century. It still seems hardly credible to me when I observe today how naturally they chat as equals with their teachers, how they hurry to school without a care, whereas we were constantly filled with a feeling of inadequacy; how they may freely express the desires and inclinations of their young and curious souls both at home and in school—free, independent and natural beings, whereas all of us, as soon as we stepped into the hated building, were forced to cringe lest we strike our foreheads against an invisible yoke. For us school was compulsion, ennui, dreariness, a place where we had to assimilate the "science of the not-worth-knowing" in exactly measured portions—scholastic or scholastically manufactured material which we felt could have no relation to reality or to our personal interests. It was a dull, pointless learning that the old pedagogy forced upon us, not for the sake of life, but for the sake of learning. And the only truly joyful moment of happiness for which I have to thank my school was the day that I was able to shut the door behind me forever.

It was not that our Austrian schools were bad in themselves. On the contrary, after a hundred years of experience, the curriculum had been carefully worked out and, had it been transmitted with any inspiration, could have been the basis for a fruitful and fairly universal education. But because of their accurate arrangement and their dry formulary our lessons were frightfully barren and lifeless, a cold teaching apparatus which never adapted itself to the individual, but automatically registered the grades, "good," "sufficient," and "insufficient," depending on how far we had complied with the "requirements" of the curriculum. It was exactly this lack of human affection, this empty impersonality and the barracks-like quality of our surroundings, that unconsciously embittered us. We had to learn our lessons and were examined on what we had learned. For eight years no teacher asked us even once what we personally wished to learn, and that encouraging stimulus, for which every young person secretly longs, was totally lacking.

This sobriety was outwardly expressed in our schoolhouse, a functional building which fifty years before had been quickly, cheaply, and thoughtlessly thrown together. With its cold, badly whitewashed halls, its low classrooms without pictures or any other decoration that might have delighted the eye, its toilets that perfumed the whole house, this learning-mill was something like an old hotel which had been used by countless numbers before us, and would be used by as many more, no less indifferent and reluctant. Even today I cannot forget the musty, moldy smell that clung to this house as it did to all official buildings in Austria. We called it the "treasury" smell. It was an odor of overheated, overcrowded rooms, never properly aired, which first attached itself to our clothes and then to our souls. We sat in pairs like galley slaves, on low wooden benches that twisted our spines, and we sat until our bones ached. In the winter the bluish light of the open gas jets flickered over our books, whereas in the summer the windows were carefully covered so that we could not dreamily enjoy the view of the little square of blue sky. That century had not yet discovered that young, unformed bodies required air and exercise. A pause of ten minutes in the cold, narrow halls was thought sufficient in a period of four or five hours of motionless squatting. Twice a week we were led into the gymnasium; and there, with the windows carefully closed, we marched stupidly around on the wooden floor, and every step sent the dust high into the air. With that the demands of hygiene had been satisfied and the State had done its "duty" towards us, so far as *mens sana in corpore sano* was concerned. For years after, whenever I passed by the gloomy, cheerless building I felt a sense of relief that I was no longer forced to enter this prison of our youth. And when the fiftieth anniversary of this exalted institution was being celebrated and I, as an erstwhile star pupil, was asked to deliver the address of the day in the presence of the Minister and the Burgomaster, I politely declined. I had no reason to be thankful to this school, and every word of that sort would have been a lie.

Nor were our teachers to blame for the dreariness of the institution. They were neither good nor bad; they were not tyrants, nor on the other hand were they helpful comrades, but poor devils who were slavishly bound to the schedule, the officially designated curriculum. They had to accomplish their task as we had to do ours, and—we felt this clearly—they were as happy as we were when in the afternoon the school bell rang and gave them, and us, freedom. They did not love us, they did not hate us, and why should they, for they knew nothing about us; even after a year or two they knew only a few of us by name. According to the teaching methods of those times, they had nothing to do but to determine how many mistakes we had made in our last lesson. They sat up at their desks and we sat below, they questioned and we had to reply, and there was no other relation between us. For between teacher and pupil, between teacher's desk and school bench, the visible above and the visible below, stood the invisible barrier of "authority" which prevented all contact. For a teacher to regard a pupil as an individual (which would have demanded particular attention to the special qualities of the pupil, or the preparation of "reports" or written observations about him, which is a matter of course today) would at that time have exceeded not only the teacher's authority but his capabilities as well. On the other hand, a private conversation would have lessened the teacher's authority, for this would have placed the scholars on the same level with him, the superior. In my opinion nothing is more characteristic of the total lack of spiritual and intellectual relationship between our teachers and ourselves than the fact that I have forgotten all their names and faces. With photographic precision my memory still retains the picture of the teacher's desk and the classbook, into which we always tried to peep because it contained our marks. I can see the little red notebook in which the grades were entered, I can see the short black pencil with which our marks were recorded, and I can see my own book strewn with the teacher's corrections in red ink, but I can no longer see a single one of their faces—possibly for the reason that we always stood before them with eyes indifferent or cast down.

~

This dissatisfaction with school was by no means a personal attitude. I cannot recall a single one of my comrades who would be reluctant to admit that our interests and good intentions were wearied, hindered and suppressed in this treadmill. It was only much later that I realized that this unfeeling and soulless method of the education of our youth was not due to the carelessness of the authorities, but represented a definite, and what is more, a carefully guarded secret intention. The world about and above us, which directed all its thoughts only to the fetish of security, did not like youth; or rather it constantly mistrusted it. Proud of its systematic "progress" and of its order, bourgeois society proclaimed moderation and leisure in all forms of life as the only effective virtues of man; all hasty efforts to advance ourselves were to be avoided. Austria was an old State, dominated by an aged Emperor, ruled by old Ministers, a State without ambition, which hoped to preserve itself unharmed in the European domain solely by opposing all radical changes. Young people, who always instinctively desire rapid and radical changes, were therefore considered a doubtful element which was to be held down or kept inactive for as long a time as possible. And so there was no reason for making our school years pleasant; we were first to earn every form of advancement by patient waiting. Being thus constantly pushed back, the various age groups were valued quite differently than they are today. An eighteen-year-old student at the *Gymnasium* was treated like a child; he was punished if he was caught with a cigarette, and he had to raise his hand obediently if he wished to leave the room. But a man of thirty was also regarded as an unfledged person, and even one of forty was not yet considered ripe for a position of responsibility. Once, when a surprising exception occurred and Gustav Mahler was appointed Director of the Imperial Opera at thirty-eight, the frightened whisper and astonished murmur went through Vienna that the first artistic institution of the city had been entrusted to "so young a man" (completely forgetting that Schubert at thirty-one, and Mozart at thirty-six, had already finished their life's work). This distrust that every young man was "not quite reliable" was felt at that time in all circles. My father would never have taken a young man into his business, and whoever was unfortunate enough to appear young had to overcome this distrust on all sides. So arose the situation, incomprehensible today, that youth was a hindrance in all careers, and age alone was an advantage. Whereas today, in our changed state of affairs, those of forty seek to look thirty, and those of sixty wish to seem forty, and youth, energy, determination and self-confidence recommend and advance a man, in that age of security everyone who wished to get ahead was forced to attempt all conceivable methods of masquerading in order to appear older. The newspapers recommended preparations which hastened the growth of the beard, and twenty-four- and twenty-five-year-old doctors, who had just finished their examinations, wore mighty beards and gold spectacles even if their eyes did not need them, so that they could make an impression of "experience" upon their first patients. Men wore long black frock coats and walked at a leisurely pace, and whenever possible acquired a slight *embonpoint,* in order to personify the desired sedateness; and those who were ambitious strove, at least outwardly, to belie their youth, since the young were suspected of instability. Even in our sixth and seventh school years we refused to carry school bags, and used briefcases instead so that we might not be recognized as attending the *Gymnasium.* All those qualities which today we look upon as enviable possessions—freshness, self-assertion, daring, curiosity, youth's lust for life— were regarded as suspect in those days that only had use for "substance."

It is from this unusual attitude alone that we can understand how the State exploited the schools as an instrument for the maintenance of its authority. Above all else we were to be educated to respect the existing as perfect, the opinion of the teacher as infallible, our father's words as uncontradictable, the provisions of the State as absolute and valid for all eternity. A second cardinal principle of the pedagogy of those times, which also was applied within the family, directed that young people were not to have things too easy. Before any rights were allowed them they were to learn that they had duties, and above all others the obligation of complete docility. It was to be impressed upon us from the very start that we, who had not yet accomplished anything in life and were entirely without experience, should simply be thankful for all that was granted to us, and had no right to ask or demand anything. In my time this stupid method of intimidation was practiced from earliest childhood. Servants and ignorant mothers frightened three- and four-year-old children with the threat of calling a "policeman" if they did not at once stop being naughty. When we were still in the *Gymnasium* and brought home a poor mark in some unimportant subject, we were threatened with being taken out of school and put to learning a trade—the worst threat in a middle-class world, a return to the proletariat. When young people, in an honest desire for education, sought explanation of some earnest, timely problem from adults, they were rebuffed with a haughty "you can't understand that yet." Everywhere this technique was utilized, at home, in school, and in the State. They never tired of drilling into a young person that he was not yet "mature," that he did not understand anything, that he was merely to listen credulously but never to enter into a conversation or to contradict. And for this reason also the poor devil of a teacher, who sat up at his desk, had to remain an unapproachable idol, and to confine our entire feeling and conduct to the curriculum. Whether we were happy at school or not was unimportant. Its true mission, according to the spirit of the times, was not to advance but to retard us, not to form us inwardly but to fit us with as little opposition as possible into the ordered scheme, not to increase our energy but to discipline it and to level it off.

Such psychological or, rather, unpsychological pressure upon youth can have only one of two effects: it can be paralyzing or it can be stimulating. We can look into the records of the psychoanalysts to see how many "inferiority complexes" this absurd method of teaching brought about. It is perhaps not chance that this complex was discovered by men who themselves went through our old Austrian schools. Personally I thank this pressure for the early emergence of a passion to be free—vehement to a degree that is scarcely known to present-day youth—and a hatred for all authority, for all "talking down," which has accompanied me throughout my lifetime. For years and years this aversion to the apodictic and the dogmatic was merely instinctive, and I had already forgotten its origin. But once, on one of my lecture tours, when the large auditorium of the university had been chosen for me, and when I suddenly discovered that I was to speak from the rostrum while my listeners were to sit down below on the benches like good schoolboys who did not speak or contradict, I was suddenly filled with discomfort. I remembered how I had suffered during my school years under this uncomradely, authoritative, doctrinaire "talking down," and I was filled with anxiety lest my speech, delivered from the rostrum, might be as impersonal in its effect as was that of our teachers upon us. Because of this obstacle, that speech was the worst of my life.

～～

Until our fourteenth or fifteenth year we still felt ourselves perfectly at home in school. We made fun of the teachers and we learned our lessons with cold curiosity.

But then the hour struck when school began to bore and disturb us. A remarkable phenomenon had quietly taken place: we, who had entered the *Gymnasium* as ten-year-olds, had intellectually outgrown the school already, in the first four of our eight years. We felt instinctively that there was nothing more of importance to be learned from it, and that in many of the subjects which interested us we knew more than our poor teachers, who had not opened a book out of personal interest since their own student years. But there was another contrast which became more apparent from day to day: on the benches, where no more of us than our breeches was sitting, we heard nothing new or nothing that to us seemed worth knowing, and outside there was a city of a thousand attractions, a city with theaters, museums, bookstores, universities, music, a city in which each day brought new surprises. And so our pent-up desire for knowledge, our intellectual, artistic and sensuous inquisitiveness, which found no nourishment in school, passionately yearned for all that went on outside of school. At first only two or three of us discovered in themselves such artistic, literary and musical interests, then a dozen, and finally nearly all of us.

For among young people enthusiasm is a kind of catching phenomenon. In a class at school it infects one after another like scarlet fever or measles, and while the neophytes, with childish, vain ambition, try to outdo each other as rapidly as possible in their knowledge, they lead each other on. It is therefore merely a matter of chance which direction these passions take: if there is a stamp collector in one class he will soon make a dozen as foolish as himself, and if three rave about dancers, the others will daily stand before the stagedoor of the Opera. Three years after us came a class which was possessed with a passion for football, and before ours there was another that was wholly devoted to

Tolstoy or socialism. By chance I entered a class in which my comrades were art enthusiasts; and this may possibly have been decisive for the development of my life. In itself this enthusiasm for the theater, for literature and for art was quite natural in Vienna. The newspapers devoted special space to all the cultural events that took place in the city, and wherever we went, right and left, we heard the grown-ups discuss the opera or the Burgtheater. The pictures of the great actors were on display in all the stationery stores. Sport was still considered to be a brutal affair of which a student of the *Gymnasium* should rightly be ashamed, and the cinema with its mass ideals had not yet been invented. At home there was no opposition to be feared; literature and the theater belonged to the "innocent" passions, in contrast to playing cards or friendships with girls. Finally, my father, like all Viennese fathers, had also been smitten with the theater, and had attended the performance of *Lohengrin* under Richard Wagner with the same enthusiasm that we felt at the premières of Richard Strauss and Gerhart Hauptmann. For it was to be expected that we *Gymnasium* students should throng to each première; how ashamed we would have been before our more fortunate colleagues had we not been able to report every single detail on the morrow! Had our teachers not been completely indifferent, it would have occurred to them that on the afternoon of an important première— we had to stand in line at three o'clock to secure standing room, the only places available to us—two-thirds of all the students were taken with some mysterious illness. With strict attention they would also have discovered that the poems of Rilke were stuck between the covers of our Latin grammars, and that we used our mathematics notebooks to copy the loveliest poems out of books which we had borrowed. Daily we invented new techniques for using the dull school hours for our reading. While the teacher delivered his time-worn lecture about the "naïve and sentimental poetry" of Schiller, under our desks we read Nietzsche and Strindberg, whose names the good old man had never heard. A fever had come over us to know all, to be familiar with all that occurred in every field of art and science. In the afternoon we pushed our way among the university students to listen to the lectures, we visited all of the art exhibitions, we went in to the anatomy classrooms to watch dissections. We sniffed at all and everything with inquisitive nostrils. We crept in to the rehearsals of the Philharmonic, we hunted about in the antique shops, we examined the booksellers' displays daily, so that we might know at once what had turned up since yesterday. And above all, we read! We read everything that came into our hands. We got books from all of the public libraries, and lent each other whatever we had been able to discover. But the coffeehouse was still the best place to keep up with everything new.

In order to understand this, it must be said that the Viennese coffeehouse is a particular institution which is not comparable to any other in the world. As a matter of fact, it is a sort of democratic club to which admission costs the small price of a cup of coffee. Upon payment of this mite every guest can sit for hours on end, discuss, write, play cards, receive his mail, and, above all, can go through an unlimited number of newspapers and magazines. In the better-class Viennese coffeehouse all the Viennese newspapers were available, and not the Viennese alone, but also those of the entire German Reich, the French and the English, the Italian and the American papers, and in addition all of the important literary and art magazines of the world, the *Revue de France* no less than the *Neue Rundschau,* the *Studio,* and the *Burlington Magazine.*

And so we knew everything that took place in the world at first hand, we learned about every book that was published, and every production no matter where it occurred; and we compared the notices in every newspaper. Perhaps nothing has contributed as much to the intellectual mobility and the international orientation of the Austrian as that he could keep abreast of all world events in the coffee-house, and at the same time discuss them in the circle of his friends. For, thanks to the collectivity of our interests, we followed the *orbis pictus* of artistic events not with two, but with twenty and forty eyes. What one of us had over-looked was noticed by another, and since in our constant childish, boastful, and almost sporting ambition we wished to outdo each other in our knowledge of the very latest thing, we found ourselves actually in a sort of constant rivalry for the sensational. If, for example, we discussed Nietzsche, who then was still scorned, one of us would suddenly say with feigned superiority, "But in the idea of egotism Kierkegaard is superior to him," and at once we became uneasy: "Who is Kierkegaard, whom X knows and of whom we know nothing?" The next day we stormed into the library to look up the books of this time-obscured Danish philosopher, for it was a mark of inferiority not to know some exotic thing that was familiar to someone else. We had a passion to be the first to discover the latest, the newest, the most extravagant, the unusual, which had not yet been dwelt upon at length, particularly by the official literary critics of our daily papers. I personally was a slave to this mania for many years. Anything that was not yet generally recognized, or was so lofty as to be attainable only with difficulty, the new and radical times, provoked our particular love. And nothing was so hidden or remote that it could not be brought forth from its hiding place by our collective, eager, competitive curiosity. At the time when we were attending the *Gymnasium*, the works of Stefan George or Rilke, for example, had appeared in editions of no more than two or three hundred copies, and of these three or four at most had found their way to Vienna; no bookseller kept them in stock and none of the official critics had ever mentioned Rilke's name. But through a miracle of determination our group knew every verse and every line. We beardless, immature boys, who were forced to sit all day long on our school benches, were actually the ideal audience a young poet might dream of; we were curious, critically understanding, and quick to rapture. Our capacity for enthusiasm was boundless; during our school hours, on our way to and from school, in the coffee-house, in the theater, on our walks, we half-grown young colts did nothing but discuss books, pictures, music, and philosophy. Whoever was in the public eye as actor or conductor, whoever had published a book or written for a newspaper, was a star in our firmament. I was almost frightened when many years later I found the following sentence in Balzac's description of his youth: *"Les gens célèbres étaient pour moi comme des dieux qui ne parlaient, ne mangeaient pas comme les autres hommes."* For we felt exactly the same way. To have seen Gustav Mahler on the street was an event that we proudly reported to our comrades the next morning as a personal triumph; and when as a boy I was once introduced to Johannes Brahms and he patted me on the shoulder in a friendly fashion, I was dazed for some days after by the astonishing experience. For although at twelve I was not quite certain what he had achieved, the mere fact of his reputation, the aura of the creative, exercised overwhelming power over me. A première of Gerhart Hauptmann's in the Burgtheater had our entire class on edge for weeks before the rehearsals began. We slipped in to the actors and understudies to be

the first—before the others!—to know the plot and learn
about the cast. We had (I do not hesitate to report upon
absurdities) our hair cut by the barber of the Burgtheater,
so that we could gather secret information about Wolter or
Sonnenthal, and a pupil in one of the lower classes was
particularly spoiled by us older boys and bribed with all
sorts of attentions, merely because he was the nephew of
one of the lighting inspectors at the Opera, and through
him we were sometimes smuggled on to the stage during
rehearsals—the shock of treading on that stage exceeded that
of Virgil when he mounted into the holy circles of Paradise. The radiant power of fame was so strong for us that
even if it were seven times removed from us, it still forced
us to respect it; a certain poor little old woman seemed like
an immortal being to us because she was a grand-niece of
Franz Schubert, and on the street we gazed respectfully at
Josef Kainz's valet because he had the good fortune to be
close to the most beloved and most genial of all actors.

～～

Of course today I know exactly how much absurdity
there was in this haphazard enthusiasm, how much was
merely mutual imitation, how much was merely a sporting
desire to outbid each other, how much childish pride there
was in feeling oneself arrogantly above the ordinary world
of relatives and teachers which surrounded us. But even
today I am still surprised how much we young lads learned
through this exaggerated literary passion, how prematurely
we acquired a faculty of critical discernment through our
endless discussion and analysis. At seventeen I not only
knew every poem of Baudelaire and Walt Whitman, but
I knew each of the important ones by heart, and I believe
that never in my later years have I read as intensely as I
did during my school and university years. As a matter of

fact we were familiar with names that were not commonly honored until ten years later, and even the most ephemeral remained in our memory because we had acquired it with such zeal. Once I told my revered friend Paul Valéry how old my literary acquaintanceship with him was; that thirty years before I had known and loved some of his verses. Valéry laughed at me kindly and said, "Do not try to deceive me, dear friend, my verses did not appear until 1916." He was astonished when I described to him in detail the color and format of the little literary magazine in Vienna in which we had found his first verses in 1898. "But hardly anyone in Paris knew them," he said with wonderment, "how could you have got hold of them in Vienna?" "Just as you did when you were a *Gymnasium* student in your provincial town, and were able to find the poems of Mallarmé, who was also as little known in official literature," I was able to reply. And he agreed with me that "young people discover their poets because they wish to discover them." In fact we scented the wind before it crossed the frontier, because we constantly lived with quivering nostrils. We found the new because we desired the new, because we hungered for something that belonged to us alone, and not to the world of our fathers, to the world around us. Youth, like certain animals, possesses an excellent instinct for change of weather, and so our generation sensed, before our teachers and our universities knew it, that in the realm of the arts something had come to an end with the old century, and that a revolution, or at least a change of values, was in the offing. So far as we were concerned, the good, solid masters of our fathers' time— Gottfried Keller in literature, Ibsen in the drama, Johannes Brahms in music, Leibl in painting, Eduard von Hartmann in philosophy—were as suspect as the rest of the world of security. In spite of their technical and intellectual mastery, they no longer interested us. Instinctively we felt that their cool, well-tempered rhythm was alien to our restless blood and no longer in keeping with the accelerated tempo of our time. Just then there lived in Vienna the most vigilant spirit of the younger German generation, Hermann Bahr, who lay about him furiously as the intellectual champion of all that was forming but still unborn. With his help the "Secession" was opened in Vienna, and, to the horror of the old school, exhibited the Impressionists and the Pointillists of Paris, Munch of Norway, Rops of Belgium, and all the other extremists imaginable. And with this the way was opened for their neglected predecessors, Grünewald, El Greco, and Goya. Suddenly one learned a new way of seeing, and at the same time a new rhythm and tone through Moussorgsky, Debussy, Strauss, and Schönberg. In literature realism broke through with Zola and Strindberg and Hauptmann, the Slavic genius with Dostoievsky, and with Verlaine, Rimbaud, and Mallarmé a hitherto unknown sublimation and refinement of the lyric art of words. Nietzsche revolutionized philosophy, and a more daring, freer architecture was announced by the unadorned functional building, instead of the classical over-adornment. Suddenly the old, comfortable order was disturbed, its former and infallible norms of the "aesthetically beautiful" (Hanslick) were questioned, and while the official critics of our correct bourgeois newspapers were dismayed by the often daring experiments and sought to dam the irresistible stream with such epithets as "decadent" and "anarchistic," we young ones threw ourselves enthusiastically into the surf where it foamed at its wildest. We had the feeling that a time had set in for us, our time, in which youth had finally achieved its rights. And so suddenly our restless, seeking, perceptive passion had a meaning: we youngsters on the school bench would take part in this wild and often rabid struggle for the new art. Wherever an experiment was attempted, perhaps a Wedekind production, or the reading of some new lyrics, unfailingly we were on the spot with all the power not only of our souls but with that of our hands as well. I was present at a première of one of Arnold Schönberg's early atonal works, when a gentleman energetically hissed and whistled, and when my friend Buschbeck gave him an equally energetic slap in the face. Everywhere we were the vanguard and the shock troops of every sort of new art, merely because it was new, merely because it wished to change the world for us, whose turn had now come to live our lives. Because we felt that *"nostra res agitur."*

But there was something else that interested and fascinated us so boundlessly in this new art: it was almost exclusively the art of young people. In the generation of our fathers, the poet, the musician, or the critic only achieved recognition when he had been "tried," when he had adapted himself to the leisurely, proved taste of bourgeois society. All the men whom we were taught to respect behaved and acted respectably. Wilbrandt, Ebers, Felix Dahn, Paul Heyse, Lenbach, these long-forgotten favorites of that epoch, wore their handsome beards tinged with gray over their poetic velvet jackets. They had themselves photographed with pensive expressions, always in a "worthy" and "poetic" pose; they behaved like privy councilors and excellencies, and like them were covered with decorations. But young poets, painters, or musicians were at best alluded to as "hopeful talents," and positive recognition was temporarily put on ice. That age of circumspection did not like to distribute its favors prematurely to anyone, before he had proved himself by long years of "solid" achievement. But all the new poets, musicians, and painters were young. Gerhart Hauptmann, who had suddenly appeared out of nowhere, reigned over the German stage at the age of thirty; Stefan George and Rainer Maria Rilke had achieved literary fame and a fanatic following at twenty-three, even before they reached their majority according to Austrian law. In our own city there appeared overnight the group known as "Young Vienna" with Arthur Schnitzler, Hermann Bahr, Richard Beer-Hofmann, Peter Altenberg, in whom the specific Austrian culture, through a refinement of all artistic means, had for the first time found European expression. Above all there was one figure that fascinated, enticed, roused, and captivated us, that wonderful and unique phenomenon, Hugo von Hofmannsthal, in whom our youth saw not only its highest ambitions but also absolute poetic perfection come into being, in the person of one of its own age.

~~

The emergence of the young Hofmannsthal is and remains remarkable as one of the great wonders of early perfection. In universal literature I know no example of anyone, with the exception of Keats and Rimbaud, who at so early an age reached a like flawless mastery of speech, such elevation of ideals, or such saturation with the substance of poetry even in the least of his random lines, as this majestic genius, who in his sixteenth and seventeenth years had inscribed himself upon the eternal rolls of the German language, with verses that will not die, and with a prose that has not yet been excelled in our day. His sudden beginning and immediate perfection constituted a phenomenon that rarely occurs twice in one and the same generation. His appearance was a preternatural event, and those who first had news of it were amazed. Hermann Bahr has often told me of his astonishment when he received an essay by one "Loris" (the *Gymnasium* did not permit us to publish anything under our own name), which came from Vienna for his magazine. Among contributions from all over the world he had never received a piece written in such winged, noble speech, and showing at the same time such a wealth of thought. He wondered who this unknown "Loris" might be. Undoubtedly it was an old man who for years and years had silently distilled his thoughts and had, in some cell apart, worked the sublimest essence of the language into an almost sensuous magic. And so wise a man, so blessed a poet, lived in the same city and he had never heard of him! Bahr wrote at once to the unknown and arranged for a meeting in a coffeehouse—the famous Café Grienstadl, the chief meeting place of the young literati. One day a slender, beardless *Gymnasium* student in short trousers approached his table with quick, light steps, bowed, and, in a high voice which had not yet broken, said briefly and to the point, "Hofmannsthal! I am 'Loris.' " For years after, when Bahr spoke of his astonishment, he was moved to excitement. At first he could not believe it. A *Gymnasium* student endowed with such art, such breadth and depth of vision, such a stupendous knowledge of life with life still before him! And Arthur Schnitzler told me practically the same thing. He was still a practicing physician, since his first literary successes had as yet by no means guaranteed him a livelihood; but even then he was looked upon as the head of "Young Vienna," and those who were still younger gladly turned to him for counsel and judgment. He had met the gangling young *Gymnasium* student through some casual acquaintances, and remarked him because of his nimble wit. When the young student asked him the favor of being permitted to read a short play in verse to him, he kindly invited him to his bachelor quarters, obviously without great expectations—it was probably nothing but a *Gymnasium* student's play, sentimental or pseudo-classical, he thought. He asked several friends to join them. Hofmannsthal appeared in his short trousers, somewhat nervous and ill at ease, and began to read. "After a few minutes," Schnitzler told me, "we riveted our attention on him, and exchanged astonished, almost frightened glances. We had never heard verses of such perfection, such faultless plasticity, such musical feeling, from any living being, nor had we thought them possible since Goethe. But more wondrous than this unique mastery of form (which has never since been achieved by anyone else in the German language) was his knowledge of the world, which could only have come from a magical intuition in a youth whose days were spent sitting on a school bench." When Hofmannsthal had finished, all remained silent. "I had the feeling," Schnitzler said, "of having encountered a born genius for the first time in my life, and never again during my entire lifetime was I so overwhelmed." Whoever at sixteen had thus begun—or rather had not begun, but was perfected in beginning—would indeed become a brother of Goethe and Shakespeare. And in truth this perfection seemed to grow even more perfect. After this first piece in verse, *Gestern,* came the majestic fragment, *Tod des Tizian,* in which the German language was raised to the harmony of Italian; then the verses, each one of which was an event for us—today, years afterwards, I know them line for line by heart; then the short dramas and those essays whose wealth of knowledge, faultless understanding of art, and world visions were magically compressed into the wondrously ordered space of a few dozen pages. All that this *Gymnasium* pupil, this university student wrote was like crystal, glowing from within, dark and luminous at once. Verse and prose bent in his hands like perfumed wax of Hymettus. By some unrepeatable miracle each poem always had its correct measure, never too much, never too little.

One always felt that an unknown something, an incomprehensible mystery had led him by this way into a hitherto untrodden land.

I can hardly describe how such a phenomenon fascinated us, who had taught ourselves to sense values. For what can be more intoxicating for a young generation than to realize that the born, the pure, the sublime poet was in their midst in the flesh—the poet whom they imagined only in the legendary forms of Hölderlin and Keats and Leopardi, unapproachable, already half dream and half vision? That is why I can so clearly recall the day on which I saw Hofmannsthal in person. I was sixteen years old, and since we avidly pursued everything that our ideal mentor did, I was unusually aroused by a small notice hidden in the newspaper, announcing a lecture by him on Goethe in the Scientific Club (incomprehensible it was to us that such a genius was to speak in so modest a place; in our schoolboy adoration we had expected that the largest hall would be filled to overflowing when a Hofmannsthal allowed himself to be seen in public). On this occasion I was again aware of how far in advance of the public at large and the official critics we little *Gymnasium* students were in our evaluation, our instinct, proved here and elsewhere, for the thing that would survive. All in all, about ten to twelve dozen listeners had gathered in the narrow hall, and so it would not have been necessary for me in my impatience to start out half an hour too early to be sure of a seat. We waited for a little while, when suddenly a slim, inconspicuous young man passed between the seats towards the desk, and began so unexpectedly that I hardly had time to look at him carefully. Hofmannsthal, with his soft, incipient mustache and his elastic figure, appeared to be even younger than I had expected him to be. His sharply profiled, dark, somewhat Italian face was nervously tense, and the impression of tension was heightened by the unrest of his very dark, velvety, markedly near-sighted eyes. With one plunge he threw himself into his talk like a swimmer into a familiar stream, and the more he spoke the freer his gestures became, and the more assured his demeanor. No sooner was he in his intellectual element (and I often noticed this later in our private conversations) than his initial nervousness was overcome by an amazing lightness and soaring of speech, as is always the case with men who are inspired. It was only in his opening sentences that I was aware of the fact that his voice was unlovely, ofttimes close to a falsetto and near to breaking; soon his talk bore us aloft high and free, so that we were barely aware of his voice or his face. He spoke without a script, without notes, and possibly without careful preparation, but out of his natural feeling for form each sentence was rounded out to perfection. Brilliantly the most daring antitheses unfolded only to dissolve themselves in clear, though amazing, formulations. Perforce we had the feeling of an overpowering abundance; we knew that what was being cast by chance before us was but part of a much greater fullness, and that inspired as he was and uplifted into a higher sphere, he could continue to talk thus for hours on end without impoverishing himself or descending from his level. Later on in private conversations I again experienced the magic power of this "inventor of rolling speech," as Stefan George called him. Restless, fiery, sensitive, exposed to every movement of the air, often moody and nervous in private, he was not easy to get close to. But the very moment that a problem interested him, it was like a spark; with a gleaming, sparkling, rocket-like flight he carried every discussion aloft into the sphere that was his own and attainable only to him. With the exception of several conversations with Valéry, who thought more clearly and with more measure,

and the *élan* of Keyserling, I have never experienced any
conversation on so high an intellectual plane. In these truly
inspired moments, everything was objectively close to his
daemonic awareness, every book that he had read, every
picture that he had seen, every landscape. One metaphor
was bound to the next as naturally as hand to hand. Per-
spectives arose like unexpected stage sets behind the horizon
one had already believed was reached. On the occasion of
that lecture and later in personal encounters, I sensed in
him the true afflatus, the enlivening, inspiriting breath of
the incommensurable, the something that cannot be grasped
fully by reason alone.

In a certain sense, Hofmannsthal never surpassed the
unique wonder that he was between his sixteenth and his
twenty-fourth years. I do not less admire many of his later
works, the lovely essays, the fragment of *Andreas,* that torso
of what was probably the most beautiful novel in the German language, and individual portions of his dramas. But
his stronger ties to the real theater and the interests of his
time, with his definite consciousness and the ambitiousness
of his plans, something that was akin to dream-walking,
something purely inspirational in those early boyish
poems, which had been the ecstasy and exhilaration of our
youth, disappeared. With that magical knowledge which
is peculiar to the immature, we had known in advance that
this miracle of our youth was unique and without recurrence in our life.

～～

Balzac has incomparably described how the example of
Napoleon electrified an entire generation in France. To
Balzac the brilliant rise of the insignificant Lieutenant
Bonaparte to the rank of emperor of the world meant not
only the triumph of an individual, but the victory of the

idea of youth. That one did not have to be born a prince or a duke to achieve power at an early age, that one might come from any humble and even poor family and yet be a general at twenty-four, ruler of France at thirty and of the entire world, caused hundreds, after this unique success, to abandon petty vocations and provincial abodes. Lieutenant Bonaparte had fired the minds of an entire generation of youth. He drove them to aspire to higher things, he made the generals of the Grande Armée the heroes and careerists of the *comédie humaine*. It is always an individual young person who achieves the unattainable for the first time in any field, and thus encourages all the youngsters around him or who come after him, by the mere fact of his success. In this sense Hofmannsthal and Rilke signified an unusual impulse for our as yet unfermented energies. Without hoping that any one of us could ever repeat the miracle of Hofmannsthal, we were none the less strengthened by his mere physical existence. It proved tangibly that a poet was possible in our time, in our city, in our midst. For after all, his father, a banker, came from the same Jewish middle class as the rest of us; this genius had grown up in a house similar to our own, with similar furniture and similar manners, he had gone to a similarly sterile *Gymnasium*, he had studied out of the same textbooks and had sat for eight years on the same wooden benches, impatient as we had been, similarly impassioned for all intellectual values; and lo, while he was still fraying his trousers on the benches and was forced to march around in the *Gymnasium*, he had succeeded in transcending space and its confines, city and family, by his flight into the boundless. Through Hofmannsthal it was to some extent demonstrated to us, *ad oculos*, that in principle it was possible, even at our age and in the prison-atmosphere of an Austrian *Gymnasium*, to create poetry, and even to create perfection. It was even possible—a terrific temptation for a youthful temperament—to be published, to be celebrated, to become famous, while at home and in school one was still considered a half-grown, unimportant being.

Rilke stood for a different sort of encouragement and supplemented that of Hofmannsthal in a comforting fashion. It would have seemed blasphemous for even the most daring of us to try to rival Hofmannsthal. We knew that he was a unique miracle of premature perfection, which could never be repeated, and when we sixteen-year-olds compared our rhymes with the highly renowned verses which he had written at the same age, we quaked with shame. In the same way we felt humbled in our knowledge of the eagle's flight with which he coursed through cosmic space while he was still in the *Gymnasium*. On the other hand, Rilke had begun to write and publish his poems at an equally early age—when he was seventeen or eighteen. But Rilke's early verses, in comparison with Hofmannsthal's, and even in an absolute sense, were immature, childish and naïve, and only forbearance could find a few slender golden traces of talent in them. It was only gradually, in his twenty-second and twenty-third years, that the personality of this majestic poet, so boundlessly loved by us, began to emerge; and that was an enormous consolation for us. It was not necessary therefore to attain perfection while still in the *Gymnasium* as Hofmannsthal had done, but like Rilke we could feel our way, experiment for ourselves, and climb upward. We did not have to give up in immediate despair because for the time being our writing was unripe, irresponsible and inadequate, and perhaps instead of the miracle of Hofmannsthal we could repeat in ourselves the serener, more normal rise of Rilke.

For as was to be expected, we had long since begun to write or to create verses, to compose music or to recite;

every passive passionate attitude is of itself an unnatural one for youth, for it is in its being not only to take up impressions but to reproduce them actively. For a young man to love the theater means that he will at least desire or dream to work for, or in, the theater. To admire talent ecstatically in all its forms irresistibly leads to introspection, to see if it is not possible to discover some trace or possibility of this choicest of essences in one's unexplored body or still cloudy soul. And so it occurred in our class at school that, in keeping with the Viennese atmosphere and the particular limitations of the times, the impulse to creative production became positively epidemic. Each one of us sought some talent within himself and endeavored to unfold it. Four or five of us wished to be actors. They imitated the diction of the Imperial players, they recited and declaimed without ceasing, secretly took lessons in acting, and, during the recesses at school, distributed parts and improvised entire scenes from the classics, while the rest of us formed a curious but exacting audience. Two or three were splendidly accomplished musicians but had not yet decided whether they would become composers, virtuosi, or conductors. I owe to them my first knowledge of the new music which then was still generally scorned at the official concerts of the Philharmonic, whereas they, in turn, came to us for the texts for their songs and choruses. Another, the son of a fashionable painter who was quite famous at that time, spent hours at school filling our notebooks with sketches, and drew portraits of all of the future geniuses of the class. But the literary endeavors were the strongest. Owing to our mutual stimulation to a constantly more rapid perfection and the exchange of criticisms of every single poem, the level which we seventeen-year-olds had attained was far superior to the merely dilettante and, in some cases, actually approached a truly valid accomplishment, as was

proven by the fact that our productions were not only
accepted by obscure provincial papers, but by the leading
reviews of the new generation; they were accepted, published, and—this is the most convincing proof—paid for.
One of my comrades, Ph. A., whom I worshiped as a
genius, shone in the first place in *Pan,* that sumptuous
de luxe publication, side by side with Dehmel and Rilke.
Another, A. M., under the pseudonym of August Oehler,
had gained admission to the most unapproachable and most
eclectic of all the German reviews, the *Blätter für die
Kunst,* which Stefan George reserved exclusively for his
sacrosanct circle. A third, encouraged by Hofmannsthal,
had written a drama about Napoleon, a fourth a new
aesthetic theory and important sonnets; I myself had gained
admission to *Gesellschaft,* the leading magazine of the
"Moderns," and to Maximilian Harden's *Zukunft,* the
weekly which was most determining for the political and
cultural history of the new Germany. If I look back today,
then I must objectively confess that the sum of our knowledge, the refinement of our literary technique, and our
artistic level were really astounding for seventeen-year-olds
and only explicable by the inspiring example of Hofmannsthal's fantastic prematurity, which forced us to a
passionate exertion towards giving the very best in order
to maintain some show of respect in each other's eyes. We
were masters of all the tricks, the extravagances, the ven-
turesomeness of the language, we possessed the technique
of every verse form, and in countless attempts had tested
every style from Pindaric pathos to the simple diction of
the folksong. Each day we showed each other our work,
mutually pointed out the slightest discrepancies, and discussed every metric detail. While our good teachers were
unsuspectingly correcting our essays with red ink for missing commas, we practiced criticism on each other with a

severity, a knowledge of art, and an exactitude such as none of the official pontiffs of literature on our biggest newspapers applied to the classical masterpieces. In our last school years we went far ahead of the appointed and famous critics in professional judgment and in our capacity for stylistic expression.

This factual and truthful description of our literary prematurity might lead to the opinion that we had been a particular wonder class. By no means! At that time one could observe the same phenomenon, the same fanaticism and the same premature talent in a dozen neighboring schools in Vienna. That could not have been chance. It was a particularly propitious atmosphere, conditioned by the artistic soil of the city, the unpolitical era, the emerging constellation of intellectual talents and the new literary orientation at the turn of the century; and it was chemically related in us to the immanent will to produce which perforce belongs to that stage of life. In the age of puberty, the poetic, or the impulse toward the poetic, goes through every young person, usually of course like a passing wave; only rarely does such an inclination outlive youth, since in itself it is only an emanation of youth. None of our five actors on the school bench later became actors on the real stage; the poets of *Pan* and the *Blätter für die Kunst,* after that first astonishing beginning, bogged down as sober lawyers or officials, and perhaps today they smile with irony or melancholy at their former ambitions. I am the only one of the whole group in whom the productive passion remained and in whom it became the meaning and quintessence of an entire life. But how thankfully I think of that comradeship! How much it helped me! How those fiery discussions, that wild rivalry, that mutual admiration and criticism gave practice to my hand and nerve, how it widened and heightened my view of the intellectual cosmos, how it gave all of us wings to rise above the emptiness and wretchedness of our school! "Thou noble art! how oft, when sorrow thrill'd me . . ." Whenever that immortal song of Schubert resounds, in a sort of plastic vision I see us sitting slump-shouldered on our miserable school benches, and then on our way home, with glowing, excited faces, criticizing poems, reciting, passionately forgetting all bonds of time and space, truly "into a better world upborne."

~

Such an artistic monomania, such overvaluation of the aesthetic, carried to the point of absurdity, could only exist at the expense of the normal interests of our age. If I ask myself today when we found time to read all those books, crammed full as our days were with school and private lessons, it becomes clear to me that it was mostly at the expense of our sleep and therefore of our bodily vigor. Although I had to get up at seven, I never put down my book before one or two in the morning—the bad habit of reading for one or two hours no matter how late at night it may be has remained with me ever since. I cannot recall ever having raced to school except with too little sleep, my face hardly washed, devouring my breakfast roll as I ran; small wonder that with all our intellectuality we looked haggard and green as unripe fruit. What is more, our clothes were fairly shabby, for every penny of our pocket money was spent on the theater, concerts, or books, and, on the other hand, we attached but little weight to pleasing young girls, since we thought to impress higher tribunals. It seemed to us that walking with the girls was time lost, for in our intellectual arrogance we looked from the start upon the other sex as being mentally inferior, and did not wish to waste our precious hours in inane conversation. It would not be easy to make a young person of today understand to what degree we ignored all sport and even disdained it. To be sure, in the last century the sport wave had not yet reached our continent from England. There were as yet no stadiums where a hundred thousand people went wild with joy when one boxer hit another on the chin. The newspapers did not yet send reporters to fill columns with Homeric rapture about a hockey game. Fights, athletic clubs, and heavyweight records were still regarded in our time as a thing of the outer city, and butchers and porters really made up their audience; at best the noble and more aristocratic sport of racing drew the so-called "good society" several times a year to the racetrack, but could not lure us who looked upon every physical activity as a plain waste of time. At thirteen, when this intellectual-literary infection set in, I stopped skating, and used for books the money which my parents allowed me for dancing lessons. At eighteen I could not yet swim, dance, or play tennis; and today I still can neither ride a wheel nor drive a car, and in all sports any ten-year-old could put me to shame. Even now, in 1941, I am highly confused as to the difference between baseball and football, hockey and polo, and the sporting page of a newspaper with its inexplicable figures seems to me to be written in Chinese. In the matter of all speed and ability records in sport, I have always been of the same opinion as the Shah of Persia who, when urged to attend the Derby, replied with Oriental wisdom: "Why? I know that one horse can run faster than another. It makes no difference to me which one it is." We were as contemptuous about throwing away our time in playing games as we were about training our bodies. Chess alone found favor in our eyes, because it required mental exertion, and what was more absurd, although we felt ourselves to be, at least potentially, the coming poets, we bothered but little about nature. During my first twenty years I saw practically nothing of the wonderful surroundings of Vienna; the loveliest and warmest summer days had a particular appeal for us because on such days the city was empty, we got more papers and magazines in the coffeehouses, and got them more quickly. It took me years and decades to find the balance for this childishly eager overexcitement and to overcome my unavoidable bodily clumsiness. But all in all, I have never regretted that fanaticism of my *Gymnasium* period—that living through one's eyes and on one's nerves. It infused into my blood a passion for the intellectual which I should never care to lose, and all I have since read and learned stands on the firm foundation of those years. What one's muscles have missed can be made up later; the *élan* toward the intellectual, the soul's inner grasping power, is set in motion in those decisive formative years, and only he who has learned early to spread his soul out wide may later hold the entire world within himself.

~

That something new was in the course of preparation in the arts, something that was more passionate, more problematical, more alluring than all that had satisfied our parents and the world around us, was the particular experience of our young years. Fascinated by this one aspect of life, we did not notice that these transitions in the aesthetic realm were nothing but trends and foreshadowings of more far-reaching changes, which were to shake the world of our fathers, the world of security, and finally to destroy it. A remarkable shifting began to prepare itself in our old sleepy Austria. The masses, which had silently and obediently permitted the liberal middle classes to retain the leadership for decades, suddenly became restless, organized themselves

and demanded their rights. And it was just in the last decade
that politics broke into the calm of easy living with sharp
and sudden blasts. The new century wanted a new order,
a new era.

The first of these great mass movements in Austria was
the socialist movement. Up to that time the erroneously
denominated "universal suffrage" was only permitted to the
well-to-do, who had to submit proof of ability to pay a set
minimum tax. The advocates and landholders chosen from
this class truly and honestly believed that they were the
spokesmen and representatives of "the people" in parliament. They were very proud of being educated—some
had had an academic training—they placed weight on
dignity, decency, and good diction; for this reason the ses-
sions of parliament were like the discussion evenings in a
fashionable club. Because of their liberal belief in the
unfailing progress of the world through tolerance and reason, these middle-class democrats honestly thought that with
small concessions and gradual improvements they were
furthering the welfare of all subjects in the best way possible. But they had completely forgotten that they represented only fifty or a hundred thousand well-situated people
in the large cities, and not the hundreds of thousands and
millions of the entire country. In the meantime the machine
had done its work and had gathered the formerly scattered
workers around industry. Under the leadership of an
eminent man, Dr. Viktor Adler, a Socialist Party was created in Austria to further the demands of the proletariat,
which sought a truly universal suffrage. Hardly had this
been granted, or rather obtained by force, before it became
apparent how thin though highly valuable a layer of liberalism had been. With it conciliation disappeared from
public political life, interests hit hard against interests,
and the struggle began.

I can still recall from my earliest childhood the day which marked the turning point in the rise of the Socialist Party in Austria. The workers, in order to demonstrate visibly for the first time their strength and numbers, had given out word that the first of May was to be declared the working people's holiday, and they had decided to march in closed ranks in the Prater, in whose main avenue, a lovely, broad, chestnut-lined boulevard, usually only the carriages and equipages of the aristocracy and the wealthy middle classes appeared. This announcement paralyzed the good liberal middle classes with fright. Socialists! The word had a peculiar taste of blood and terror in the Germany and Austria of those days, like "Jacobin" before and "Bolshevik" since. At first it was thought impossible for this rabble of the faubourgs to carry out its march without setting houses on fire, plundering shops, and committing every sort of atrocity imaginable. A kind of panic set in. The police of the entire city and the surroundings were posted in the Prater, and the military were held in reserve, ready to shoot. Not a carriage, not a cab, dared to come near the Prater; the merchants let down the iron shutters in front of their shops, and I can remember that our parents strictly forbade us children to go out on the streets on this day of terror which might see Vienna in flames. But nothing happened. The workers marched in the Prater with their wives and children in closed ranks, four abreast, with exemplary discipline, each one wearing a red carnation in his buttonhole as a party emblem. While marching they sang the "Internationale," and the children, who trod on the lovely green of the Nobelallée for the first time, chanted their carefree school songs. No one was insulted, no one was struck, no fists were clenched; and the police and the soldiers smiled at them like comrades. Thanks to this circumspect conduct, the middle classes were no longer able to brand the workers as "revolutionary rabble" and they came to mutual concessions, as always in wise old Austria. The present-day system of suppression and extirpation had not yet been discovered, and the ideal of humanity (although it had already begun to fade) was alive even among political leaders.

Hardly had the red carnation made its appearance as a party emblem, when another flower began to appear in button-holes, the white carnation, the sign of membership in the Christian Social Party! (Is it not touching that flowers were then still chosen as party emblems instead of top-boots, daggers and death's heads?) The Christian Social Party, a lower middle-class party throughout, was actually only the organic counterpart of the proletarian movement and, like it, was fundamentally a product of the victory of the machine over manual crafts. For while the machine, through the aggregation of large masses in the factories, brought power and a social rise to the workers, at the same time it threatened the small handicrafts. The large department stores and mass production were the ruin of the bourgeoisie and the small employers and their manufacture by hand. An able and popular leader was Dr. Karl Lueger, who mastered this unrest and worry and with the slogan "the little man must be helped," carried with him the entire small bourgeoisie and the disgruntled middle class, whose envy of the wealthy was markedly less than the fear of sinking from its bourgeois status into the proletariat. It was exactly the same worried group which Adolf Hitler later collected around him as his first substantial following. Karl Lueger was also his prototype in another sense, in that he taught him the usefulness of the anti-semitic catchword, which put an opponent before the eyes of the broad classes of the bourgeoisie, and at the same time imperceptibly diverted their hatred from the great landed gentry and the

feudal wealthy class. The entire vulgarization and brutaliza-
tion of present-day politics, the horrible decline of our
century, is demonstrated in the comparison of these two
figures. Karl Lueger, with his soft, blond beard, was an
imposing person—*der schöne Karl,* the Viennese called him.
He had been academically educated in an age that placed
intellectual culture over all else; and he had not gone to
school in vain. He could speak in a way that appealed to
the people; he was vehement and witty, but even in the
most heated speeches—or at least, those that were thought
to be heated at that time—he never overstepped the bounds
of decency. His Streicher, a certain mechanic named
Schneider, who operated with legends of ritual murders
and similar vulgarities, was carefully held in check. Lueger
was modest and above reproach in his private life. He always
maintained a certain chivalry towards his opponents, and
his official anti-semitism never stopped him from being helpful and friendly to his former Jewish friends. When his
movement had finally captured the Viennese town council
and he, after Emperor Franz Josef (who detested the anti-
semitic tendency) had twice refused to sanction him, was
appointed burgomaster, his city administration remained
perfectly just and even typically democratic. The Jews,
who had trembled at this triumph of the anti-semitic party,
continued to live with the same rights and esteem as always.
The poison of hatred, and the will to mutual and unspar-
ing destruction, had not yet entered into the blood stream
of the time.

But soon a third flower appeared, the blue cornflower,
Bismarck's favorite flower, and the emblem of the German
National Party, which—although not then recognized as
such—was consciously a revolutionary party, and worked
with brutal forcefulness for the destruction of the Austrian
monarchy in favor of a Greater Germany under Prussian

and Protestant leadership, such as Hitler dreams of. Whereas the Christian Social Party in Vienna and throughout the country was anchored in the industrial centers, the German National Party had its followers in the Bohemian and Alpine border districts; weak in numbers, it compensated its unimportance by wild aggression and unbridled brutality. Its few representatives became the terror and (in the old sense) the shame of the Austrian parliament. In their ideas and technique, Hitler, also a border-Austrian, had his origin. He took over the cry *"Los von Rom!"* from Georg Schönerer. At that time thousands of German Nationals had followed him with German obedience by going over from Catholicism to the Protestant religion in order to annoy the Emperor and the clergy. Hitler also took over from him the anti-semitic racial theory—"In that race lies swinishness," his illustrious prototype had said. But above all else, he took from the German Nationals the beginning of a ruthless storm troop that blindly hit out in all directions, and with it the principle of terroristic intimidation by a small group of a numerically superior but humanely more passive majority. What the S. A. men, who broke up meetings with rubber clubs, attacked their opponents by night and felled them to the ground, accomplished for the National Socialists was provided for the German Nationals by the Corps Students [Tr.: Students' Club or Association with distinctive colors and emblems, such as caps and ribbons] who, under the cover of academic immunity, instituted an unparalleled campaign of violence, and who were organized as a militia to march in, at beck and call, upon every political action. Grouped into so-called *Burschenschaften* [Tr.: German Students' Association founded in 1815 in opposition to the Corps], scar-faced, drunken, and brutal, they dominated the University Hall, for they did not wear the cap and ribbon like the others, but were armed with hard, heavy sticks. Unceasingly aggressive, they attacked the Jewish, the Slavic, the Catholic, and the Italian students turn by turn, and drove them, defenseless, out of the University. On the occasion of every *Bummel* (as the Saturday student spree was called) blood flowed. The police, who because of the ancient privilege accorded the University were not allowed to enter the Hall, had to look on inactively from without and see how these cowardly ruffians worked havoc, and could do no more than carry off the wounded who were thrown bleeding down the steps into the street by these nationalist rowdies. Wherever this tiny though loud-mouthed party of the German Nationals wished to obtain anything by force in Austria, they sent this student storm troop on ahead. When Count Badeni, with the approval of the Emperor and the parliament, had concluded a language decree calculated to bring about peace between Austria's national groups, and which, in all probability, would have prolonged the existence of the monarchy for decades, this handful of young hotheaded fellows occupied the Ringstrasse. The cavalry was called out, swords were drawn and shots fired. But so great was the abhorrence of that tragically weak and touchingly human era for any violent tumult or the shedding of blood, that the Government retired in the face of the German National terror. The Minister-President resigned, and the thoroughly laudable language decree was rescinded. The invasion of brutality into politics thus chalked up its first success. All of the underground cracks and crevices between the classes and races, which the age of conciliation had so laboriously patched up, broke open once again and widened into abysses and chasms. In reality it was during the last decade preceding the new century that the war of all against all had already begun in Austria.

We young people, however, completely wrapped up in

our literary ambitions, noticed little enough of these dangerous changes in our homeland: we had eyes only for books and pictures. We did not have the slightest interest in politics and social problems: what did these shrill wranglings mean in our lives? The city was aroused at the elections, and we went to the libraries. The masses rose, and we wrote and discussed poetry. We did not see the fiery signs on the wall, and like King Belshazzar of old we feasted without care on the precious dishes of art, not looking anxiously into the future. And only decades later, when roof and walls fell in upon us, did we realize that the foundations had long since been undermined and that together with the new century the decline of individual freedom in Europe had begun.

III

Eros Matutinus

DURING the eight years of our higher schooling, something had occurred which was of great personal importance to each one of us: we ten-year-olds had grown into virile young men of sixteen, seventeen, and eighteen, and Nature began to assert its rights. The awakening of puberty appears to be a purely private matter which each growing person has to fight out in his own fashion, and at first glance does not seem at all suitable for public discussion. As far as we were concerned, that crisis grew beyond its proper sphere. At the same time it brought about an awakening in another sense: for the first time it taught us to observe more critically the social world in which we had grown up, and its conventions. Children and even young people are at first inclined to adapt themselves respectfully to the laws of their surroundings. But they submit to the conventions demanded of them only so long as they see that these are honestly observed by everyone else. A single untruthfulness on the part of teachers or parents inevitably leads a young person to regard his entire surroundings with a suspicious and therefore a sharper eye. It did not take us long to discover that all those authorities in whom we had previously confided—school, family, and public morals—manifested an astonishing insincerity in this matter of sex. But what is more, they also demanded secrecy and reserve from us in this connection.

For they thought differently about these things thirty or forty years ago than they do now. It is quite possible that there is no sphere of public life in which a series of factors—the emancipation of women, Freudian psychoanalysis, physical culture, the independence of youth—have brought about so complete a change within one generation as in the relationship between the sexes. If we attempt to differentiate between the middle-class morality of the nineteenth century, which was essentially a Victorian morality, and the freer and unaffected views of today, we shall probably come closest if we say that that epoch anxiously evaded the sexual problem out of an inner feeling of uncertainty. Earlier religious ages, that still were honest, and strict Puritanism in particular, made things easier for themselves. Filled with an upright conviction that sensual desire was the sting of the Devil, and that bodily lust was unchaste and sinful, the authorities of the Middle Ages approached the problem fairly and squarely with harsh interdictions: and—particularly in Calvinist Geneva—they enforced their strict morality with cruel punishments. Our century, however, being an epoch that no longer believed in the Devil and scarcely believed in God, had no heart for so drastic an anathema, but looked upon sexuality as an anarchical and therefore disturbing element, which had no place in its ethics and which was not allowed to see the light of day, because every form of free and extra-marital love was in opposition to middle-class "decency." In this dilemma the times invented a remarkable compromise. It limited its morality, not by forbidding a young man to carry on his *vita sexualis,* but by demanding of him that this painful matter be attended to in as inconspicuous a manner as possible. If it was not feasible to do away with sexuality, then at least it must not be visible in the world of morality. A silent pact was therefore reached, by which the entire bothersome affair was not mentioned in school, in the family, or in public, and everything which brought its existence to mind was suppressed.

It is easy for us, who since the time of Freud know that whoever seeks to suppress the consciousness of natural desires not only fails to remove them but dangerously displaces them into the subconscious, to laugh at the unenlightenment of that naïve technique of concealment. But the nineteenth century labored under the illusion that all conflicts could be solved by rationalization, and that the more we hid the natural, the more we could temper our lawless powers. Therefore, if young people were not enlightened about the presence of these forces, they would forget their own sexuality. In this illusion of control through ignoring, all authorities were united in a boycott of hermetic silence. School and church, salon and courts, newspapers and books, modes and manners, in principle avoided every mention of the problem, and even science, whose real task should have been to approach all problems impartially, shamefully subscribed to the *naturalia sunt turpia*. Science also surrendered with the excuse that it was beneath its dignity to handle such improper themes. In paging through books of those times, philosophical, legal, or even medical, we find that they consistently and scrupulously avoided any mention of the subject. When professors of criminal law, in their meetings, discussed more humane methods in prisons and the injurious moral effects of incarceration there, they shyly passed by the main problem. Nor did the nerve specialists, although in many cases they were fully aware of the etiology of some hysterical illnesses, dare to admit how matters really stood. We read in Freud that even his own respected teacher, Charcot, had privately admitted to him that although he knew the true cause, he had never spoken of it in public. But least of all did the so-called *belles lettres* of the times dare to represent things honestly, for the aesthetically beautiful alone had been apportioned to them as their proper domain. Whereas in earlier centuries a writer had not been afraid to give an honest and inclusive cultural picture of his times, and while in the writings of Defoe, the Abbé Prévost, Fielding and Rétif de la Bretonne, one still meets with unvarnished descriptions of conditions as they actually were, our epoch thought that it could only portray the "sentimental" and the "sublime," but not the painful and the true. For this reason we find, in the literature of the nineteenth century, only the merest trace of all the perils, shadows, and confusions of the city youth. Even if a writer boldly mentioned prostitution, he thought it necessary to ennoble it, and perfumed the heroine as a veritable Camille. So we are confronted with the amazing fact that if, wishing to know how the young of the last century, and even the century before that, fought their way through life, a young man of today picks up the novels of the greatest masters of those times, the works of Dickens and Thackeray, Gottfried Keller and Björnson—with the exception of Tolstoy and Dostoievsky, who being Russian stood outside of European pseudo-idealism—he will find nothing but sublimated and toned-down events described there, for the entire generation was inhibited in its freedom of speech by the pressure of the times. And nothing shows more clearly the almost hysterical overexcitement of the morality of our forefathers and its incredible atmosphere than the fact that even this literary reticence was not sufficient. Is it possible for us to understand that so objective a novel as *Madame Bovary* was forbidden by a French court as being indecent, or that in the time of my youth Zola's novels were held to be pornographic, and that even so calm and epic a writer as Thomas Hardy had raised storms of indignation

in England and America? As reticent as they were, these
books had already revealed too much of reality.

⟨But we grew up in this sticky, perfumed, sultry, un-
healthy atmosphere.⟩ This dishonest and. unpsychological
morality of secrecy and hiding hung over us like a nightmare, and since true literary and culturally historical documents are lacking because of the universality of this
technique of concealment, it may not be easy to reconstruct
what already has become incomprehensible. A certain clue,
however, is available. We need merely look at the fashions,
for the modes of a century, with their trends in visual taste,
unintentionally also reveal its morals. It is no mere chance
that today, in the year 1941, when men and women of
society of the year 1900 are shown on the cinema screen
in the costumes of their time, audiences in every city and
in every village of Europe or America break out into uncontrolled laughter. Even the most naïve persons of today
laugh at them as caricatures. These strange figures of yester-
year appear as unnaturally, uncomfortably, unhygienically,
and unpractically dressed fools. And even to us who still
saw our mothers and aunts and friends in these absurd
costumes (to say nothing of the fact that we ourselves went
about as ridiculously attired), it seems like a ghost-like
dream that an entire generation could have submitted itself
to such stupid fashions without a murmur. The male
fashions alone—the high, stiff collar, the "choker" which
made any easy motion impossible, the buttoned-up black
frock coats with their flapping skirts, and the high "stove-
pipe" hats—are cause for mirth, to say nothing of the "lady"
of former times in her careful and complicated attire, violat-
ing Nature in every single detail! The middle of her body
laced into a wasp's shape in a corset of stiff whalebone,
blown out like a huge bell from the waist down, the neck
closed in up to the chin, legs shrouded to the toes, the hair

towering aloft with countless curls, locks, and braids under
a majestically swaying monstrosity of a hat, the hands
encased in gloves, even on the warmest summer day, this
long since archaic being, the "lady," in spite of the jewelry
with which she was bespangled, in spite of the perfume
which surrounded her, the costly laces, the ruchings and
other adornments, was an unhappy, pitifully helpless person.
At first glance one is aware that a woman, once she is
encased in such a toilette, like a knight in armor, could no
longer move about freely, gracefully and lightly. Every
movement, every gesture, and consequently her entire conduct, had to be artificial, unnatural and affected in such a
costume. The mere make-up of such a "lady"—to say
nothing of her social education—the putting on and taking
off of these robes, was a troublesome procedure and quite
impossible without the help of others. First a countless
number of hooks and eyes had to be fastened in the back
from waist to neck, and the corset pulled tight with all the
strength of the maid in attendance. The long hair (must
I remind the young people that thirty years ago, with the
exception of a few dozen Russian students, every woman
in Europe could let her hair down to her waist?) was curled,
brushed, combed, flattened, piled up, with the aid of a
legion of hairpins, barrettes, and combs and with the
additional help of a curling iron and curlers, by a hair-
dresser who called daily, before one could swathe and build
her up with petticoats, camisoles, jackets, and bodices like
so many layers of onion skin, until the last trace of her
womanly and personal figure had fully disappeared. But this
nonsense had a secret reason. The true lines of the body
of a woman had to be so completely hidden that even her
bridegroom at the wedding banquet could not have the
faintest idea whether his future life-partner was straight or
crooked, whether she was fat or lean, short-legged, bow-

legged, or long-legged. This "moral" era by no means regarded as impermissible the building up of the bosom, the hair, or the use of a bustle for reasons of deception or as an adaptation to the common ideal of beauty. The more of a "lady" a woman was to be, the less was her natural form to be seen. Fundamentally, the mode, with this as its obvious motive, merely obeyed the general moral tendency of the time, whose chief care was dissembling and concealment.

But this wise morality completely forgot that if one shuts the front door on the Devil, he usually forces an entrance through the chimney or the back door. What catches the more impartial eye of today, looking at these fashions which sought in despair to cover up every trace of naked skin and honest growth, is not their decency but, on the contrary, their minutely provocative revelation of the radical difference between the sexes. Whereas the young man and young woman of our day, both tall and slim, both beardless and with short hair, have a certain conformity even in their outward appearance, the sexes in those days set themselves as far apart as they could. The men sported long beards or at least twirled a mighty mustache, so that their manhood was apparent even from afar, while in the case of woman the corset ostentatiously outlined the bosom, the chief characteristic of her sex. The stronger sex was accentuated over the weaker one in the bearing demanded of each, the man vigorous, chivalrous, and aggressive, the woman shy, timid and on the defensive, the hunter and his prey, instead of their being equal. By this unnatural differentiation in external habits the inner tension between the poles, the erotic, was necessarily strengthened, and thus, by its unpsychological method of concealment and reticence, the society of that time achieved the directly opposite effect. While in its incessant fear and prudishness it was constantly tracking down the indecent in all forms of life, literature, art, and dress, in order to avoid every possible incitement, it was actually forced to think constantly of the indecent. Since it searched without interruption for all that was "improper," it found itself in a constant state of alert; to the world of that day "decency" was always in mortal danger, in every word and in every gesture. Perhaps we can still understand that in those days it would have been a crime for a woman to wear a pair of trousers at play. The possibility of two young people of the same social class, but of different sexes, going on an excursion together without proper supervision was unthinkable; or rather, the first thought would have been that "something might happen." Such companionship was only permissible if some chaperone, a mother or a governess, followed the young people step by step. That even in the hottest summers young girls should play tennis in clothes that permitted freedom to their legs or with naked arms, would have been scandalous, and when a well-behaved woman crossed her feet in society, custom found this to be horribly improper, because her ankles might be disclosed under the hem of her dress. Even the elements, sun, water, and air, were not permitted to touch the skin of a woman. In the open sea women made painful progress in heavy suits which covered them from top to toe, and in the boarding schools and convents the young girls, in order to forget that they had bodies, were forced to bathe in long, white shirts. It is neither legendary nor exaggerated to say that old women died, the lines of whose shoulders or knees no one had ever seen, with the exception of the midwife, their husbands, and the undertaker. Yet after forty years all this must appear to be either a fairy tale or humorous exaggeration. But this fear of everything physical and natural dominated the whole people, from the highest to the lowest, with the violence of an actual neurosis. Can one still imagine

today that at the turn of the century when women first
ventured to ride a bicycle or rode a man's saddle, these
daring creatures were stoned by peasants? Or that once,
when I still went to school, the Viennese papers printed
columns of discussion about the proposed horribly indecent
innovation—the ballerinas of the Imperial Opera were to
dance without stockings? Or that it was an incomparable
sensation when Isadora Duncan, in her highly classical
dances, for the first time showed the soles of her feet below
her white tunic (which fortunately floated all the way
down!) instead of wearing the customary silk slippers? And
now think of the young people who grew up with eyes wide
open in such an era, and how ridiculous these fears over
the constant threat to decency must have seemed to them,
as soon as they discovered that the cloak of morality, which
had been thought to conceal all these things, was threadbare and full of holes. After all, it was unavoidable that
one of the fifty *Gymnasium* students would occasionally
meet his professor in a dimly lighted back street, or that
in the family circle we heard that this one or that one, who
was particularly haughty in our presence, had various
lapses from grace on his conscience. As a matter of fact,
nothing increased and troubled our curiosity as much as
this clumsy business of concealment; and since all that was
natural was not permitted to run its course freely and
openly, in a big city curiosity created its own not very
clean underground outlets. In all classes, through this
suppression of youth, an overexcitation was felt which
worked itself out in a childish and helpless fashion. There
was scarcely a fence or a privy that was not besmeared with
obscene words and drawings, hardly a bathing pool in which
the wooden wall of the women's quarters was not bored
full of peepholes. Entire industries, which have perished
today now that customs are more natural, flowered secretly.

"Art" and nude photographs in particular were offered to half-grown boys for sale under the table by peddlers in every café. Since serious literature was forced to be careful and idealistic, pornographic literature of the very worst sort called *sous le manteau,* printed on bad paper and written in bad language, none the less found a tremendous public, as did magazines of a racy nature. None can be found today as vile and repulsive as they were. In addition to the Imperial Theater, which had to serve the ideal of the times with all its nobility of purpose and its snow-white purity, there were theaters and cabarets given over exclusively to obscenity. Everywhere the suppressed sought byways, loopholes, and detours. In the final analysis that generation, to whom all enlightenment and all innocent association with the opposite sex was prudishly denied, was a thousand times more erotically inclined than the younger generation of today with its greater freedom of love. For it is only the forbidden that occupies the senses, only the forbidden excites desire; and the less the eyes manage to see and the ears to hear, the more the mind will dream. The less air, light, and sun were allowed to the body, the more the senses were troubled. To sum up, the pressure of society on our youth, instead of bringing about a higher morality, brought forth nothing but mistrust and bitterness against all authorities. From the very first day of our awakening, we had felt instinctively that this dishonest morality, with its concealment and reticence, wished to take something that rightly belonged to our age away from us, and our will to honesty was sacrificed to a convention which had long since become false.

～～

This "social morality," which, on the one hand privately presupposed the existence of sexuality and its natural course, but on the other would not recognize it openly at any price, was doubly deceitful. While it winked one eye at a young man and even encouraged him with the other "to sow his wild oats," as the kindly language of the home put it, in the case of a woman it studiously shut both eyes and acted as if it were blind. That a man could experience desires, and was permitted to experience them, was silently admitted by custom. But to admit frankly that a woman could be subject to similar desires, or that creation for its eternal purposes also required a female polarity, would have transgressed the conception of the "sanctity of woman-hood." In the pre-Freudian era, therefore, the axiom was agreed upon that a female person could have no physical desires as long as they had not been awakened by man, and that, obviously, was officially permitted only in marriage. But even in those moral times, in Vienna in particular, the air was full of dangerous erotic infection, and a girl of good family had to live in a completely sterilized atmos-phere, from the day of her birth until the day when she left the altar on her husband's arm. In order to protect young girls, they were not left alone for a single moment. They were given a governess whose duty it was to see that they did not step out of the house unaccompanied, that they were taken to school, to their dancing lessons, to their music lessons, and brought home in the same manner. Every book which they read was inspected, and, above all else, young girls were constantly kept busy to divert their attention from any possible dangerous thoughts. They had to practice the piano, learn singing and drawing, foreign languages, and the history of literature and art. They were educated and overeducated. But while the aim was to make them as educated and as socially correct as possible, at the same time society anxiously took great pains that they remain innocent of all natural things to a degree unthinkable today. A young girl of good family was not allowed to have any idea of how the male body was formed, or to know how children came into the world, for the angel was to enter into matrimony not only physically untouched, but completely "pure" spiritually as well. "Good breeding," for a young girl of that time, was identical with ignorance of life; and this ignorance ofttimes lasted for the rest of their lives. I am still amused by a grotesque story of an aunt of mine who, on the night of her marriage, stormed the door of her parents' house at one o'clock in the morning. She never again wished to see the horrible creature to whom she had been married. He was a madman and a beast, for he had seriously attempted to undress her. It was only with great difficulty that she had been able to escape from this obviously perverted desire.

Now I cannot conceal the fact that this innocence lent the young girls of those days a secret charm. These unfledged creatures sensed that besides their own world there was another of which they knew nothing and were not permitted to know anything, and this made them curious, dreaming, yearning, and covered them with an alluring confusion. When we greeted them on the street they blushed—are there any young girls today who blush? When they were among themselves, they giggled and whispered and laughed incessantly as if they were slightly tipsy. Full of expectation for all this unknown experience from which they were locked out, they dreamed their lives romantically, but at the same time they were bashful lest someone discover how much their bodies yearned for a tenderness of which they knew nothing clearly. A sort of mild confusion constantly irritated their conduct. They walked differently from the girls of today whose bodies have been steeled by sports, who move about freely with young men of their own kind; in those days one could distinguish at a distance a young girl from a woman who had already known a man, simply by the way she walked. They were more girlish, and less womanly, than the girls are today. In their nature they were akin to the exotic delicacy of a hothouse plant cultivated under glass in an artificially over-warmed atmosphere, protected against any strong gust of wind, the artfully tended product of a definite education and culture.

And that is how the society of those days wished young girls to be, silly and untaught, well educated and innocent, curious and shy, uncertain and unpractical, and predisposed to this education without knowledge of the world from the very beginning, to be led and formed by a man in marriage without any will of their own. Custom seemed to preserve them as a symbol of its most secret ideals, as an emblem of womanly chastity, virginity, and unworldliness. But what a tragedy it was if one of these young girls missed her time, if she was not yet married at twenty-five or thirty! Custom pitilessly demanded of women of thirty and forty years of age that for the sake of "family" and "morality" they maintain this condition of inexperience and freedom from desire, of naïveté, although it no longer suited their age. But then the sweet picture usually turned into a sharp and cruel caricature. The unmarried maiden became an article left on the shelf, and the left-over became an old maid, the butt of the shallow derision of all the comic papers. Whoever picks up a volume of the *Fliegende Blätter,* or any one of the humorous magazines of that period, will shudder at their stupid jeering at aging maidens, who with nerves disturbed did not know how to conceal their natural desire for love. Instead of recognizing the tragedy which beset these sacrificed lives, which for reasons of family and good name were forced to suppress the demands of Nature and the desire for love and motherhood, people ridiculed them with a lack of understanding that disgusts us today. For a society is always most cruel to those who disclose and reveal its secrets, when through dishonesty society itself has outraged Nature.

~

Although middle-class usage strove frantically to uphold the fiction that a well-born woman neither possessed sexual instincts nor was permitted to possess any as long as she remained unmarried—anything else would have made her an "immoral person," an outcast from the family—it was obliged to admit the existence of such desires on the part of young men. Since experience had taught that those who had grown to manhood could not be hindered from carrying on their sexual life, the only restriction was the modest wish that they accomplish their unworthy pleasures outside the walls of sacred morality. Just as cities, under the cleanly swept streets with their handsome *de luxe* shops and elegant promenades, hide a system of subterranean sewers which carry off their filth, so the entire sexual life of youth was supposed to go on under the moral surface of "society." The perils to which a young man was exposed, and the company into which he might come, were a matter of indifference; school and family carefully avoided enlightening the young man in this connection. Occasionally, in later years, there were cautious or "enlightened" fathers, as they were then called, who, the moment their sons showed the first signs of a sprouting beard, wished to guide them into the right path. Then the family physician was called in, and at the proper time bade the young man come into the room, polished his glasses unnecessarily before he began his lecture on the dangers of venereal diseases, and admonished the young man, who usually at this point had long since taught himself, to be moderate and not to overlook certain preventive measures. Other fathers used an even more astonishing method; they engaged a pretty servant girl for the house whose task it was to give the young lad some practical experience. It seemed best to them that the youngster take care of this bothersome matter under their own roof, for it not only preserved decorum outwardly, but also averted the danger of his falling into the hands of some designing person. One method of enlightenment was frowned upon by all the authorities: the open and honest method.

~

What possibilities actually existed for a young man of the middle-class world? In all the others, in the so-called lower classes, the problem was no problem at all. In the country the farmhand slept with a maid when he was seventeen, and even if the affair had any consequences, it was of no further importance. In most of our Alpine villages the number of natural children greatly exceeded the legitimate ones. Among the proletariat, the worker, before he could get married, lived with another worker in free love. Among the orthodox Jews of Galicia, a bride was given to the seventeen-year-old, that is, at the normal age of puberty, and it was possible for him to be a grandfather at forty. It was only in our middle-class society that such a remedy as an early marriage was scorned. No father of a family would have entrusted his daughter to a twenty- or twenty-two-year-old man, since so "young" a man was not considered sufficiently mature. Here too, an inner dishonesty disclosed itself, for the middle-class calendar in no way agreed with that of Nature. As far as society was concerned, a young man did not reach manhood until he had secured a "social position" for himself—that is, hardly before his twenty-fifth or twenty-sixth year. And so there was an artificial interval of six, eight, or ten years between actual manhood and manhood as society accepted it; and in this interval the young man had to take care of his own "affairs" or adventures.

Those days did not give him too many opportunities. Only a very few particularly rich young men could afford the luxury of keeping a mistress, that is, taking an apartment and paying her expenses. And only a very few fortunate young men achieved the literary ideal of love of the times—the only one which it was permitted to describe in novels—an affair with a married woman. The others helped themselves for the most part with shopgirls and waitresses, and this offered little inner satisfaction. For at that time, before the emancipation of women and their active participation in public life, it was only the girls of the very poorest proletarian background who were sufficiently unresisting on the one hand, and had enough freedom on the other, for such passing relationships without serious thoughts of marriage. Badly dressed, tired after a twelve-hour day of poorly paid work, unkempt (a bathroom in those days was still only the privilege of the rich), and brought up in narrow circumstances, these poor creatures were so much below the standing of their lovers that these in turn were mostly ashamed of being seen openly with them. But convention, always cautious, had invented its own measures for this painful situation, the so-called *chambres séparées,* where one could dine unseen with a girl; the rest was accomplished in the dark side streets in the little hotels which were equipped for these purposes exclusively. But all these meetings had to be fleeting and without any real beauty, more sex-drive than *eros,* for they were always hasty and secret as all forbidden things are. Then, of course, there was still the possibility of an affair with one of those amphibious creatures who were half inside, half outside society—actresses, dancers, and artistes, the only "emancipated" women of the times. But generally speaking, prostitution was still the foundation of the erotic life outside of marriage; in a certain sense it constituted a dark underground vault over which rose the gorgeous structure of middle-class society with its faultless, radiant façade.

~~~

The present generation has hardly any idea of the gigantic spread of prostitution in Europe before the World War. Whereas today it is as rare to meet a prostitute on the streets of a big city as it is to meet a wagon in the road, then the sidewalks were so sprinkled with women for sale that it was more difficult to avoid than to find them. To this was added the countless number of "closed houses," the night clubs, the cabarets, the dance parlors with their dancers and singers, and the bars with their "come-on" girls. At that time female wares were offered for sale at every hour and at every price, and it cost a man as little time and trouble to purchase a woman for a quarter of an hour, an hour, or a night, as it did to buy a package of cigarettes or a newspaper. Nothing seems to me to confirm the greater honesty and naturalness of our present-day life and love forms than the fact that it is possible and almost normal for the youth of today to do without this once indispensable institution. It is not the police nor the laws that have restricted prostitution in our world. This tragic product of a pseudo-morality, except for a small remnant, has liquidated itself because of a decreased demand.

The official attitude of the State and its morality towards this shady affair was never a very comfortable one. From the moral point of view, the State did not dare acknowledge the right of a woman to sell herself, and from the hygienic viewpoint, on the other hand, prostitution could not be spared because it canalized the troublesome extra-marital sexuality. And so the authorities sought to avail themselves of an ambiguity, in that a distinction was made between private prostitution, which the State prosecuted as being immoral and dangerous, and legalized prostitution, which it supplied with a sort of trade license and which it taxed. A girl who had decided to become a prostitute was given a particular concession by the police and received her own book as a qualifying certificate. Inasmuch as she submitted to police control and complied with her duty of being examined by a physician twice each week, she had acquired the business right to lease out her body at any price she saw fit. Prostitution was recognized as a profession among the other professions; but—and here is the rub of morality— it was not quite fully recognized. So, for example, a prostitute who sold her wares, that is, her body, to a man and later did not receive the price agreed upon, had no right to sue him. For then suddenly her suit—*ob turpem causam* as the law saw it—had become an immoral one and stood without the protection of the law.

It was in such matters that one felt the duplicity of a concept which, although it incorporated these girls into a legally permitted profession, still considered them personally as outcasts beyond the law. But the actual dishonesty lay in the fact that these limitations applied only to the poorer classes. A ballet dancer, who was available for any man at any hour in Vienna for two hundred crowns, just as the girl of the streets was available for two crowns, obviously did not need a trade license. The great *demi-mondaines* were even mentioned in the papers as among those present at the Derby or the trotting-races, because they were already a part of "society." And again, certain of the most fashionable go-betweens, who furnished the Court, the aristocracy, and the rich with luxury wares, were above the law, though usually procuring was punished with a heavy prison sentence. The strict discipline, the pitiless surveillance, the social ostracism, applied only to the army of thousands and thousands who defended, with their bodies and their humiliated souls, an old and long since undermined moral prejudice against free and natural love.

~~~

This gigantic army of prostitution, like the real army, was made up of various branches, cavalry, artillery, infantry, and siege artillery. In the ranks of prostitution the siege artillery was the group which had occupied certain streets in the city as their quarter. They were for the most part the places where in the Middle Ages the gallows had stood, or a leper hospital, or a cemetery had been, or where the "freemen" and other social outcasts had found shelter. In other words, vicinities which the citizens had preferred to avoid as residential quarters. There the authorities had set up certain streets as a love market; door after door, in the twentieth century, from two to five hundred women sat as they did in the Yoshiwara of Japan or the Fish Market in Cairo, one next to the other on display at the windows of their dwellings at street level—cheap goods which were worked in two shifts, day and night.

The cavalry or infantry was made up of the roving prostitutes, the countless girls who sought their clients on the streets. In Vienna they were commonly called "line girls" because the sidewalks had been marked off by the police with an invisible line where they might carry on their trade. By day and by night until the gray of the dawn, they dragged their dearly bought false elegance over the streets, in rain and snow, constantly forced to twist their tired, badly painted faces into an alluring smile for every passer-by. Every city appears to me to be lovelier and more humane since these droves of hungry, unhappy women no longer populate the streets, without pleasure offering pleasure for sale, and after all their wandering from one· corner to another finally going one and the same inevitable way, the way to the infirmary.

But even these masses did not suffice for the steady demand. There were some who wished to be more comfortable and more discreet than in chasing these fluttering bats or sorry birds of paradise on the streets. They wanted love at their ease, with light and warmth, with music and dancing and an appearance of luxury. These clients had their "closed houses" or brothels. There the girls were assembled in a so-called *salon,* furnished in counterfeit luxury, some in evening gowns, others in unreticent negligées. A piano player supplied the music; there was drinking and dancing and conversation before the pairs discreetly retired to a bedroom. In some of the more fashionable houses, particularly in Paris and Milan, which had a sort of international reputation, a naïve person could labor under the illusion of having been invited to a private house with some very merry ladies of society. Outwardly the girls in these houses were better off than the roving girls of the streets. They did not have to wander through wind and rain, through filthy alleys, they sat in warm rooms, were given good clothes, ample food, and, in particular, ample drink. But in return, they were actually the prisoners of their landladies, who forced the clothes they wore upon them at exorbitant prices, and did such magic tricks of arithmetic with the rent and board that even the most industrious and persevering girl remained in debt and could never leave the house of her own free will.

To write the intimate history of some of these houses would be interesting and also of documentary importance for the culture of that period, for they held the strangest secrets, well known to the otherwise strict authorities. There were hidden doors and a special stairway by which the members of the highest society—and, it was whispered, even members of the Court—could pay their visits without being seen by other mortals. There were mirrored rooms and some that offered a hidden view of the neighboring room, in which a couple were unsuspectingly enjoying themselves. There were the weirdest changes of costumes, from the habit of a nun to the dress of a ballerina, locked away in closets and chests for particular fetishists. And this was the same city, the same society, the same morality, that was indignant when young girls rode bicycles, and declared it a disgrace to the dignity of science when Freud in his calm, clear, and penetrating manner established truths that they did not wish to be true. The same world that so pathetically defended the purity of womanhood allowed this cruel sale of women, organized it, and even profited thereby.

We should not permit ourselves to be misled by sentimental novels or stories of that epoch. It was a bad time for youth. The young girls were hermetically locked up under the control of the family, hindered in their free bodily as well as intellectual development. The young men were forced to secrecy and reticence by a morality which fundamentally no one believed or obeyed. Unhampered, honest relationships—in other words, all that could have made youth happy and joyous according to the laws of Nature—were permitted only to the very few. And anyone of that generation who wishes to look back honestly upon his first meetings with women will recall but few episodes that he can think about with unmixed pleasure. For in addition to the social pressure, which constantly enforced precaution and secrecy, there was at that time another element that overshadowed the happiest moments: the fear of infection. Here too, the youth of that era was neglected

in comparison with those of today, for it must not be forgotten that forty years ago sexual diseases were spread a
hundred times more than they are today, and that they
were a hundred times more dangerous and horrible in effect,
because medicine did not yet know how to approach them
clinically. Science could not yet cure them quickly and
completely as it does today, so that now they are no more
than episodes. Whereas today, thanks to Paul Ehrlich's
therapy, in the clinics of the small and medium-sized universities weeks often pass by in which the professor is unable
to show his students a freshly infected case of syphilis, the
statistics of those days show that in the army and in the
big cities at least one or two out of every ten young men
had fallen victim to infection. Youth was reminded incessantly of the danger. Going through the streets of Vienna,
one could read on the door of every sixth or seventh house,
Specialist for Skin and Venereal Diseases, and to the fear of
infection was added the horror of the disgusting and degrad-
ing forms of the erstwhile cures, of which the world of
today also knows nothing. For weeks on end the entire
body of anyone infected with syphilis was rubbed with
mercury, the effect of which was that the teeth fell out and
other injuries to health ensued. The unhappy victim of a
severe encounter felt himself not only physically but spiritually spotted, and even after so horrible a cure, he could
never be certain that the cunning virus might not at any
moment awake from its captivity and paralyze the limbs
from the spine, or soften the brain. Small wonder then that
at that time many young people, once the diagnosis had
been made, reached for their revolvers because they could
not stand the feeling that they were suspected of being
incurable. Then there were the other sorrows of a *vita
sexualis* carried on in secret. Though I try hard to remember, I cannot recall a single comrade of my youth who did

not come to me with pale and troubled mien, one because
he was ill or feared illness, another because he was being
blackmailed because of an abortion, a third because he
lacked the money to be cured without the knowledge of his
family, the fourth because he did not know how to pay
hush money to a waitress who claimed to have had a child
by him, the fifth because his wallet had been stolen in a
brothel and he did not dare to go to the police. The youth
of those pseudo-moral times were much more romantic and
yet more unclean, much more excited and yet more depressed, than the novels and dramas of their official writers
depict them. In the sphere of *eros*, in school and home,
youth was rarely given the freedom and happiness to which
its years entitled it.

All this has to be set down in an honest picture of the
times. For often when I converse with younger comrades
of the post-war generation, I must convince them almost
by force that our youth was by no means specially favored
in comparison with their own. True, we had more freedom
in the political sense than the present generation, which is
compelled to submit to military service, compulsory labor,
and in many countries to mass ideologies, and in almost
all countries is helplessly delivered up to the arbitrary
power of world politics. We were able to devote ourselves
to our art and to our intellectual inclinations, and we were
able to mold our private existence with more individual
personality. We could live a more cosmopolitan life and the
whole world stood open to us. We could travel without a
passport and without a permit wherever we pleased. No one
questioned us as to our beliefs, as to our origin, race, or
religion. I do not deny that we had immeasurably more
individual freedom and we not only cherished it but made
use of it as well. But as Friedrich Hebbel once so aptly said:
"Now we lack the wine, now we lack the cup." One and the

same generation is rarely granted both. If morality gives man freedom, then the State confines him. If the State permits him freedom, then morality attempts to enslave him. We lived better and tasted more of the world, but the youth of today lives and experiences its own youth more consciously. When today I see young people come out of their schools and their colleges with their heads high, with happy faces, when I see boys and girls in free, untroubled companionship, without false modesty and false shame, at their studies, sport, and play, coursing over the snow on skis, competing classically with one another in the swimming pool, racing over the country in pairs in automobiles, akin in all forms of healthy, carefree life without any inner or outer burden, then each time it seems as if not forty, but a thousand years stand between them and us who, in order to procure or to receive love, always had to seek shadows and hiding places. I am genuinely happy to see how tremendous a moral revolution has occurred in favor of youth, how much freedom in loving and living they have regained, and how much they have recovered physically and spiritually in this freedom. The women appear to be more beautiful since it is permitted them to display their figures, their walk is more erect, their eyes clearer, their talk less artificial. What a different sense of security this new generation possesses, since its members need not give an accounting of their conduct to anyone but themselves, having wrung control from mothers and fathers and aunts and teachers, and no longer dream of all the suppression, intimidation, and tension that was forced upon us, no longer know anything of the bypaths and secretiveness with which we had to secure the forbidden, which they correctly conceive to be their right. Happily it enjoys its age with that vivacity, that freshness, that ease, and that carefreeness which are fitting to this age. But the loveliest thing about this happiness seems to be that it need not lie to others, and may be honest with itself, honest to its natural feelings and desires. It may well be that through this freedom from care with which these young people go through life, some of that respect for intellectual things, which animated us, may be lacking in them. It may well be that through this modern and natural give-and-take, something which seemed particularly precious and attractive to us may be lost to them in love—a secret reticence of modesty and shame, some kindliness and gentleness. Perhaps they do not even suspect that awe of the forbidden and self-denial secretly increase enjoyment. But all this seems little to me in contrast to the one saving change, that the youth of today is free of fear and depression and enjoys to the full that which was denied us in our time: the feeling of candor and self-confidence.

IV

Universitas Vitae

THE LONG desired moment finally came with the last year of the old century, and we were able to slam the door of the hated *Gymnasium* behind us. When we had passed our examinations with difficulty—for what did we know of mathematics, physics, and other scholastic subjects?—the director of the school favored us, ceremoniously attired in frock coats for the occasion, with a stirring address. We were now grown up and were to do honor to our fatherland with diligence and zeal. And so a comradeship of eight years was broken up, and I have seen very few of my fellow galley slaves again since that time. Most of them enrolled at the University, and those who had to content themselves with other vocations and occupations looked upon us with envy.

For in those long forgotten times the university in Austria was still surrounded with a certain romantic nimbus. To be a university student accorded definite rights to the young academician and conferred upon him privileges far beyond those of the others of his own age. This antiquated oddity is probably but little known in non-German countries, and the outmoded absurdity may well require some explanation. Most of our universities were founded in the Middle Ages, that is, at a time when being occupied with the learned sciences was considered unusual, and in order to attract young people to study, certain class privileges were conferred upon them. The medieval scholars were not subject to the jurisdiction of the ordinary courts; officers of the law could not seek them out or molest them in their colleges.

They wore special dress, and had the right to fight duels with impunity. They were recognized as a closed guild with certain rules of conduct, or misconduct, of their own. In time, with the increasing democratization of public life, when all of the other medieval guilds and corporations were being dissolved, these academic prerogatives were done away with throughout Europe. In Germany and in German Austria alone, where class consciousness always predominated over the democratic idea, the students stubbornly clung to these long outdated privileges, and even evolved their own student code. Above all else, the German student assumed a sort of "student honor" in addition to the civil and common code of honor. Whoever insulted him was forced to give the student satisfaction—in other words, to meet him in a duel—but only if he were "qualified" to give satisfaction. But again, according to this self-assumed evaluation, "qualified" did not apply to merchants or bankers, for example, but only to those who had an academic education, graduates and officers. Among the millions, no others were permitted to share the particular honor of crossing swords with a stupid and beardless youth. On the other hand, being a real student meant giving proof of one's manhood by participating in as many duels as possible, and bearing the evidence of such heroic deeds in the shape of scars on one's face; smooth cheeks and a nose that had not been disfigured were not worthy of a genuine Germanic academician. The color students, that is those who belonged to an association that wore ribbons, in order to duel with new opponents, were constantly forced to provoke each other, as well as the other completely peaceable students and officers. In the students' associations each new student was coached in the fencing room for this principal activity and initiated in the other customs of the *Burschenschaft*. Every *Fuchs*, or freshman, was assigned to a Corps member whom he had to obey slavishly, and who in return instructed him in all the regulations prevailing among the students: to drink to the point of illness, to empty a heavy stein of beer to the last drop in one draught, thus to harden himself lest he become a weakling, to roar out the student songs in chorus and to brawl at night on the streets, marching in goose step and hooting at the police. All this was thought to be "manly," "academic" and "German," and when the members of the *Burschenschaft* gathered on Saturdays for their *Bummel*, with their flags flying and their colored caps and ribbons, these silly fellows, elated with a senseless pride by their conduct, felt that they were the true representatives of the intellectual youth. They looked with disdain upon the "rabble" who could not properly appreciate this academic culture and German virility.

This exuberant and joyous student life must have appeared to be the quintessence of all romance to a young student coming as a greenhorn to Vienna from a provincial *Gymnasium*. As a matter of fact, for years afterwards aging lawyers and doctors sat in their villages, their maudlin stares fixed on the crossed foils and colored ribbons that hung in their rooms, proudly bearing their scars as a sign of their academic rank. But the effect of this inane and brutal activity was highly repulsive, and whenever we met one of these beribboned hordes, we prudently turned the corner; for to us, who cherished the freedom of the individual as the most sacred of all things, this passion for the aggressive, which was likewise servility to mob rule, too plainly manifested the worst and the most dangerous elements of the German spirit. What is more, we knew that this artificial romantic mummery hid slyly calculated and practical aims, for membership in a dueling *Burschenschaft* assured the members the protection of the "old boys" of the association in high positions and eased the way to careers later on. Membership in the "Borussia" of Bonn was the only certain way to German diplomacy; the Catholic brotherhoods in Austria led to the choice sinecures of the ruling Christian Social Party; and most of these "heroes" well knew that in the future their colored ribbons would prove substitutes for what they had neglected in their studies, and that a few scars on their forehead could be far more advantageous when applying for a post than what lay behind it. The mere sight of these rude militarized cliques, these slashed, bold, provoking faces, spoiled my visits to the university rooms; and all the other students whose earnest aim was to learn whenever they went to the university library avoided the main hall and preferred the unpretentious back door in order to escape any possible meeting with these sorry heroes.

~

That I was to study at the university had been decided from the very beginning by the family council. But which Faculty was I to choose? My family allowed me complete freedom of choice. My elder brother had already gone into my father's business, and so there was no need for the second son to hurry. After all, it was merely a question of some doctorate or other to assure the family honor; any one would do. And surprisingly enough the choice was equally indifferent to me. Inasmuch as I had long since dedicated my soul to literature, not one of the accredited special university courses interested me, and anyway I had a secret distrust of all academic activity which has remained with me to this day. Carlyle's axiom that the true university of these days is a good collection of books has remained valid as far as I am concerned, and even today I am convinced that one can become an excellent philosopher, historian, philologist, lawyer, or what you will, without having attended a university or even a *Gymnasium*. Countless times I have seen it proved in daily life that a secondhand dealer will know more about books than professors of literature, that art dealers know more than art historians, that a goodly portion of the important discoveries and inspirations in all fields are made by outsiders. As practical, useful and beneficial as an academic career may be for those of average talent, it is superfluous for individually productive natures, for whom it may even develop into a hindrance. And in particular, in a university such as ours in Vienna, which was so overcrowded with its six or seven thousand students that fruitful personal contact between teacher and scholar was hindered from the very outset, and which had remained behind the times because of its all too great adherence to tradition, I did not see a single teacher who could make his branch of learning irresistible to me. And so the actual ground for my choice was not which branch of knowledge would interest me most, but, on the contrary, which would inconvenience me the least, and would give me a maximum of time and freedom for my true passion. I finally decided upon philosophy—or "exact" philosophy as it was called in the old curriculum—but surely not because I felt it was an inner call, my capacity for purely abstract thinking being insignificant. Without exception, my thoughts are developed by objects, events and persons, and the purely theoretical and metaphysical remains beyond my ken. Nevertheless the actual performance required in this domain was the smallest possible, and attendance at lectures and seminars in exact philosophy was the easiest to evade. All that was necessary was to hand in a dissertation and to take one examination at the end of eight semesters. And so I began by arranging a time schedule for myself: not to bother about studying at the University for three years; then, in the last year, to exert myself and master the scholastic material, and quickly produce some sort of dissertation! Then the

University would have given me the only thing that I wanted: a few years of complete freedom for my own life and for my endeavors in art: *universitas vitae.*

~

When I look back upon my life I can recall but few moments as happy as those first years when I was a university student without a university. I was young and for that reason did not as yet have any feeling of obligation to achieve perfection. I was fairly independent; the day had twenty-four hours and all of them belonged to me. I could read and study what I wished, without having to give an accounting to anyone. The cloud of an academic examination had not yet appeared upon the bright horizon. How long three years can be when compared to nineteen years of life, how rich and replete, and how filled with surprises and gifts one can make them!

The first thing I did was to make a selection—pitilessly, as I thought—of my verses. I am not ashamed to admit that to the nineteen-year-old boy who had just graduated from the *Gymnasium,* the sweetest smell on earth, sweeter than the oil of the Rose of Shiraz, was the smell of printer's ink. Every acceptance of one of my poems by a newspaper had given a new uplift to my self-confidence, unsteady by nature as it was. Should I not now grit my teeth and attempt the publication of an entire volume? The encouragement of my comrades, who believed more in me than I did in myself, finally determined me. Rashly I sent the manuscript to the very publisher who was the most representative of German poetry, Schuster & Löffler, the publishers of Liliencron, Dehmel, Bierbaum, and Mombert, that entire generation who, together with Rilke and Hofmannsthal, had created the new German lyric poetry. And—wonders will never cease!—one after the other came those unforgettable moments of happiness in the life of a writer which never repeat themselves even after his greatest successes, the arrival of a letter with the seal of the publisher, which I held in my trembling hands, lacking the courage to open it. The minute arrived when, with bated breath, I read that the publisher had decided to publish my book and even stipulated an option for later ones. The package with the first set of proofs came and was untied in great excitement, so as to see the type, the type-page, the very embryo of the book and then, after a few weeks, the book itself, the first copies. One never tired of looking at them, touching them, comparing them, again and again and again. And then the childish visits to the bookstores to see if copies were already on display, whether they were resplendent in the center of the shop or hidden bashfully at the side. And then to await the first letters, the first notices, the first reply from the unknown, the incalculable. I secretly envy the young man all his suspense, excitement and enthusiasm, who casts his first book into the world! But my rapture was merely being in love with the first moment and by no means self-satisfaction. What I soon thought of these early verses is shown by the simple fact that I not only never allowed *Silberne Saiten* to be reprinted (the title of my now forgotten first-born), but did not include a single one of its poems in my *Collected Poems.* They were verses of vague premonition and instinctive feeling, not created out of my own experience, but rather born of a passion for language. But still they showed a certain musicality and enough feeling for form to win notice in interested circles, and I could not complain of a lack of encouragement. Liliencron and Dehmel, who were then the leading lyric poets, gave the nineteen-year-old hearty and fraternal recognition. Rilke, whom I idolized, reciprocated for the "nicely presented book" with a copy of a special edition of his latest verses, inscribed "gratefully,"

STEFAN ZWEIG
AS A YOUNG MAN

which I safely rescued from the ruins of Austria as one of the most precious recollections of my youth and took to England with me. Where may it be today! It is truly eerie that this first gift of Rilke's friendship—the first of many—is now forty years old and that the familiar writing greets me out of the land of the dead. But the most unexpected surprise of all was that Max Reger, then the greatest living composer except Richard Strauss, asked my permission to set six of the poems of this volume to music. And how often since then have I heard one or the other in concerts—my own long forgotten and discarded verses, carried through time by the fraternal art of a master!

~~~

These unexpected approbations, which were also accompanied by friendly published notices, encouraged me to a step which, because of my incurable mistrust of myself, I would otherwise never have undertaken, or at least not at so early an age. Even during my *Gymnasium* period I had published short stories and essays besides verses in the literary publications of the "Moderns," but I had never dared to offer any of my efforts to a powerful or widely read newspaper. In Vienna there was really only one journal of high grade, the *Neue Freie Presse*, which, because of its dignified principles, its cultural endeavors and its political prestige, assumed in the Austro-Hungarian monarchy a role not unlike that of the *Times* in England or the *Temps* in France. No paper, even in the German Reich, was as particular about its intellectual level. Its editor, Moritz Benedikt, a man of phenomenal powers of organization and untiring industry, put his entire, almost daemonic energy into excelling all the German papers in the fields of culture and literature. No expense was spared if he wanted something from a noted author; he would send telegram after tele-

gram, and would agree in advance to any fee. The holiday
numbers at Christmas and New Year were complete volumes
with their literary supplements and included the greatest
names of the time: Anatole France, Gerhart Hauptmann,
Ibsen, Zola, Strindberg, and Shaw found themselves associated in this paper, which accomplished so immeasurably
much for the literary orientation of the city and the whole
country. As a matter of course it was progressive and liberal
in its views, prudent and cautious in its politics; and it represented the high cultural aspirations of the old Austria in
an exemplary fashion.

This temple of progress preserved another sacred relic in
the so-called *feuilleton;* like the great Parisian dailies such
as the *Temps* and the *Journal des Débats,* it printed admirable and authoritative essays on poetry, theater, music, and
art in the lower half of the front page, separated sharply
from the ephemera of politics and the day by an unbroken
line that extended from margin to margin. In this space only
the long-established authorities were permitted to express
themselves. Sound judgment, the comparative experience of
years, and finished artistic form alone could summon an
author to this holy place after years of probation. Ludwig
Speidel, a master of the pen, and Eduard Hanslick had the
same pontifical authority in the theater and music as Sainte-
Beuve had in his *Lundis* in Paris. Their yes or no in Vienna
decided the success of a work, a play, or a book, and with
it that of the author. Each of these essays was the talk of the
day in intellectual circles. They were discussed, criticized,
admired, or attacked, and whenever a new name bobbed
up among the time-honored and accepted *feuilletonists,* it
was an event. Of the younger generation Hofmannsthal
alone succeeded, with a few of his capital essays, in gaining
admission. Other young authors had to be content to sneak
in and find refuge in the literary section at the back. He who

appeared on the first page had hewn his name in marble, as far as Vienna was concerned.

It is no longer comprehensible to me how I found the courage to offer a small article on poetry to the *Neue Freie Presse,* the oracle of my fathers and the temple of the high priests. But after all nothing worse than having it rejected could happen to me. The editor of the *feuilleton* received visitors only once a week between two and three o'clock, because the constant succession of famous and established collaborators seldom left space for the work of an outsider. It was not without a beating heart that I walked up the iron circular staircase which led to his office and had myself announced. After a few moments the attendant returned and said that the *feuilleton* editor would see me and I walked into the small narrow room.

~~

The *feuilleton* editor of the *Neue Freie Presse* was Theodor Herzl, and he was the first man of world importance whom I had encountered in my life—although I did not then know how great a change his person was destined to bring about in the fate of the Jewish people and in the history of our time. At that time his stand was still divided and uncertain. He began as a young poet, and soon gave evidence of a startling, astounding journalistic talent. At first he was the Paris correspondent and later the *feuilletonist* of the *Neue Freie Presse,* and as such had become the darling of the Vienna public. His essays are still enchanting in their wealth of sharp and ofttimes wise observations, their stylistic animation, and their aristocratic charm. Whether light or critical, they never lost their innate nobility; and they were the most cultivated in journalism, and were the delight of a city that had schooled itself to every subtlety. He had been successful with a play given at the

Burgtheater and now he was a man of fame, adored by the young, respected by our fathers, till one day the unexpected happened. Destiny always knows how to find the way to a man whom it needs for its secret purposes, even if he desires to hide himself.

In Paris Theodor Herzl had had an experience which convulsed his soul, one of those hours that change an entire existence. As a newspaper correspondent he witnessed the public degradation of Alfred Dreyfus, had seen them tear the epaulets from the pallid man while he cried aloud: "I am innocent." At that moment he knew in the depth of his heart that Dreyfus was innocent and that he had brought the horrible suspicion of treason on himself merely by being a Jew. Indeed in his upright and manly pride Theodor Herzl had already suffered under the Jewish lot when he was a student; moreover by his prophetic instinct he had foreseen the entire tragedy of his race at a time when it had not appeared to be an inevitable fate. With the feeling of being born to leadership, which his imposing presence no less than his grandiose thinking and his worldly knowledge seemed to confirm, he had then formulated the fantastic plan to end the Jewish problem once and for all: Jewry was to unite itself with Christianity by means of a mass baptism. Always thinking dramatically, he had pictured to himself how he would lead the thousands and thousands of Jews of Austria, in an exemplary symbolic act, in long procession to the Cathedral of St. Stephen, there to absolve the persecuted, homeless people of the curse of separation and hatred for all time. Soon he realized the unfeasibility of this plan, and years of his own work diverted him from the original problem of his life, the solution of which he had recognized as his true task. But now at the moment of Dreyfus's degradation the thought of the eternal exile of his people entered his breast like the thrust of a dagger. If separation was inevitable, he said to himself, then let it be a complete one. If humiliation is to be our constant fate, then let us face it with pride. If we suffer because of our homelessness, then let us build our own homeland! And so he published his pamphlet, "The Jewish State," in which he proclaimed that all attempts at assimilation and all hope for total tolerance were impossible for the Jewish people. They had to create a new homeland of their own in their old home, Palestine.

I was still in the *Gymnasium* when this short pamphlet, penetrating as a steel shaft, appeared; but I can still remember the general astonishment and annoyance of the bourgeois Jewish circles of Vienna. What has happened, they said angrily, to this otherwise intelligent, witty and cultivated writer? What foolishness is this that he has thought up and writes about? Why should we go to Palestine? Our language is German and not Hebrew, and beautiful Austria is our homeland. Are we not well off under the good Emperor Franz Josef? Do we not make a decent living, and is our position not secure? Are we not equal subjects, inhabitants and loyal citizens of our beloved Vienna? Do we not live in a progressive era in which in a few decades all sectarian prejudices will be abolished? Why does he, who speaks as a Jew and who wishes to help Judaism, place arguments in the hands of our worst enemies and attempt to separate us, when every day brings us more closely and intimately into the German world? The rabbis thundered passionately from the pulpits, the head of the *Neue Freie Presse* forbade the very mention of the word Zionism in his "progressive" newspaper. Karl Kraus, the Thersites of Viennese literature, the master of invective, wrote a pamphlet called "The King of Zion," and when Theodor Herzl entered a theater, people whispered sneeringly: "His Majesty has arrived!"

At first Herzl could rightly feel himself misunderstood—Vienna, where he thought himself most secure because he had been beloved there for so many years, not only deserted him but even laughed at him. But then the answer roared suddenly back with such force and such ecstasy that he was almost frightened to see how mighty a movement, already growing beyond his control, he had brought into being with his few dozen pages. True, it did not come from the well-situated, comfortable bourgeois Jews of the West but from the gigantic masses of the East, from the Galician, the Polish, the Russian proletariat of the ghetto. Without realizing it, Herzl with his pamphlet had brought to flame the glowing coal of Judaism, long smoldering in the ashes, the thousand-year-old messianic dream, confirmed in the Holy Books, of the return to the Promised Land. This is the hope and the religious certainty which have made life worth living for the persecuted and enslaved millions. Whenever anyone—prophet or deceiver—throughout the two thousand years of exile plucked this string, the entire soul of the people was brought into vibration, but never as forcefully as upon this occasion, never with such a roaring and rushing echo. By means of a few dozen pages a single person had united a dispersed and confused mass.

The first moment, while the idea was still a dream of vague outline, was decidedly the happiest in Herzl's short life. As soon as he began to fix his aims in actual space, and to unite the forces, he was made to realize how divided his people had become among various races and destinies—the religious on the one hand, the free thinkers on the other, here the socialist, there the capitalistic Jews—all competing eagerly with one another in all languages, and all unwilling to submit to a unified authority. In the year 1901, when I saw him for the first time, he stood in the midst of this struggle and perhaps he was even struggling with himself; he did not have sufficient faith in its success to relinquish the position that fed him and his family. He still had to divide himself between his petty journalistic duties and the task which was his true life. It was still the *feuilleton* editor Theodor Herzl who received me in the beginning of 1901.

～～

Theodor Herzl rose to greet me, and unwittingly I realized that the ironic witticism "the King of Zion" had some truth in it. He actually looked regal with his broad high forehead, his clear features, his long, black, almost blue-black, priestly beard and his dark brown, melancholy eyes. The ample, somewhat theatrical gestures that he employed did not appear to be artificial because they were part of his natural majesty, and the occasion was not one which particularly required his being impressive. Even at this old desk, covered with papers, in this narrow editorial office, with its one window, he appeared like a Bedouin sheik of the desert, and a flowing white burnoose would have been as fitting as his carefully tailored black cutaway, obviously fashioned along Parisian lines. After a short, deliberate pause—he liked these small effects, as I often noticed later, and he had probably studied them at the Burgtheater—he extended his hand with condescension and yet not without friendliness. Motioning to the chair next to him, he asked: "I think that I have heard or read your name somewhere. Poetry, isn't it?" I had to admit it. "Well," he said, leaning back, "what have you brought me?"

I replied that I wished to submit a short piece of prose to him and handed him the manuscript. He looked at the title page, turned over to the last page in order to measure its length, and sank deeper into his chair. To my astonishment (I had not expected it) I noticed that he had already begun to read the manuscript. He read slowly, putting aside each leaf without looking up. When he had read the last page, he slowly gathered the leaves and, still without looking at me, carefully put them into an envelope on which he wrote something with a blue pencil. It was only then, after having kept me in suspense for a sufficiently long time with these occult passes, that he raised his handsome, dark countenance towards me, and with deliberate dignity he said slowly: "I am happy to tell you that your fine piece is accepted for the *feuilleton* of the *Neue Freie Presse.*" It was as if Napoleon had pinned the Knight's Cross of the Legion of Honor upon a young sergeant on the battlefield.

This would seem to be a small, inconsequential episode. But one had to be a Viennese, and a Viennese of that generation, to understand what a step upward this promotion signified. In my nineteenth year I had suddenly achieved a prominent position overnight, and Theodor Herzl, who remained kindly disposed towards me from that moment on, took the opportunity of writing in one of his next essays that Vienna need not fear the decadence of art. On the contrary, besides Hofmannsthal, there was an entire platoon of young talent of whom the best was to be expected; and he mentioned my name at the head. I have always felt it as a particular honor that a man of such outstanding importance as Theodor Herzl was the first to champion me publicly from his exposed and therefore responsible position, and it was difficult for me to determine—ungratefully, it might seem—not to join his Zionist movement actively and in the responsible capacity that he would have wished.

The right relation never presented itself. I was estranged above all else by the disrespect, of a kind hardly comprehensible today, with which his own party associates treated

Herzl. Those of the East charged him with not understanding Judaism and not even knowing its customs; the economists looked upon him as a *feuilletonist;* each one had his own objection and they were not always the most respectful. I realized how important and necessary it would have been to Herzl to have persons and particularly young people around him who were completely submissive, but the quarreling and dogmatic spirit, the constant opposition, the lack of honest, hearty subordination in this circle, alienated me from the movement which I had only approached curiously for Herzl's sake. Once when we were speaking about the subject, I frankly admitted my dislike of the lack of discipline in his ranks. He smiled somewhat bitterly and said: "Do not forget that we have been accustomed for centuries to play with problems and to struggle with ideas. In the two thousand years of our history we Jews have not had any practice in creating anything real in this world. One must first learn unconditional devotion, and I myself have not yet mastered it, for I still keep on writing *feuilletons,* and I am still the *feuilleton* editor of the *Neue Freie Presse,* whereas it would be my duty to have only one thought and not to put another pen-stroke on paper for anything but that one thought. But I am on the way to improve myself. I must first learn unconditional devotion, and perhaps the others will learn with me." I can remember that these words made a deep impression upon me, for people could not understand why Herzl was so slow to make up his mind to resign from the *Neue Freie Presse*—we thought it was for his family's sake. That this was not so, and that he had sacrificed his private fortune to the cause, was not known to the world until much later. How greatly he had suffered under the discord was revealed not only by this conversation but also by many entries in his diaries.

I saw him a number of times afterwards, but only one

meeting remains important and unforgettable in my memory, perhaps because it was the last. I had been abroad and had only been in correspondence with Vienna, when I finally met him one day in the Stadtpark. He had obviously come from his office, he was walking very slowly and stooped slightly; it was no longer the old swinging step. I saluted him politely and was about to pass on, but he straightened up and came rapidly towards me, holding out his hand: "Why do you hide yourself? You don't have to do that." He approved my having escaped abroad so often. "It's the only thing for us to do," said he. "All that I know, I learned abroad. It is only there that one learns to think in terms of distance. I am convinced that I never would have had the courage for that first idea, they would have destroyed it when it was still budding and growing. But thank God, when I brought it here, all was finished, and they could do nothing more than try to trip me up." He then spoke very bitterly about Vienna; he had found the greatest obstructions here and he would already have wearied if new impulsion had not come from abroad, from the East and, in particular, from America. "Anyway," he said, "it was my mistake that I started too late. Viktor Adler was leader of the Social Democrats at thirty, in his best fighting years, to say nothing of the great in history. If you knew how I suffer at the thought of the lost years, and that I did not approach my task sooner. If my health were as good as my will, then all would be well; but one cannot buy back lost years." I accompanied him all the way to his house. There he stood still, gave me his hand and said: "Why do you not come to see me? You have never been in my house. Call me up first and I will see to it that I am free." I promised him although I was determined not to keep my promise, for the more I love a person the more I respect his time. I was fully determined not to go to him.

But I did go to him—and only a few months later. The illness which had, at the time of that meeting, begun to bend him, broke him off suddenly, and it was only to the cemetery that I was able to accompany him. It was a singular day, a day in July, unforgettable to those who participated in the experience. Suddenly, to all the railroad stations of the city, by day and by night, from all realms and lands, every train brought new arrivals. Western, Eastern, Russian, Turkish Jews; from all the provinces and all the little towns they hurried excitedly, the shock of the news still written on their faces; never was it more clearly manifest what strife and talk had hitherto concealed—it was a great movement whose leader had now fallen. The procession was endless. Vienna, startled, became aware that it was not just a writer or a mediocre poet who had passed away, but one of those creators of ideas who disclose themselves triumphantly in a single country, to a single people at vast intervals. A tumult ensued at the cemetery; too many had suddenly stormed to his coffin, crying, sobbing, screaming in a wild explosion of despair. It was almost a riot, a fury. All regulation was upset through a sort of elementary and ecstatic mourning such as I had never seen before nor since at a funeral. And it was this gigantic outpouring of grief from the depths of millions of souls that made me realize for the first time how much passion and hope this lone and lonesome man had borne into the world through the power of a single thought.

～～

The real significance of my formal admission to the *feuilleton* of the *Neue Freie Presse* lay in its effect on my life. It achieved for me an unexpected security in relation to my family. My parents occupied themselves but little with literature and laid no claims to any judgment of it. For them, as well as for the entire Viennese bourgeoisie, only that was of importance which was praised in the *Neue Freie Presse,* and only what was ignored or attacked there was inconsequential. Whatever appeared in the *feuilleton* seemed vouched for by the highest authority, because those who sat in judgment there commanded respect by their mere position. Conjure up a family that glances at this first page of the paper each day with awe and anticipation, and one morning stumbles on the discovery that the rather untidy nineteen-year-old at their table, who was none too good at school, and whose scribbling they looked upon indulgently as harmless play (safer than cards or dalliance), was permitted to voice his opinions (which up to then had received small attention at home) in this circle of the tried and famous. If I had written the most beautiful poems of Keats or Hölderlin or Shelley, it could not have brought about so complete a transformation in my entire surroundings; when I entered a theater, people pointed out this curious Benjamin who in some mysterious fashion had penetrated the holy precincts of the elders and worthies. And since I appeared in the *feuilleton* often and almost regularly, I was soon in danger of becoming a local celebrity, a danger which I was able to escape in time by surprising my parents one morning with the announcement that I wished to study in Berlin during the coming semester. And my family had too much respect for me, or rather for the *Neue Freie Presse* in whose golden shadow I stood, not to grant my wish.

~

Of course I had no intention of "studying" in Berlin. As in Vienna, I went to the university only twice during the semester, once to enroll for the lectures, and the second time to secure a certificate of my supposed attendance. What I sought in Berlin was neither colleges nor professors, but a higher and more complete sort of freedom. In Vienna I still felt myself tied to my surroundings. The literary colleagues with whom I associated were nearly all from the same Jewish bourgeois class as myself; in the constricted city, where everyone knew about everyone else, I was always the son of a "good" family, and I was tired of the so-called "good" society. I even longed for a pronouncedly "bad" society, an unforced, uncontrolled kind of existence. I had not even looked in the catalogue to see who was teaching philosophy at the university in Berlin; it sufficed for me to know that the "new" literature was more active and impulsive there than at home, that one might meet Dehmel and the other poets of the younger generation there, that magazines, cabarets and theaters were constantly being started— that, in a word, "something was doing."

As a matter of fact I came to Berlin at a very interesting historical moment. Since 1870, when Berlin had changed from the rather small, sober, and by no means rich capital of the Kingdom of Prussia into the seat of the German Emperor, the homely town on the Spree had taken a mighty upswing. But the leadership in artistic and cultural matters had not yet fallen to Berlin; Munich, with its painters and poets, was considered the real center of art, the Dresden Opera dominated the music field and the small capitals drew valuable elements to themselves. Vienna above all, with its century of tradition, its concentrated power, and its innate talent, was still predominant over Berlin. But of recent years, with the rapid economic rise in Berlin, a new page had turned. The large concerns and the wealthy families moved to Berlin, and new wealth, paired with a strong sense of daring, opened to the theater and to architecture greater opportunities than in any other large German city. The museums enriched themselves under the patronage of Emperor Wilhelm, the theater found an exemplary direc-

tor in Otto Brahm, and just because there was no real tradition, no century-old culture, youth was tempted to try its
hand. For tradition always means repression. Vienna, bound
to the old and worshiping its own past, was cautious and
non-committal with respect to young men and daring experiments. But in Berlin, which wished to form itself more
rapidly and more personally, novelty was sought after. So
it was natural that the young people of the entire Reich and
even Austria thronged to Berlin, and results proved to the
talented among them that they were right. The Viennese
Max Reinhardt would have had to wait patiently for two
decades to achieve the position in Vienna that he assumed
in two years in Berlin.

It was just at this period of its transition from a mere
capital to a world city that I came to Berlin. Coming after
the lush beauty of Vienna, inherited from great ancestors,
the first impression was rather disappointing. The exodus
to the West End, where the new architecture was soon to
become manifest as against the pretentious houses of the
Tiergarten quarter, had but just begun, and the architec-
turally tedious Friedrichstrasse and Leipzigerstrasse, with
their clumsy ostentation, were still the center of the city.
Suburbs such as Wilmersdorf, Nicolassee, and Steglitz were
only accessible by a tiresome journey on the street cars, and
it was almost an expedition in those days to reach the lakes
of the Mark with their sharp beauty. Other than the old
Unter den Linden there was no real center, no promenade
like our Graben and, thanks to the old Prussian thrift,
there was no suggestion of general elegance. Women went
to the theater in unattractive home-made dresses, and
everywhere one missed the light, deft, and lavish hand which
in Vienna, as in Paris, could create an enchanting abundance out of very little. In every detail one felt the closefist-
edness of Frederician husbandry. The coffee was thin and

bad because every bean was counted, the food was unimagi-
native, without strength or savor. Cleanliness and rigid and
accurate order reigned everywhere instead of our musical
rhythm of life. Nothing seemed more characteristic to me
than the contrast between my landladies in Vienna and in
Berlin. The Viennese was a cheerful, chatty woman who did
not keep things too clean, and easily forgot this or that, but
was enthusiastically eager to be of service. The one in Berlin
was correct and kept everything in perfect order; but in
my first monthly account I found every service that she had
given me down in neat, vertical writing: three pfennigs
for sewing on a trouser button, twenty for removing an ink-
spot from the tabletop, until at the end, under a broad
stroke of the pen, all of her troubles amounted to the neat
little sum of 67 pfennigs. At first I laughed at this; but it was
characteristic that after a very few days I too succumbed to
this Prussian sense of orderliness and for the first, and last,
time in my life I kept an accurate account of my expenses.

My Viennese friends had given me a whole series of introductions, but I did not deliver a single one of them. After
all, it was the real intent of my adventure to evade any
assured and bourgeois atmosphere and, freed of this, to be
entirely dependent upon myself. I wanted to meet people
exclusively through my own literary efforts, and the most
interesting people at that. I had not read *La Bohème* for
nothing, without wishing, at twenty, to live a similar life.

It did not take me long to find such a wild and casually
assorted crowd. While still in Vienna I had collaborated
on the leading paper of the Berlin "moderns," which not
without irony was named *Society* and was run by Ludwig
Jacobowski. This young poet, shortly before his early death,
had founded a club which bore the alluring name of "The
Coming Ones" and which met once a week on the second
floor of a café in Nollendorfplatz. In this huge circle,

fashioned after the Parisian *Closerie des Lilas,* the most heterogeneous throngs gathered, poets and architects, snobs and journalists, young girls who styled themselves sculptresses or art experts, Russian students and snow-blond Scandinavians who wished to perfect themselves in the German language. Germany itself was represented by all its provinces; strong-limbed Westphalians, sober Bavarians, Silesian Jews: all these mixed in wild discussions with complete freedom. Occasionally poems or plays were read aloud, but the main thing for all was getting to know each other. In the midst of these young people who played the Bohemians sat an old gray-bearded man much like Santa Claus, respected and loved by all because he was a true poet and a true Bohemian: Peter Hille. With his blue dog-like eyes the septuagenarian looked gently and innocently around at this amazing crowd of children, always wrapped in his gray greatcoat which covered a very ragged suit and very dirty linen. Gladly he yielded to our entreaties, and brought forth crumpled manuscripts from his coat pockets and read his poems. They were uneven poems, actually the improvisations of a lyric genius, but too loose, too casually formed. He wrote them down in pencil in the streetcars or the cafés, forgot them then, and had great difficulty, while reading them out loud, in finding the words again in the stained and blurred scraps of paper. He never had any money, but it meant nothing to him. He would sleep here and there, as he was invited, and his forgetfulness of the world and absolute lack of ambition were touchingly genuine. We did not quite understand when and how this good man of the woods had happened into the large city of Berlin and what he sought there. He wanted nothing, he had no desire to be famous or celebrated and, thanks to his poetic dreaming, he was more footloose and carefree than any person I ever knew later on. The ambitious debated and out-shouted

each other around him; he listened quietly, argued with
none, sometimes lifted his glass with a friendly word toward
one, but hardly ever entered into the conversation. We had
the impression that throughout the wildest tumult within
his disheveled and rather weary head verses and words
were seeking each other, without ever touching or meeting.

The genuine and childish quality that emanated from
this naïve poet—who in Germany today is almost forgotten—
perhaps diverted my attention from the elected chairman
of "The Coming Ones," and yet he was a man whose words
and ideas were to be formative in the lives of many people.
In Rudolf Steiner, whose disciples were later to build
magnificent schools and academies for the propagation of
the teachings of the founder of Anthroposophy, for the
first time since Theodor Herzl I approached a man to whom
destiny had given the mission of guiding millions of people.
Personally he was not so much of a leader as Herzl had
been, but he was more engaging. A hypnotic power lay in
his dark eyes and I listened to him better and more
critically when not looking at him, for his ascetic, thin
face, carved by spiritual suffering, was well disposed to be
convincing—and not only to women. At that time Rudolf
Steiner had not yet formulated his theories, he was still
seeking and learning. On occasion he recited for us com-
mentaries on the color-theories of Goethe, whose portrait,
as he drew it, became more Faustian, more Paracelsian. It
was exciting to listen to him, for his education was stupendous and quite different from our own, which was
confined to literature alone. I always returned home from
his lectures, and from many good, private conversations,
both enraptured and somewhat depressed. However, if I
ask myself today whether I would have foretold for that
young man his great philosophical and ethical effect upon
the masses, I must admit, to my shame, that I would not.

I had expected great things from his questing intellect, and I would not have been in the least astonished to hear of some important biological discovery which his intuitive spirit had accomplished; but when many years later I saw the grandiose Goetheanum in Dornach, this "school of wisdom," which his pupils had founded as a platonic academy of anthroposophy, I was rather disappointed that his power had run to material and sometimes even into the commonplace. I do not claim any judgment of anthroposophy, for even today I am not quite clear as to what it seeks or means, and I believe that on the whole its seductive power is bound up not with an idea, but with the fascinating personality of Rudolf Steiner. Nevertheless, meeting a man of such magnetic personality at so early a stage, when he yielded himself to the younger people around him in friendship and without dogmatizing, was an incalculable gain for me. In his fantastic and at the same time profound knowledge I realized that true universality, which we, with the overweening pride of high school boys, thought we had already mastered, was not to be gained by flighty reading and discussion, but only by years of burning endeavor.

But in that receptive period, when friendships are easily made and social or political differences have not yet hardened, a young man learns the most important things better from those who strive with him than from his superiors. And again I felt—but on a higher and more international plane than in the *Gymnasium*—how fruitful collective enthusiasm can be. Whereas most of my Viennese friends had come from the middle classes and nine-tenths of them from the Jewish bourgeoisie, which meant that we merely duplicated or multiplied our inclinations, the young people of this new world came from directly opposite classes, from above and from below, one a Prussian aristocrat, another the son of a Hamburg shipping man, the third from Westphalian peasant stock. Unawares, I found myself in a circle where actual poverty existed, with torn clothing and worn-out shoes, a sphere which I had never touched in Vienna. I sat at the same table with heavy drinkers, homosexuals, morphine addicts. I shook hands—quite proudly—with a fairly well-known swindler who had been in jail, and who because of his published memoirs had become one of us. All the seemingly impossible characters of realistic fiction pushed and thronged together in the small cafés and drinking places into which I was introduced, and the worse a man's reputation was, the more eager my interest to meet its bearer. This particular love or curiosity for men who live dangerously has accompanied me throughout my entire life; even in the years when it would have been fitting to be more selective, my friends berated me for associating with such immoral, undependable and compromising persons. Perhaps it was just the substantial sphere from which I came, and my feeling that I too was burdened to a certain degree with a complex of "security," that caused me to be fascinated by those who were wasteful and almost disdainful of their lives, their time, their money, their health, and their good name, these passionate individuals whose only mania was mere existence without a goal; and perhaps you may notice in my novels and short stories my predilection for all intense and unruly natures. To this was added the attraction of the exotic, the foreign; nearly every one of them contributed to my eager curiosity from a strange world. In the artist E. M. Lilien, the son of a poor orthodox Jewish wood turner from Drohobycz, I encountered for the first time an Eastern Jew, and a Judaism which in its strength and stubborn fanaticism had hitherto been unknown to me. A young Russian translated the most beautiful portions of *The Brothers Karamazov,* then unknown in Germany. A young Swedish girl showed me my first pictures by Munch. I frequented the studios of painters (although poor ones) to observe their methods. One of the faithful led me to a spiritualist séance—in a thousand forms and aspects I experienced life, and could not get enough. The intensity which had spent itself in the *Gymnasium* in mere forms, in rhymes and verses and words, now hurled itself against men; in Berlin I was constantly with new and with different people, enraptured, disappointed, and even swindled by them. I believe that I never enjoyed so much intellectual companionship in ten years as I did in that one short semester in Berlin, my first in complete freedom.

~~

It would appear to be quite logical that this uncommon variety of stimulation should bring about an unusual increase in my desire to produce. Actually what happened was the exact opposite; my self-confidence, which had been raised by our mutual extolment in the *Gymnasium*, declined appreciably. Four months after it had appeared, I could no longer understand where I had found the courage to publish that volume of immature verses. I still thought that the verses were good, apt, and in part even remarkable works of art, created out of an ambitious joy in playing with form, but unreal in their sentimentality. And also, after this contact with actuality, I divined a scent of perfumed paper in my first stories; written in total ignorance of reality, they always followed a technique copied at second hand. A novel, finished except for the last chapter, which I had brought with me to Berlin and with which I had thought to make my publisher happy, soon heated the stove, for my faith in the competence of my *Gymnasium* class had received a heavy blow with my first glimpse of real life. I felt as if I had been put back several years at school. As a matter of fact, six years elapsed after my first volume of verses before I published another, and it was only after three or four years that my first book of prose appeared. Following Dehmel's advice, for which I am thankful to this day, I used my time in translating from foreign languages, and even now I hold this to be the best way for a young poet to understand more deeply and more creatively the spirit of his own language. I translated the verses of Baudelaire, a few of Verlaine, Keats, William Morris, a short drama by Charles van Lerberghe, a novel by Camille Lemonnier, *pour me faire la main.* Just because every strange language at first offers opposition in its most personal turnings to those who would copy it, it invites forces of expression which, otherwise unsought, would never come to light; and this struggle to wrest from a strange language its most intimate essence and to mold it as plastically into one's own language, was always a particular artistic desire on my part. Because this silent and actually thankless work requires patience and perseverance, virtues which I had neglected in the *Gymnasium* through ease and boldness, it became particularly dear to me; for in this humble activity of transmitting the highest treasures of art I experienced for the first time the assurance of doing something truly useful, a justification of my existence.

～

Inwardly, my way for the next years had become quite clear; to see much, to learn much, and only then to begin! First to learn the essentials of the world, rather than step before the world with premature publications! Berlin, with its strong brine, had only increased my thirst. I looked around me for a country in which to take a summer trip. My choice fell upon Belgium. At the turn of the century this country had felt an uncommon artistic impulse, and in a certain sense had even overshadowed France in intensity, Knopf and Rops in painting, Constantin Meunier and Minne in the plastic arts, van der Velde in the applied arts, Maeterlinck, Eekhoud, and Lemonnier in poetry, provided a magnificent measure of the new strength in Europe. But above all others, it was Emile Verhaeren who fascinated me, because he pointed out a wholly new way to the lyric muse. I had, so to speak, discovered him in private, for then he was completely unknown in Germany and the official literature had confused him with Verlaine, just as it had confused Rolland with Rostand. And to love someone alone is to love doubly.

It will perhaps be necessary to pause briefly here. Our time lives too rapidly and experiences too much to possess a good memory, and I do not know if the name of Emile Verhaeren means anything today. Verhaeren was the first of all the French poets who endeavored to give Europe what Walt Whitman had given America: a profession of faith in the times, in the future. He had begun to love the modern world and wished to conquer it for poetry. Whereas for others the machine was evil, the cities ugly, and the present unpoetical, he was enthusiastic for every new invention and every technical accomplishment, and he was enraptured with his own rapture. He did so knowingly in order to experience this passion the more strongly. And the little poems of the beginning grew into great, outpouring hymns. *Admirez-vous les uns les autres,* was his advice to the nations of Europe. All the optimism of our generation, an optimism no longer comprehensible in the present day with our dreadful decline, found in him its first poetic expression, and some of his best poems will give evidence for a long time to come of the Europe and the humanity we then dreamed of.

My real reason for going to Brussels was to become

acquainted with Verhaeren. But Camille Lemonnier, that powerful and today unjustly forgotten poet of the *"mâle,"* one of whose novels I had translated into German, told me regretfully that Verhaeren came to Brussels from his little village only rarely, and that he was absent at that moment. To make up for my disappointment, he gave me the most gracious introductions to other Belgian artists. I saw the aged master, Constantin Meunier, that heroic worker and the strongest portrayer of labor, and after him van der Stappen, whose name today is almost forgotten in the annals of art. But what a friendly person he was, this small chubby-faced Fleming, and how cordially they received me, young as I was, he and his big, broad, jolly Dutch wife! He showed me his works, and we talked at length on that bright morning about art and literature; and the kindness of these two soon removed all of my shyness. Openly I spoke of my regret at having missed the one person I had come to Brussels to meet—Verhaeren.

Had I said too much? Had I said something that was foolish? At any rate, I noticed that both van der Stappen and his wife had begun to laugh silently and to exchange furtive glances. I sensed a secret understanding between them, caused by my words. I became embarrassed and wished to take my leave, but they both insisted that I remain for lunch. Again that curious smile passed from one to the other. I felt that if there was a secret here it was a friendly one, and gladly gave up my intended trip to Waterloo.

It was soon midday and we were already sitting in the dining room—it was level with the ground as in all Belgian houses, and one could look out through the colored panes onto the street—when a shadow suddenly halted in front of the window. A finger tapped on the colored glass and at the same time the bell began to ring sharply. *"Le voilà,"* said Mrs. van der Stappen and got up. I did not know what she meant, but already the door opened and a man walked in with a heavy, strong tread: it was Verhaeren. At first glance I recognized the face with which I had long been familiar from photographs. As so often before, Verhaeren was again their house guest; and when they heard that I had been seeking him in vain in the entire vicinity, they had agreed with the exchange of a rapid glance not to say anything to me, but to surprise me with his presence. Now he stood facing me, smiling at the successful trick which he had quickly taken in. For the first time I felt the strong clasp of his vigorous hand, and for the first time I saw his clear, kindly glance. He came home laden as always with adventures and enthusiasm. He began to talk while he was still attacking the food. He had called upon friends and visited a gallery and he was still all aflame with that hour. He always came home that way, elated by anything and everything, even a casual event, and this enthusiasm had grown into a sacred habit; like a flame it sprang again and again from his lips and he knew wondrously well how to outline his words with telling gestures. With the first word he seized upon his hearers, because he was entirely open, receptive to all that was new, declining nothing, prepared for everything. He threw himself, so to speak, out of himself towards another with his entire being; upon hundreds and hundreds of occasions, as in this first hour, I have happily experienced this stormy, overpowering contact of his being. As yet he knew nothing about me, but still he offered me his confidence merely because he heard that I was close to his work.

After lunch the first good surprise was followed by a second. Van der Stappen had long wished to fulfill his own and Verhaeren's desire to make a bust of the latter; the last sitting was to be today. My presence, so van der Stappen said, was a friendly gift of fate, for he needed someone to talk with this much too unruly model while he sat, so that his face might become enlivened in speaking and listening. So for two hours I gazed deep into this face, this unforgettable, lofty brow, already plowed by the furrows of evil years, and over this a wealth of rust-brown locks. The structure of his face was strong and tightly covered by a brownish skin tanned by the wind; his chin jutted forth like a rock, and over his slim lips hung his mighty Vercingetorix mustache. His nervousness lay in his hands, those slender, gripping, fine yet powerful hands in which the pulse beat strongly under the sparse flesh. The entire force of his will-power stemmed from his broad peasant shoulders for which the small, vigorously boned head seemed almost too small; it was only when he got up that one saw his power. When I look at the bust today—nothing of van der Stappen's ever turned out better than the work of that hour—I know how genuine it is and how completely it embraces his nature. It is a document of his poetic greatness, the monument of an immortal power.

～

In those three hours I learned to love the man as I have loved him throughout my entire lifetime. There was an assurance in him that did not, for a single instant, seem like self-satisfaction. He remained independent of money, and preferred living his country life to writing a single line. He remained independent of success, made no effort to increase it by means of concessions or favors or conviviality—his friends and their loyal adherence sufficed him. He even remained independent of the dangerous temptations of his character, of fame when it finally came to him at the peak of his life. He remained open in every sense, was burdened by no repression and confused by no pride, a free joyous person, easily given to every rapture;

when one was with him one felt enlivened in his own desire
for life.

So there before me—youth that I was—stood the poet in
the flesh as I had wished it, as I had dreamed of him. In
the very first hour of our meeting I had come to a decision:
to serve this man and his work. It was actually a daring
decision, for this hymnographer of Europe was then but little known in Europe, and I knew in advance that the translation of his monumental poetical work and his three
dramas in verse would take away two or three years from my
own work. But in resolving to devote my entire energy, time
and passion to the translation of a foreign work, I did myself
the best of services, by assuming a moral task. My uncertain
seeking and striving now began to make sense. And if today
I were to counsel a young writer who is still unsure of his
way, I would try to persuade him first to adapt or translate
a sizable work. In all sacrificing service there is more assurance for the beginner than in his own creation, and nothing
that one has ever done with devotion is done in vain.

~

During the two years which I devoted almost exclusively
to the translation of Verhaeren's poetical works and to the
preparation of his biography, I traveled much in between,
at times giving public lectures. Soon I received unexpected
thanks for my apparently thankless devotion to the work
of Verhaeren; his friends abroad, and soon my friends also,
took note of me. One day I was visited by Ellen Key. She
was the wonderful Swedish woman who with unequaled
boldness fought for the emancipation of women in those
benighted, opposition-filled days, and who, long before
Freud, pointed out the spiritual vulnerability of youth in
her *Century of the Child*. Through her I was introduced
to Giovanni Cena and his poetic circle in Italy and won

an important friend in the Norwegian Johan Bojer. Georg Brandes, the international master of the history of literature, disclosed a kindly interest in me, and soon the name of Verhaeren began to be better known in German than it was in his mother tongue. Kainz, the greatest of all actors, and Moissi recited his poetry in public, using my translation, and Max Reinhardt presented Verhaeren's *Cloister* on the German stage. I had reason to feel satisfied.

But it was now high time for me to remember that I had undertaken another obligation besides the one to Verhaeren. I had finally to terminate my university career and to bring home the doctor's hood. Now I had to work up in a few months all the scholastic material on which the more stable students had labored for almost four years. With Erwin Guido Kolbenheyer, a literary friend of my youth, who may today not like to be reminded of it because he has become one of the public poets and academicians of Hitler's Germany, I crammed through the nights. But my examination was not made difficult for me. The kindly professor, who knew too much about my public literary activity to vex me with petty detail, said to me in a private conversation beforehand, smiling: "You would prefer not to be examined in exact logic"; and then, as a matter of fact, led me over into fields in which I felt more sure of myself. It was the first time that I passed an examination with honors, and the last time as well. And now I was *outwardly* free and all the years up to the present have been devoted to one struggle—a struggle which in our times grows constantly more difficult—to remain equally free *inwardly*.

V

Paris, the City of Eternal Youth

I HAD promised myself Paris as a gift for the first year of my newly won freedom. I knew this inexhaustible city only slightly from two earlier visits and I knew that whoever had lived there for a year as a young man would carry away with him an incomparably happy memory that would remain for all time. Nowhere else did a young man breathe the very atmosphere of youth as he did in this city, which yields itself to all, yet allows none to fathom it.

I know that this exhilarated and exhilarating Paris of my youth is no more; possibly that wonderful nonchalance will never be restored since the hardest hand on earth pressed the branding iron down upon it. In the hour in which I began writing these lines, the German armies and the German tanks began to roll in like a gray horde of termites to eradicate the divine colorfulness, the joyous spirit, the glowing and imperishable bloom of this most harmonious phenomenon. And it has happened: the swastika waves from the Eiffel Tower, the black storm troops parade provokingly through Napoleon's Champs Elysées. From afar I sympathize with the hearts throbbing convulsively in the home, and with the humiliated gaze of the once good-natured citizens when the conqueror's boots stamp through their beloved *bistros* and cafés. Hardly any other misfortune has touched, shaken, and grieved me so much as the degradation of this city which possessed a special grace to give happiness to everyone who approached it. Will it ever again be able to give to future generations what it gave

126

to us—the wisest lesson, the most wonderful example of how to be free and creative at the same time, so open-handed and yet always becoming richer in its lovely extravagance?

I know, I know, it is not Paris alone that suffers today; the rest of Europe as well for decades to come will not be what it was before the First World War. A certain shadow has never quite disappeared from Europe's once so bright horizon. Bitterness and distrust of nation for nation and people for people remained like an insidious poison in its maimed body. In spite of the social and technical progress of this quarter of a century between world war and world war, there is not a single nation in our small world of the West that has not lost immeasurably much of its *joie de vivre* and its carefree existence. It would take days to describe how confiding, how childishly joyous the Italian people once were, even in the depth of poverty, how they laughed and sang in their *trattorie,* how wittily they derided the bad *governo;* and now they march sullenly with their chins thrust forward and, wrath in their hearts. Can one still imagine an Austria so lax and loose in its joviality, so piously confiding in its Imperial master and in the God who made life so comfortable for them? The Russians, the Germans, the Spaniards, not one of them can remember how much freedom and joy the soulless, voracious bogy of the "State" has sucked from the very marrow of their soul. All peoples feel only that a strange shadow hangs broad and heavy over their lives. But we, who once knew a world of individual freedom, know and can give testimony that Europe once, without a care, enjoyed its kaleidoscopic play of color. And we shudder when we think how over-cast, overshadowed, enslaved and enchained our world has become because of its suicidal fury.

But nowhere did one experience the naïve and yet won-

drously wise freedom of existence more happily than in
Paris, where all this was gloriously confirmed by beauty
of form, by the mildness of the climate, by wealth and
tradition. Each one of us youngsters took into himself a
share of that lightness and in so doing contributed his own
share; Chinese and Scandinavians, Spaniards and Greeks,
Brazilians and Canadians, all felt themselves at home on
the banks of the Seine. There was no compulsion; one
could speak, think, laugh, and scold as one wished; all lived
as they pleased, convivially or alone, wastefully or frugally,
luxuriously or *à la bohème*. There was room for the unusual
and provision for all opportunities. There were the sublime
restaurants, with all kinds of culinary magic, and vintage
wines for two or three hundred francs, and sinfully expensive cognacs from the days of Marengo and Waterloo. But
one could eat and carouse as well at any wine shop around
the corner. In the crowded student restaurants of the Latin
Quarter, for a few *sous* you could get the choicest bits before
and after your juicy beefsteak, and in addition you had
red or white wine and a long stick of marvelous white
bread. One could dress as one pleased; the students prom-
enaded about with their rakish berets along the Boul'
Mich', the *rapins* or painters wore wide, huge mushroom
hats and romantic black velvet jackets, the workers wandered about unconcernedly in their blue blouses or in their
shirt sleeves on the most fashionable boulevards, the nurses
in their broad pleated Breton caps, the wine shop keepers
in their blue aprons. It did not have to be the Fourteenth
of July for a young couple to begin dancing on the street
after midnight while the police stood by laughing. The
street belonged to everybody. No one was embarrassed in
the presence of anybody, the prettiest girls were not ashamed
to go arm in arm with a coal-black Negro or a slant-eyed
Chinese into the nearest *petit hôtel*—in Paris who cared

about the bogies that were to be made much of later on, race, class, and birth? One walked, one talked, one slept with whomever one pleased, and cared not a hoot about others. Oh, one needed to know Berlin first in order to love Paris properly, and to experience the innate servility of Germany with its angular and painfully sharp-edged class consciousness. There the officer's wife did not associate with the wife of the teacher, nor the latter with the merchant's, nor she in turn with the wife of the workman. But in Paris the inheritance of the Revolution was still in the blood. The proletarian worker felt himself as free and important a citizen as his employer. In the café the waiter cordially shook the hand of the gold-braided general, the small solid sober bourgeoise did not stick up her nose at the prostitute who lived on the same floor, but chatted with her daily on the staircase, and the children gave her flowers. In a fashionable restaurant—it was Larue's, near the Madeleine—I once saw some wealthy Norman peasants who had come from a christening. They came thundering in with heavy boots like hooves, in their village dress, their hair so thickly pomaded that it could be smelled as far as the kitchen. They talked animatedly and the conversation took on volume the more they drank, and unashamed they laughingly poked their fat wives in the ribs. Being true peasants, it did not trouble them in the least to sit among men in elegant tails and beautifully gowned women. Even the smooth-shaven waiter did not turn up his nose as he would have done in Germany or England in the presence of such rural company, but served them as politely and as perfectly as he did the Ministers and the Excellencies, and the maître d'hotel took a special delight in welcoming the somewhat unconventional guests quite heartily. Paris knew only a mixture of contrasts, no above and no below; there was no visible barrier between the luxurious streets and the unswept alleys, and in each there was equal life and gaiety. In the courtyards of the faubourgs the street musicians made their music and one heard the *midinettes* through the open windows singing while they worked. Always and everywhere there was laughter in the air or a friendly greeting. If on occasion two cabbies got into a row they afterwards shook hands, drank a glass of wine together and ate a few ridiculously cheap oysters. Nothing was difficult or stiff. Relations with women were easily started and as easily ended; every Jack found his Jill, every young man a happy girl untrammeled by convention. Oh, how easily, how well, one lived in Paris, particularly if one was young! Merely walking about was a pleasure and a lesson at the same time, for everything was within reach. You could walk into a secondhand bookshop and spend a quarter hour turning the pages without the dealer's grumbling or complaining. You could go into the small galleries and the art shops and browse around as you wished, you could look in on the auctions at the Hôtel Drouot, and chat with the governesses in the parks. It was not easy to stop once you had started strolling, for the street drew you on magnetically; it was a kaleidoscope, constantly disclosing something new. If you were tired you could sit on the terrace of one of the ten thousand cafés and write letters on stationery which was supplied free of charge and at the same time have the street vendors trying to sell you their entire stock of baubles and gadgets. The only difficult thing was to stay home or to go home, especially when it was spring and the lights shone soft and silvery over the Seine, and the trees on the boulevards were beginning to bud, and the girls were wearing bunches of violets which they had bought for a penny. But it was not necessarily spring that put you in a good mood in Paris.

At the time that I learned to know the city it was not as completely welded together as it is today, as a result of the subways and the automobile. It was principally the mighty omnibuses with their heavy steaming horses that dominated the traffic. However, Paris was never more comfortably explored than from the top of those wide coaches, the "Imperials," or from the open cabs which, similarly, never progressed too madly. Then it was still something of a trip from Montmartre to Montparnasse, and in view of the frugality of the Parisian bourgeois, I readily believe the legend that there were still Parisians on the right bank who had never been on the left, and that there were children who played only in the Luxembourg Gardens and had never seen those of the Tuileries or the Parc Monceau. The seasoned citizen or concierge preferred remaining *chez soi,* in his own *quartier.* He built up his small Paris in the greater Paris, and for that reason each of the districts retained its distinctive and even provincial character. So it became something of a question for a stranger to choose where to pitch his tent. The Latin Quarter no longer enticed me. Thither I had raced from the station when I was twenty, on an earlier brief visit. The very first evening I sat in the Café Vachette and looked with awe at Verlaine's chair and the marble table which, when in his cups, he beat angrily with his stick, thus to command proper respect. Abstaining acolyte that I was, I drank a glass of absinthe in his honor although the greenish brew was not to my taste. But I felt that as a young devotee in the Latin Quarter I was obliged to conform to the ritual of the lyric poets of France. At that time I should have liked above all—because of my sense of the fitness of things—to live in a sixth-floor attic room near the Sorbonne, so as to participate faithfully in the Latin Quarter life as I had conceived it from books. But at twenty-five I was no longer so naïvely romantic, and the students' quarter seemed to be too international, too un-Parisian. Above all I had no wish to choose my permanent quarters according to my literary reminiscences but rather to do my own work as best I could. I looked about carefully. The elegant Paris of the Champs Elysées was not at all suited to this purpose, and even less so the quarter surrounding the Café de la Paix where all the well-to-do foreigners from the Balkans congregated, and no one spoke French but the waiters. The quiet district of Saint Sulpice, overshadowed by churches and convents, where Rilke and Suarez liked to live, had more charm for me; but most of all I would have liked to take lodgings on the Ile Saint Louis so as to be connected with both sides of Paris, the right and the left banks. But while out walking one day during the first week of my stay, I was lucky enough to find something even better. Strolling through the galleries of the Palais Royal, I discovered what had once been a fashionable palace among the uniformly constructed houses in the huge square, erected by Prince Egalité in the eighteenth century, and which had declined until now it was a small, somewhat primitive hotel. I looked at one of the rooms, and noticed to my delight that the window gave on the garden of the Palais Royal, which was locked at dusk. I could hear only the slight murmur of the city, faint and rhythmic as the breaking of waves on a distant shore. The statues glistened in the moonlight, and in the early morning hours the wind sometimes wafted the spicy aroma of vegetables from the near-by Halles. It was in this historic quarter of the Palais Royal that the poets and statesmen of the eighteenth and nineteenth centuries had lived. Directly opposite was the house where Balzac and Victor Hugo so often climbed the hundred narrow steps to the mansard of Marceline Desbordes-Valmore, the poetess I loved so

much. There glistened the marble where Camille Des-
moulins had aroused the people to storm the Bastille, there
was the covered passage where the poor little Lieutenant
Bonaparte sought a patroness among the strolling, not
always virtuous ladies. Here the history of France spoke
from every stone; besides, only one street distant was the
Bibliothèque Nationale, where I spent my mornings, and
close by, too, were the Louvre with its pictures, and the
boulevards with their streams of people. I had finally found
the place where I wished to live; in innermost Paris, where
for centuries, warm and rhythmical, the heart of France had
been beating. I recall that André Gide once visited me and,
wondering at this stillness in the heart of Paris, said: "It
takes strangers to show us the loveliest spots in our own
city." And truly, I could not have found anything more
Parisian, and at the same time more secluded, than this
romantic study in the innermost city.

～

How I roamed about the streets in those days, how much
I saw, how much I sought in my impatience—for I did not
wish to know only the Paris of 1904! In my mind and in
my heart, I looked for the Paris of Henri IV and Louis XIV,
and of Napoleon and the Revolution, the Paris of Rétif de
la Bretonne and Balzac, Zola, and Charles-Louis Philippe,
with all its streets, its personalities, and its events. I felt
here, as everywhere in France, how much of immortality
a great and truthful literature can confer upon a people,
for I was intellectually familiar in advance with everything
in Paris through the descriptive and almost plastic ren-
dering of its poets, its novelists, its historians, and its writers
on modes and manners, before I had seen it with my own
eyes. It was merely brought to life by coming face to face
with it; and seeing it physically was really nothing but a

recognition, that delight of the Greek *anagnorismos* which Aristotle lauds as the greatest and most mysterious of all artistic satisfactions. Yet still, you never know a people or a city in its depth and its most hidden qualities through books, nor even most persistent poking about in its nooks and crannies, but only through its best people. It is only through an intellectual friendship with the living that one gains insight into the true connection between folk and land; all observation from without can give no more than a spurious premature view.

Such friendships were given me, and the best was that of Léon Bazalgette. Because of my intimate connection with Verhaeren, whom I visited twice each week in Saint Cloud, I was saved from falling in with the windy circle of international painters and writers as most foreigners did—for after all, here they were no different than in Munich, Rome, and Berlin. With Verhaeren, however, I visited those painters and poets who lived in the midst of this temperamental and sybaritic city, each one living for his work in a creative stillness, as if he were on a lonely island. I even saw Renoir's studio, and the best of his pupils. Externally, the existence of these Impressionists, whose work today fetches thousands of dollars, differed in no way from that of the *rentiers* and the middle class; a small house with a studio attached, no such pretension as Lenbach and the other celebrities in Munich displayed with their imitation Pompeian villas. The painters lived as simply as the poets with whom I soon became familiar. They all had small governmental jobs in which there was little actual work. The great respect for intellectual activity which is apparent in France from the highest to the lowest for years inspired the intelligent system of conferring inconspicuous sinecures upon poets and writers whose work brought them only a small revenue; they were, for example,

appointed librarians in the Ministry of Marine or in the
Senate. Here they were given a small salary, and little
work, for it was only rarely that a senator asked for a book,
so that the fortunate possessor of such a benefice could sit
quietly and comfortably in front of his window in the
stylish old senatorial palace in the Luxembourg Gardens
and write his verses during working hours without worrying
about his earnings. And this modest security was enough.
Others were physicians, as Duhamel and Durtain were
later, or they had a small picture gallery like Charles
Vildrac, or they were Lycée professors like Romains and
Jean-Richard Bloch; or, like Paul Valéry, they put in a
few hours at the Havas Agency or read for publishers.
But none of them had pretensions like their successors
who, spoiled by the cinema and huge editions, attempted
to win sovereign independence at the first stirring of an
artistic inclination. What these poets sought from their
small unambitious professions was nothing but a little
security for their outer life which guaranteed them freedom
for their inner work. Because of this modest security they
could pass up the great corrupt Parisian dailies with disdain,
and write without pay for their small magazines which were
maintained only through personal sacrifice; and they could
be content with having their plays given in the small literary
theaters and at first getting no publicity outside their own
circle. For decades only a small élite had known of Claudel,
of Péguy, Rolland, Suarez, and Valéry. In the midst of this
hustling and bustling city, they were the only ones who
were not in a hurry. Living quietly and working quietly
for a quiet circle outside of the *foire sur la place* was more
important to them than pushing themselves forward, and
they were not ashamed to live frugally and in middle-class
circles in return for the right to think and work freely and
adventurously in the world of art. Their wives did the

cooking and ran the house; everything was simple and for that reason more convivial at their evening gatherings. We sat on inexpensive wicker chairs around a carelessly set table covered with a checkered cloth, no more fashionable than the plumber on the same floor, but we felt free and unhindered. They had no telephone, no typewriter, no secretaries, they avoided all mechanical tools just as they did the intellectual apparatus of propaganda. They wrote by hand as they did a thousand years ago, and even at the large publishers', such as the Mercure de France, there was no stenography and no elaborate organization. Nothing was wasted for show, for prestige, or for impressiveness. All these young French poets, like the rest of the people, lived for the joy of living in its sublimest form, the creative joy in work. How the simple human integrity of these newly won friends revised my idea of the French poet! How different was their style of living from that described by Bourget and the other famous novelists of the period, for whom the *salon* was identical with the world! And how their women taught me to see through the criminally false picture that we had conceived at home out of books, of the French woman as a *mondaine* who cared only for adventures, extravagance, and staring at herself in a mirror. I have never seen better or quieter housekeepers than in that fraternal circle—frugal, modest, and gay even in the tightest circumstances, working minor miracles on a tiny stove, taking care of the children and yet always intellectually akin to their husbands. Only someone who has lived in these circles as a friend and comrade knows the true France.

My friend of friends was Léon Bazalgette, whose name is improperly omitted from most accounts of modern French literature, in which it stood for something exceptional, namely that he exclusively employed his creative

energy in fostering the work of others, and thus saved up
his truly amazing intensity for the persons he loved. In
him, a born comrade, I found the highest type of self-
sacrificing person in flesh and blood, truly devoted, considering his life's work to be nothing but to help the natural
talents of his time to realize themselves and bear fruit, and
never even aspiring to the justifiable pride of being renowned as their discoverer and promoter. His active
enthusiasm was simply a natural function of his moral
consciousness. Somewhat soldierly in appearance, although
he was an ardent anti-militarist, in his associations he had
the cordiality of a true comrade. Always ready to help and
to advise, incorruptible in his honesty, punctual as clock-
work, he was concerned about everything that concerned
another, but never to his own advantage. Time meant
nothing to him, money meant nothing, when friendship
was concerned, and he had friends in all parts of the world,
a small but select number. He had devoted ten years to
making Walt Whitman known to the French by translating
all his poems and by his monumental biography. His life's
aim was to carry the intellectual outlook of his nation
beyond its frontiers, and to make his compatriots more
manly and more comradely, with this example of a free
world-loving man; the best of Frenchmen, he was at the
same time a passionate anti-nationalist.

We soon became close and fraternal friends, for neither
of us thought nationally, we both liked to further foreign
works with devotion and without any ulterior advantage,
and we looked upon intellectual independence as the alpha
and omega of living. It was in him that I learned to know
the "underground" France. When I later read in Rolland
how Olivier met the German Jean Christophe, I almost
thought I was reading an account of our own personal
experience. But the nicest thing about our friendship, and

the thing that remained unforgettable, was that it always had to overcome a ticklish point, whose constant resistance under normal circumstances would usually have hindered any honest and cordial intimacy between two writers. The ticklish point was this, that Bazalgette, with his amazing honesty, decisively rejected all that I wrote at that time. He liked me personally and had the greatest respect imaginable for my devotion to the work of Verhaeren. Whenever I came to Paris, he awaited me faithfully at the station and was the first to greet me. Whenever he could be of help to me he was there and we agreed more heartily on important things than brothers usually do. But upon my own work he pronounced a decided "no." He knew some of my poems and prose in the translations of Henri Guilbeaux (who played an important role in the World War and as a friend of Lenin), and frankly and abruptly turned them down. Steadfastly he admonished me that my product had no connection with reality, it was esoteric literature (which he hated thoroughly) and he was annoyed that just I chose to write that. Unconditionally honest with himself, he made no concessions on this point, not even that of politeness. When, for example, he was editing a review, he asked my help—that is, he asked me to secure important collaborators for him in Germany, in other words, contributions that were better than mine; he neither demanded nor published a single line from me, his closest friend, although at the same time out of pure friendship he devoted himself, without remuneration, to the revision of the French translation of one of my books for a publisher. That our fraternal comradeship did not suffer for a moment throughout ten years because of this peculiar circumstance made it doubly dear to me. And no one's approval ever pleased me more than Bazalgette's when during the World War I turned my back on all my earlier efforts and finally achieved some sort of personal expression. For I knew that his "yes" to my new works was just as honest as his sharp "no" had been throughout the ten years.

～～～

If I set down the precious name of Rainer Maria Rilke in these pages of the Paris days, although he was a German poet, it is because I saw him most often and to the best advantage there and because I always see his face, as in old pictures, against the background of that city which he loved more than any other. When I think of him today, and of those other masters of words hammered as if by the noble goldsmith's art—when I think of those honored names which shone over my youth like the farthest constellations in the sky, I cannot escape the melancholy question: will such pure lyricists again be a possibility in this era of turbulence and universal destruction? Is it not a lost tribe that I am bemoaning, a tribe without visible successors in this day of exposure to every storm of fate? These were poets who made no demands on society—neither the regard of the masses nor decorations, honors or profit—who sought only to bind verse to verse in silent yet passionate effort, every line saturated with music, flaming with color, glowing with images. They constituted a guild, an almost monastic order in the midst of our clattering time; to them, awaredly rejecting life's workaday round, nothing in the whole universe was more significant than the note—delicate, yet surviving the booming of the age—emitted when rhyme joining rhyme created the indescribable stir, softer than the sound of a leaf falling in the wind, that vibrates to the most distant soul. How elevating for us young people was the presence of these men, true to themselves, exemplary servitors and custodians of the language, whose sole devotion was to the ringing word, not the word of the moment and of the newspaper but proper to the lasting and the everlasting. We were abashed to gaze upon them, for they lived obscurely, insignificantly, invisibly, one peasant-like in the country, another in some petty vocation, a third wandering abroad like a passionate pilgrim, all known to but a few, but loved the more earnestly by those few! One was in Germany, another in France, another in Italy, and yet they were all in the same homeland, for they lived in poetry alone; and, in the firm renunciation of the ephemeral their life, through art, became itself a work of art. More and more it seems a wonder to me that we had such immaculate poets amongst us in our youth. And that is why I also ask myself repeatedly, with a kind of private anxiety: will it be possible for such personalities, completely devoted to the lyric art, to exist in our time, in our new forms of life, which drive men out murderously from all inner contemplation as a forest fire drives wild animals from their hidden lairs? I know full well that the miracle of a poet repeats itself in all times, and Goethe's moving consolation in his elegy on Lord Byron remains eternally true: "For the Earth will conceive them again, as she has always conceived them." Again and again such poets will arise in blessed recurrence, for from time to time immortality lends so precious a pledge to even the most unworthy era. But is not ours a time which does not grant, even to the purest and the most secluded, any quiet for waiting and ripening and contemplation and collecting one's self, as it was still granted to the men of the better and calmer European pre-war period? I do not know how much all those poets, Valéry, Verhaeren, Rilke, Pascoli, Francis Jammes, count today, or how much they mean to a generation into whose ears, instead of that gentler music, the clatter of the propaganda mill has rumbled for years and years, and twice the thunder of cannons. I only know and feel the necessity of avowing publicly how great a lesson and how great a joy it was for us to have the presence of such saints, sworn to perfection, in the midst of a world that had already begun to mechanize itself. And looking back upon my life, I am aware of no more precious possession than the privilege of being humanly close to some of them, and of having my early reverence often grow into lasting friendships.

Of all of these men, perhaps none lived more gently, more secretly, more invisibly than Rilke. But it was not willful, nor forced or assumed priestly loneliness such as Stefan George celebrated in Germany; silence seemed to grow around him, wherever he went, wherever he was. Since he avoided every noise, even his own fame—that "sum of all misunderstanding, that collects itself about a name," as he once expressed it—the approaching wave of idle curiosity moistened only his name and never his person. It was difficult to reach Rilke. He had no house, no address where one could find him, no home, no steady lodging, no office. He was always on his way through the world, and no one, not even he himself, knew in advance which direction he would take. To his immeasurably sensitive soul, every positive decision, all planning and every announcement were burdensome. It was always by chance that one met him. You stood in an Italian gallery and felt, without being aware whence it came, a gentle, friendly smile. And only then you recognized his blue eyes which, when they looked at you, lit up his otherwise unimpressive countenance with an inner light. But this unimpressiveness was precisely the deepest secret of his being. Thousands may have passed by this young man, with his slightly melancholy drooping blond mustache and his somewhat Slavic features, undistinguished by any single trait, without dreaming that this was a poet and one of the greatest of our generation; his individuality, his unusual demeanor were only apparent in a closer association. He had an indescribably gentle way of approaching and talking. When he entered a room where people were gathered together, it was so noiselessly that hardly anyone noticed him. He sat there quietly listening, lifted his head unconsciously when anything seemed to occupy his thoughts, or when he himself began to speak, always without affectation or raised voice. He spoke naturally and simply, like a mother telling a fairy tale to her child, and just as lovingly; it was wonderful how, listening to him, even the most insignificant subject became picturesque and important. But no sooner did he feel that he was the center of attention in a larger circle than he stopped speaking and once again sank down into his silent, attentive listening. Every movement, every gesture was soft; even when he laughed it was no more than a suggestion of a sound. Muted tones were a necessity to him, and nothing annoyed him so much as noise and, in the realm of feeling, all violence. "They exhaust me, these people who spit out their feelings like blood," he once said; "that's why I swallow Russians, like liqueur, in small doses." No less than measured conduct, orderliness, cleanliness and quiet were physical necessities; to ride in an overfilled streetcar, or to have to sit in a noisy public place, disturbed him for hours thereafter. All that was vulgar was unbearable to him, and although he lived in restricted circumstances, his clothes always gave evidence of care, cleanliness, and good taste. At the same time they showed thought and poetic imagination; they were a masterpiece of unpretension, always with an unobtrusive personal touch, a little something additional which gave him pleasure, such as perhaps a thin silver bracelet around his wrist. For his aesthetic sense of perfection and symmetry entered into the most intimate and the most personal details. Once I watched him in his rooms prior to his departure—he declined my help as superfluous—as he was packing his trunk. It was like mosaic work, each individual piece gently put into the carefully reserved space; I would have felt it to be an outrage to disturb this flowerlike arrangement by a helping hand. And his sense of the elements of beauty accompanied him to the most insignificant detail. It was not only that he wrote his manuscripts on the best of paper with his calligraphic round hand so that every line was related to another as if measured with a ruler; the choicest paper was selected for even an occasional letter, and even, clean and round his calligraphic writing filled the space. Even in the most hurried notes, he did not permit himself to strike out a word and whenever a sentence or an expression did not seem correct, he wrote the letter a second time with his marvelous patience. Rilke never allowed anything to leave his hands that was not perfect.

This muted and yet integrated quality of his being impressed itself upon anyone who came close to him. It was as impossible to think of Rilke being noisy as it was to imagine a man in his presence who did not lose his loudness and arrogance through the vibrations that emanated from Rilke's quietness. For his conduct vibrated like a secret, continuous, purposive, moralizing force. After every fairly long talk with him one was incapable of any vulgarity for hours or even days. On the other hand, of course, this constant temperateness of his nature, this never-wishing-to-give-himself-completely put an early end to any particular cordiality; I believe that few people may boast of having been Rilke's "friends." In the six published volumes of his letters, one rarely finds such form of address, and the brotherly, familiar *du* was hardly ever applied to anyone after his school days. To permit anyone or any-

thing to approach him too closely burdened his extraordinary sensitivity and everything that was pronouncedly masculine caused him physical discomfort. He gave himself'
more easily to women in conversation. He wrote often and
gladly to them and was much more free in their presence.
Perhaps it was the absence of the guttural in their voices
that pleased him, for he suffered particularly from unpleasant voices. I can still see him before me in conversation with a high aristocrat, completely bent over, his
shoulders tortured and even his eyes cast down, so that
they might not betray how much he suffered physically
from the gentleman's unpleasant falsetto. But how good
to be with him when he was kindly disposed toward someone! Then one sensed his inner goodness—although he
remained sparing of words and gestures—like a warm,
healing outpouring deep into one's soul.

Shy and retiring, Rilke seemed most receptive in Paris,
this heart-warming city, and perhaps it was because here
his name and his work were still unknown and because he
always felt freer and happier when he was anonymous. I
visited him there in two different lodgings which he had
rented. Each was simple and without ornament and yet
immediately assumed character and calm through his
dominant sense of beauty. It was never a huge house with
noisy neighbors, rather an old, even though less comfortable, one, in which he could feel at home; and no
matter where he was, his sense of orderliness made the
place meaningful and harmonized it with his being. There
were only a very few things around him, but flowers always
shone in a vase or bowl, perhaps the gift of women, perhaps
tenderly brought home by himself. Books gleamed from
the walls, beautifully bound or carefully jacketed in paper,
for he liked books as he liked dumb animals. Pencils and
pens lay on the desk in a straight line, and clean sheets of

paper perfectly straightened; a Russian icon and a Catholic crucifix, which, I believe, accompanied him on all his travels, gave his working cell a slightly religious character, although his religiousness was not connected with any specific dogma. One felt that everything had been carefully chosen and as carefully preserved. If you lent him a book with which he was unfamiliar, it was returned faultlessly wrapped in tissue paper and tied with colored ribbon like a gift. I can still recall how he brought the manuscript of *Die Weise von Liebe und Tod* into my room as a precious gift. I have kept the ribbon that was around it. But it was nicest to walk with Rilke in Paris, for that meant seeing the most insignificant things with eyes enlightened to their meaning. He noticed every detail, and he liked to repeat aloud the firm names on the signs if they seemed rhythmic to him. It was his passion—almost the only one that I ever observed in him—to know every nook and cranny of this Paris. Once, when we met at the home of mutual friends, I told him that on the day before I had chanced upon the old Barrière where the last victims of the guillotine had been buried in the Cimetière de Picpus, and André Chénier among them. I described to him the affecting little meadow with its scattered graves, rarely seen by strangers, and told him how on the way back I had seen in one of the streets through the open door of a convent a sort of *béguine,* silently telling her rosary as in a pious dream. It was one of the few times when I saw this gentle composed man almost impatient. He had to see the grave of André Chénier and the convent. Would I take him there? We went the next day. He stood in a sort of entranced silence before the lonesome cemetery and called it "the most lyric in Paris." On our way back the door of the convent was closed. And now I had an opportunity of testing the silent patience which he had mastered in his life no less than in his work.

"Let us wait for an opportunity," he said. With head slightly bent, he stood so that he could look through the door when it opened. We waited for perhaps twenty minutes. One of the sisters of the order came down the street and rang the bell. "Now," he whispered softly, with excitement. But the sister had become aware of his silent waiting—I have already said that one sensed everything about him from afar—and came up to him and asked if he was waiting for someone. He smiled at her with his gentle smile that immediately created confidence, and said warmly that he much desired to see the convent corridor. She was sorry, the sister smiled in turn, but she could not let him in. However, I advised him to go to the little house of the gardener next door where he would have a good view from a window in the upper story. And so this too, like so much else, was granted him. Our paths crossed a number of times thereafter, but whenever I think of Rilke, I see him in Paris. He was spared the experience of its saddest hour.

~~

Men of this rare mold were a great benefit to a novice; but I still had to receive a determining lesson, one which was to have an effect for my entire lifetime. It was a gift of chance. At Verhaeren's we had got into a discussion with an art historian who complained that the era of great sculpture and art had passed. I contradicted him warmly. Was not Rodin still in our midst, no less important a creator than the great of the past? I began to enumerate his works and fell, as always when one meets contradiction, into an almost angry tone. Verhaeren smiled to himself. "Anyone who likes Rodin so much should really meet him," he said finally. "Tomorrow I am going to his studio. If you wish, I will take you with me."

If I wished! I could not sleep for happiness. But at

Rodin's, the words stuck in my throat. I could not say a single thing to him, and stood among his statues like one of them. Strangely enough, my embarrassment seemed to please him, for at parting the old man asked me if I did not want to see his real studio in Meudon, and even asked me to dine with him. My first lesson had been taught me— that the greatest men are always the kindest.

The second was that nearly always they are the simplest in their manner of living. At the home of this man, whose fame was universal, and of whose work every line was as familiar to men of our generation as an old friend, we ate as simply as at a plain farmer's; a good piece of meat, a few olives and copious fruit, and some *vin du pays* with it. That gave me more courage, and at the end I spoke freely, as if this old man and his wife had been known to me for years.

After dinner we went over into the studio. It was a huge room, which contained replicas of most of his works, but amongst them lay hundreds of precious small studies—a hand, an arm, a horse's mane, a woman's ear, mostly only clay models. Today I can still recall exactly some of these sketches, which were made for his own practice, and could talk about them for an hour. Finally the master led me to a pedestal on which, covered with wet cloths, his latest work, a portrait of a woman, was hidden. With his heavy, furrowed peasant's hand he removed the cloths, and stepped back. "Admirable" escaped from my lips, and at once I was ashamed of my banality. But with quiet objectivity in which not a trace of pride could have been found, he murmured, looking at his own work, merely agreeing: *"N'est-ce pas?"* Then he hesitated. "Only there at the shoulder . . . just a moment." He threw off his coat, put on a white smock, picked up a spatula and with a masterly stroke on the shoulder smoothed the soft material so that it seemed the skin of a living, breathing woman. Again he stepped back. "And now here," he muttered. Again the effect was increased by a tiny detail. Then he no longer spoke. He would step forward, then retreat, look at the figure in a mirror, mutter and utter unintelligible sounds, make changes and corrections. His eyes, which at table had been amiably inattentive, now flashed with strange lights, and he seemed to have grown larger and younger. He worked, worked, worked, with the entire passion and force of his heavy body; whenever he stepped forward or back the floor creaked. But he heard nothing. He did not notice that behind him stood a young man, silent, with his heart in his throat, overjoyed that he was being permitted to watch this unique master at work. He had forgotten me entirely. I did not exist for him. Only the figure, the work, concerned him, and behind it, invisible, the vision of absolute perfection.

So it went on for a quarter or a half hour, I cannot recall how long. Great moments are always outside of time. Rodin was so engrossed, so rapt in his work that not even a thunderstroke would have roused him. His movements became harder, almost angry. A sort of wildness or drunkenness had come over him; he worked faster and faster. Then his hands became hesitant. They seemed to have realized that there was nothing more for them to do. Once, twice, three times he stepped back without making any changes. Then he muttered something softly into his beard, and placed the cloths gently about the figure as one places a shawl around the shoulders of a beloved woman. He took a deep breath and relaxed. His figure seemed to grow heavier again. The fire had died out. And then the incomprehensible occurred, the great lesson: he took off his smock, again put on his house-coat and turned to go. He had forgotten me completely in that hour of extreme concentration. He no longer knew that a young man whom he

himself had led into the studio to show him his work had
stood behind him with bated breath, as immovable as his
statue.

He stepped to the door. As he started to unlock it, he
discovered me and stared at me almost angrily: who was
this young stranger who had slunk into his studio? But in
the next moment he remembered and, almost ashamed,
came towards me. "Pardon, Monsieur," he began. But I did
not let him finish. I merely grasped his hand in gratitude.
I would have preferred to kiss it. In that hour I had seen
the Eternal secret of all great art, yes, of every mortal
achievement, made manifest: concentration, the collection
of all forces, all senses, that *ecstasis,* that being-out-of-the-
world of every artist. I had learned something for my entire
lifetime.

~~~

It had been my intention to leave Paris at the end of May
for London; but I was forced to take my trip two weeks
earlier because my enchanting room had become uncomfortable through an unexpected circumstance. This came
about through a peculiar episode, which amused me greatly
and at the same time gave me instructive insight into the
mental processes of widely varying French milieus.

I had been away from Paris for the two holidays at
Whitsuntide, in order to admire with friends the lovely
cathedral at Chartres, which I had not yet seen. When I
returned to my hotel room on Tuesday morning, and wished
to change my clothes, I found that my portmanteau, which
had been standing peaceably in the corner for all these
months, was missing. I went down to the owner of the small
hotel, who took turns with his wife sitting in the porter's
room during the daytime. He was a small, chubby, red-
faced Marseillais, with whom I often joked and sometimes

played his favorite game—backgammon—in the café across the way. He became terribly excited at once, banged the table, and cried out mysteriously: "So that's it!" While hastily putting on his coat—as always, he had been sitting in his shirt sleeves—and exchanging his comfortable slippers for his shoes, he told me what had happened. But I ought first to recall a peculiarity of Parisian houses and hotels in order to make things comprehensible. The smaller hotels and most of the private houses do not supply latch keys. The *concierge,* or porter, unlocks the door automatically from his room when the bell is rung outside. In the smaller hotels and houses the owner or the *concierge* does not remain in the porter's room all night but opens the door from his bedroom by pressing a button, mostly when half asleep. Whoever leaves the house has to call out, *"Le cordon, s'il vous plaît,"* and those coming in have to mention their name, so that theoretically no stranger can slip in at night. At two o'clock one morning the outside bell had rung in my hotel, and someone upon entering had called a name that sounded like that of one of the guests and had removed a key that was hanging in the porter's room. This Cerberus should have verified the identity of the late-comer through the glass partition, but apparently he had been too tired. But when an hour later someone had called, *"Cordon, s'il vous plaît,"* it had appeared strange to him, after having released the door, that anyone would leave the house after two o'clock. He had risen and, looking out on the street, had seen someone carrying a heavy bag and immediately started in pursuit in his dressing gown and slippers. But on seeing that the man had turned the corner and gone into a little hotel in the Rue des Petits Champs, he had no longer thought of a thief or robber and peacefully returned to his bed.

Excited at his error, he hurried with me as he was to the

nearest police station. Inquiries were immediately made at the hotel in the Rue des Petits Champs and it was ascertained that my portmanteau was still there, but not the thief, who probably had gone out to get his morning coffee in a neighboring bar. Two detectives watched for the culprit in the porter's room of his hotel; and when, unsuspecting, he returned after half an hour, he was apprehended.

Now both of us, the landlord and I, had to go to the police station to attend the official inquiry. We were led into the room of the prefect, an unusually stout, pleasant, mustached gentleman, who sat with unbuttoned coat at an untidy desk covered with papers. The entire office smelled of tobacco, and a large bottle of wine on the table showed that the prefect by no means belonged to the cruel and murderous guardians of the sacred *Hermandad*. At his command, the bag was brought in and I was to ascertain if anything of importance was missing. The only object of value was my letter of credit in the amount of two thousand francs which had been sorely damaged by my five months' stay, and which as a matter of fact was quite useless to any stranger; it lay at the bottom of the bag untouched. After a report had been drawn up that I had identified the portmanteau as my own and that nothing had been taken from it, the prefect ordered the thief to be brought in, and I looked forward to seeing him with no little curiosity.

And I was well rewarded. Between two mighty sergeants, who made his puny weakness appear even more grotesque, a poor devil appeared, badly dressed, collarless, with a small drooping mustache and a pale, half-starved, mousy face. He was also, if I may say so, a poor thief, which was proven by his ineptness in not making off in the early morning with the booty. He stood with eyes cast down, trembling slightly as if he were freezing, in front of the huge prefect, and be it said to my shame that I not only felt sorry for him but even experienced a sort of sympathy with him. My compassionate interest was increased as a police official spread out the various objects that had been found upon him when he was searched. A strange collection came to light: a very dirty and torn handkerchief, a key ring with a number of pass-keys and skeleton keys that struck against each other musically, a worn pocketbook, but fortunately no weapon, a sign that this thief carried on his profession in an expert but peaceable fashion.

The pocketbook was the first to be examined in our presence. The result was astonishing. Not that there were thousand- or hundred-franc notes, or even a single banknote—it held no less than twenty-seven pictures of famous dancers and actresses in extreme *décolleté,* as well as three or four nude photographs, whereby no more serious crime was manifest than that this gaunt, sorry lad was a passionate lover of beauty, and at least wanted the stars of the Parisian theater world, whom he could not otherwise attain, to rest in pictures upon his heart. Although the prefect examined the photographs with a seemingly stern glance, it did not escape me that the peculiar collector's passion of a delinquent of such a class amused him as much as it did me. For my sympathy for the poor thief had increased greatly through his predilection for the aesthetically beautiful. And when the prefect asked me formally, his pen in hand, if I wished to *porter plainte*—to lodge a complaint against the robber—of course I answered with a quick "no."

In order to understand the situation another explanation may be necessary. While in Austria and in many other countries when a crime is committed, the complaint follows automatically, that is, the State officially takes justice in its own hands, in France it remains the free choice of the injured party to press or refuse to press a charge. To me personally this manner of legal interpretation seems more just than the so-called rigid justice. For it offers the possibility of forgiving a man for an injury he may have committed, whereas, for example, if in Germany a woman injures her lover in a fit of jealousy, all the begging and pleading of the victim cannot save her from being convicted. The State steps in, tears the woman from the side of the man, though because of her action she may be more deeply in love than ever, and throws her into jail, while in France, the two would walk off arm in arm after being reconciled, and would look on the matter as one to be settled between themselves.

No sooner had I spoken my decided "no," when three things occurred. The haggard creature between the two policemen gave me an indescribable look of gratitude that I shall never forget. The prefect contentedly laid down his pen; it was obviously quite agreeable to him that my refusal to prosecute had saved him much additional writing. But my landlord behaved quite differently. He became purple in the face and began to yell at me that I should not do this, that these rascals, *cette vermine,* must be exterminated, that I had no idea how much damage that type did. Day and night decent people had to be on the watch, and if I let one thief escape it meant encouraging a hundred others. It was the honesty and sobriety and at the same time the pettiness of a bourgeois who had been disturbed in his business which thus exploded. And in view of the nuisance he had suffered because of the affair, he practically demanded that I revoke my pardon. But I remained steadfast. I had, I said with determination, recovered my goods; and so no damage had been done, and everything was settled. I had never in my life brought charges against anyone, and I would consume a beefsteak with much more appetite that noon for knowing that another was not eating prison fare because of me. My landlord's wrath grew and when the prefect declared that I, and not he, had to decide and that my refusal had settled the matter, he turned abruptly, left the room and banged the door behind him. The prefect arose, smiled at the man's anger, and shook my hand in silent agreement. The official act had been performed and I was already reaching for my portmanteau to carry it home. Quickly the thief approached me and said humbly, "Oh, no, Monsieur, I will carry it to your house." And so I marched off with the grateful thief carrying the large bag behind me through the streets to my hotel.

In this fashion it seemed as if an affair which had begun disagreeably had ended happily and amusingly. But in rapid succession it brought about two sequels for which I was grateful, since they enriched my knowledge of French psychology appreciably. When I called on Verhaeren the next day he greeted me with a malicious smile. "You do have strange adventures here in Paris," he said jokingly. "But I did not know what a wealthy fellow you are." I did not understand what he meant. He handed me a newspaper and, behold, the entire affair of the day before was printed there, although I could not gather the facts as they were from the romantic account it gave. With great journalistic art it described how in a hotel in the inner city a fashionable stranger—I had become fashionable to be more interesting—had been robbed of his trunk which contained many very valuable objects and among them a letter of credit for twenty thousand francs—the two thousand had increased tenfold overnight—as well as other irreplaceable objects (actually there was nothing but shirts and ties). At first it had been impossible to find a clue, for the thief had done his job with great precision and apparently with an exact knowledge of the locality. But the prefect of the district had undertaken all the necessary measures with his "well-known energy" and his *"grande perspicacité."* Within an hour every hotel and boarding house in Paris had been notified and, instructions having been put into effect with their usual precision, the criminal had been apprehended in a very short time. The president of the police had rewarded this excellent piece of work on the part of the efficient officer with special recognition, for through his actions and far-sightedness he had once again given an enlightening example of the masterful organization of the Paris police. Nothing in the report was true, for the good prefect did not have to leave his desk for a single minute, and we furnished him the thief and the bag in his office. But he had taken the opportunity to gain as much publicity as he could out of the matter.

Yet, though it all ran off pleasantly enough for the thief and the police authorities, it was not so pleasant for me. From that hour on my formerly jovial landlord did his best to spoil my further stay in the hotel. I came downstairs and greeted his wife politely in the porter's room; she did not reply and turned away as though insulted. The valet no longer cleaned my room properly, and letters disappeared mysteriously. Even in the neighboring stores and in the *bureau de tabac* where I was usually greeted as a regular *copain* because of my large consumption of tobacco, I suddenly met with icy faces. The insulted middle-class morality not only of the house, but of the entire street and even the entire district, stood firmly against me for having "helped" a thief. Nothing remained for me but to depart with the portmanteau I had rescued and to leave the comfortable hotel as wretchedly as if I had been the criminal.

~~~

After Paris, London affected me as when, on a hot day, one suddenly steps into the shade; at the first moment I shook with cold, but eyes and mind quickly adjusted themselves. From the very beginning I had allotted two or three months to London as part of my duty—for how can we understand our world and evaluate its forces without knowing the country that had kept the world rolling on its tracks for hundreds of years? Then too, I had hoped to give some polish to my rusty English (which, moreover, never really became fluent) by industrious conversation and social activity. But alas, that never happened; like all Continentals I had but few literary contacts on the other side of the Channel, and in all the breakfast conversations and small talk in our boarding house I felt myself woefully uninformed about the Court and racing and parties. When they discussed politics I was unable to follow, for they spoke of Joe (I was unaware that they meant Chamberlain), and in like fashion they alluded to Sirs by their first names. As for the Cockney of the coachmen, on the other hand, my ears were as if plugged with wax. And so I did not make the rapid progress I had hoped. I endeavored to learn a bit of good diction from the preachers in the churches, two or three times I listened in at court trials, and I went to the theater to hear real English—but I was always forced to seek out with difficulty that which had overwhelmed me in Paris: sociability, comradeship, and joyousness. I found no one with whom to discuss the things that were important to me; and on the other hand I must have seemed to the well-meaning among the English a fairly rough and dry person with my bottomless indifference to sport, play, and politics as well as everything else that occupied them. Nowhere did I succeed in connecting myself with any circle or any group. I spent nine-tenths of my time in London in my room or in the British Museum.

At first I tried walking. In the first week I had covered London until the soles of my feet burned. I rattled off all the noteworthy sights in the Baedeker from Madame Tussaud's to the Houses of Parliament with a schoolboyish sense of duty, I learned to drink ale and replaced the Parisian cigarettes with the indigenous pipe, I tried in a hundred different ways to acclimatize myself. But I found no real contact, either social or literary; and anyone who sees England from the outside passes by the essentials— passes by the rich firms of the City and sees no more than the well-polished traditional brass plate. Having been put up at a club, I did not know what to do there; the very sight of the deep leather chairs, like the whole atmosphere, lured me into a sort of intellectual somnolence, for I had not, like the others, earned that wise relaxation by concentrated activity or sport. Unless he was able to raise leisure to a social art by means of millions, this city energetically eliminated the idler, the mere observer, as a foreign body, instead of permitting him, as in Paris, to amble along contentedly in its bustling life. My mistake was, and I did not realize it until too late, that I failed to take up some sort of activity during my two months in London, as a volunteer in a business, or as secretary in a newspaper, for then I would have penetrated at least a finger-breadth deep into English life. As a mere observer from without I experienced but little, and it was only many years later, during the war, that I gained some knowledge of the real England.

Arthur Symons was the only one of England's poets whom I got to see. He, in turn, arranged an introduction to W. B. Yeats, whose poems I liked very much and a part of whose delicate poetic drama, *The Shadowy Waters*, I had translated for the pure joy of doing so. I did not know that it was to be a poetry reading; a small circle of select people had been invited, we sat fairly crowded in a not very large room, and some even had to sit on folding chairs and on the floor. Finally Yeats began, after two huge altar candles had been lighted next to the black or black-covered reading desk. All the other lights in the room had been extinguished so that the energetic head with its black locks appeared plastically in the candlelight. Yeats read slowly with a melodious somber voice, without becoming declamatory, and every verse received its full value. It was lovely. It was truly ceremonious. The only thing that disturbed me was the preciousness of the presentation, the black monkish garb which made Yeats look quite priestly, the smoldering of the thick wax candles which, I believe, were slightly scented. And so the literary enjoyment—and this afforded me a new charm—became more of a celebration of poems than a spontaneous reading. I was reminded involuntarily of how Verhaeren read his poems—in shirt sleeves, in order the better to mark the rhythm with his vigorous arms, without pomp or staging; or how Rilke occasionally recited a few poems out of a book, simply, clearly, in tranquil service to the word. It was the first "staged" poetry reading that I had ever attended, and in spite of my love for his work I was somewhat distrustful of this cult treatment. Nevertheless, Yeats had a grateful guest.

But the actual poetic discovery that came to me in London did not concern a living poet, but an artist who at that time was very much forgotten—William Blake, that lonely and problematical genius who, with his mixture of helplessness and sublime perfection, still fascinates me. A friend had advised me to look at the books illustrated in color in the Print Room of the British Museum, which was then directed by Laurence Binyon, "Europe," "America," and "The Book of Job," which, today, have become the great rarities at the dealers, and I was enchanted. Here for the first time I saw one of those magic natures who, without planning their own way in advance, are borne on angel's wings by visions through all the wilderness of phantasy.

For days and weeks I tried to penetrate more deeply into the labyrinth of that soul, at once naïve and yet daemonic, and to reproduce some of the poems in German. I yearned to own a single page from his hand, but at first it seemed no more possible than a dream. One day my friend Archibald G. B. Russell, already then the best Blake expert, told me that in the exhibition which he was putting on one of the visionary portraits was for sale—in his (and my) opinion the master's loveliest pencil drawing, the "King John." "You will never tire of it," he promised me; and he was right. From the ruins of my library and my pictures, this one leaf has accompanied me for more than thirty years; and how often the magic flashing glance of this mad king has looked down from the wall at me. Of all that is lost and distant from me, it is that drawing which I miss most in my wandering. The genius of England, which I tried in vain to recognize in streets and cities, was suddenly revealed to me in Blake's truly astral figure. And now I had added another to my many world loves.

VI

Bypaths on the Way to Myself

Paris, England, Italy, Spain, Belgium, and Holland—this inquisitive nomadic wandering was not only pleasant in itself but in many respects highly productive as well. Yet after all—and I realize this better than ever today when my roaming through the world is no longer a thing of choice but a flight from the hounds—one has to have an anchorage from which one can set out and to which one can always return. In the years since my school days, I had assembled a small library, and pictures and souvenirs, and my manuscripts began to pile up; but I could not drag this desirable burden around in my trunks all over the world. And so it was that I took a small apartment in Vienna, not as a permanent residence but merely as a *pied-à-terre,* as the French so aptly call it. For up to the time of the World War the feeling that everything was merely temporary dominated my life in some secret fashion. Nothing that I undertook, so I convinced myself, was the real, the actual thing, either in my work, which I looked upon as sketches leading to the real thing, or with women with whom I was friendly. In so doing I gave to my youth a sense of not yet being definitely burdened with responsibilities and, at the same time, the *diletto* for unhampered tasting, testing, and enjoyment. Arrived at an age when others had already long been married and had children and held important positions, and were obliged to produce the best that was in them with all their energy, I still regarded myself as youthful, a beginner who faced immeasurable time, and I was hesitant about final

decisions of any kind. Just as I looked on my work as preparatory to the "real thing," as a visiting card which was to
announce my existence to the world of literature, so my
rooms were to be nothing more than an address for the time
being. I chose small quarters at the city's edge intentionally,
so that my freedom was not weighted by costliness. The furniture that I bought was not particularly good, for I had no
desire to "tend" it as my parents had done in their home,
where every chair had its own slip cover which was only
removed when company came. It was also my intention not
to settle down in Vienna lest I might become sentimentally
bound to a definite place. For many years I looked back on
this self-training for the temporary as a mistake, but when
later I was compelled once again to leave each home that I
created for myself and when I saw everything about me
crumbling, this enigmatic instinct not to bind myself
proved an aid. Acquired early, it made all loss and all leave-
taking easier for me.

I did not yet have many valuables to stow away in my
first abode. The Blake drawing which I had secured in
London hung on the wall and one of Goethe's loveliest
poems, written in his flowing freehand, was at that time the
jewel in my autograph collection which I had already begun
in the *Gymnasium*. In the same herd spirit with which our
entire literary group had written poetry, we hounded poets,
actors, and singers for their autographs, and although most
of us had given up the sport as we had given up writing
poetry when we left school, the passion for these earthly
shadows of genial personalities increased and intensified
itself in my case. The mere signatures meant nothing to me,
nor did the degree of international fame or value of any
person interest me; what I sought was the originals or the
sketches for poems or compositions, because the problem
of the creation of a work of art, both in its biographical

and psychological forms held my attention more than anything else. That mysterious moment of transition in which
a verse, a melody, emerges out of the invisible, out of the
vision and intuition of a genius, and is graphically fixed in
a material form—where else can it so well be examined
and observed as in the tortured or trance-born manuscript
of the master? I do not know enough about an artist if I am
familiar only with his finished work, and I agree perfectly
with Goethe when he says that to understand completely
great creations one must have seen them not only in their
perfection but have pursued the process of their creation.
The sight of one of Beethoven's first sketches with its wild
impatient strokes, its chaotic mixture of motifs begun and
discarded, and with the creative fury, the superabundance
of his genius, compressed into a few pencil strokes is
physically exciting to me because it is mentally exciting. I
can look at such a scribbled page of hieroglyphics with
enchantment and love, as others gaze upon a perfect picture.
A proof sheet of Balzac in which practically every sentence
is torn apart, every line plowed through, the white margin
blackened with strokes, signs and words, represents to me
the eruption of a human Vesuvius; and to see any poem
that I have loved for years in its first draft, in its first
earthly realization arouses a religious awe in me and I
hardly dare to touch it. The pride of owning a few such
leaves was accompanied by the sporting desire to acquire
them, to hunt for them at auctions or in catalogues. How
many tense hours do I owe to that chase, how many exciting
incidents! Here I had come a day too late, there a desired
piece proved to be a forgery, and again a miracle would
occur. I had secured a small manuscript of Mozart's but
with joy impaired, for a scrap of the music had been cut
away. Suddenly the missing portion which had been removed fifty or a hundred years before by some loving vandal

turned up in a Stockholm auction, and now the aria could be put together just as Mozart had left it a hundred and fifty years ago. Of course in those days my literary income obviously did not suffice to buy things in the grand manner, but every collector knows how much the joy of possessing a certain piece is enhanced if a sacrifice must be made to procure it. Furthermore, I demanded toll of all of my poet friends. Rolland gave me a volume of his *Jean Christophe,* Rilke his most popular work *Die Weise von Liebe und Tod,* Claudel his *L'Annonce faite à Marie,* Gorky a lengthy sketch, Freud a dissertation. They all knew that no museum could preserve their manuscripts more lovingly. How much of all this is scattered to the four winds today, with other lesser joys!

I discovered only later, by chance, that the most unusual and most valuable literary museum-piece was treasured not in my closet yet in the same house. Above me, in an equally modest apartment, there lived a gray-haired, elderly spinster, a music teacher by profession. One day she spoke to me pleasantly on the stairs saying that it worried her that I was an involuntary listener to her lessons, and that she hoped my work was not too much disturbed by the imperfect art of her pupils. In the course of our conversation I learned that her mother lived with her. Half blind and unable to leave her room, this eighty-year-old lady was no less a person than the daughter of Goethe's physician Doctor Vogel, and in 1830 Ottilie von Goethe, with Goethe present, was sponsor at her christening. I almost fainted—there was still one person on earth in the year 1910 on whom Goethe's sacred glance had rested. Now there had always been a particular sense of reverence in me for every earthly manifestation of genius, and besides my manuscripts I collected whatever relics I could lay hands on. At a later time, in my "second life," one room in my house was devoted to my cult, if I may so call it. There stood Beethoven's desk and the little money-box out of which, when in bed, he drew the necessary change for the maid with a trembling hand already touched by death. There were also a page from his household book and a lock of his graying hair. For years I carefully preserved one of Goethe's quill pens under glass to avoid the temptation of taking it into my own unworthy hand. But how far beyond comparison with these inanimate objects was a person, a breathing, living being who had looked into Goethe's dark round eyes, knowingly and lovingly—a last thin thread, that might break at any moment, by chance united the Olympian world of Weimar with a modest house, Kochgasse 8, through this frail, earthly creature. I asked permission to call upon Mrs. Demelius. The old lady received me kindly and hospitably, and in her room I found many of the immortal's belongings which had been given to her by Goethe's grandchild, a friend of her youth: a pair of candlesticks that had stood on Goethe's table, and similar tokens of the house in the Frauenplan in Weimar. But was not she herself the real miracle, this old lady with a Biedermeier cap covering her thin white hair, as with her wrinkled mouth she gladly told how she had spent the first fifteen years of her youth in the house in the Frauenplan (which then had not yet become the museum it is today) guarding these things untouched since the hour when the greatest of German poets left his house and the world, forever? As old people always do, she looked back upon her youth with intense objectivity; her indignation because the Goethe Society had perpetrated a grave indiscretion in having "so soon" published the love letters of her childhood friend, Ottilie von Goethe, was touching. "So soon!" She had forgotten that Ottilie had been dead for fifty years. To her, Goethe's darling was still alive and still young, things that long since had become historic and legendary to us were still reality to her. I always felt a ghostlike atmosphere in her presence. Here I lived in this stone house, spoke over the telephone, burned electric lights, wrote letters on a typewriter, and but twenty-two steps above I was transported into another century and stood in the holy shadow of the world of Goethe!

Later, I met many other women whose white heads reached upward into the heroic and Olympian world: Cosima Wagner, the daughter of Liszt, hard, strong, and yet majestic with her pathetic gestures; Elisabeth Förster, Nietzsche's sister, dainty, petite, and coquette; Olga Monod, the daughter of Alexander Herzen who, as a child, had often sat on Tolstoy's knee. I have heard such an old man as Georg Brandes tell of meetings with Walt Whitman, Flaubert, and Dickens, or Richard Strauss describe how he saw Richard Wagner for the first time. But nothing touched me so much as the face of this venerable woman, the last among the living whom Goethe's eye had deliberately looked upon. And perhaps I myself am now the last person who may say that I knew someone on whose head Goethe's hand had rested gently for a moment.

~

A haven between journeys had now been found. More important, however, was another home that I had discovered at the same time—the publishing house that preserved and promoted all my work for thirty years. Such a choice is critical in the life of an author, and it could not have happened more fortunately for me. Some years earlier a poetic dilettante of fine culture conceived the idea of utilizing his wealth for an intellectual purpose rather than for a racing stable. Alfred Walter Heymel, who was not of great importance as a poet himself, had decided to establish in Germany, where publishing was carried on mainly on a commercial basis, a publishing house which would make the criterion for the publication of a work not its commercial value but its content, with no view to material gain but rather the prospect of continued losses. Light literature, profitable as it might be, was to be excluded; contrariwise even the most subtle and experimental was to be welcomed. To accept only works of the purest artistic expression in its purest form was the motto of this exclusive publishing house, which at first depended on a small clientele of real connoisseurs. With conscious pride in its isolation it called itself *Die Insel* (the Island) and, later, the Insel-Verlag. Its books were not to be factory-made but every opus was to be given an external distinction in the printed form which suited its inner perfection: thus the title page, the letter press, the face of type and the paper for each book presented a new and individual problem. Even the prospectuses and the stationery of this ambitious publishing firm became the object of passionate pondering. I cannot recall, for example, that throughout thirty years I ever found a single printer's error in one of my books or even a corrected line in a letter from the firm. Everything, even the smallest detail, aspired to be model.

Hofmannsthal and Rilke were united in their lyric work in the Insel-Verlag, and their presence set the highest standard as the only valid one. One can readily imagine my joy and my pride in being honored, at twenty-six, with permanent citizenship in this "island." The external significance of this relationship was literary promotion; inwardly it meant increased responsibility. Whoever stepped into this select circle had to practice discipline and reticence, no literary flightiness was permitted him, he dared not be guilty of any journalistic haste, for the Insel-Verlag's colophon implied, at first for thousands and later for hundreds of thousands, not only a guarantee of textual quality, but also exemplary perfection of everything pertaining to the printer's art.

Nothing happier can occur to an author than, when still young, to come upon a young publishing house and to grow up with it; only such a common development truly creates an organic connection between him, his work, and the outside world. Soon I was bound by hearty friendship to the director of the Insel-Verlag, Professor Kippenberg, our friendship being strengthened by mutual understanding of our private collector's instincts and predilections. Kippenberg's Goethe collection developed parallel with the increase of my autograph collection for thirty years, and became the most monumental ever brought together by a private person. He gave me valuable advice and often valuable warnings—and on the other hand, because of my special observation of foreign literature, I was able to give him important suggestions. So it was that the Inselbücherei, with its many millions of copies, was built like a mighty cosmopolis around the original "ivory tower," making the Insel the most distinguished of German publishing houses, as the result of an idea that I proposed. After thirty years things looked different than when we had begun; the slender undertaking had become one of the mightiest publishing houses, and the author who once appealed to only a limited circle after all was one of the most widely read in Germany. And in truth, it took a world catastrophe and the most brutal exercise of law to sever what had been a happy and congenial association for both of us. I must confess that it was easier for me to leave house and home than no longer to see the familiar imprint on my books.

~~~

The path lay clear before me. I had begun to publish at an unseemly early age yet I had an inner conviction that at twenty-six I had not created anything of substance. The finest conquest of my young manhood, the association and friendship with the best creative minds of the time, strangely enough became a dangerous hindrance to my productivity. I had learned true values all too well, and that made me hesitant. Because of this lack of courage everything which I had heretofore published, except for translations, had been carefully limited to smaller forms such as short stories and poems; I was not bold enough to start a novel (that did not happen until nearly thirty years later). My first larger venture was in the dramatic field; and with this first attempt came a great temptation and certain favorable auguries that pressed toward succumbing to it. In the summer of 1905 or 1906 I had written a play—naturally, in the style of our time it was a drama in verse in the classic mode. It was called *Thersites.* My present opinion of that play which now possesses only conventional significance is evidenced by the fact that—as with nearly all of my books written before my thirty-second year—I have never permitted it to be reprinted. Nevertheless, this drama announced a certain personal trait in my inner attitude which invariably never champions the so-called hero but rather always see tragedy only in the conquered. In my stories it is always the man who succumbs to destiny, in my biographies the personality of one who succeeds not in a worldly way but in the moral sense. Erasmus and not Luther, Mary Stuart and not Elizabeth, Castellio and not Calvin. That is what prompted me even then not to take Achilles as protagonist, but the least imposing of his antagonists, the suffering Thersites, instead of the figure who, through his power and self-certainty, makes others suffer. I did not show the finished work to any actor, even to those amongst my friends, for I was sufficiently worldly-wise to know that dramas in blank verse and in Greek costume, even those by Sophocles or

Shakespeare, are not good box-office in the commercial theater. In a merely formal way I sent copies to a few of the important theaters, and then I forgot the matter.

Great was my astonishment when, after about three months, I received a letter on whose envelope was printed: "Königliches Schauspielhaus Berlin." What can the Prussian State Theater want of me, I thought. To my amazement the director, Ludwig Barnay, formerly one of the greatest German actors, informed me that the play had impressed him profoundly, and that it was particularly welcome since in Achilles he had finally found the long-sought part for Adalbert Matkowsky. He asked me therefore to grant the rights for the première to the Royal Theater in Berlin.

I was almost terrified with delight. At that time, Germany had two great actors, Adalbert Matkowsky and Josef Kainz; the former a North German, unequaled in the primitive force of his personality, his overpowering passion, the latter, our Viennese Josef Kainz, in whom audiences rejoiced for his intellectual grace, his inimitable diction, and the mastery of the vibrant as well as the metallic voice. And now that Matkowsky was to personify my hero and speak my verses, and the principal theater of the capital of the German Reich was to be godfather for my drama, a glowing dramatic career, unsought by me, seemed to present itself.

Since then I have learned never to anticipate the joys of a première before the curtain finally goes up. True, the actual rehearsals had begun, one after the other, and friends assured me that Matkowsky had never been more superb, never more masculine than at these rehearsals when speaking my verses. I had already reserved a berth in a sleeper for Berlin when a telegram arrived at the last moment: postponement because of the illness of Matkowsky. I believed it to be an excuse common in the theater when one wants to evade a promise or a date. But a week later the newspapers published the news of Matkowsky's death. My verses were the last that his wonderful lips had spoken.

Finished, I said to myself. *Vorbei*—it's over with. Although two other important Court theaters, Dresden and Cassel, wanted the play, my interest had become languid. I did not wish to think of an Achilles other than Matkowsky. Just then even more startling news arrived. A friend woke me one morning to tell me that Josef Kainz had sent him to say that he had chanced upon the play and saw a part in it for himself, not the Achilles that Matkowsky wished to play, but the tragic opposite role of Thersites. He was going to get in touch with the Burgtheater at once. Its manager, Schlenther, a pioneer of the then-current realism, had come from Berlin and (to the annoyance of the Viennese) directed the Court theater on realistic principles. He wrote to me promptly that although he was aware of what was interesting in my drama, unfortunately he did not see the possibility of any success beyond the première.

Finished, I said to myself again, skeptical as I had always been towards myself and my literary work. Kainz, on the other hand, was bitter. He invited me to call upon him at once and for the first time I saw before me the god of my youth whose hands and feet we *Gymnasium* students would have liked to kiss, his body pliant as a feather, his face spiritual and lit up by handsome dark eyes, even in his fiftieth year. It was a joy to hear him speak. Every word, even in private conversation, had its purest outline, every consonant its sharp-cut precision, every vowel vibrated fully and clear. Even now, I cannot read such poems as I had once heard him recite, without his voice speaking at the same time, with its measured power, its perfect rhythm, its heroic vibration; never since has it been such joy to hear the German language. And this man, whom I adored as a

god, apologized to me, a novice, because he had not succeeded in putting through my play. But from now on, he
said with emphasis, we were not to lose sight of each other.
As a matter of fact, he had a request to make—I almost
laughed that Kainz should request something from me!—
he was playing frequent guest engagements and had two
one-act plays for those occasions. He needed a third; and
what was shadowed in his mind was a short piece, in verse if
possible, and preferably with one of those lyric cascades
such as only he among German actors, because of his grandiose diction, could pour forth crystalline at one breath
before an audience that was itself breathless. Could I not
write such a one-act play for him?

I promised to try. The will to do can sometimes, as
Goethe says, "command poesy." I outlined a sketch of a one-
act play, *Der verwandelte Komediant* (*The Transformed
Comedian*), a featherweight rococo affair with two big
lyrico-dramatic monologues incorporated. Involuntarily I
felt myself influenced by his desire in every word, and identified myself enthusiastically with Kainz's being and even
sought to make his diction mine. Hence this made-to-order
work became one of those happy accidents which come
about not through mere craftsmanship but by enthusiasm
alone. After three weeks I was able to show Kainz the half-
finished sketch with one of the "arias" in its setting. Kainz
was genuinely enthusiastic. He immediately recited the
"cascade" twice, the second time with to me unforgettable
perfection. How much time did I need, he asked, visibly
impatient. A month. Excellent! That suited him perfectly.
He was going on tour for a few weeks to Germany and upon
his return he would begin rehearsals without delay, for this
was to be a Burgtheater play. Then he promised me that he
would include in it his repertory wherever he went, for it
fitted him like a glove. "Like a glove!" again and again he

repeated these words, shaking my hand heartily three times.

It was obvious that he had made the Burgtheater rebellious before his departure, for the director telephoned me in person, asked me to show him the one-act play in outline form, and accepted it in advance. The parts supporting Kainz were given to the cast so that they might read them. Again it seemed as if I were winning a grand prize on a modest stake—the Burgtheater, the pride of our city, and an actor, who, with Duse, was the greatest of the times, in a play by me; it was almost too much for a beginner. There was only one possible danger, that Kainz might change his mind when the play was completed, but how improbable that was! Nevertheless, the impatience was now on my side. At last I read in the paper that Josef Kainz had returned from his guest tour. For the sake of politeness I waited two days so as not to rush in on him immediately upon his return. But on the third day I took courage and handed my visiting card to the familiar old porter of the Hotel Sacher where Kainz was staying at the time: *Zu Herrn Hofschauspieler Kainz!* The old man stared at me over his glasses in astonishment. "But haven't you heard, Herr Doktor?" No, I had not heard anything. "They took him to the sanatorium this morning." He told me that Kainz had returned very ill from his tour, during which he had played his great parts, for the last time heroically mastering the most terrible pains before an unsuspecting audience. The next day he was operated on for cancer. According to the newspaper bulletins we could still hope for his recovery, and I visited him on his sickbed. He lay there tired, emaciated, his dark eyes looking larger than usual in his wasted face, and I was shocked; his eternally young, eloquent lips were outlined with an icy gray mustache, and I saw an old, dying man before me. Sadly he smiled at me. "Do you think the Lord will grant that I act in that piece of ours? That could make me well." But a few weeks later we stood at his coffin.

~~~

One can readily understand my uneasiness at remaining in the dramatic field and the anxiety which ensued every time I presented a new piece to a theater. The fact that the two greatest actors of Germany had died while rehearsing my verses made me (I am not ashamed to confess it) superstitious. It was only after some years that I again took courage to enter the field of the theater, and when the new manager of the Burgtheater, Alfred Baron Berger, an eminent man of the theater and a master of declamation, immediately accepted the drama, I scanned the selected cast anxiously and, paradoxically, sighed with relief: "Thank God, not a famous name there!" There was no one upon whom fate could wreak her wrath. But none the less, the improbable occurred. If one shuts the door upon misfortune it will sneak in through another. I had thought only of the actors and not of the manager, who had intended himself to direct my tragedy, *Das Haus am Meer (The House by the Sea)*, and had already prepared the prompt book. I had not thought of Alfred Baron Berger. Truly enough, a fortnight before the date of the first rehearsal he was dead. The curse that seemed to hang over my dramatic works was still operating. Even when, more than a decade later, *Jeremiah* and *Volpone* coursed the earth after the war in every possible language, I felt none too sure. And I acted consciously against my own interests when, in 1931, I completed a new piece, *Das Lamm des Armen (The One Ewe Lamb)*. One day, after I had sent the manuscript to him, I received a telegram from my friend Alexander Moissi asking that I reserve the lead for him for the première. Moissi, who had brought from his Italian homeland a sensuous euphony such as had never before been heard on the German stage, was then the only great successor to Josef Kainz. Enchanting in appearance, clever, alive, and moreover a kindly and inspiring person, he invested every play with some of his own personal magic. I could not have asked for a more ideal actor for the part. And yet, when he had made this proposal to me, the memory of Matkowsky and Kainz stirred within me, and I declined on a pretext without telling him the real reason. I knew that he had inherited from Kainz the Iffland ring, which is always bequeathed by Germany's greatest actor to his greatest successor. Was he also to inherit Kainz's fate? In any case, as far as I was concerned I had no wish to be the cause of misfortune for a third time to the greatest German actor of the time. And so, because of superstition and out of love for him, I renounced what would have been the most perfect interpretation of my play. And yet, I was unable to protect him by my renunciation, although I refused to give him the part, and though I have never given a new piece to the stage since that time, I was still to be enmeshed in the misfortune of others without the slightest fault on my part.

~

I am quite aware that I shall be suspected of telling a ghost story; Matkowsky and Kainz, these might be explained as being cruel chance. But why Moissi after them, when I had not given him the part and had not written a new drama since? This is what happened: years later—and I am getting ahead of my story—I was in Zurich, in the summer of 1935, when, with no previous warning, I received a telegram from my friend Moissi from Milan, telling me that he was coming to see me that evening and that I was to await him without fail. How strange, I thought. What can be so pressing? I had no new play and had been more than indifferent towards the theater for years. Naturally I awaited his coming with pleasure, for I loved this warm, affectionate man like a brother. He rushed up to me from the train and we embraced in the Italian fashion. We were still in the automobile on the way from the station when he began, with his marvelous impatience, to tell me what it was that I could do for him. Pirandello had done him a special honor by giving him the rights for the première of his new play, *Non si sa mai*. It was not for the Italian première, but for the world première, which was to take place in Vienna in the German language. It was the first time that such an Italian master had given precedence to a non-Italian country, he had never even accorded it to Paris. But Pirandello had a particular wish. He feared that in the translation the musical quality, the subtleties of his prose might be lost, so it was his desire that I, whose lingual art he had long valued, translate the piece into German and not some chance translator. Pirandello had, naturally, hesitated to approach me; how could he expect me to waste my time with translations? he had said. And so Moissi had taken it upon himself to transmit Pirandello's wish. As a matter of fact I had been done with translating for years. But I respected Pirandello, with whom I had had some pleasant meetings, too much to disappoint him and above all it was a pleasure to be able to give so close a friend as Moissi a token of comradeship. I put my own work aside for a week or two and not many weeks later Pirandello's play, in my translation, was announced for the world première in Vienna, an event which, for political reasons, too, was to be made particularly impressive. Pirandello had promised to be present, and as Mussolini was then still the avowed patron of Austria, every official of consequence, led by the Chancellor, announced his attendance. The evening was to be made the occasion of demonstrating Austro-Italian friendship (in truth, the protectorate of Italy over Austria).

When the rehearsals were to begin I happened to be in Vienna. I looked forward with pleasure to seeing Pirandello again, and I was curious to hear the words of my translation in Moissi's musical voice. But with ghostlike similarity there occurred, after a quarter of a century, the same event. When I opened my newspaper early in the morning, I read that Moissi had arrived from Switzerland suffering with a severe attack of grippe and that the rehearsals would have to be postponed because of his illness. Grippe, I thought— that cannot be serious. But my heart began to race as I approached the hotel—this time, thank God, the Grand Hotel and not the Hotel Sacher!—to visit my sick friend. The memory of my futile visit to Kainz made me shudder. And again, after some twenty-five years, the same thing occurred to the greatest of German actors. It was too late to see Moissi, for he was already delirious. Two days later, as had been the case with Kainz, I stood at his coffin instead of at his rehearsal.

～～

I have related out of turn the last fulfillment of the mysterious spell connected with my theatrical efforts. Naturally I see in this recurrence nothing more than chance. But undoubtedly the closely succeeding deaths of Matkowsky and Kainz had a definite effect upon the direction of my life at that time. If Matkowsky in Berlin, and Kainz in Vienna, had acted in the first dramas of a twenty-six-year-old, then it is quite possible that, thanks to their great art which could have made a success of even the weakest play, I would rapidly have become widely known and perhaps undeservedly so and would thus have been deprived of years of slow learning and experience of the world. It was natural enough for me to think that I was being persecuted by fate, since at the very start the theater had so temptingly offered me undreamed-of possibilities only to snatch them cruelly from me at the last moment. But it is only early in life that one believes fate to be identical with chance. Later one knows that the actual course of one's life was determined from within; however confusedly and meaninglessly our way may deviate from our desires, after all it does lead us inevitably to our invisible goal.

VII

Beyond Europe

DID time go more quickly in the past than it does today, when it is packed with events that will change our world to the very vitals for hundreds of years to come? Or do the last years of my youth before the first European war seem somewhat blurred because they were spent in regular work? I wrote, I published, my name was known in Germany and, to some extent, abroad, I had a following and, what is better testimony to a certain individuality, I already had opponents. All the great newspapers of the Reich were open to me, and I no longer had to proffer material, but was asked to contribute. But I cherish no secret belief that what I did and wrote in those years would have significance today; all our ambitions, our sorrows, our disappointments and exasperations look Lilliputian now. Perforce the dimensions of this day have changed our point of view of things. Had I begun this book some years ago, I would have written of conversations with Gerhart Hauptmann, with Arthur Schnitzler, Beer-Hofmann, Dehmel, Pirandello, Wassermann, Schalom Asch, and Anatole France (the last-named, by the way, was very amusing; the old gentleman told us improper stories the whole afternoon, but with meditative seriousness and an indescribable grace). I could tell of great premières, those of Gustav Mahler's Tenth Symphony in Munich, the *Rosenkavalier* in Dresden, those of Karsavina and Nijinsky—for I got about much and was an eager witness of many "historical" artistic events. But all that remains unrelated to the problems of the present day is out of date when measured by our stricter standard of importance. Today, those men of my youth who held my attention to literature seem far less important than those who drew it away towards reality.

Chief among them was a man who had to govern the destiny of the German Reich in one of its most tragic epochs, and who was struck by the National Socialists' first murderous shot eleven years before Hitler seized power: Walter Rathenau. Our friendly relations were of long standing and very cordial; they had begun in an unusual manner. Maximilian Harden, whose magazine *Die Zukunft* was a determining influence in the last decades of Emperor Wilhelm's empire, was one of the first persons to whom I owed advancement at the age of nineteen. It was Harden whom Bismarck himself had pushed into politics—the Chancellor liked using him as his mouthpiece or lightning-rod—who broke Ministers, who brought about the explosion of the Eulenburg Affair, and caused the Imperial Palace to tremble each week for fear of new attacks and disclosures. Yet for all this, Harden's real love was the theater and literature. One day there appeared in the *Zukunft* a series of aphorisms, signed with a pseudonym that I can no longer recall, which struck me because of their unusual wisdom and compact expression. As one of his regular contributors, I wrote to Harden: "Who is this new man? I have not read such finely polished epigrams in years."

The reply did not come from Harden, but from one who signed himself Walter Rathenau, and who, as I learned from his letters and from other sources, was none other than the son of the almighty director of the Berlin Electric Company, and was himself an industrialist and a director in countless companies—one of the new German "far-sighted" merchants, to use a term of Jean Paul's. He wrote to me very cordially and appreciatively that mine had been his first encouragement for a literary endeavor. Although he was at least ten years older than I, he confided his doubts whether to publish an entire book of his thoughts and aphorisms at that time. He was an outsider, he felt, and until then had concentrated his activity in the field of economics. I encouraged him wholeheartedly, we continued to correspond, and when I next visited Berlin I called him on the telephone. A hesitant voice replied: "Ah, it is you! What a pity, I am leaving for South Africa at six tomorrow morning . . ." I interrupted, saying: "Then of course we will meet some other time." But the voice continued slowly and reflectively: "No, wait a minute . . . my afternoon is taken up with conferences . . . tonight I must go to the Ministry and then to a club dinner . . . could you come here at 11:15?" Of course I agreed. We chatted until two the next morning. He left at six—on behalf of the German Emperor, as I learned later—for Southwest Africa.

I relate this detail because it is so characteristic of Rathenau. This very busy man always had time. I saw him during the direst days of war and shortly before the Locarno Conference, and a few days before his assassination I rode with him in the same automobile and through the same street in which he was murdered. Although every minute of his day was always allocated he was ready to turn from one subject to another without the least effort, for his mind was always on the alert, an instrument of such precision and rapidity as I have never seen in anyone else. He spoke fluently as if he were reading from an invisible page, and yet each individual sentence was so plastically and clearly formed that, had it been taken down in shorthand, his conversation would have been a perfect exposition, ready for the press. He spoke French, English, and Italian as well as he did German. His memory never failed him, and he required no special preparation for any subject.

In speaking with him, one felt stupid, faultily educated, uncertain and confused in the presence of his calm, deliberate, and clear-thinking objectivity. But there was something in the blinding brilliance, the crystal clarity of his thinking, just as there was something in the choice furniture and the fine pictures in his home, that made one feel uncomfortable. His mind had the effect of an ingeniously contrived apparatus, his home that of a museum. One could never really get warm in his feudal Queen Louise palace in Brandenburg: its order was too obvious, its arrangement too studied, its cleanliness too clean. His thinking had the transparency of glass, hence seemed unsubstantial; rarely have I sensed the tragedy of the Jew more strongly than in his personality which, with all of its apparent superiority, was full of a deep unrest and uncertainty. My other friends, for example Verhaeren, Ellen Key, and Bazalgette, were not a tenth as clever, not a hundredth as universal or as worldly-wise as he was, but they were secure within themselves. In Rathenau's case I always felt that, in spite of his immeasurable cleverness, his feet were not firmly on the ground. His entire existence was a single conflict of constantly changing contradictions. He had inherited all imaginable power from his father and yet had no wish to be his heir, he was a merchant but fancied himself an artist; he had millions and toyed with socialistic ideas; he felt himself to be a Jew and flirted with Christ. He thought internationally and worshiped Prussianism, he dreamt of the people's rule and yet was highly honored every time he was received and consulted by Emperor Wilhelm, whose weaknesses and vanity he saw through intuitively without being able to master his own vanity. And so it was perhaps that his ceaseless activity was nothing but an opiate to cover up an inner nervousness and to deaden the loneliness that surrounded his inner life. It was only in the hour of responsibility, when in 1919, after the breakdown of the German armies, the most difficult task in history—that of leading the disorganized Republic from chaos to new life—fell to him, that the tremendous potential forces within him suddenly became a single force. And in staking his life on a single idea, the salvation of Europe, he attained the greatness which was innate to his genius.

~~

Besides many a glance into far lands in the course of enlivening conversations, which in intellectual intensity and lucidity could perhaps only be compared with those of Hofmannsthal, Valéry, and Count Keyserling, I also owe to Rathenau, who broadened my horizon from the purely literary to the contemporary historical, my first impulse to go outside of Europe. "You cannot understand England," he said to me, "as long as you merely know the Island. Nor our continent unless you have gone beyond it at least once. You're a free man, make use of your freedom. Literature is a wonderful profession because haste plays no part in it. A year more or less is of no importance for a real book. Why don't you go to India, and to America?" This chance remark sank in, and I determined to follow his advice without delay.

India itself had a more sinister and depressing effect upon me than I would have thought possible. I was shocked by the misery of the emaciated figures, the joyless seriousness in their somber glances, the often cruel monotony of the landscape and, more than all else, the rigid division of classes and races of which I had already had a taste on board ship. Two charming girls, black-eyed and slim, well educated and well mannered, discreet and elegant, were on the same vessel. I noticed on the very first day that they kept at a distance, or were kept at a distance by some invisible barrier. They did not appear at the dances, they did not enter a general conversation, but sat apart reading English or French books. It was only on the second or third day that I became aware that it was not they who avoided the society of the English, but the others who drew back from these half-castes, although these two attractive girls were the daughters of a Parsi merchant and a Frenchwoman. For two or three years, in a boarding school in Lausanne and in a finishing school in England, there had been no discrimination, but on the ship going to India a cool, invisible but none the less horrid social exile had set in. This was my first sight of the pest of the racial purity mania which has become more dangerous for our world of today than the actual plague had been centuries ago.

This encounter served to sharpen my observation from the outset. With some shame I partook of the respect—long since vanished through our own fault—shown the European as if he was some sort of white god; who, when on a tourist trip such as up Adams Peak in Ceylon, had a retinue of twelve or fourteen servants, for a lesser number would be beneath his "dignity." I could not rid myself of the uneasy feeling that the coming decades and centuries would bring about transformations and changes in these absurd conditions, which we Europeans in our comfortable and fondly imagined security did not dare to dream about. Because of this impression I did not see India as something "romantic," as Pierre Loti did through rose-colored spectacles, but as an admonition; it was not the beautiful temples, the weathered palaces, nor the Himalaya landscapes, which gave me the most on this trip as far as my education was concerned, but the people whom I met, people of other sorts and other worlds than a writer from the European interior commonly met. Whoever traveled outside Europe in those days, when one spent more frugally and before Cook's Tours had spread over the world, was usually an outstanding person in

his particular class. The merchant would not be a small re-
tailer with the restrictions of his level but a wholesaler;
the physician was likely to be a real scientist; the *entrepre-
neur* of the race of the Conquistadores, daring, lavish, ruthless; and even the writer a man of superior intellectual
curiosity. Throughout the long days and nights of the trip
—there was not yet the radio to fill them with chatter—I
learned more in my association with these novel types about
the push and pull that move the world than I did from a
hundred books. Distance from home alters spiritual standards. Many a detail that had formerly occupied me unduly
seemed petty after my return, and I ceased to regard our
Europe as the eternal axis of the universe.

~~

One of the men whom I met on my trip to India has
achieved an immeasurable even if not publicly apparent
influence upon the history of our time. From Calcutta to
Indo-China, and on a river boat headed up the Irrawaddy,
I spent hours every day with Karl Haushofer and his wife.
He was on his way to Japan as German Military Attaché.
Erect and slim, spare-faced and eagle-nosed, he gave me my
first insight into the unusual qualities and the intrinsic
discipline of a German General Staff officer. I had, of course,
sometimes associated with military men in Vienna, amiable,
cordial and even jolly young fellows who, for the most part,
had come from families of restricted means and had taken
refuge in the uniform and sought to derive such pleasure as
the service could yield. Haushofer, however (as one sensed
at once), came from middle-class people of culture—his
father had published some poems and was, I believe, a university professor—and his education, besides military science, was comprehensive. Ordered to make a firsthand
study of the various theaters of the Russo-Japanese War, he

and his wife had familiarized themselves with the Japanese language and even its literature. He exemplified the fact that every science, even the military, when pursued profoundly, must necessarily push beyond its own limits and impinge on all the other sciences. He worked all day on board ship, followed the landscape with binoculars, kept a diary, made notes, consulted dictionaries; I rarely saw him without a book in hand. A precise observer, he was well able to describe things effectively. In conversation with him I learned much of the enigmatic Orient. After my return home, I kept up cordial relations with the Haushofer family; we exchanged letters and visited each other in Salzburg and Munich. A severe pulmonary illness which confined him for a year to Davos or Arosa kept him from the army and compelled him to go over to science; but he recovered, and was able to take a command in the World War. At the time of the collapse, I often thought of him with great sympathy. I could easily imagine how much he, who had labored for years at building up German mastery and perhaps also at its war machine in his obscure retirement, must have suffered in seeing Japan, where he had made many friends, among the victorious opponents.

Soon it was evident that he was one of the first to think systematically and in a broad-gauge way of the rebuilding of Germany's position. He edited a journal of geopolitics, and, as is so often the case, I failed to understand the deeper meaning of this new movement at its inception. I honestly believed that it was concerned only with the play of forces in the co-operation of nations, and I took the expression *Lebensraum* of nations, which I think Haushofer coined, in Spengler's sense, as the relative energy, changing with the ages, which every nation once in its life cycle produces. And Haushofer's summons to study the individual traits of the nations more closely, and to create a permanent

educational apparatus on a scientific basis, appeared quite
proper to me, for I conceived such investigations as calculated to draw nations closer together. Who knows, Haushofer's original intentions may have been quite unpolitical.
However that may be, I read his books (he quotes me once
in them) with great interest and without the least suspicion,
and heard objectively thinking persons praise his lectures
as being unusually instructive. No one charged that he intended his ideas to serve a new policy of power and aggression; they were meant simply to give new ideological motivation to the old Greater Germany claims. But one day in
Munich when I chanced to mention his name, someone
said, in a matter-of-course tone, "Ah, Hitler's friend."
Nothing could have astonished me more. First of all, Haushofer's wife was by no means "racially pure" and his talented and very agreeable sons could never have met the
requirements of the Nuremberg Jewish laws. Moreover, I
could see no basis of intellectual relation between a highly
cultivated, cosmopolitan scholar and a rabid agitator who
was mad on the subject of Germanism in its narrowest
and most brutal sense. But one of Haushofer's pupils had
been Rudolf Hess, and he had brought about the connection. Hitler, though himself far from receptive to unfamiliar
ideas, possessed, from the outset, the instinct to appropriate
whatever might serve his personal ambitions. Therefore,
National Socialist politics accepted geopolitics and pumped
it dry, Hitler using as much as fitted his purpose. It was
always the technique of National Socialism to supply
an ideological and pseudo-moral foundation for its thoroughly unequivocal egotistical instinct for power. The word
Lebensraum finally proved a neat cloak for its naked will to
aggression, an apparently innocent but only vaguely defin-
able word that would justify any annexation, no matter
how arbitrary, as an ethical and ethnological necessity. So it

was my old traveling companion who—whether consciously and willingly I do not know—was responsible, to the world's detriment, for that fundamental change in Hitler's aims, originally strictly directed to nationalism and racial purity, which, through the *Lebensraum* theory, took form in the slogan: *Zuerst erobern wir Deutschland und dann die ganze Welt* (First we will conquer Germany and then the entire world). This was as senseless an example of the transformation of a single pregnant formula into deed and destiny through the power immanent in language as the earlier formulation of the Encyclopedists of the rule of *raison,* which finally changed to its very opposite, terror and mass emotion. As far as I know, Haushofer never held a prominent position in the party; perhaps he never was a party member; at any rate I cannot, like the imaginative journalists, see him as a cunning "Gray Eminence" who, concealed in the background, invents the most dangerous schemes and whispers them to the Führer. But there can be no doubt that it was his theories, rather than any of Hitler's most rabid advisers, which either consciously or unconsciously drove the aggressive policy of National Socialism from the narrow national to the universal; only posterity, with better documentation than is available to our contemporaries, will be able to place him in the proper perspective of history.

~~

Before long this first overseas trip was followed by another, this time to America. It, too, was prompted by no other purpose than to see the world and, if possible, a bit of the future which lay before us. I truly believe that I was one of the very few writers who went over not to earn money or to exploit America journalistically, but solely to compare a rather uncertain impression of the new continent with the reality.

My impression—I declare it frankly—was a fairly romantic one. For me America was Walt Whitman, the land of the new rhythm and the coming world brotherhood. Once again before I sailed I read the wild, cataractic pour of the great "camerado's long lines"; and so I entered Manhattan with an open fraternal feeling instead of the usual arrogance of the European. I remember that the first thing that I did when I got to the hotel was to ask the porter to direct me to Walt Whitman's grave, but my desire greatly embarrassed the poor Italian who had never even heard the name.

My first impression was overpowering, although New York did not yet have the enchanting night beauty which it now has. The rushing cascades of light in Times Square were not yet present, nor the city's dreamlike heaven which, with its billions of artificial stars, glitters at the real ones in the sky. The appearance of the city as well as the traffic lacked the daring grandeur of today, for the new architecture was only trying itself out uncertainly with an occasional skyscraper and the astonishing development of taste in show windows and decorations had only modestly set in. But to look down from the Brooklyn Bridge, with its constant gentle swaying, at the harbor and to wander about in the stone canyons of the avenues, was discovery and excitement enough. But after two or three days it gave way to another more pronounced feeling: that of extreme solitude. I had nothing to do in New York, and at that time a leisured person could not have been more out of place anywhere. There were not yet cinemas in which to while away an hour, nor the small comfortable cafeterias, nor so many art galleries, libraries, and museums as there are now. In matters cultural everything was still far behind our Europe. After two or three days of loyally "doing" the museums and other notable sights, I was swept along like a rudderless boat in the icy, windy streets. Finally this sense of the aimlessness of my wandering became so strong that I could overcome it only by some positive artifice. I invented a game for myself. I pretended that I was friendless and alone, a jobless emigrant with my last seven dollars in my pocket. Do then, I said to myself, what they have to do. Imagine that you are forced to earn your own living after three days. Look around and see how one begins here as a stranger without connections or friends to find a position. So I wandered from agency to agency and examined the lists tacked on their doors. Here a baker was wanted, there a temporary clerk who knew French and Italian, here a clerk for a bookshop; this last, incidentally, was the first opportunity for my imaginary self. And so I climbed up three flights of iron stairs, asked about the salary and compared it with the prices for a room in the Bronx which I had seen advertised in the newspaper. After two days of job hunting I had theoretically found five jobs by which I could have made my living. In this manner I had convinced myself more vividly than by mere strolling about how much room, how much opportunity there was in this young country for anyone willing to work, and that impressed me. Also through this experience at agencies and interviews in shops and offices, I gained an insight into the divine freedom of the country. No one had asked me about my nationality, my religion, my origin, and—fantastic as it may seem to the world of today with its fingerprinting, visas, and police certificates—I had traveled without a passport. But here were jobs that but waited for takers; that spoke volumes. Without the hindering interference of the State or formalities, or trade unions, in that now legendary freedom a deal was made in a minute. Through this "job hunting," I learned more about America in those very first few days than in all the succeeding weeks when I traveled comfortably to Philadelphia, Boston, Baltimore, and Chicago. I was always alone except in Boston, where I spent a few convivial hours with Charles Loeffler, who had composed the music for some of my poems. On only one occasion was the complete anonymity of my existence interrupted by a surprise. I remember the moment clearly. I was strolling down a broad avenue in Philadelphia and halted before a large bookshop to find at least in the names of the authors something known or familiar to me. Suddenly I started. In the window six or seven German books stood on the left, and from one of them my name jumped out at me. I stared as if enchanted, and began to meditate. Something of this self of mine that was being driven through these strange streets unknown and apparently futilely, unknown and observed by none, something of this self had preceded me; the bookseller must have written my name on an order slip and so caused my book to make the ten days' journey over the ocean. My desolation left me for the moment, and when two years ago I again visited Philadelphia, I instinctively sought this window again and again.

I had lost courage to go as far as San Francisco—Hollywood had not yet been invented—but at least there was one other spot from which I could fulfill my longing to see the Pacific Ocean, for since my childhood I had been fascinated by the accounts of the early circumnavigators. What is more, it was a spot that has since disappeared which mortal eye will never behold again—the lost mounds of earth of the Panama Canal which was then still building. I had gone down there in a small ship by way of Bermuda and Haiti. Through Verhaeren our poetic generation had learned to admire the technical wonders of our age with the same enthusiasm with which our ancestors admired Roman antiquity. Panama itself was an unforgettable sight, the river bed excavated by machinery, its ocher yellow burning the eye even through dark glasses, the infernal air filled with millions and billions of mosquitoes whose victims could be seen in endless rows in the cemetery. How many had died for this enterprise which Europe had begun and America was to complete! And only now, after thirty years of catas- trophes and disappointments, it was becoming a reality. A few more months of final labor on the sluices, and then pressure on an electric button and the two oceans, after thousands of years, would unite for eternity. But I was one of the last of this day to see them still separate while fully aware of what was to come. It was a good leave-taking from America, this sight of its greatest creative accomplishment.

VIII

Light and Shadow over Europe

I HAD now lived through ten years of the new century and had seen India, Africa and part of America; it was with a new, more informed pleasure that I began to look at our Europe. I never loved that old earth more than in those last years before the First World War, never hoped more ardently for European unity, never had more faith in its future than then, when we thought we saw a new dawning. But in reality it was the glare of the approaching world conflagration.

It may perhaps be difficult to describe to the generation of today, which has grown up amidst catastrophes, collapses, and crises, to which war has been a constant possibility and even a daily expectation, that optimism, that trustfulness in the world which had animated us young people since the turn of the century. Forty years of peace had strengthened the economic organism of the nations, technical science had given wings to the rhythm of life, and scientific discoveries had made the spirit of that generation proud; there was sudden upsurge which could be felt in almost identical measure in all countries of Europe. The cities grew more beautiful and more populous from year to year. The Berlin of 1905 no longer resembled the city that I had known in 1901; the capital had grown into a metropolis and, in turn, had been magnificently overtaken by the Berlin of 1910. Vienna, Milan, Paris, London, and Amsterdam on each fresh visit evoked new astonishment and pleasure. The streets became broader and more showy, the public buildings more impressive, the shops more luxurious and tasteful. Everything manifested the increase and spread of wealth. Even we writers experienced it in the editions of our works which, within some ten years, had increased three-, five- and ten-fold. New theaters, libraries, and museums sprang up everywhere; comforts such as bathrooms and telephones, formerly the privilege of the few, became the possession of the more modestly placed, and the proletariat emerged, now that working hours had been shortened, to participate in at least the small joys and comforts of life. There was progress everywhere. Whoever ventured, won. Whoever bought a house, a rare book, or a painting saw it increase in value; the more daring and the larger the scale on which an enterprise was founded, the more certain a profit. A wondrous unconcernedness had thus spread over the world, for what could interrupt this rapid ascent, restrict the *élan*, which constantly drew new force from its own soaring? Never had Europe been stronger, richer, more beautiful, or more confident of an even better future. None but a few shriveled graybeards bemoaned, in the ancient manner, the "good old days."

Not only the cities, the people too looked handsomer and healthier because of sports, better nutrition, shorter working hours, and a closer tie with Nature. Winter, formerly a dreary time which men spent in ill-humor at cards in the cafés, or bored in over-heated rooms, had been rediscovered on the mountain-tops as a fount of filtered sunshine, as nectar for the lungs, as delight for the flushed and ruddy skin. The mountains, the lakes, the ocean were no longer as far away as formerly; the bicycle, the automobile, and the electric trains had shortened distances and had given the world a new spaciousness. On Sundays thousands and tens of thousands in gaudy sport coats raced down the snow-banks on skis and toboggans; sport-palaces and swimming

pools appeared everywhere, and it was just in the pools that
the transformation was most noticeable; whereas in my
youth a really well-built man attracted attention among the
thick necks, the fat bellies and the sunken chests, now
persons athletic, lithe, browned by the sun and steeled
through sport vied with one another in gay competition as
in the days of antiquity. None but the very poorest remained at home on Sundays, and all of youth hiked,
climbed, and gamboled, schooled in every type of sport.
People on vacation no longer restricted themselves to some
nearby resort or at best to the Salzkammergut, as in the days
of my parents, for they had become curious about the world,
curious to see whether it was as beautiful everywhere, and
whether there were varieties of beauty. Whereas formerly
only the privileged few had ventured abroad, now bank
clerks and small trades-people would visit France and Italy.
Traveling had become cheaper and more comfortable. But
above all it was the new courage, the new spirit of adventure that made people more daring in their travels, and less
fearful and parsimonious in their living; one was even
ashamed to appear anxious. The world began to take itself
more youthfully and, in contrast to the world of my parents,
was proud of being young. Suddenly beards began to disappear among the young, then the elders followed lest they
appear old. To be young and fresh, and to get rid of pompous dignity, was the watchword of the day. The women
threw off the corsets which had confined their breasts, and
abjured parasols and veils since they no longer feared air
and sunshine. They shortened their skirts so that they could
use their legs freely at tennis, and were no longer bashful
about displaying them if they were pretty ones. Fashions
became more natural; men wore breeches, women dared to
ride astride and people no longer covered up and hid them-

selves from one another. The world had become not only more beautiful, but more free.

This health and self-confidence of the generation that succeeded mine won for itself freedom in modes and manners as well. For the first time girls were seen without governesses on excursions with their young friends, or participating in sports in frank, self-assured comradeship; they were no longer timid or prudish, they knew what they wanted and what they did not want. Freed from the anxious control of their parents, earning their own livelihood as secretaries or office workers, they seized the right to live their own lives. Prostitution, the only love institution which the old world sanctioned, declined markedly, for because of this newer and healthier freedom all manner of false modesty had become old-fashioned. In the swimming places the wooden fences which had inexorably separated the women's section from the men's were torn down, and men and women were no longer ashamed to show how they were built. More freedom, more frankness, more spontaneity had been regained in these ten years than in the previous hundred years.

For a different rhythm prevailed in the world. None could foretell all that might happen in a single year! One discovery, one invention, followed another, and instantly was directed to the universal good; for the first time the nations sensed in common that which concerned the commonweal. On the day that the Zeppelin made its first flight I happened to be in Strassburg on my way to Belgium when, amidst the jubilant roaring of the crowd, it circled the cathedral as if to pay homage to the thousand-year-old edifice. That night at Verhaeren's in Belgium came the news that the ship had crashed in Echterdingen. Verhaeren had tears in his eyes and was terribly moved. He was not indifferent to the German catastrophe as if, being a Belgian, it concerned him less, but as a European of our time he shared the common victory over the elements as he now did the common trial. In Vienna we shouted with joy when Blériot flew over the Channel as if he had been our own hero; because of our pride in the successive triumphs of our technics, our science, a European community spirit, a European national consciousness was coming into being. How useless, we said to ourselves, are frontiers when any plane can fly over them with ease, how provincial and artificial are customs-duties, guards and border patrols, how incongruous in the spirit of these times which visibly seeks unity and world brotherhood! This soaring of our feelings was no less wonderful than that of the planes, and I pity those who were not young during those last years of confidence in Europe. For the air about us is not dead, is not empty, it carries in itself the vibration and the rhythm of the hour, it presses them unknowingly into our blood and directs them deep into our heart and brain. In those years each one of us derived strength from the common upswing of the time and increased his individual confidence out of the collective confidence. Perhaps, thankless as we human beings are, we did not realize then how firmly and surely the wave bore us. But whoever experienced that epoch of world confidence knows that all since has been retrogression and gloom.

〜〜〜

Marvelous was this tonic wave of power which beat against our hearts from all the shores of Europe. But there was danger too in the very thing that brought joy, although we did not perceive it. The storm of pride and confidence which rushed over Europe was followed by clouds; perhaps the rise had come too quickly, the States and cities had become powerful too hastily. The sense of power always leads men as well as States to use or to abuse it. France was puffed up with wealth; it wanted yet more, wanted a colony even though there was no superfluous population for the old ones; it almost went to war over Morocco. Italy wanted Cyrenaica, Austria annexed Bosnia, Serbia and Bulgaria pushed toward Turkey, and Germany, still excluded for the time being, raised its paw for an angry blow. In all these States there was a congestive rush of blood to the head. Out of the fruitful will for internal union there developed everywhere, simultaneously, an infectious greed for expansion. The French industrialists with their big profits agitated against the Germans who were fattening no less fast, because both of them, Krupp and Schneider-Creusot, wanted to produce more cannon. The Hamburg shipping interests with their huge dividends worked against those of Southampton, the Hungarian agriculturists against the Serbians, one corporation against another. The critical juncture everywhere evident had made them frantic for more and more. Calmly reflecting on the past, if one asks why Europe went to war in 1914, neither reasonable ground nor even provocation can be found. It had nothing to do with ideas and hardly even with petty frontiers. I cannot explain it otherwise than by this surplus of force, a tragic consequence of the internal dynamism that had accumulated in those forty years of peace and now sought violent release. Every State suddenly had the feeling of being strong and forgot that every other State had the same feeling, each wanted more and wanted something from the other. And the worst was that just the sentiment which we most highly valued—our common optimism—betrayed us. For each one thought that in the last moment the other would draw back affrightedly; and so the diplomats began their game of bluff. Four or five times, at Agadir, in the Balkan War, in Albania, it remained a game; but the great coalitions drew together always more tightly and more militaristically. In Germany a war tax was introduced in the midst of peace, in France the period of military service was prolonged. The surplus energy had finally to discharge itself and the vanes showed the direction from which the clouds were already approaching Europe.

It was not yet panic, but there was a constantly swelling unrest; we sensed a slight discomfort whenever a rattle of shots came from the Balkans. Would war really come upon us without our knowing why and wherefore? Slowly—all too slowly, all too timidly, as we are now aware!—the opposing forces assembled themselves. There was the Socialist Party, millions of people here and millions there, whose program disavowed war, there were the mighty Catholic groups under the leadership of the Pope and several internationally interlocked concerns, there were a very few sensible politicians unfriendly to subterranean trickery. We writers, too, stood up against war, although as always individualistically isolated instead of united and determined. The stand of most of the intellectuals was unfortunately an indifferently passive one, because our optimism blinded us to the problem of war with all of its moral consequences; in no important book or pamphlet by prominent writers of that time is a single discussion of principles or a single passionate warning to be found. We thought we were doing enough when we thought as Europeans and fraternized internationally, when we professed in our sphere the ideal of peaceful understanding and intellectual brotherhood beyond language and frontier, seeking only indirectly to affect the affairs of the day. And it was just the new generation which attached itself most firmly to this European idea. In Paris I found my friend Bazalgette surrounded by a group of young people who, in contrast to earlier generations, had renounced all narrow nationalism and aggressive imperialism.

Jules Romains, who was to address the great poem to Europe during the war, Georges Duhamel, Charles Vildrac, Durtain, René Arcos, Jean-Richard Bloch, gathered together first in the *Abbaye* and then in the *Effort libre,* were all passionate champions of the Europe to come and, as the fiery trial of war proved, steadfast in their hatred of all militarism. Rarely had France conceived a youth that was more courageous, more talented, more morally determined. In Germany, it was Werfel who gave world brotherhood its strongest lyric accent with his *Weltfreund;* René Schickele, an Alsatian, placed by fate between the two nations, labored passionately for an understanding; from Italy G. A. Borgese hailed us as a comrade, and encouragement came from the Scandinavian and the Slavic countries as well. "Why don't you come over here!" a great Russian writer said in a letter. "Show the Panslavists who are trying to egg us into the war that you Austrians are against it." Oh, we loved our inspired time well enough and we loved our Europe! But this blind belief that reason would balk the madness at the last minute, established itself as our one shortcoming. True, we did not regard the handwriting on the wall with sufficient misgiving, but is it not the very essence of youth not to be distrustful but to believe? We relied on Jaurès, on the Socialist International, we believed that the railroad men would rather tear up the tracks than transport their comrades to the front as so much cattle to be slaughtered, we counted on the women, who would refuse to sacrifice their children and husbands to Moloch, we were convinced that the spiritual and moral forces of Europe would reveal themselves triumphantly at the critical moment. Our common idealism, our optimism based on progress, led us to misjudge and contemn the common danger.

Moreover, we lacked an organizer who could unerringly unite the latent energy within us; we had amongst us but a

single man to sound a warning, a single person of percep-
tion and vision. But the curious thing was this, that he lived
among us long before we knew anything about him whom
destiny was to appoint as our leader. It was a fateful stroke
of luck that I discovered him for myself at the last moment;
and it was difficult to discover him, for he lived apart from
the *foire sur la place* in the heart of Paris. If anyone once
undertakes the writing of a straightforward history of
French literature in the twentieth century he must not dis-
regard the astonishing phenomenon that, although all imaginable authors and big names were then being praised in
the Paris papers, three of the most important remained unknown or were mentioned in a misleading connection. From
1900 to 1914 I never saw a reference to Paul Valéry as a
poet in either *Figaro* or *Le Matin;* Marcel Proust was looked
upon as the dandy of the salons, and Romain Rolland as a
well-informed scholar in music. They were almost fifty years
of age before the first timid ray of renown touched their
names, and their great work had been accomplished in
shadow in the center of the most inquisitive, most intellectual city in the world.

~~

It was mere chance that I had discovered Romain Rolland
opportunely. A Russian sculptress in Florence had invited
me to tea, to show me her work and also to attempt to make
a sketch of me. I arrived promptly at four, forgetting that
she was a Russian and as such beyond all time and punctuality. An old *babushka,* who, as I learned, had already been
her mother's nurse, led me into the studio in which the most
colorful thing was its disorder, and bade me wait. In all
there were but four small pieces of sculpture about and I
had looked at them in two minutes. And so, in order not to
waste any time, I reached for a book, or rather a few little

brown books, that lay about. They were called *Cahiers de la Quinzaine* and I recalled having heard the name before in Paris. But who could possibly keep up with all the little reviews that popped up all over the country like so many short-lived idealistic flowers, only to disappear again? I leafed through the volume—*L'Aube,* by Romain Rolland— and began to read it, my interest and astonishment constantly increasing. Who was this Frenchman who knew Germany so well? Soon I was thankful to the good Russian for being late. My first question, when she finally made her appearance, was: "Who is this Romain Rolland?" She could not give me any exact information, and it was only when I had procured the remaining volumes (the rest of the work was still in progress) that I knew that here was a work that was not to serve but one European nation but all of them and their brotherhood. Here was the man, the poet, who brought all the moral forces into play—a loving mutual knowledge and an honest will to that knowledge, proven and refined justice and a soaring faith in the unitive mission of art. While we had frittered away our time with small manifestoes, he had calmly and patiently proceeded to show to all, the individual and most lovable traits of each. It was the first consciously European novel that was achieved here, the first decisive appeal towards brotherhood, more effective because it reached broader masses than the hymns of Verhaeren, more penetrating than all the protests and pamphlets; here the thing that we had all subconsciously hoped for, longed for, had been accomplished in silence.

The first thing I did in Paris was to inquire about him, mindful of Goethe's words: "He has learned, he can teach us." I asked my friends about him. Verhaeren thought that he remembered a drama, *The Wolves,* that had been given in the socialist Théâtre du Peuple. Bazalgette, on the other hand, had heard that Rolland was a musicologist and that he had written a small book about Beethoven. In the catalogue of the Bibliothèque Nationale I had found a dozen works about modern and old music, seven or eight dramas, all of which had been brought out by small publishers or had appeared in the *Cahiers de la Quinzaine*. Finally, in order to establish some connection, I sent him one of my books. Soon a letter came asking me to come to see him, and so a friendship began which, together with that of Freud and Verhaeren, was the most fruitful and, at certain times, the most decisive for the future course of my life.

Momentous days in life glow more powerfully than ordinary ones. I can recall that first visit quite clearly. Up five narrow winding flights in an unpretentious house near the Boulevard Montparnasse, and in front of the door I felt a particular stillness. The hum of the boulevards was hardly more audible than that of the breeze that came in under the windows through the trees of an old monastery garden. Rolland opened the door and led me into his small room filled to the ceiling with books. For the first time I saw his remarkable, shining blue eyes, the clearest and kindest eyes I have ever seen in anyone; in conversation they draw fire and color from his inner emotions, they cloud darkly in sorrow, grow darker in contemplation and sparkle in excitement, these singular pupils between somewhat reddened eyelids overtired with reading and waking, that could glow with a wondrously communicative and beneficent light. I observed his figure somewhat anxiously. Very tall and slim, he walked with a slight stoop, as if the countless hours at his desk had bent his neck; he looked somewhat sickly, with his sharply chiseled pallid features. He spoke very softly, just as he spared his body in all things to the utmost. He hardly ever went walking, ate little, neither smoked nor drank, and avoided all physical exertion; and I realized later with admiration how much perseverance dwelt in that ascetic body, how much intellectual labor capacity lay behind this apparent weakness. For hours on end he wrote at his small, heaped-full desk, for hours he would read in bed, never allowing his tired body more than four or five hours' sleep, and music was the sole relaxation he permitted himself. He played the piano beautifully with an unforgettably soft touch, caressing the keys as if he wished to entice the tones, not to force them out. No virtuoso—and I have listened to Max Reger, Busoni, and Bruno Walter in the most intimate setting—ever gave me such a feeling of direct communication with the beloved masters.

His varied knowledge put one to shame; actually living only through his reading eye, he mastered literature, philosophy, history, and the problems of all nations and times. He knew every measure in music; he was familiar with even the least works of Galuppi and Telemann, of sixth- and seventh-rate musicians, and yet took lively part in the events of the present. In this simple, almost monastic cell, the world was mirrored as in a *camera oscura.* Humanly he had enjoyed the confidence of the great of his time, had been a pupil of Renan, a guest in Wagner's house, a friend of Jaurès; Tolstoy had written that famous letter to him which as a human profession of faith deserves rank with his literary work. I sensed, with the joy that such recognition always gives me, a human, moral superiority, an inner freedom without pride, the taken-for-granted freedom of an independent soul. At first glance I recognized in him—and time has proven me right—the man who was to be Europe's conscience in a crucial hour. We spoke about *Jean Christophe.* Rolland told me that in it he had tried to fulfill a threefold duty—his gratitude to music, his profession of faith in European unity, and an appeal to the nations to awake to consciousness. There was a task for each to do, each in his own position, in his own country, in his own language. The time

had come to be alert and ever increasingly so. The powers
of hatred were more vehement and aggressive, because of
their baser nature, than those of reconciliation, and there
were material interests behind them that in themselves were
less scrupulous than our own. Obscurantism was visibly at
work, and the battle against it was even more important
than our art. I felt his mourning—for the brittleness of the
mundane structure was doubly bitter—this man whose
entire work celebrated the imperishability of art. "Art can
bring us consolation as individuals," he said, "but it is
powerless against reality."

~~

   That was in the year 1913. It was the first conversation in
which I faced our duty not to meet the constant possibility
of a European war without preparation and action. In the
decisive moment nothing gave Rolland such tremendous
moral superiority over all others as the fact that he had
painfully steeled his soul in advance. And perhaps we in our
circle had also accomplished something. I had translated
much, had called attention to the poets among our neighbors, and had accompanied Verhaeren on a lecture tour
throughout all Germany in 1912, which shaped up into
something like a symbolic Franco-German fraternization; in
Hamburg, Verhaeren and Dehmel, the greatest French lyricist and the great German lyricist, embraced each other publicly; I had won over Reinhardt for Verhaeren's new drama;
our collaboration home and abroad had never seemed more
cordial, more intensive, more impulsive, and in many hours
of enthusiasm we labored under the misconception that we
had charted the way to the world's salvation. But the world
bothered little about such literary manifestations, and went
its own evil path. The electric crackling of an invisible friction ran through the timbers. Again and again a spark would

appear—the Zabern Affair, the crises in Albania, a stupid interview—it was always nothing but a spark, yet each one could have ignited the piled-up explosives. We in Austria were particularly aware of being in the center of the zone of unrest. In 1910 Emperor Franz Josef had passed his eightieth year. The aged man, long since become a symbol, could not last much longer and a mystical feeling began to spread universally that after his passing the dissolution of the thousand-year-old monarchy could no longer be stayed. Within, the pressure of nationalities against each other grew, and outside waited Italy, Serbia, Rumania, and in a certain sense Germany as well, to divide the Reich. The Balkan War, where Krupp and Schneider-Creusot rehearsed their cannon against foreign "human material," as later the Germans and Italians rehearsed their planes in the Spanish Civil War, drew us closer and closer to the cataract. Again and again we started up, only to breathe again: "Not yet, this time—and let us hope, never!"

~

We know from experience that it is a thousand times easier to reconstruct the facts of an era than its spiritual atmosphere. Its traces are not to be found in official events, but rather in the small, personal episodes such as I should like to include here. At that time, to be frank, I did not believe war would come. But twice I had had waking dreams of it, and started up with terrified soul. The first was at the time of the Redl Affair, which, like all background episodes in history, is but little known.

I had known Captain Redl, the hero of a most complicated espionage drama, very slightly. He lived only one street away from me in the same district, and one day in a café the kindly-looking, cigar-smoking gentleman had been introduced to me by District Attorney T. Since that time we had greeted each other in passing. It was only later that I discovered how greatly we are surrounded with mystery in the midst of life, and how little we know about our next-door neighbor. This captain, externally a good, average Austrian officer, was the confidant of the heir-apparent; his was the important duty of directing the secret service of the army, and of offsetting that of the opposing parties. It leaked out that in 1912, during the Balkan War crisis when Russia and Austria were mobilizing against each other, the most important secret document of the Austrian Army, the Plan of March, had been sold to Russia. In case of war this would have brought about an unparalleled catastrophe, for the Russians knew every step, every tactical move, that the attacking Austrian Army intended to make. The panic in the General Staff at this piece of treason was terrifying; Captain Redl, as the chief expert, was assigned to discover the betrayer, who could only have been found within a very narrow circle. The Foreign Ministry, not quite trusting the ability of the military authorities, gave orders—a typical example of the jealous counterplay of the various departments—for an independent investigation of its own, without notifying the General Staff of its action, and ordered the police, among other things, to open every letter from abroad addressed in care of General Delivery, disregarding the inviolability of the mails.

One day a letter arrived at a post office from the Russian border station Podvolochiska, with only a code address: "Opera Ball." It proved to contain not a letter but six or eight new Austrian thousand-crown notes. This suspicious discovery was reported to the authorities and a detective was detailed to arrest whoever claimed the dubious letter.

For a moment the tragedy took on the characteristics of a Viennese light comedy. At noon a man appeared at the post-office window and asked for a letter addressed to "Opera

Ball." The official immediately gave the signal agreed upon to the waiting detective. But the detective had just gone out for his lunch, and when he had returned, all that could be ascertained was that the stranger had taken a cab and had driven off in an unknown direction. The second act of the comedy soon followed. In the time of the *Fiaker,* those fashionable, elegant cabs drawn by two horses, the cabdriver looked upon himself as too important a personage to wash his own cab, consequently each cab-stand had a so-called *Wasserer,* whose function it was to feed the horses and wash the cabs. One of these boys, happily enough, had noticed the number of the cab that had just driven off; promptly every police station was notified, and the cab was found. The driver gave a description of the gentleman who had driven to the Café Kaiserhof, where I had always met Captain Redl; furthermore, by a fortunate chance the pocket knife with which the unknown had slit open the letter lay in the cab. The detectives rushed to the Café Kaiserhof. The gentleman whom they described had already gone. With perfect assurance, the waiters declared that he could be none other than their good and steady patron, Captain Redl, and that he had driven to the Hotel Klomser.

The detectives stood rooted to the spot. The secret had been solved. Captain Redl, the highest espionage chief of the Austrian Army, was at once the paid spy of the Russian General Staff. Not only had he sold various secrets and the Plan of March as well, but it also suddenly became clear why all the Austrian spies whom he had sent to Russia in the past year had been captured and condemned. A wild round of telephoning began, until finally Konrad von Hötzendorf, the Chief of the Austrian General Staff, was reached. An eye-witness of this scene told me that at the very first words the Chief of Staff turned white as a sheet. A telephone conversation with the Imperial palace ensued, and conference followed upon conference. What was to be done? In the meantime, the police had taken precautions to prevent Captain Redl's escape. When he again left the Hotel Klomser, and while he was talking to the porter, a detective approached him unobtrusively, held out the pocket knife, and asked politely: "Did not the Captain forget this knife in the cab?" In that second Redl knew that all was lost. Wherever he went he saw the familiar faces of the secret police who were watching him, and when he returned to the hotel, two officers followed him into his room and laid down a pistol. It had been decided upon in the palace that this affair, with its scandalous implications for the Austrian Army, was to be terminated as quietly as possible. Until two in the morning the two officers walked up and down outside of Redl's room in the Hotel Klomser. Then they heard the pistol shot.

The next day the evening papers carried a short obituary of the capable officer, Captain Redl, who had died suddenly. But too many people had been involved in the investigation for the secret to be kept. Bit by bit a number of details were revealed that psychologically explained a great deal. Captain Redl, unknown to his superiors and friends, was a homosexual and for years had been at the mercy of blackmailers who finally drove him to his desperate act. The army was shocked to the core. All knew that in case of war this one man might have been the cause of the death of hundreds of thousands, and of the monarchy being brought to the brink of the abyss; it was only then that we Austrians realized how breath-takingly near to the World War we already had been for that past year.

～～

That was the first time that terror clutched at my throat. By chance, the very next day I met Berta von Suttner, that

majestic and grandiose Cassandra of our time. An aristocrat
of one of the first families, in her early youth she had experienced the cruelty of the War of 1866 in the vicinity of her
native family palace in Bohemia. And with the passion of a
Florence Nightingale she saw but one task for herself in
life: to hinder a second war, or any war at all. She wrote a
novel, *Lay Down Your Arms,* which met with universal success; she organized countless pacifist meetings, and the triumph of her life was that she had aroused the conscience of
Alfred Nobel, the inventor of dynamite, to such an extent
that, to compensate for the evil that he had caused with his
dynamite, he had established the Nobel Prize for Peace and
International Understanding. She came up to me in great
excitement. "The people have no idea what is going on!"
she cried quite loudly on the street, although she usually
spoke quietly and with deliberation. "The war is already
upon us, and once again they have hidden and kept it from
us. Why don't you do something, you young people? It is
your concern most of all. Defend yourselves! Unite! Don't
always let us few old women to whom no one listens do
everything." I told her that I was going to Paris; perhaps
one could really attempt a common manifesto. "Why only
'perhaps'?" she pressed on. "Things are worse than ever, the
machine is already in motion." Being disturbed myself, I
had difficulty in quieting her.

But it was just in France that I was to be reminded, by a
second personal episode, with what prophetic clarity the old
lady, who was not taken seriously in Vienna, had seen into
the future. It was a very small episode, but most impressive
to me. In the spring of 1914 I had gone with one of my
friends from Paris to spend a few days in Touraine, in order
to visit the grave of Leonardo da Vinci. We had roamed
along the mild and sunny banks of the Loire for hours, and
at night were fairly tired. And so we decided to go to the

cinema in the sleepy city of Tours, after first paying our respects to Balzac's birthplace.

It was a small suburban cinema, utterly different from the modern palaces of chromium and glass; a sparsely fitted hall, filled with humble folk, workers, soldiers, market women—the plain people—who chatted comfortably, and in spite of the "no smoking" sign blew thick, blue clouds of Scaferlati and Caporal into the sticky air. First the "News of All the World" appeared on the screen. A boat race in England; the people chattered and laughed. Then there was a French military parade: here also the people paid but little attention. The third picture was "Emperor Wilhelm Visits Emperor Franz Josef in Vienna." Suddenly I saw the familiar platform of the ugly West Station in Vienna on the screen, with a few policemen who were awaiting the arrival of the train. Then a signal: the aged Emperor Franz Josef appeared, walking between the guard of honor to receive his guest. When the old emperor appeared on the screen, a bit bent, a bit shaky, walking along the platform, the people of Tours began to laugh heartily at the aged party with the white whiskers. Then the train came on the screen, the first coach, the second, and the third. The door of the compartment was thrown open, and out stepped Wilhelm II in the uniform of an Austrian general, his mustache curled stiffly upwards.

The moment that Emperor Wilhelm appeared in the picture, a spontaneous wild whistling and stamping of feet began in the dark hall. Everybody yelled and whistled, men, women, and children, as if they had been personally insulted. The good-natured people of Tours, who knew no more about the world and politics than what they had read in their newspapers, had gone mad for an instant. I was frightened. I was frightened to the depths of my heart. For I sensed how deeply the poison of the propaganda of hate must have advanced through the years, when even here in a small provincial city the simple citizens and soldiers had been so greatly incited against the Kaiser and against Germany that a passing picture on the screen could produce such a demonstration. It only lasted a second, a single second. Other pictures followed and all was forgotten. The people laughed at the Chaplin film with all their might and slapped their knees with enjoyment, roaring. It had only been a second, but one that showed me how easily people anywhere could be aroused in a time of a crisis, despite all attempts at understanding, despite all efforts.

My whole evening was spoiled. I could not sleep. If this had occurred in Paris, it would also have made me uneasy, but I would not have been so shocked. I shuddered at the thought that this hatred had eaten its way deep into the provinces, deep into the hearts of the simple, naïve people. A few days later I told my friends about the episode. Most of them did not take it seriously: "How we Frenchmen laughed at fat Queen Victoria, and yet two years later we formed an alliance with England. You don't know the French, politics do not enter into them too deeply." Only Rolland saw things in a different light. "The more naïve a people are, the easier it is to get around them. Things are bad since Poincaré was elected. His trip to Petersburg will not be a pleasure jaunt." We spoke at length about the socialist congress which had been called for that summer in Vienna, but here too Rolland was more skeptical than the others. "Who knows how many will remain steadfast once the mobilization order has been nailed up? We live in a time of mass emotion, mass hysteria, whose power in the case of war cannot be estimated."

But as I have already said, such moments of anxiety were swept away like cobwebs in the wind. We did think of war occasionally, but no more than we did of death—as a possibility, yet probably a distant one. And Paris was too beautiful in those days, and we were too young and too happy. I can recall an enchanting farce which Jules Romains had thought up, in which, in order to ridicule the *prince des poètes,* a *prince des penseurs* was to be crowned, a good, though simple, man who permitted himself to be led by the students with all pomp to the Rodin statue in front of the Panthéon. That night we reveled like schoolboys at the sham banquet. The trees were in blossom, the air was mild and sweet; who had any desire in the presence of so much rapture to think of the inconceivable? My friends were better friends than ever, and new ones had been made in the stranger—the "enemy"—country. The city was more carefree than ever before and, being carefree ourselves, we loved the city for being carefree. During those last days I accompanied Verhaeren to Rouen where he was to lecture. At night we stood in front of the cathedral; its spire gleamed like magic in the moonlight—did such gentle wonders belong to only one "fatherland," did they not belong to all? At the station in Rouen, where two years later one of the machines whose praises he had sung was to tear him to pieces, we parted. He embraced me. "I will see you on the first of August at 'Caillou qui bique'!" I promised, for I visited him each year at his country place there, in order to translate his verses with him at my side. Why not this year as well? Without a care I took leave of my other friends and of Paris, a simple, unsentimental leave-taking, as if going from one's own home for a few weeks. My plan for the next months was clear. To retire to the country somewhere in Austria and there to continue my work on Dostoievsky (it was not to appear until five years later) and thus to complete my book, *Drei Meister,* which was to depict each of the great nations in their greatest novelists. Then to go to Verhaeren, and in the winter, perhaps, to undertake the long-planned trip to Russia, in order to organize a group for intellectual co-operation there. All lay clear and plain before me in this, my thirty-third year. The world offered itself to me like a fruit, beautiful and rich with promise, in that radiant summer. And I loved it for its present, and for its even greater future.

Then, on June 29, 1914, in Sarajevo, the shot was fired which in a single second shattered the world of security and creative reason in which we had been educated, grown up and been at home—shattered it like a hollow vessel of clay.

IX

The First Hours of the War of 1914

THE summer of 1914 would have been memorable for us even without the doom which it spread over the European earth. I had rarely experienced one more luxuriant, more beautiful and, I am tempted to say, more summery. Throughout the days and nights the heavens were a silky blue, the air soft yet not sultry, the meadows fragrant and warm, the forests dark and profuse in their tender green; even today, when I use the word summer, I think involuntarily of those radiant July days which I spent in Baden near Vienna. In order that I might concentrate on my work I had retired for the month of July to this small romantic town where Beethoven loved to spend his summer holidays, planning to pass the remainder of the season with my honored friend Verhaeren in his little country house in Belgium. In Baden one does not have to leave the city to enjoy the country. The lovely, hilly forest insinuates itself between the low Biedermeier houses which have retained the simplicity and the charm of the Beethoven period. At all the cafés and restaurants one sat in the open and could mingle at pleasure with the light-hearted visitors who strolled about the Kurpark, or slip into a solitary path.

Already on the eve of that twenty-ninth of June, which Catholic Austria celebrates as the feastday of Saints Peter and Paul, many guests had arrived from Vienna. In light summer dress, gay and carefree, the crowds moved about to the music in the park. The day was mild; a cloudless sky lay over the broad chestnut trees; it was a day made to be happy. The vacation days would soon set in for the people and children, and on this holiday they anticipated the entire summer, with its fresh air, its lush green, and the forgetting of all daily cares. I was sitting at some distance from the crowd in the park, reading a book—I still remember that it was Merejkovsky's *Tolstoy and Dostoievsky*—and I read with interest and attention. Nevertheless, I was simultaneously aware of the wind in the trees, the chirping of the birds, and the music which was wafted toward me from the park. I heard the melodies distinctly without being disturbed by them, for our ear is so capable of adapting itself that a continuous din, or the noise of a street, or the rippling of a brook adjusts itself completely to our consciousness, and it is only an unexpected halt in the rhythm that startles us into listening.

And so it was that I suddenly stopped reading when the music broke off abruptly. I did not know what piece the band was playing. I noticed only that the music had broken off. Instinctively I looked up from my book. The crowd which strolled through the trees as a single, light, moving mass, also seemed to have undergone a change; it, too, had suddenly come to a halt. Something must have happened. I got up and saw that the musicians had left their pavilion. This too was strange, for the park concert usually lasted for an hour or more. What could have caused this brusque conclusion? Coming closer I noticed that the people had crowded excitedly around the bandstand because of an announcement which had evidently just been put up. It was, as I soon learned, the text of a telegram announcing that His Imperial Majesty, the successor to the crown, Franz Ferdinand, and his wife, who had gone to the maneuvers in Bosnia, had fallen victims of a political assassination there.

More and more people pressed toward the placard; the

unexpected news was passed on from one to the other. But to be honest, there was no particular shock or dismay to be seen on their faces, for the heir-apparent was not at all well-liked. From the very earliest days of my youth I can recall another day when Crown Prince Rudolf, the Emperor's only son, had been found shot dead in Mayerling. Then the whole city was in a tumult of despair and excitement, tremendous crowds thronged to witness his lying-in-state, the expression of shock and sympathy for the Emperor was overwhelming, that his only son and heir, who had been looked upon as an unusually progressive and humane Habsburg of whom much was expected, had passed on in the prime of life. But Franz Ferdinand lacked everything that counts for real popularity in Austria; amiability, personal charm and easygoingness. I had often seen him in the theater. There he sat in his box, broad and mighty, with cold, fixed gaze, never casting a single friendly glance towards the audience or encouraging the actors with hearty applause. He was never seen to smile, and no photographs showed him relaxed. He had no sense for music, and no sense of humor, and his wife was equally unfriendly. They both were surrounded by an icy air; one knew that they had no friends, and also that the old Emperor hated him with all his heart because he did not have sufficient tact to hide his impatience to succeed to the throne. My almost mystic premonition that some misfortune would come from this man with his bulldog neck and his cold, staring eyes, was by no means a personal one but was shared by the entire nation; and so the news of his murder aroused no profound sympathy. Two hours later signs of genuine mourning were no longer to be seen. The throngs laughed and chattered and as the evening advanced music was resumed at public resorts. There were many on that day in Austria who secretly sighed with relief that this heir of the aged Emperor had been removed in favor of the much more beloved young Archduke Karl.

Of course the newspapers printed lengthy eulogies on the following day, giving fitting expression to their indignation over the assassination. But there was no indication that the event was to be used politically against Serbia. The immediate concern of the Imperial house was quite another one, namely the solemn obsequies. According to his rank as heir-apparent, and especially since he had died in the service of the monarchy, his burial place would obviously have been the Capuchin vault, the historic place of interment of the Habsburgs. But Franz Ferdinand had married a Countess Chotek in the face of a long and bitter struggle on the part of the Imperial family. She was a high aristocrat, but according to the secret, ancient family laws of the Habsburgs, she was not considered of equal birth with her husband, and at all the great official functions the archduchesses stubbornly clung to their precedence over the wife of the heir-apparent, whose children were not entitled to the succession. The court pride even followed them in death. What?—a Countess Chotek to be buried in the Imperial vault of the Habsburgs? Perish the thought! A mighty intrigue set in; the archduchesses stormed the old Emperor. Whereas official mourning was expected from the populace, within the palace there was a wild cross-play of bitterness and rancor and, as usual, the dead were in the wrong. The masters of ceremony invented the assertion that it had been the express desire of the deceased to be buried in Artstetten, a provincial hole; and with this pseudo-pious excuse, they were able cautiously to evade the public lying-in-state, the funeral cortege and all the disputed questions of precedence that went with it. The coffins of the murdered royalty were quietly taken to Artstetten and interred there. Vienna, whose perpetual fondness for a show was thus deprived of a great opportunity, had already begun to forget the tragic occurrence. After all, the violent death of Queen Elizabeth and of the Crown Prince, and the scandalous flight of all sorts of members of the Imperial house, had long since accustomed Vienna to the thought that the old Emperor would outlive his Tantalidean house in imperturbable solitude. Only a few weeks more and the name and the figure of Franz Ferdinand would have disappeared for all time out of history.

In less than a week, however, attacks suddenly began to appear in the newspapers, and their constantly mounting crescendo was regulated too consistently for them to have been entirely accidental. The Serbian government was accused of collusion in the assassination, and there were veiled hints that Austria would not permit the murder of its supposedly beloved heir-apparent to go unavenged. One could not escape the impression that some sort of action was being prepared in the newspapers, but no one thought of war. Neither banks nor business houses nor private persons changed their plans. Why should we be concerned with these constant skirmishes with Serbia which, as all knew, arose out of some commercial treaties concerned with the export of Hungarian pigs? My bags were packed so that I could go to Verhaeren in Belgium, my work was in full swing, what did the dead Archduke in his catafalque have to do with my life? The summer was beautiful as never before and promised to become even more beautiful—and we all looked out upon the world without a care. I can recall that on my last day in Baden I was walking through the vineyards with a friend, when an old wine-grower said to us: "We haven't had such a summer for a long time. If it stays this way, we'll get better grapes than ever. Folks will remember this summer!"

He did not know, the old man in his blue cooper's smock, how gruesomely true a word he had spoken.

~~~

In Le Coq, the small seaside resort near Ostend where I had planned to stay for two weeks before paying my annual visit to Verhaeren's country home, the same unconstraint reigned as elsewhere. The happy vacationists lay under their colored tents on the beach or went in bathing, children were flying kites, and the young people were dancing in front of the cafés on the *digue.* All nationalities were peaceably assembled together, and one heard a good deal of German in particular, for vacationists from the near-by Rhineland had long shown a preference for the Belgian seacoast. The only disturbance came from the newsboy who, to stimulate business, shouted the threatening captions in the Parisian papers: *L'Autriche provoque la Russie, L'Allemagne prépare la mobilisation.* We could see the faces of those who bought copies grow gloomy, but only for a few minutes. After all, we had been familiar with these diplomatic conflicts for years; they were always happily settled at the last minute, before things grew too serious. Why not this time as well? A half-hour later, one saw the same people splashing about in the water, the kites soared aloft, the gulls fluttered about and the sun laughed warm and clear over the peaceful land.

But the bad news piled up and constantly became more threatening. First it was Austria's ultimatum to Serbia, and the evasive reply to it, then an exchange of telegrams between the monarchs, and finally the barely hidden mobilization. The village became irksome to me; every day I would take the little electric train for Ostend to be closer to the news, and it grew increasingly worse. People were still bathing, the hotels still full, the *digue* still crowded with strolling, laughing, chatting summer visitors. But for the first time now, however, a new element appeared; one saw Belgian soldiers who had never before been seen on the beach, and machine guns in small carts drawn by dogs, this being a peculiarity of the Belgian army.

At that time I was sitting in a café with some Belgian friends, a young painter and the poet Crommelynck. We had spent the afternoon at the house of James Ensor, Belgium's greatest painter, a very reticent and retiring sort of man, who was much prouder of the poor and petty waltzes and polkas that he composed for the military band than he was of his fantastic paintings in glowing colors. He had shown us his work, indeed rather unwillingly, for the thought that somebody might possibly purchase one of them dejected him in a buffoonist sort of way. His ideal, so his friends laughingly told me, was to sell them at a high price and then be permitted to keep them, for he was as avaricious about money as he was about his work. Whenever he was forced to part with a painting, he was plunged into despair for several days. With all his curious crotchets this genial Harpagon had made us quite jolly; and when a troop of soldiers happened to pass by with its machine gun harnessed to a dog, one of us got up to stroke the dog. This disgusted the officer in charge who feared that this petting of an adjunct of war might possibly damage the dignity of a military institution. "Why all this stupid marching about?" one of our group muttered. But another immediately replied with excitement: "One has to be prepared. They say that in case of war the Germans intend to invade us." "Out of the question!" I said with honest conviction, for in that old world one still believed in the sanctity of treaties. "If something were to happen and France and Germany were to destroy each other to the last man, you

Belgians would still keep your feet dry!" But our pessimist did not give in. There must be sufficient reason, he continued, if such measures had been ordered in Belgium. Years ago they had already got wind of a secret plan of the German General Staff, whereby, in case of an attack on France, Belgium was to be invaded despite all ratified treaties. But neither would I give in. It appeared completely ridiculous to me that while thousands and tens of thousands of Germans were enjoying at their leisure the hospitality of this small, impartial country, an army should stand in readiness at the frontier prepared to march in. "Nonsense!" I said. "You can hang me to this lamp post if the Germans march into Belgium!" Today I am still grateful to my friends that they did not take me at my word when the time came.

Then came the critical last days of July and each hour brought conflicting news—the telegrams of Emperor Wilhelm to the Tsar, the telegrams of the Tsar to Emperor Wilhelm, Austria's declaration of war on Serbia, the murder of Jaurès. One sensed the serious situation. At once an icy wind of fear blew over the beach and swept it bare. People by the thousands left the hotels and stormed the trains, and even the most optimistic began to pack their bags with speed. I too booked a ticket the moment that I learned of Austria's declaration of war on Serbia, and it was high time for this. The Orient Express was the last train from Belgium to Germany. We stood in the corridors, excited and impatient, everybody talking to everybody else. No one could remain quiet or read, and at each station we would rush out of the train to get the latest news, filled with the secret hope that some determined hand would restrain the Fates that had been unleashed. We still did not believe there would be war and even less in the possibility of an invasion of Belgium. We could not believe it because we did not wish to believe in such madness. We had passed through Verviers, the Belgium border station, and gradually the train approached the frontier. A German crew got on, and in ten minutes we would be on German soil.

Half-way to Herbesthal, the first German station, the train suddenly stood still in the middle of an open field. We hurried into the corridor to the windows. What had happened? In the darkness I saw one freight train after another coming towards us, open cars covered with tarpaulins, under which I thought I could indistinctly see the threatening outlines of cannon. My heart missed a beat. It could be nothing but the advance of the German army. But perhaps, I comforted myself, it was only a precautionary measure, merely a threat of mobilization, and not mobilization itself. Always in time of danger, the renewed will to hope becomes enormous. Finally we heard the signal "All clear!" and the train rolled on into the station at Herbesthal. I leapt down the steps with one jump to get a newspaper and to learn what was going on. But the military had occupied the station. When I wished to enter the waiting-room, an official, white-bearded and grave, stood in front of the locked door: no one was permitted to enter the station buildings. But I had already heard the rattling and clanking of swords behind the carefully covered glass panes and the hard thud of grounded rifles. No longer any doubt, the monstrous thing, the German invasion of Belgium contrary to every provision of international law, was in progress. Shuddering, I went back to the train and rode on, back to Austria. Now there was no more doubt: I was riding into the war.

～

The next morning I was in Austria. In every station placards had been put up announcing general mobilization.

The trains were filled with fresh recruits, banners were flying, music sounded, and in Vienna I found the entire city in a tumult. The first shock at the news of war—the war that no one, people or government, had wanted—the war which had slipped, much against their will, out of the clumsy hands of the diplomats who had been bluffing and toying with it, had suddenly been transformed into enthusiasm. There were parades in the street, flags, ribbons, and music burst forth everywhere, young recruits were marching triumphantly, their faces lighting up at the cheering —they, the John Does and Richard Roes who usually go unnoticed and uncelebrated.

And to be truthful, I must acknowledge that there was a majestic, rapturous, and even seductive something in this first outbreak of the people from which one could escape only with difficulty. And in spite of all my hatred and aversion for war, I should not like to have missed the memory of those first days. As never before, thousands and hundreds of thousands felt what they should have felt in peace time, that they belonged together. A city of two million, a country of nearly fifty million, in that hour felt that they were participating in world history, in a moment which would never recur, and that each one was called upon to cast his infinitesimal self into the glowing mass, there to be purified of all selfishness. All differences of class, rank, and language were flooded over at that moment by the rushing feeling of fraternity. Strangers spoke to one another in the streets, people who had avoided each other for years shook hands, everywhere one saw excited faces. Each individual experienced an exaltation of his ego, he was no longer the isolated person of former times, he had been incorporated into the mass, he was part of the people, and his person, his hitherto unnoticed person, had been given meaning. The petty mail clerk, who ordinarily sorted

letters early and late, who sorted constantly, who sorted
from Monday until Saturday without interruption; the
clerk, the cobbler, had suddenly achieved a romantic possibility in life: he could become a hero, and everyone who
wore a uniform was already being cheered by the women,
and greeted beforehand with this romantic appellation by
those who had to remain behind. They acknowledged the
unknown power which had lifted them out of their everyday existence. Even mothers with their grief, and women
with their fears, were ashamed to manifest their quite
natural emotions in the face of this first transformation. But
it is quite possible that a deeper, more secret power was at
work in this frenzy. So deeply, so quickly did the tide
break over humanity that, foaming over the surface, it
churned up the depths, the subconscious primitive instincts
of the human animal—that which Freud so meaningfully
calls "the revulsion from culture," the desire to break out
of the conventional bourgeois world of codes and statutes,
and to permit the primitive instincts of the blood to rage at
will. It is also possible that these powers of darkness had
their share in the wild frenzy into which everything was
thrown—self-sacrifice and alcohol, the spirit of adventure
and the spirit of pure faith, the old magic of flags and
patriotic slogans, that mysterious frenzy of the millions
which can hardly be described in words, but which, for the
moment, gave a wild and almost rapturous impetus to the
greatest crime of our time.

~

Today's generation, which has only observed the outbreak of the Second World War, may ask: why was our
experience different? Why did not the masses in 1939 flare
up with the same rapturous madness as in 1914? Why did
they respond to the call only with gravity and determination,

fatalistically and in silence? Was it not the same thing, were not even holier and higher aims at stake in our present war, which is one of ideas and not merely concerned with frontiers and colonies?

The answer is simple: because the world of 1939 does not possess so much childishly naïve credulity as did that of 1914. Then the people had unqualified confidence in their leaders; no one in Austria would have ventured the thought that the all-high ruler Emperor Franz Josef, in his eighty-third year, would have called his people to war unless from direct necessity, would have demanded such a sacrifice of blood unless evil, sinister, and criminal foes were threatening the peace of the Empire. The Germans, on the other hand, had read the telegrams of their Emperor to the Tsar in which he struggled for peace; a mighty respect for the "authorities," the ministers, the diplomats, and for their discernment and honesty still animated the simple man. If war had come, then it could only have come against the wishes of their own statesmen; they themselves were not at fault, indeed no one in the entire land was at fault. Therefore the criminals, the war mongers must be the other fellows; we had taken up arms in self-defense against a villainous and crafty enemy, who had "attacked" peaceful Austria and Germany without the slightest provocation. In 1939, however, this almost religious faith in the honesty or at least in the capacity of one's own government had disappeared throughout Europe. Diplomacy was despised, since one had seen with bitterness how the possibility of a lasting peace had been betrayed at Versailles; nations remembered all too clearly how they had been shamefully cheated of the promises of disarmament and the abolition of secret diplomacy. In truth, there was not a single statesman in 1939 for whom anyone had respect and none in whom one would confidently entrust his destiny. The humblest French crossing-sweeper ridiculed Daladier, and in England, since Munich—"peace in our time"—all confidence in Chamberlain's perspicacity had vanished; in Italy and in Germany the masses looked upon Mussolini and Hitler with anxiety: Where will he drive us now? To be sure, they had no choice, the Fatherland was at stake: and so the soldiers shouldered their guns, the women let their children go, but not with the unswerving belief of other times that this sacrifice had been unavoidable. They obeyed but without rejoicing. They went to the front, but without the old dream of being a hero; the people, and each individual, already knew that they were naught but the victims either of mundane, political stupidity or of an incomprehensible and malicious force of destiny.

Besides, what did the great mass know of war in 1914, after nearly half a century of peace? They did not know war, they had hardly given it a thought. It had become legendary, and distance had made it seem romantic and heroic. They still saw it in the perspective of their school readers and of paintings in museums; brilliant cavalry attacks in glittering uniforms, the fatal shot always straight through the heart, the entire campaign a resounding march of victory—"We'll be home at Christmas," the recruits shouted laughingly to their mothers in August of 1914. Who in the villages and the cities of Austria remembered "real" war? A few ancients at best, who in 1866 had fought against Prussia, which was now their ally. But what a quick, bloodless, far-off war that had been, a campaign that had ended in three weeks with few victims and before it had well started! A rapid excursion into the romantic, a wild, manly adventure—that is how the war of 1914 was painted in the imagination of the simple man, and the young people were honestly afraid that they might miss this most wonderful and exciting experience of their lives; that is why they hurried and thronged to the colors, and that is why they shouted and sang in the trains that carried them to the slaughter; wildly and feverishly the red wave of blood coursed through the veins of the entire nation. But the generation of 1939 knew war. It no longer deceived itself. It knew that it was not romantic but barbaric. It knew that it would last for years and years, an irretrievable span of time. It knew that men did not storm the enemy, decorated with oak leaves and ribbons, but hung about for weeks at a time in trenches or quarters covered with vermin and mad with thirst and that men were crushed and mutilated from afar without ever coming face to face with the foe. The newspapers and cinemas had already made the new and devilish techniques of destruction familiar: people knew how the giant tanks ground the wounded under in their path, and how airplanes destroyed women and children in their beds. They knew that a World War of 1939, because of its soulless mechanization, would be a thousand times more cruel, more bestial, more inhuman than all of the former wars of mankind. Not a single individual of the generation of 1939 believed any longer in a God-decreed justice of war: and what was worse they no longer believed in the justice and permanence of the peace it was to achieve. For they remembered all too well the disappointments that the last war had brought; impoverization instead of riches, bitterness instead of contentment, famine, inflation, revolts, the loss of civil rights, enslavement by the State, nerve-destroying uncertainty, distrust of each against all.

That is what made the difference. The war of 1939 had a spiritual meaning, a question of freedom and the preservation of moral possessions; and to fight for an idea makes man hard and determined. The war of 1914, on the other hand, knew nothing of realities, it still served a delusion, the dream of a better, a righteous and peaceful world. And it is only delusion, and not knowledge, that bestows happiness. That is why the victims, crowned with flowers and with oak leaves in their helmets, marched jubilating on their way to the shambles through streets that rumbled and sparkled as if on a holiday.

That I myself did not succumb to this sudden rapture of patriotism was not due to any unusual sobriety or discernment on my part, but rather because of my former manner of life. Two days earlier I had still been in "enemy" country and could convince myself that the great masses in Belgium were just as peaceful and unaware as our own people. What is more, I had lived too internationally to be able suddenly, overnight, to hate a world that was as much mine as my fatherland. I had long been dubious of politics, and especially during recent years I had discussed countless times with my French and Italian friends the stupidity of a possible war. I was inoculated to some extent against the infection of patriotic enthusiasm and, being thus prepared against this fever of the first hours, I remained fully determined not to allow this war of brothers, brought about by clumsy diplomats and brutal munitions-manufacturers, to affect my conviction of the necessity of European unity.

As a result, I was inwardly secure from the very beginning of my world citizenship; it was more difficult to determine my course as a citizen of the State. Although only thirty-two, I had no military obligations for the time being, for at all physical examinations I had been declared unfit, which ever on those past occasions had made me heartily glad. These rejections saved me from wasting a year in stupid army service and furthermore, it struck me as a criminal anachronism to let myself be trained in the use of implements of murder in the twentieth century. The right thing for a man of my convictions would have been to declare myself a conscientious objector, a course which, in Austria, invited the heaviest punishments imaginable and would have demanded a martyr's steadfastness of soul. It happens —and I am not ashamed to admit this fault—that there is nothing heroic in my nature. My natural attitude to all dangerous situations has always been to evade, and it was not only on this occasion that I had to accept, perhaps justly, the reproach of indecision that so often was made to my revered master of an earlier century, Erasmus of Rotterdam. On the other hand, it was equally unbearable to me as a comparatively young man, to wait until they dug me out of my retirement and planted me in some inept spot. So I looked around for some activity in which I could serve to advantage without being militarily active, and the fact that one of my friends, an officer of rank, was in the War Archives, procured my assignment there. I worked in the library, where my knowledge of languages was useful, and styled and improved publicity releases—certainly not a glorious occupation, I readily concede, but at least one that seemed to suit me better than pushing a bayonet into the entrails of a Russian peasant. But the deciding factor was that I had sufficient time after these none-too-arduous duties to devote to what I believed was the most important service in the war: the preparation for the understanding to come.

～～

My position among my Viennese friends was much more difficult than my official one. Limited in their experience of Europe as a whole and living entirely within the German circle of thought, most of our writers believed that their best contribution was to strengthen the enthusiasm of the masses and support the supposed beauty of war with poetic appeals or scientific ideologies. Nearly all the German authors, led by Hauptmann and Dehmel, felt themselves obligated, like the bards of the ancient Germani, by songs

and runes to inflame the advancing warriors with enthusiasm for death. Poems poured forth that rhymed *Krieg* with
Sieg and *Not* with *Tod*. Solemnly the poets swore never
again to have any cultural association with a Frenchman or
an Englishman; they went even further, they denied overnight that there had ever been any French or English culture. All that was insignificant and valueless in comparison
with German character, German art, and German thought.
But the savants were even worse. The sole wisdom of the
philosophers was to declare the war a "bath of steel" which
would beneficially preserve the strength of the people from
enervation. The physicians fell into line and praised their
prosthesis so extravagantly that one was almost tempted to
have a leg amputated so that the healthy member might
be replaced by an artificial one. The ministers of all creeds
had no desire to be outdone and joined in the chorus, at
times as if a horde of possessed were raving, and yet all of
these men were the very same whose reason, creative power,
and humane conduct one had admired only a week, a
month, before.

The most shocking thing about this madness was that
most of these persons were honest. For the most part, too
old or physically unfit for military service, they thought
themselves in decency obliged to take part in every supporting effort. All that they had achieved they owed to
the language and thus to the people. And so they desired
to serve their people by means of the language and let them
hear what they wished to hear: that justice was solely on
their side in this struggle, and injustice on the other, that
Germany would triumph and the enemy be ignominiously
conquered—quite oblivious of the fact that in so doing they
were betraying the true mission of the poet, the preserver
and defender of the universal humanity of mankind. Of

course many felt the bitter taste of disgust on their tongues at their own words as soon as the fumes of the initial enthusiasm had evaporated. But in the early months those who raved the loudest attracted most attention, and so they sang and yelled in a wild chorus here, there and everywhere.

To my mind, the most typical and most moving case of such honest and at once inane ecstasy, was that of Ernst Lissauer. I knew him well. He wrote short, incisive, brittle poems, and was the most kindly person imaginable. Even today I can recall how I had to bite my lips to hide my smile on the occasion of his first visit. Arbitrarily, judging by his pithy Germanic verses which strove for the utmost brevity, I had pictured him as a slim, raw-boned young man. Instead, there toddled into my room a round little man, a jolly face above a double double-chin, bubbling over with self-importance and exuberance, stuttering in his haste, and so possessed with poetry that nothing could keep him from citing and reciting his verses again and again. But for all the laughable things he did, I had to like him because he was warm-hearted, comradely, honest and demoniacally attached to his art.

He was of a wealthy German family, had been educated in the Friedrich Wilhelm-Gymnasium in Berlin, and possibly he was the most Prussian, or Prussian-assimilated Jew I had ever known. He spoke no other living tongue and had never been outside of Germany. Germany was his world and the more Germanic anything was, the more it delighted him. York, Luther, and Stein were his heroes, the German War of Liberation his favorite topic, and Bach his musical god; he played him beautifully in spite of his small, short, thick, spongy fingers. No one was more familiar with German poetry, and no one was more enamored of, more enchanted with the German language; like so many

Jews whose families had entered German culture late, he had more faith in Germany than the most devoted of Germans.

When the war broke out, his first act was to hurry to the barracks to enlist. I can well imagine the laughter of the sergeants and corporals when this fat body came puffing up the stairs. He was promptly rejected. Lissauer was in despair but, like the others, he at least wished to serve Germany with his muse. Everything that the newspapers and the German army communiqués published was gospel truth to him. His country had been attacked, and the worst criminal—as cast by Wilhelmstrasse—was that perfidious Sir Edward Grey, the British Foreign Minister. This feeling, that England was the arch enemy of Germany and responsible for the war, found expression in his "Hymn of Hate," a poem—I do not have a copy before me—that in hard, short, impressive stanzas raised the hatred against England to an eternal oath never to forgive her for her "crime." It was soon fatefully apparent how easy it is to work hatred (this blinded, fat little Jew, Lissauer, anticipated Hitler's example). The poem exploded like a bomb in a munitions depot. Possibly no other poem in Germany, not even the "Watch on the Rhine," got around as quickly as this notorious "Hymn of Hate." The Kaiser was enraptured and bestowed the Order of the Red Eagle upon Lissauer, the poem was reprinted in all the newspapers, teachers read it out loud to the children in school, officers at the front read it to their soldiers, until everyone knew the litany of hate by heart. As if that were not enough, the little poem was set to music and, arranged for chorus, was sung in the theaters; among Germany's seventy millions there was hardly one person who did not know the "Hymn of Hate" from the first line to the last, and soon it was known—with less rapture, be it said—to the entire world. Overnight Ernst

Lissauer had achieved the greatest renown won by any poet in that war—but, to be sure, a renown that later was to burn him like the shirt of Nessus. For no sooner had the war ended, with merchants seeking to resume trade and politicians making honest efforts towards mutual understanding, everything was done to disclaim the poem which had demanded eternal enmity with England. And to shake off one's own culpability, poor "Hate-Lissauer" was pilloried as the sole culprit of this insane hysteria of hate, which in fact everyone from the highest to the lowest had shared in 1914. All who had celebrated him in 1914 turned from him pointedly in 1919. The newspapers ceased to print his poems, and when he appeared among his fellows a marked silence fell. Finally he was driven out by Hitler from the Germany to which he had been attached with every fiber of his heart, to die forgotten, the tragic victim of the one poem which had raised him so highly only to dash him to the lowest depths.

~~

The rest were just like Lissauer. Their emotions were honest and they thought they were acting honestly, the professors and poets, the sudden patriots of that time. I do not deny it. But it took little time for it to become apparent how terrible a disaster had been caused by these songs in praise of war and orgies of hatred. In 1914 all the warring nations were already in a state of over-excitation and the worst rumor was immediately transformed into truth, the most absurd slander believed. In Germany men by the dozen swore that they had seen with their own eyes automobiles laden with gold going from France to Russia shortly before the outbreak of the war; the tales of gouged-out eyes and severed hands which appear on the third or fourth day of every war filled the newspapers. They did not know, those innocents who spread such lies, that the accusation of every possible cruelty against the enemy is as much war matériel as are munitions and planes, and that they are systematically taken out of storage at the beginning of every war. War does not permit itself to be coordinated with reason and righteousness. It needs stimulated emotions, enthusiasm for its own cause and hatred for the adversary.

It lies in human nature that deep emotion cannot be prolonged indefinitely, either in the individual or in a people, a fact that is known to all military organizations. Therefore it requires an artificial stimulation, a constant "doping" of excitement; and this whipping up was to be performed by the intellectuals, the poets, the writers and the journalists, scrupulously or otherwise, honestly or as a matter of professional routine. They were to beat the drums of hatred and beat them they did, until the ears of the unprejudiced hummed and their hearts quaked. In Germany, in France, in Italy, in Russia, and in Belgium, they all obediently served the war propaganda and thus the mass delusion and mass hatred, instead of fighting against it.

The results were disastrous. At that time, propaganda not yet having worn itself thin in peace time, the nations believed everything that they saw in print in spite of thousands of disillusionments. And so the pure, beautiful, sacrificial enthusiasm of the opening days became gradually transformed into an orgy of the worst and most stupid impulses. In Vienna and Berlin one "fought" France and England in the Ringstrasse and the Friedrichstrasse, which was definitely more comfortable. The French and English signs on the shops were made to disappear and even a convent Zu den Englischen Fräulein had to change its name because the people were aroused, not knowing that *englische* referred to the angels and not the Anglo-Saxons. Sober merchants stamped or pasted *Gott strafe England* on their letters, and society ladies swore, (so they wrote to the news-papers), that never again would they speak a single word of French. Shakespeare was banned from the German stage, Mozart and Wagner from the French and English concert halls, German professors declared that Dante had been Ger-manic, the French that Beethoven had been a Belgian, intellectual culture was requisitioned without scruple from the enemy countries like grain and ore. It was not enough that thousands of peace-loving citizens were kill-ing each other daily at the front. In the hinterland there was mutual berating and slandering of the great dead of the enemy countries, who had been slumbering in their graves for centuries. The mental confusion increased in absurdity. The cook at her stove, who had never been out-side the city and had never looked at an atlas since her schooldays, believed that Austria could not endure without Sanchschak (a small frontier hamlet somewhere in Bosnia). Cabdrivers argued on the streets about the reparations to be imposed on France, fifty billions or a hundred, without knowing how much a billion was. There was no city, no group that had not fallen prey to this dreadful hysteria of hatred. The ministers preached from their pulpits, the Social Democrats, who but a month before had branded militarism as the greatest crime, clamored perhaps louder than all the others so as not to be classed as "people without a fatherland" in the words of Emperor Wilhelm. It was the war of an unsuspicious generation, and the greatest peril was the inexhaustible faith of the nations in the single-sided justice of their cause.

~~~

It soon became impossible to converse reasonably with anybody in the first war weeks of 1914. The most peaceable and the most good-natured were intoxicated with the smell of blood. Friends whom I had looked upon as decided individualists and even as philosophical anarchists, changed over night into fanatic patriots and from patriots into insatiable annexionists. Every conversation ended in some stupid phrase such as: "He who cannot hate cannot really love," or in coarse inculpations. Comrades with whom I had not quarreled for years accused me rudely of no longer being an Austrian; why did I not go over to France or Belgium? They even hinted cautiously that sentiments such as that the war was a crime ought to be brought to the attention of the authorities, for "defeatists"—that nice word had just been invented in France—were the worst betrayers of the fatherland.

Nothing remained but to withdraw into one's self and to keep silent while the others ranted and raved. It was not easy. For even in exile—I have experienced it to the full— it is not as difficult to live alone as it is in one's own country. In Vienna I had estranged my old friends and this was no time to seek new ones. It was only with Rainer Maria Rilke that I sometimes had talks of intimate understanding. It had become possible to secure him, too, for our War Archives, for with his over-delicate nerves he would have been the most impossible soldier, since filth, smells, and noise actually produced physical nausea in him. I always have to smile when I remember him in uniform. One day there was a knock at my door. A timid soldier stood outside. For the moment I was frightened: Rilke—Rainer Maria Rilke, in military disguise! He looked so touchingly awkward, his collar too tight, disturbed by the thought that he had to salute every officer, clicking his heels together. And since, in his high impulse to perfection, he wished to perform even this insignificant formality of the ritual in as exemplary a manner as possible, he found himself in a perpetual state of confusion. "I have always hated this military uniform," he said to me in his soft tone of voice, "since my time in the military academy. I thought that I had escaped it once and for all. And now again, at almost forty!" Fortunately there were helping hands to protect him and, thanks to a benevolent medical examination, he was soon discharged. Once more he came into my room, this time to take leave—back in civilian clothes again—it seemed almost as if he had been wafted in, so noiseless were his movements. He wished to thank me for endeavoring, through Rolland, to rescue his library which had been confiscated in Paris. For the first time he no longer looked young; it was as if the thought of all this horror had exhausted him. "Abroad," he said, "if one could only go abroad! War is always prison." Then he left. Again I was all alone.

After a few weeks, determined to escape this dangerous mass psychosis, I moved to a rural suburb to commence my personal war in the midst of war, the struggle against the betrayal of Reason by the current mass passion.

X

The Struggle for Intellectual Brotherhood

Retirement in itself proved useless. The atmosphere remained oppressive. And just because of that I became aware that mere passive non-participation in this wild derogation of the enemy, was not conclusive. After all, one was a writer and had the gift of words, and with it the duty of expressing one's convictions as far as that was possible under the censorship. I attempted to do so. I wrote an article called "To Friends Abroad" in which, in direct and blunt contrast to the accustomed fanfares of hate, I announced to all friends in foreign countries that, although relations were now impossible, I would remain loyal to them so that, at the very first opportunity, we might again collaborate in the reconstruction of European culture. I sent it to the most widely-read German paper. To my amazement, the *Berliner Tageblatt* did not hesitate to print it entire. Only one passage—"no matter who may be victorious"—was censored, because even the slightest doubt that Germany would emerge victorious from the World War was not permitted at that time. But even without this limitation, my article brought me a number of indignant letters from superpatriots; they could not understand how one could have anything in common with those rascally opponents in such an hour. I was not very much hurt. Throughout my life it had never been my purpose to convert others to my opinions. It sufficed for me to be permitted to express them, and to express them openly. Two weeks later when I had almost forgotten about my article, I received a letter with a Swiss postage stamp and marked "Passed by Censor," and the familiar handwriting told me that it came from Romain Rolland. He must have read my article, for he wrote: *Non, je ne quitterai jamais mes amis.* I sensed immediately that these few lines were an attempt to see if it were possible to correspond with an Austrian friend in war time. I replied at once. From that time on we wrote to each other regularly, and our correspondence continued for more than twenty-five years until the second war—more brutal than the first—disrupted all connections between nations.

This letter was one of the high points of happiness in my life: it came to me like a white dove out of the ark of bellowing, stamping, raging wild beasts. I no longer felt alone but once again linked with someone of my own convictions. I felt myself strengthened by Rolland's greater spiritual strength. I knew how wonderfully Rolland was proving his humanity beyond the frontier. He had found the only right path for a writer to take in such times: not to participate in destruction and murder, but—following the great example of Walt Whitman, who served as a hospital orderly in the Civil War—to be active in works of assistance and humanity. Living in Switzerland, exempt from all military duty because of his poor health, he had immediately offered his services to the Red Cross in Geneva where he happened to be at the outbreak of the war, and labored there in the over-crowded rooms day after day in the magnificent work for which I later tried to express thanks publicly in an article called "The Heart of Europe." After the murderous battles of the first weeks, all connections were broken off; in all countries relatives did not know whether or not their sons, their brothers, their fathers had fallen, or were merely missing or prisoners, and they did not know where to inquire, for no answer was to be expected from the "enemy." The Red Cross took over the task of alle-

viating the harrowing uncertainty about the fate of one's
loved ones—the worst misery in the midst of horror and
cruelty—by directing letters from prisoners of war to their
homelands in the opposing countries. However, the organization which had been operating for decades, was unpre-
pared for such tremendous numbers; daily, hourly, the number of volunteer workers had to be augmented, for every
hour of suspense seemed an eternity to those concerned.
At the end of December 1914, thirty thousand letters came
in daily, and finally twelve hundred people crowded
together in the little Musée Rath in Geneva to answer and
take care of the daily mail. And among them, instead of
selfishly doing his own work, labored the most human of
poets: Romain Rolland.

But he had not forgotten his other duty, the duty of the
artist to express his convictions even in the face of opposition of his own country and that of the entire belligerent
world. In the Autumn of 1914, when most writers were out-
shouting each other in hatred, and spat and bellowed at
one another, he wrote that notable avowal *Au-dessus de la
Mêlée,* in which he fought against intellectual hatred
between nations and demanded justice and humanity from
all artists even in the midst of war. It was an article which,
like no other of its time, aroused opinion and resulted in a
controversial literature of its own.

For this was the favorable difference between the First
World War and the second: in the first the word still had
power. It had not yet been done to death by the organization
of lies, by "propaganda," and people still considered the written word, they looked to it. Whereas in 1939 not a single pro-
nouncement by any writer had the slightest effect either
for good or evil, and up to the present no book, pamphlet,
essay, or poem has stirred the masses to their core. In 1914

a forty-eight line poem like Lissauer's "Hymn of Hate," an inane manifesto like that of the "93 German Intellectuals," or an eight-page essay such as Rolland's *Au-dessus de la Mêlée,* or a novel like Barbusse's *Le Feu,* became an event. The moral conscience of the world had not yet become as tired or washed-out as it is today. It reacted vehemently to every obvious lie, to every violation of international law and of humanity, with the whole force of centuries of conviction. A violation such as Germany's invasion of neutral Belgium, which today, since Hitler elevated lying to a matter of course and anti-humanitarianism to law, would hardly be complained of seriously, could then still arouse the world from end to end. The shooting of Edith Cavell and the torpedoing of the *Lusitania* were more harmful to Germany than a battle lost, thanks to the universal outburst of moral indignation. And so it was by no means vain for the poet, the writer, to speak out at that time when the ear and the soul had not yet been flooded with the incessant chattering waves of the radio. On the contrary, the spontaneous manifestation of a great poet was a thousand times more effective than all of the official speeches of the statesmen, who were known to be geared tactically and politically to the immediate moment and to speak half-truths at best. In this feeling of confidence in the poet as the highest guarantee of pure sentiments, there was infinitely more belief on the part of that generation that later was to be so disappointed. Aware of this authority of the poet, military leaders and officials sought to secure the services of the men of moral and intellectual prestige for their purposes. They were needed to declare, to prove, to confirm, that all the injustice, all the evil was piled up on the other side, and that all truth and all righteousness were on the side of their own nation. They could not get Rolland to do this.

He did not see it as his duty to intensify the atmosphere
sultry with hatred and heavy through every kind of incitement but, on the contrary, to purify it.

Whoever reads the eight pages of the famous *Au-dessus
de la Mêlée* today will in all probability no longer comprehend its tremendous effect. All that Rolland postulated in it
connotes, if read cooly and clearly, nothing but the most
obvious of obvious truths. But these words were written in a
time of mass insanity that can hardly be reconstructed today.
When the article appeared, the French super-patriots cried
out as if they had picked up a red hot iron by mistake. In
a trice Rolland was boycotted by his oldest friends, the booksellers no longer dared to display *Jean Christophe,* the military authorities, who needed hatred to stimulate their
soldiers, were already considering measures against him.
One pamphlet after the other appeared with the argument:
*Ce qu'on donne pendant la guerre á l'humanité est volé de
la patrie.* But as always, the outcry proved that the blow had
struck home. The discussion as to the attitude of the intellectuals in the war could no longer be halted, and the problem was posed inescapably before every individual.

～

I regret nothing more in these memoirs than that I no
longer have access to Rolland's letters of those years; the
thought that they may be destroyed or lost in this new
Deluge weighs upon me as a heavy responsibility. For much
as I love all his works, I believe that the time may come
when those letters will be counted among the loveliest and
the most humane that his great heart and passionate reason
ever brought forth. Out of the measureless despair of a
compassionate soul, out of the entire force of powerless bitterness, written to a friend beyond the border, officially an
"enemy," they may possibly be the most penetrating moral

documents of a time where understanding was a gigantic manifestation of strength, and loyalty to one's own beliefs in itself demanded grandiose courage. Our friendly correspondence soon crystallized into a definite project: Rolland suggested that we attempt to invite the important intellectual personalities of all nations to a conference in Switzerland, in order to achieve a more uniform and dignified attitude and perhaps, even, to address a united appeal for conciliation to the world. He, for his part, was prepared to invite the French and those of other lands to participate, and I was to take care of the Austrians and Germans in so far as they had not already compromised themselves by taking an open part in the propaganda of hate. I went to work at once. The most important and most representative German poet at that time was Gerhart Hauptmann. In order to make it easier for him to accept or to decline, I did not wish to approach him directly. So I wrote to our common friend Walter Rathenau, asking him to sound out Hauptmann confidentially. Rathenau refused—I never learned whether he did so with or without Hauptmann's knowledge —saying that the time for an intellectual understanding was not ripe. With that the whole plan faded, for then Thomas Mann was in the other camp, and had just expressed the German legal point of view in an article on Frederick the Great. Rilke, who I knew was on our side, refused to participate in any public and joint action as a matter of principle. Dehmel, the former socialist, proudly, with juvenile patriotism, signed his letters "Lieutenant Dehmel," and private conversations had convinced me that we could not count on Hofmannsthal or Jacob Wassermann. There was not much to be hoped for on the German side and Rolland was hardly more successful in France. In 1914 and 1915 it was still too early, and for the people of the hinterland the war was still too distant. We stood alone.

Alone, yet not entirely alone. We had yet accomplished something through our exchange of letters—a preliminary survey of the few dozen people in the warring or neutral nations upon whom we could count and who thought along our lines. We could direct each other's attention to books, articles, and pamphlets here and there. A certain crystallization point had been assured, to which—hesitatingly at first, but always more strongly because of the ever-growing pressure of the times—new elements could adhere. This feeling of not being entirely in the void encouraged me from time to time to write articles that would draw answers and reactions from the isolated and hidden people who sympathized with us. In spite of all, the important newspapers of Germany and Austria were at my disposal, which assured an important sphere of activity; and strangely enough there was no danger of opposition in principle from the authorities, for I never touched on current politics. Because of the effect of the liberal spirit, respect for all things literary was still very great, and when I re-read the articles which I was then able to smuggle out into the open I cannot withhold my respect for the generosity of the Austrian military authorities. It was possible for me in the midst of the World War to give enthusiastic praise to Berta von Suttner, the founder of pacifism, who had branded war as a crime of crimes, and to report in detail on Barbusse's *Le Feu* in an Austrian newspaper. Obviously we had to utilize a certain technique in spreading our inopportune views to the general public in a time of war. In order to picture the horrors of the war to the indifferent hinterland it was, of course, necessary for me to dwell upon the sufferings of a *French* soldier in my article *Le Feu,* but hundreds of letters from the Austrian front proved how clearly our people had recognized their own fate in that description. Or, in order to express our own convictions, we adopted a method of

apparently attacking one another. For example, one of my
French friends took issue with my "To Friends Abroad"
in the *Mercure de France*. By this attack, in which he
printed every single word of my article in translation, he had
succeeded in smuggling it over into France where everyone
could read it; and that, of course, had been his intention.
In such manner signal lights went up which were nothing
but signs of mutual recognition. How clearly they were understood by those for whom they were intended, was later
demonstrated to me by a slight incident. When in May
1915 Italy declared war upon Austria, its former ally, a
wave of hatred ensued. Everything Italian was insulted,
Dante was annexed (that is, it was ceremoniously declared
that the only great, supposedly Italian poet, had been a
Teuton) just as France had suddenly claimed Beethoven as
a Belgian. It chanced that in the memoirs of a young Italian
of the time of the Risorgimento, Carlo Poerio by name,
which had just appeared, there was a description of a visit
to Goethe. In order to point out, in the midst of all this
manifestation of hate, that the Italians had always been
closely and sympathetically allied to our culture, I wrote a
rather pointed article called "An Italian Visits Goethe,"
and as the book had an introduction by Benedetto Croce
I took the opportunity of devoting a few words to my high
esteem for the latter. Words of admiration for an Italian
uttered in Austria at a time when one was not supposed to
pay homage to any enemy writer or scholar could not but
signify something ulterior and as such they were recognized
beyond our borders. Croce, who was then in the Italian
Government told me later how one of the employees of the
Ministry, who could not read German, had informed him
in some dismay that Croce had been attacked in the principal enemy newspaper (for he could not conceive of a reference to the Minister as being other than unfriendly). Croce

ordered a copy of the *Neue Freie Presse* and was at first astonished to read words of admiration instead, then pleasantly amused.

~~

It is far from my purpose to overestimate these small, isolated essays. It goes without saying that they had not the slightest effect upon the course of events. But they helped us as well as many an unknown reader. They eased the horrible isolation, the spiritual despair, in which the truly humane person of the twentieth century found himself—as he finds himself today, after twenty-five years, again as powerless against the over-powering, if, as I fear, not even more so. At that time I was perfectly aware of the fact that I could not shake off my real burden by these small protests and devices; slowly I began to develop the plan of a work that was to enable me not only to express certain ideas, but also my considered attitude to time and race, catastrophe and war.

However, in order to describe the war in a poetic synthesis, I lacked the most important thing: I had not seen it. I had been anchored in an office for almost a year and there, in the invisible distance, the actual, true horror of war was being enacted. I had had opportunities to go to the front, and on three occasions important newspapers had offered me an assignment as war correspondent. But any sort of description would have carried the obligation to depict the war in an exclusively positive and patriotic sense, and I had sworn to myself—an oath which I still kept in 1940—never to write a single word that affirmed war or disparaged another nation. But an opportunity presented itself by chance. The great Austro-German offensive had broken through the Russian lines at Tarnow in the Spring of 1915, and Galicia and Poland had been conquered in one concentric attack. Now the War Archives wished to secure for its files all the original Russian proclamations and placards in the occupied Austrian area before they had been torn down or otherwise destroyed. The colonel, who happened to be aware of my collector's technique, asked me if I wished to undertake the task. Of course I accepted at once and I was given a passport which permitted me to travel on any military train and to move about freely wherever I chose without being assigned to any definite division and without having to report to any particular office or superior. This caused a number of the strangest occurrences, for I was not an officer but merely a titular sergeant-major, and wore a uniform without any special insignia. Whenever I produced my enigmatic document it elicited particular respect for the officers at the front and the officials thought that I must be some officer of the General Staff in disguise, or that I had been entrusted with some mysterious task. Since I avoided the officers' mess and stopped at hotels, I achieved the additional advantage of being outside of the great machine, and seeing whatever I wished to see without official "guiding."

My set task, that of collecting the proclamations, did not burden me greatly. Whenever I came into one of the Galician cities, Tarnow, Drohobycz, or Lemberg, I found a few Jews, so-called agents, whose profession it was to provide whatever one wished. It sufficed for me to tell one of these universal geniuses that I desired to obtain the proclamations and placards of the Russian occupation, and he ran off like a weasel and transmitted my wish in some mysterious fashion to dozens of other sub-agents; within three hours, without having taken a step myself, all the material had been collected for me in as complete a fashion as could be imagined. Because of this exemplary organization I had time to see much, and I saw much. Above all else, I saw the terrible misery of the civilian population, upon whose eyes the horror of what they had experienced lay like a shadow. I saw the unsuspected misery of the Jews in the ghettos, where eight or twelve of them would live in one room level with the ground or in a cellar. And, for the first time, I saw the "enemy." In Tarnow I came upon the first transport of captured Russian soldiers. Fenced within a large square, they sat about on the ground, smoking and chatting, guarded by two or three dozen mature, bearded Tyrolese militia who were as tattered and torn as their captives, and had but little in common with the smart, clean-shaven, brilliantly uniformed soldiers we saw pictured in the illustrated papers at home. But the guard had nothing martial or severe about it. The captives did not display the slightest desire to escape, nor the Austrian militia the slightest inclination to be strict about their duties. They sat about in a neighborly fashion with their captives, and the very fact that they could not understand each other's language caused huge enjoyment. They exchanged cigarettes and laughed at each other. A Tyrolese militia man was just taking some pictures of his wife and children out of a very old and dirty pocketbook and showing them to the "enemy," who passed them about amongst themselves asking the Austrian by means of their fingers if this child was three, or four. I could not escape the feeling that these simple, primitive people had understood the war more truly than our university professors and poets: namely, as a disaster that had come over them with which they had had nothing to do, and that everyone who had happened into this misfortune was somehow a brother. This knowledge comforted me on my entire trip past the shelled cities and the plundered shops, whose contents lay about in the middle of the streets like broken limbs or torn-out entrails. Then too, the well-tilled fields in between the war areas made me hope

that in a few years all the destruction would have disappeared. Obviously at that time I was unable to conceive
that just as quickly as the traces of the war would disappear
from the face of the earth, the memory of its horrors would
also as quickly disappear from the minds of men.

I did not face the actual horrors of war during those first
days, and when I did they exceeded my worst imaginings.
As there were practically no passenger trains, on occasion
I rode on an open artillery car, sitting on a caisson, or in
one of the cattle cars where men completely tired out slept
alongside and on top of each other in the midst of stench
and filth, and while they were being led to the slaughter,
already looked like slaughtered cattle. But the worst of all
were the hospital trains which I had to use two or three
times. How little they resembled the well-lighted, white,
carefully cleaned ambulance trains in which the archduchesses and the fashionable ladies of Viennese society had
their pictures taken as nurses at the beginning of the war!
What I saw to my dismay were ordinary freight cars without real windows, with only one narrow opening for air,
lighted within by sooty oil lamps. One crude stretcher stood
next to the other, and all were occupied by moaning, sweat-
ing, deathly pale men, who were gasping for breath in the
thick atmosphere of excrement and iodoform. The hospital
orderlies staggered rather than walked, for they were terribly tired; nothing was to be seen of the gleaming bed
linen of the photographs. Covered with blood-stained rags,
the men lay on straw on the hard wood of the stretchers,
and in each one of the cars there lay at least two or three
dead among the dying and groaning. I spoke with the doctor
who, as he admitted to me, had been nothing more than a
dentist in a small Hungarian village and had had no surgical
practice for years. He was in despair. He had already telegraphed ahead to seven stations for morphine. But none

was available; he had no more cotton, no fresh bandages, and it was still twenty hours away to the hospital in Budapest. He asked me to help him, for his own people were too fatigued. I tried, clumsy as I was, and found that I could at least be of some use in getting out at each station to fetch a few pails of water (bad, dirty water intended for the locomotive, but still refreshing), so that the men could be washed a bit, and the blood which was constantly dripping on the floor could be mopped up. Since all nationalities had been thrown together into this rolling coffin, the soldiers suffered additionally from the Babelish confusion of tongues. Neither the doctor nor the orderlies understood Ruthenian or Croatian. The only one who could be of some help was an old white-haired priest who—like the doctor who was in despair for want of morphine—complained for his part that he lacked the oil for the Last Sacraments. In all his long life he had never "administered" to so many people as during the past month. It was from him that I heard the words that I was never to forget, spoken in a hard, angry voice: "I am sixty-seven and I have seen much. But I would never have believed such a crime on the part of humanity possible."

~~

The hospital train in which I was returning arrived in Budapest in the early morning hours. I drove at once to a hotel to get some sleep; my only seat in the train had been my bag. Tired as I was, I slept until about eleven and then quickly got up to get my breakfast. I had gone only a few paces when I had to rub my eyes to make sure that I was not dreaming. It was one of those brilliant summer days that are spring in the morning and summer at noon, and Budapest was as beautiful and carefree as ever before.

Women in white dresses walked arm in arm with officers who suddenly appeared to me to be officers of quite a different army than that I had seen only yesterday and the day before yesterday. With the odor of iodoform of yesterday's ambulance train still in my clothes, my mouth, my nose, I saw how they bought bunches of violets and gallantly tendered them to their ladies, saw spotless automobiles with smoothly shaved and spotlessly dressed gentlemen ride through the streets. And all this but eight or nine hours away from the front by express train. But by what right could one judge these people? Was it not the most natural thing that, living, they sought to enjoy their lives?— that because of the very feeling that everything was being threatened, that they had gathered together all that was to be gathered, the few fine clothes, the last good hours! It was just because one had seen how frail and perishable man is, whose life with all its memories, ecstasies, and knowledge can be destroyed in the thousandth part of a second by a little piece of lead, that one understood why multitudes thronged to the gleaming river to join in the morning promenade, to see the sun, to feel themselves, their own blood, their own lives with perhaps heightened power. I had become almost reconciled to what at first had shocked me. But unfortunately the attentive waiter just then brought me a Viennese newspaper. I tried to read it; and only then was I filled with rage and disgust. Here were all the phrases about the inflexible will to conquer, about the petty losses of our own troops and the gigantic losses of the enemy. Here it jumped out at me, naked, towering and unashamed, the lie of the war! No, it was not the promenaders, the careless, the carefree, who were to blame, but those alone who drove the war on with their words. But we too were guilty if we did not do our part against them.

It was only now that the true impulse was given me: one had to fight against war! The material lay ready within me, only this last visible confirmation of my instinct had been lacking to make me start. I had recognized the foe I was to fight—false heroism that prefers to send others to suffering and death, the cheap optimism of the conscienceless prophets, both political and military who, boldly promising victory, prolong the war, and behind them the hired chorus, the "word makers of war" as Werfel has pilloried them in his beautiful poem. Whoever voiced a doubt hindered them in their patriotic concerns, whoever uttered a warning was ridiculed as a pessimist, whoever fought against the war in which they themselves did not suffer was branded as a traitor. It has always been the same, the eternal pack throughout the times, calling the prudent cowardly, the humane weak, only to be supine themselves in the hour of catastrophe which they themselves wantonly conjure up. It was always the same pack, the same who derided Cassandra in Troy, Jeremiah in Jerusalem, and never had I sensed the greatness and the tragedy of those figures as in these all too similar hours. From the very beginning I had no faith in victory and was certain of but one thing: that even if it could be achieved by immeasurable sacrifice, it could never justify that sacrifice. But I remained always alone among my friends with this warning, and the confused shouting about victory before the first shot, the division of the spoils before the first battle, often caused me to wonder if I alone were mad among all these wise men, or perhaps alone horribly aware in the midst of their intoxication. So it became only natural for me to describe my own situation, the tragic situation of the "defeatists"—the word had been invented to make those who strove for understanding seem to desire defeat—in a dramatic form. I chose for my symbol the figure of Jeremiah, the man of futile warnings. I had no intention of writing a "pacifist" play, or to set in words and verses the truth that peace was better than war, but to portray the man who in time of enthusiasm is despised as the weakling, the timid one, but who in the hour of defeat proves himself to be the only one able not only to endure it, but also to master it. From the time of my first play, *Thersites*, I had frequently occupied myself with the problem of the spiritual superiority of the vanquished. I was always tempted to depict the internal hardening which every form of power brings about in man, the spiritual numbness of an entire people which every victory entails, and to contrast it with the energizing power of defeat that plows through the soul so painfully and fruitfully. In the midst of war, while others, prematurely triumphant, were proving to one another the certainty of victory, I already threw myself to the lowest abyss of the catastrophe and was seeking the way out.

But in choosing a Biblical theme I had unknowingly touched upon something that had remained unused in me up to that time: that community with the Jewish destiny whether in my blood or darkly founded in tradition. Was it not my people that again and again had been conquered by all other peoples, again and again, and yet outlasted them because of some secret power—that power of transforming defeat through will, of withstanding it again and again? Had they not presaged, our prophets, this perpetual hunt and persecution that today again scatters us upon the highways like chaff, and had they not affirmed this submission to power, and even blessed it as a way to God? Had trial not eternally been of profit to all and to the individual? Happily, I realized this while working at my drama, the first of all my works that means something to me. I know

today: without all that I suffered in sympathy and in anticipation during the war, I would have remained the writer
I had been before the war, "pleasantly agitated," as certain
pieces of music are marked, but never fixed, composed and
responsive to my very vitals. Now for the first time I had the
feeling that when I spoke it came from myself and from
my time. In my effort to help others, I had helped myself
toward my most personal, most intimate work besides
Erasmus, by means of which in 1934, in the days of Hitler, I
extricated myself from a similar crisis. From the moment
when I attempted to shape them, I no longer suffered so
greatly from the tragedy of the times.

I had never believed for a single moment that my work
might have a visible success. Because of the many problems,
the prophetic, the pacifist, and the Jewish, and the choral
structure of the closing scenes which rise to a hymn of the
vanquished to his fate, the length of my poem had grown so
far beyond that of a normal drama, that an actual presentation would have required two or three evenings in the
theater. What is more, how could a play that not only
announced defeat but even praised it be given on a German
stage, while the papers were daily blasting forth "Victory
or annihilation"? It would even be miraculous if the book
were permitted to be published, but if the worst came
to the worst and nothing happened, it had at least helped
me at a dire time. I had said in poetic dialogue everything
that I had to withhold in my conversation with those around
me. I had thrown off the burden that had rested on my soul
and had been restored to myself; in the very hour in which
everything in me was "No" against the times, I had found
the "Yes" to myself.

XI

In the Heart of Europe

THE publication of my tragedy *Jeremiah* at Easter 1917, afforded me a surprise. I had written it in a spirit of exasperation against the time and had therefore to expect exasperated criticism. But just the contrary occurred. Twenty thousand copies of the book were sold at once, a fantastic quantity for a drama in book form; it received public backing not only from friends like Romain Rolland but as well from those who heretofore had stood rather on the other side, like Rathenau and Richard Dehmel. Producers to whom the drama had not even been submitted—a German production during the war was, of course, out of the question—wrote requesting that I reserve the rights for the world première for them after the war; and even the opposition of the bellicose manifested itself courteously. I had expected everything but this.

What had happened? Nothing other than in two and one-half years of war, time had effected its own cruel sobering. After the terrible blood-letting on the battlefields the fever had begun to abate. People were looking war in the face with colder, sterner eyes than during the first months of enthusiasm. The feeling of solidarity was loosening up, because there was no observable trace of the great "moral cleansing" that had been rapturously prophesied by the philosophers and poets. A deep split divided the whole people; it seemed as if the country had divided into two quite different worlds, that of the fighters at the front who were suffering the most terrible privations, and

255

the one of the stay-at-homes care-free, crowding the
theaters, and even profiting from the others' misery. Front
and hinterland contrasted with each other in growing,
intensity. Insidiously and in many disguises a repulsive
system of graft had entered officialdom; it was well known
that profitable contracts were to be had for cash or
through knowing the right people. Peasants and laborers,
already badly done in, were repeatedly driven back into
the trenches. In consequence everybody helped himself
unscrupulously as far as was possible. The prices of necessities rose daily because of shameless middlemen, food-
stuffs became scarcer and, phosphorescent above the gray
morass of mass-misery, like a will-o'-the-wisp, fluttered the
provocative luxury of the war profiteers. An embittered
distrust gradually took hold of the population: distrust of
currency, of constantly sinking purchasing power; distrust of generals, officers, and statesmen; distrust of any
report from the government or the General Staff; distrust of the newspapers and their news, distrust of the
war itself and of the need for it. Hence it was by no means
the literary content of my book that caused its surprising
success; I had merely uttered what others did not dare to
say openly: hatred of war, distrust of victory.

To express such sentiments in living, spoken words on
the stage was, however, seemingly impossible. Demonstrations would have been unavoidable and so I believed that
I would have to forego seeing this first drama against war
produced during war-time. Then, unexpectedly, I received
a letter from the director of the Zurich Stadttheater offering to produce my *Jeremiah* forthwith and inviting me
to attend the première. I had forgotten that there still was
—just as in this second war—a small but precious bit of
German earth that was blessed by the right to hold itself
aloof, a democratic land where speech was still free and

public opinion unclouded. Naturally, I assented immediately.

My acceptance, to be sure, could be no more than academic for it presupposed permission to leave my post and my country for a period. It proved lucky that each belligerent nation conducted a department—not known in this second war—under the name of Cultural Propaganda. To make clear the difference in the intellectual atmosphere between the First and Second World Wars, it becomes necessary to reiterate that the peoples, emperors, kings, who had matured in the traditions of humanity still cherished a subconscious shame about the war. One country after the other denied the charge of being or having been "militaristic" as an infamous slander; on the contrary, each one eagerly sought to show, to prove, to explain, to demonstrate that it was a "nation of culture." In 1914 the world that elevated culture above force would have rejected slogans like *sacro egoismo* and *Lebensraum* as immoral, for it held nothing to be more urgent than the appreciation of contributions to universal intellectual attainment. Thus neutral countries would be flooded with artistic offerings. Germany sent her orchestras under Furtwängler to Switzerland, to Holland, to Sweden, and Vienna its Philharmonic; the French organized exhibitions of paintings; even poets, authors, and scholars were sent abroad, but not to glorify military deeds or to foster annexationist tendencies, but solely to attest by means of their works, that the Germans were not "barbarians" and that they produced not only flame-throwers or good poison gases, but also absolute values worthy of Europe. It should be remembered that the world conscience was still a courted power in the years from 1914 to '18; the artistically productive, the moral elements of a nation, still represented a force in the war which was respected for its influence;

the nations still struggled to obtain human sympathy instead of employing inhuman terror as Germany did in 1939. My application for leave to attend a performance of a drama in Switzerland, therefore, had a good chance of being granted; if difficulties were to arise it would be only because it was an anti-war drama, in which an Austrian—even though only in symbolic form—considers defeat as a possibility. I secured an appointment with the head of my department and made my request of him. To my great surprise he immediately promised to give the necessary orders, adding this remarkable motivation: "You never were one of those stupid war-mongers, thank heaven. Well, do your best abroad to bring the thing to an end at last." Four days later I had my leave and a passport to go abroad.

~~

I had been rather surprised to hear one of the highest officials of an Austrian ministry talk so freely in the middle of the war. But, unfamiliar with the mysteries of politics, I did not suspect in 1917, that under the new Emperor Karl, a movement in the upper circles of the government had got quietly under way to cut loose from the dictatorship of German militarism which was dragging Austria, inconsiderately and against her real will, in the tow of its wild expansionism. Our General Staff hated Ludendorff's brutal domineering, our Foreign Office resisted desperately the adoption of unrestricted submarine warfare which was bound to make America our enemy, even the people muttered about "Prussian arrogance." For the time being such utterances were expressed in a cautious undertone, in seemingly purposeless remarks. But in the next few days I was to learn even more and, before anyone else, I ran unexpectedly close to one of the great political secrets of that time.

It happened thus: on the trip to Switzerland I stopped for two days in Salzburg where I had bought a house with the intention of living there after the war. In this city there was a small group of rigorously Catholic-minded men, two of whom were to play determining roles as chancellors in the post-war history of Austria, Heinrich Lammasch and Ignaz Seipel. The former was the most eminent teacher of public law of his day and had been chairman of the Peace Conference at The Hague; the other, Ignaz Seipel, a Catholic prelate of almost uncanny intelligence, was destined to take over the leadership of diminutive Austria after the collapse of the monarchy and upon that occasion give proof of his distinguished political genius. Both were pronounced pacifists, orthodox Catholics, fanatical Old-Austrians and, as such, in deep-rooted opposition to German, Prussian, Protestant militarism which they held to be incompatible with the traditional ideas of Austria and her Catholic mission. My drama, *Jeremiah*, had struck a sympathetic chord in such religious-pacifistic circles and Privy Councillor Lammasch (Seipel had just left town) asked me to visit him in Salzburg. The distinguished old scholar complimented me warmly on my book; it fulfilled our Austrian idea of conciliation, he said, and he hoped greatly that it would operate beyond its literary purpose. And to my astonishment, he confided to me, whom he had never seen before, with a frankness that testified to his intrinsic bravery, the secret that Austria stood at a decisive turning point. With the military elimination of Russia, there existed neither for Germany, if she would give up her aggressive tendencies, nor for Austria, a real obstacle to peace; the moment dare not be missed. If the pan-German clique in Germany continued to resist negotiations, Austria would have to take the initiative and act independently. He indicated that the young Emperor Karl had promised his support of their purposes; the result of his personal policy might very shortly become evident. All depended now on whether Austria could muster enough energy to put through a negotiated peace instead of the "Victorious Peace" which the German military party demanded regardless of further sacrifices. At a pinch they would have to go the limit: Austria would have to renounce its alliance in good time, before the German militarists dragged her down to catastrophe. "Nobody can accuse us of a breach of faith," he said firmly and determinedly. "More than a million of our men are dead. We have sacrificed and done enough! Now, no more human lives, not a single one for German world-domination."

It took my breath away. We had all thought those things privately many times but none had had the courage to say in broad daylight: "Let us renounce the Germans and their expansionist aims while there is time," because that would have been to "betray" our brother-in-arms. And here it was being uttered to me, practically a stranger, by one who enjoyed his Emperor's confidence at home and the esteem of those abroad who knew his participation in the Hague Conference; he spoke with such calm and determination as to convince me that an Austrian-separatist movement was no longer in the stage of preparation but actually in train. It was a bold idea to bend Germany towards negotiations by a threat of a separate peace or, in an emergency, to execute the threat; it was then, as history attests, the last and only possibility of saving the Empire, the monarchy and thus Europe. Alas, the manner of carrying it out was lacking in the determination that marked the original plan. Emperor Karl actually sent his wife's brother Prince Sixtus with a secret letter to Clemenceau, for the purpose of sounding out the chances of peace and perhaps of taking initial steps, without a prior understanding with the court in Berlin. How this secret mission became known to Germany has not yet, I think, been fully revealed; unfortunately Emperor Karl was without the courage to declare his conviction publicly, be it that Germany, as some contend, threatened a military invasion of Austria, or that he as a Habsburg feared the odium of renouncing at the decisive moment an alliance made by Emperor Franz Josef and sealed by so much blood. In any event, he did not call Lammasch or Seipel to the post of prime minister, the only ones who, as Catholic internationalists, would from inner moral conviction have had the strength to take upon themselves the odium of deserting Germany; and this hesitation became his undoing. Both of them became prime ministers only of the mutilated Austrian Republic instead of the old Habsburg Empire, yet nobody would have been better able to justify the seeming injustice before the world than this great and respected teacher of public law. If Lammasch had openly threatened to break away, or had broken away, he would not only have preserved Austria but would also have saved Germany from her innermost danger, her unbridled impulse to annex. Europe would be better off if the project which that wise and pious man then revealed to me had not been ruined by weakness and clumsiness.

～

The next day I traveled onward and crossed the Swiss frontier. It is hard to make intelligible what the transition from a walled-in and half-starved country at war to a neutral zone signified at that time. It took but a few minutes from one station to the other, but in the very first second one was sensible of such a change as that of suddenly stepping from a closed suffocating room into invigorating and snow-filled air, of something like a giddiness which trickled palpably from the brain through all one's nerves and senses. In the years that followed whenever I passed this station, Buchs, on my way out of Austria that strange sensation of sudden relief flashed into my mind. Passengers leaped from the train and found there—our first surprise!—at the buffet all the things which they had long forgotten as once belonging to the commonplaces of life; there were golden oranges, bananas; chocolate and ham, things which we were used to getting only by slinking to back doors were frankly displayed; there was bread and meat, obtainable without bread cards or meat cards —and truly like hungry beasts they attacked the cheap magnificence. There was a post and telegraph office from which one could write and wire uncensored to the four corners of the world. There lay French, Italian and English newspapers which one could buy, and read with impunity. Here the interdicted was available, while five minutes distant the available was interdicted. The whole paradox of European wars became almost physically clear to me through this contiguity. In the tiny village beyond, the posters and signs of which one could read from here with the naked eye, men had been taken out of every little house or hut and shipped to the Ukraine and Albania, to murder and to be murdered while here, within eyeshot, men of like age sat with their wives peacefully before their ivy-framed doors, smoking their pipes. I found myself asking whether the fish in this frontier rivulet were belligerents on the right bank and neutral on the left. In the moment of crossing the border I was already thinking differently, more freely, more actively, less servilely, and on the very next day I had evidence that not only our mental state but our physical organism as well declines within a world at war; the guest of relatives, after dinner I drank nonchalantly a cup of black coffee and smoked a Havana cigar when suddenly I became dizzy and experienced violent palpitations. After many months of *ersatz* supplies my body and my nerves proved unequal to real coffee and real tobacco; the change from the abnormality of war to the normality of peace called for a corporal adjustment, too.

That unsteadiness, that agreeable dizziness, carried over to the mental plane. Every tree struck me as more beautiful, every mountain bolder, every prospect as more gracious; for, inside a country at war the rhythmical calm of a meadow appears to the gloomy eye to be insolent indifference on Nature's part, each purple sunset recalls spilled blood; while here, where peace reigned normally, the noble aloofness of Nature had again become natural and I loved Switzerland as I had never loved it before. I had always enjoyed visiting the land, so magnificent within its small area and so inexhaustible in its variety. Never, however, had I been so conscious of the significance of its being; the Swiss idea of the meeting of nations on one spot without enmity; of elevating lingual and national differences to brotherhood by mutual respect and honestly realized democracy—what an example for the whole of harassed Europe! Refuge of the persecuted, the centuries-old abode of peace and freedom, hospitable to all opinions while faithfully treasuring its own particularity—how momentous the existence of this single supernational country for our world! I could well feel this to be a land blessed with beauty and opulence. None was a stranger in it; an independent human being felt more at home here in this tragic hour of world history than on his native soil. For hours at a stretch I was driven to stride through the streets of Zurich and along the lake shore. The lights radiated peace, the population pursued life in quiet composure. I seemed to sense that the walls did not shelter women lying sleepless abed for thoughts of their sons; I saw no wounded or mutilated; no young soldiers ready to be loaded into trains tomorrow or the next day—here one felt more entitled to live whereas in a country at war it had become embarrassing and almost an offense to be free of wounds.

However, it was not discussions about my production nor meetings with my Swiss and other friends that seemed most urgent. I wanted above everything to see Rolland who, I knew, could add to my firmness, clarity, and efficiency, and I wanted to thank him for what his encouragement and friendship had done for me in the days of bitter mental solitude. He was my first objective so I proceeded to Geneva at once. We "enemies" found ourselves in a somewhat complicated situation. It goes without saying that the belligerent governments did not like their subjects to have personal intercourse with those of enemy nations in neutral territory. But no law forbade it and there was no statute according to which a meeting was punishable. Only business intercourse, "trading with the enemy," the equivalent of treason was forbidden so, in order not to arouse suspicion of the slightest infraction of this ban, we would refrain, on principle, from even offering each other cigarettes, for innumerable agents were undoubtedly constantly on watch. In order to overcome any thought of fear or guilt on our part, we international friends adopted a policy of complete candor. We used no pseudonyms or secret addresses in our correspondence, we did not meet furtively at night but walked the streets and frequented the cafés together. Thus, immediately after arriving in Geneva I told the hotel *portier* my name and asked for M. Romain Rolland just because it was better that the German or French intelligence bureau should be able to report who I was and whom I was visiting; for our part it was out of the question for two old friends suddenly to avoid each other because they accidentally belonged to two different nations which accidentally were at war with each other. We felt no obligation to participate in an absurdity merely because the world behaved absurdly.

At last, then, I was in his room—almost it seemed to me to be the one in Paris. Here, too, stood the table and chair covered with books. Magazines, letters, and papers spilled from the writing table; the unpretentious, monastic working surroundings were the emanation of his very being, and were the same wherever he might be. For a moment words failed me, we merely clasped hands; his was the first French hand I had touched in years. It was three years since I had spoken to a Frenchman, yet in that period Rolland and I had approached each other more closely than ever. I spoke more intimately and frankly in the foreign language than I had with anyone at home. I was fully aware that the friend with whom I stood face to face was the most important man of this crucial hour, that in him the moral conscience of Europe was speaking. It was only now that I could survey all that he was doing and had done in his magnificent service to mutual understanding. Working night and day, always alone, without help, without a secretary, he kept in touch with all efforts everywhere, conducted a vast correspondence with people who asked for advice in matters of conscience and wrote copiously in his diary every day; like none other in his time he was conscious of the responsibility of living in a historical epoch and he regarded it as a duty to leave a record for the future. (Where may they be today, those many manuscript volumes of diaries which will once throw full light on the moral and intellectual conflicts of that First World War?) Meanwhile he published articles, of which every one excited international attention, and labored on his novel *Clerambault*—devotedly and unsparingly he staked his whole life on the great responsibility which he had assumed; to deal in every particular as an exemplar of human justice in the midst of mankind's insane fit. No letter remained unanswered, no pamphlet on current topics was left unexamined. This feeble delicate man, whose health was just then badly threatened, who could speak only in low tones and always struggled with a slight cough, who needed the protection of a shawl if he entered a corridor and had to rest after every rapid step, invoked powers which, under the strain of the claims made upon them, expanded unbelievably. Nothing agitated him, neither attack, nor treachery, his outlook on the world in turmoil was fearless and direct. In him I perceived the other heroism, the spiritual and moral, as in a living monument; in my book on Rolland it is perhaps inadequately celebrated on account of the reserve that we have about too high praise of the living. For days after I saw him in his tiny room from which invisible invigorating rays went out to every zone, I continued to feel deeply stirred and, after a fashion, purged, and I know that the uplifting, tonic-energy which Rolland evolved through his almost single-handed battle against the insane hatred of millions is to be reckoned among those imponderables which defy calculation and measurement. Only those of us who were witnesses of that epoch know what his being and his exemplary steadfastness signified. It was he who preserved the conscience of a Europe fallen into madness.

In the talks of that afternoon and the following days I was touched by the faint mourning which clothed his words; it was the same as when one discussed war with Rilke. He was bitter about politicians and those who in their national vanity were insatiable in their desire for sacrifices from others. But all the while one felt his sympathy for the countless mass who suffered and died for a purpose they themselves did not comprehend and which, after all, was purposeless. He showed me Lenin's telegram imploring him to accompany him to Russia in that notorious sealed train because of the value of Rolland's moral authority to his cause. But Rolland remained firmly determined to align himself with no group but to serve independently and alone the cause to which he had dedicated himself: the common cause. He demanded of none that they submit to his ideas and likewise he withheld commitment to others. He wanted those who loved him to remain free themselves and he wished to serve as an example in only one thing: how one can remain free and faithful to one's own conviction even against the whole world.

~~~

On my first evening in Geneva I met the little group of Frenchmen and other foreigners who were attached to two small independent newspapers, *La Feuille* and *Demain*, J. P. Jouve, René Arcos, Frans Masereel. We became close friends with that quick élan with which only youth forms friendships. But we felt instinctively that we were on the threshold of an entirely new life. Most of our old associations had been vitiated by the patriotic delusion of our former colleagues. New friends were needed and, since we were drawn up on a common front, in a common intellectual trench, against a common enemy, an ardent comradeship formed itself spontaneously; after twenty-four hours we were as close as if we had known each other for years. We were aware—"we few, we happy few, we band of brothers"—of the mixture of personal hazard and unwonted boldness that marked our association; we knew that five hours off any German who spied a Frenchman and any Frenchman who spied a German fell on him with his bayonet or destroyed him with a hand grenade and was decorated for it, that millions on both sides, dreamed only of exterminating each other, that the newspapers frothed at the mouth about the "enemy" while we, this handful among many millions, not only congregated at table peacefully but in a spirit of genuine warm fraternity. We knew that this was against official rules and regulations; we knew that such frank manifestation of friendship jeopardized us in relation to our respective countries; but the very danger whipped our presumption to an almost ecstatic ascent. We wanted to take risks and we enjoyed the pleasure of those risks, for risk alone gave weight to our protest. I went so far as to join in a public appearance in Zurich with J. P. Jouve—the event was unique in war-time—he read his poems in French, I parts of my *Jeremiah* in German; the mere fact of our laying our cards on the table was evidence of the sincerity of our audacious game. We were indifferent to the opinion of our consulates and embassies; even if it meant that we had burned our ships behind us and, like Cortez, were unable to return home. For deep in our souls we were permeated with the belief that the "traitors" were not ourselves but those who were false to the poet in his call at the fortuitous hour. And those young Frenchmen and Belgians did live heroically! There was Frans Masereel who, before our eyes, carved a lasting pictorial monument of the war in his woodcuts against the horror of war, those memorable black and white prints which, in power and wrath, are not inferior to Goya's *Desastros de la guerra.* By day and night this indefatigable man produced new figures and scenes from the mute wood; his narrow room and kitchen were already piled with wooden blocks, yet every morning a fresh graphic indictment of his appeared in the *Feuille,* none of them a charge against a particular nation but all against the common enemy: war.

It was our dream that these grim gruesome pilloryings,
wordless yet intelligible to even the lowliest, might, in
leaflet form, be showered from airplanes in place of bombs
on cities and armies; I am confident that the war would
thus have met premature death. But the pity is that they
appeared only in the little sheet, *La Feuille,* which hardly
got beyond Geneva. Whatever we uttered and attempted
was confined within Swiss limits and only became oper-
ative when it was too late. Privately we were under no
delusion about our powerlessness against the big machine
of the general staffs and the political authorities; and if
they took no action against us, it was perhaps because we
constituted no danger to them, what with speech frowned
upon and our field limited. But just our sense of fewness
and isolation, drew us closer together, shoulder to shoulder, heart to heart. Never in my riper years did I respond
to friendship with such enthusiasm as in those hours at
Geneva, and the bond has survived the years.

~~~

The most noteworthy figure of this group, from the
point of view of psychology and history but not of art, was
Henri Guilbeaux. He was a living confirmation of the
irrevocable historical law that in epochs of precipitate
overturns, particularly during wars or revolutions, pluck
and boldness often count for more in short periods than
intrinsic worth, and impetuous courage in civil life can
signify more than character and dependability. Whenever
time hurtles forward in headlong rapidity, certain natures
that know the trick throw themselves unhesitatingly on
the incoming wave and thus get the start of others. And
in those days there were many merely ephemeral personalities which time lifted over and beyond themselves—
Bela Kun and Kurt Eisner—up to a point which their true

capacity could not match. Guilbeaux, a slim, blond, little man with sharp, restless gray eyes, and the gift of gab, was not a gifted person. Even though it was he who had translated my poems into French (almost a decade earlier), I must frankly denominate his literary ability as inconsiderable. His command of language was not more than average; his education was not profound. His entire power lay in controversy. He was one of those unfortunate people who always have to be "against" something, no matter what. He was satisfied only when, like a naughty boy, he could raise a row and charge against something that was stronger than himself. In Paris, before the war, although a good-natured lad he was always involved in some contentiousness against literary movements or writers, then hung around the radical parties but none was radical enough for him. Then, with the war on, as an antimilitarist he had suddenly encountered a gigantic adversary: the World War. In the light of the fear and cowardice that marked the majority, his bold and audacious manner of entering the fight gave him a momentary importance, even indispensability. The danger that frightened others was the very thing that tempted him. In contrast with the performance of others his great daring served to stimulate his literary and controversial abilities to an abnormal level, and gave this otherwise unimportant writer a sudden greatness—a phenomenon not unlike that disclosed among the petty attorneys of the Gironde during the French Revolution. Where others were silent, where we ourselves hesitated and pondered every project, he would act, and it is to Guilbeaux's lasting merit that he established and conducted the only anti-war periodical of the First World War of intellectual substance, *Demain*, a document to be studied by all who wish really to understand the spiritual tendencies of that epoch. He supplied what we needed: a center of international, supernational discussion in the midst of the war. Rolland's backing fixed the importance of the paper and his moral leadership and his connections afforded Guilbeaux the best co-workers in Europe, America, and India. Furthermore, Lenin, Trotzky, and Lunacharsky, revolutionaries then still in exile from Russia, trusted Guilbeaux's radicalism and contributed regularly to *Demain*. For a year or two the world knew no more interesting or more independent periodical, and if it had survived the war it might have become a positive influence on public opinion. Meanwhile Guilbeaux undertook the representation in Switzerland of those French radical groups which Clemenceau had rudely gagged. At the celebrated Congresses of Kienthal and Zimmerwald at which the internationally-minded Socialists separated from those who had gone patriotic, he played a historic rôle; no Frenchman, not even that Captain Sadoul who joined the Bolsheviks in Russia, was feared and hated as much in political and military circles of Paris during the war as this little fair-haired person. The French espionage bureau managed to trip him up in the end. Blotting-paper and carbon-copies were stolen from the room of a German agent in a Berne hotel, but they were evidence of nothing more than that certain Germans had placed subscriptions to *Demain*, a fact innocent in itself because German thoroughness probably required the paper for various libraries and bureaus. But the pretext was sufficient for Paris to denounce him as an agitator in German pay and to indict him. In default of appearance he was sentenced to death, quite unjustly, as was proved by the revocation of the sentence when the trial was reviewed ten years later. But hard upon this, because of his violence and intransigence which began to endanger Rolland and the rest of us, he got into trouble with the Swiss authorities and was put into jail. Then Lenin, who liked him personally and was grateful for his assistance in dark days, saved him by a stroke of the pen which transformed him into a Russian citizen, and had him shipped to Moscow in the second sealed train. At last he had a chance to reveal his creative ability. Possessing all the badges of a genuine revolutionary—jail and death sentence *in contumacium*—he had in Moscow a second field for good work. Just as Rolland's support helped him in Geneva, he could, because of Lenin's faith in him, have made a positive contribution to the rebuilding of Russia; and again, his courageous stand during the war fitted him better than any other to wield directive influence in parliament and on the public in post-war France, because all radical groups saw him as a real, active, bold man, the born leader. The truth is that Guilbeaux turned out to be anything but a natural leader; rather, like so many war poets and revolutionists, he was no more than the product of a passing hour. Natures that are out of equilibrium always suffer collapse after an abrupt rise. In Russia Guilbeaux frittered away his talents in endless controversies, in quarrels, and petty intrigues just as he had formerly done in Paris; gradually, too, he fell out with those who had respected his courage, first with Lenin, then with Barbusse and Rolland, and eventually with all of us. He wound up in a less dramatic time, just as he began, with his pamphlets and petty quarrels; soon after his reprieve he died obscurely in Paris. He was the boldest and bravest in the war against war and if he had known how to use and be worthy of the impulse with which the time endowed him he might have become a great figure of our epoch. Today he is forgotten and perhaps I am one of the last who still remember him with gratitude for the war achievement which *Demain* constituted.

After some days in Geneva I returned to Zurich for conversations about putting my play in rehearsal. I always had loved this city for its beautiful location on the lake in the shadow of the mountains, and not less for its distinguished, a bit conservative culture. But owing to Switzerland's peaceful setting among belligerent countries Zurich had emerged from its reserve and in a trice had become the most important city of Europe, a meeting place of all intellectual trends, to be sure, it had become equally a center for every sort of trafficker, speculators, spies, propagandists who, for their sudden affection, were eyed by the native population with quite justifiable suspicion. Every language was to be heard in restaurants, cafés, streetcars and on the street. Everywhere one ran into acquaintances, desirable and undesirable ones, and whether or no, one was caught in a stream of excited argument. For all the people whom fate had washed here depended for their future on the outcome of the war; some were here for their governments, others were persecuted and proscribed; each one, however, detached from his real being and hurled into fortuitousness. Homeless as they were, they constantly sought social intercourse and, as they were in no position to shape or influence military and political events, they spent nights and days in a fever of debate which was at once stimulating and fatiguing. After years of being gagged it was pleasant to yield to the urge of setting ideas on paper, now that at last there was no censor over thinking and writing; in our high-strung state even mediocrities, (as illustrated by Guilbeaux) acquired a greater degree of interest than ever before or than they would possess in the future. All languages and every shade of political thought was present. Alfred A. Fried, bearer of the Nobel peace prize, published his *Friedenswarte* here, Fritz von Unruh, former Prussian officer, gave readings of his dramas,

Leonhard Frank wrote his provocative *Der Mensch ist gut,*
Andreas Latzko caused a sensation with his *Menschen im
Kriege,* Franz Werfel came to deliver a lecture; I met men
from all nations in my old hotel Schwerdt where Casanova
and Goethe had been guests in their time. I encountered
Russians who bobbed up later in the revolution and whose
real names I never knew, Italians, Catholic priests, uncompromising socialists and uncompromising German belligerents; the admirable Pastor Leonhard Ragaz and the poet
Roebert Faesi were among our Swiss stand-bys. At the
French book store I ran into my translator Paul Morisse,
at the concert hall the conductor Oscar Fried—all sorts
and conditions were there, all sorts of opinions were
uttered, absurd and rational, so that there was food for
annoyance, irritation, enthusiasm. Magazines were founded,
polemics fought over, extremes would meet or cause the
differences between them to intensify, coalitions formed
and others split apart; I have never since faced a more
motley and zealous medley of opinions and people in a
form so concentrated and steaming, as it were, than in
those Zurich days, nights, rather, for the debates in the
Café Bellevue or Café Odéon lasted until lights were
switched off, and often we would go to someone's home
after that. Landscape, mountains, lakes and their enfold-
ing calm went unnoticed in this bewitched world; life
meant newspapers, bulletins, and rumors, opinions, ex-
plications. And, oddly, one lived the war in one's mind
more intensively than at home in a country at war, because
here the problem became objective, and so to speak, wholly
detached from any national interest in victory or defeat.
The war was seen, no longer from a political standpoint,
but rather as a European matter, as a horrible and mighty
happening which was not merely to change some boundary
lines on the map but the form and future of our world.

The people in this circle who affected me most deeply —perhaps by way of premonition of my own future fate— were the ones without a country or, worse still, who instead of one had two or three fatherlands and were inwardly uncertain to which they belonged. A young man with a little brown beard, with keen eyes behind strikingly thick lenses sat, usually alone, in a corner of the Café Odéon; they told me that he was a highly gifted English author. When I became acquainted with James Joyce a few days after that, he harshly rejected all association with England. He was Irish. True, he wrote in the English language but did not think in English and didn't want to think in English. "I'd like a language," he said, "which is above all languages, a language to which all will do service. I cannot express myself in English without enclosing myself in a tradition." This was not quite clear to me; I did not know of his *Ulysses,* on which he was then working; he had merely lent me *A Portrait of the Artist as a Young Man,* his only copy, and his little drama *Exiles* which I had thought to translate in order to be of use to him. The better I knew him the more his incredible knowledge of languages astonished me; his round firmly sculptured brow, which shone smooth like porcelain in the electric light, stored every vocable of every idiom and he was brilliantly able to toss and keep them balanced in the air. Once when he asked how I would reproduce a difficult sentence in the *Portrait of an Artist* in German, we attempted it first in French and then in Italian; for every word he was prepared with four or five in each idiom, even those in dialect, and he knew their value and weight to the finest nuance. He was inclined to be testy, and I believe that just that irritation produced the power for his inner turmoil and productivity. His resentment against Dublin, against England, against particular persons became converted into dynamic energy and actually found release only in literary creation. But he seemed fond of his own asperity; I never saw him laugh or show high spirits. He always made the impression of a compact, somber force and when I saw him on the street, his thin lips pressed tightly together, always walking rapidly as if heading for a definite objective, I sensed the defensive, the inner isolation of his being even more positively than in our talks. It failed to astonish me when I later learned that just this man had written the most solitary, the least affined work—meteor-like in its introduction to the world of our time.

Another of those living amphibiously between two nations was Feruccio Busoni, by birth and education an Italian, by choice a German. From my early youth I had cared for none among virtuosos as much as for him; when he played the piano his eyes took on a dreamy brightness. Below, his hands, effortless, made music, unique perfection; but above, the handsome soulful head, thrown back a little, listened and drank in the music which he created. Then something like transfiguration seemed to claim him. Many times in concert halls I had regarded, fascinated, this refulgent face, while the sounds, gently lashing and silvery clear, thrust into my blood. Now I saw him again and his hair was gray and his eyes shadowed by sadness. "Where do I belong?" he asked me once. "If I wake out of a dream at night, I know that I spoke Italian in the dream. Then when I begin to write, I think in German words." His pupils were scattered all over the world—"perhaps they are shooting at each other right now"—and he dared not undertake the work before him, his opera *Doctor Faust*, because he was too distracted. He wrote a short, light, musical one-act play by way of release, but the cloud did not lift from him during the war. Only seldom did I hear his jolly vehement,

Aretinian laughter which I used to like in him so much. And late one night I saw him in the railroad station restaurant; he had drunk two bottles of wine by himself. As I passed he called to me. "Narcotic!" he said, pointing at the bottles, "not drink! But there are times when one has to take a narcotic or one can't stand it. Music won't always do it and the time isn't always propitious for good work."

The discordant situation was most burdensome for the Alsatians, and worst off among them were such as René Schickele whose hearts were loyal to France but whose language was German. The war was actually being fought over their country and the scythe cut straight through their hearts. They were being dragged to the right and to the left, they were being squeezed to declare loyalty to Germany or to France. But they loathed such "either" and "or" which was impossible for them. Like the rest of us they wanted Germany and France to be brothers; understanding, not enmity, hence they suffered from both and for both.

Surging about, besides, was the helpless crowd of the semi-aligned, those of mixed loyalties, English women married to German officers, French mothers of Austrian diplomats, with one son on this side and the other on that, where the parents here and parents there waited for letters; those whose small possessions had been confiscated on one side, those who had lost jobs on the other. All thus disrupted had escaped into Switzerland to elude the suspicion which dogged them in their old country no less than in the new. Fearing to compromise those on one side or the other, they avoided talking in either language and slunk about like shadows, destroyed and broken existences. The more European a life a man had lived in Europe, the harder he was punished by the fist that battered Europe.

Meanwhile the time for producing *Jeremiah* had come. It was a nice success and I was not greatly disquieted by the *Frankfurter Zeitung's* report to Germany that the American minister and other prominent allied personages had been present. We felt that the war, now in its third year, was suffering an internal decline and that to oppose its continuance (which Ludendorff alone compelled) was now less risky than in the early sinful days of its glory. A conclusion would have to be reached in the fall of 1918. But I no longer wished to spend this waiting time in Zurich. Little by little I had become more vigilant and more observant. In my initial enthusiasm I had thought to find earnest partisans of my opinions among all these pacifists and anti-militarists, honest, determined fellows-in-arms for European unity. Soon, however, I became aware that among seeming refugees and martyrs in heroic causes, there were some dubious characters who served the German intelligence bureau and were paid to spy and eavesdrop. It became obvious that sound and peaceful, quiet and solid Switzerland was being undermined by the mole-like activities of secret agents from both camps. The chambermaid who emptied the waste basket, the telephone operator, the grave waiter who came suspiciously close, were employed by enemy power, the same person often in the pay of both. Luggage would be mysteriously unlocked. blotters were photographed, letters disappeared on the way to or from the post office. Elegant women smiled at one invitingly in the hotel lobbies, strangely eager pacifists unknown to one would show up to request a signature to a proclamation or sanctimoniously to ask for addresses of "reliable" friends. A "socialist" offered me a suspiciously high fee for a lecture before the workingmen in Chaux de Fonds who, it proved, knew nothing about it; one had to be always on guard. It was not long before I learned how few there were who could be regarded as absolutely reliable, and as I had no desire to be dragged into politics I kept to myself more and more. But even in the society of the unimpeachable I was bored by the barrenness of the everlasting discussions and the arbitrary pigeonholing of radical, liberal, anarchist, bolshevik and non-political; this was my first proper insight into the eternal type of the professional revolutionary who feels himself lifted out of his insignificance by the mere fact of being in opposition and who clings to his dogma for want of resources within himself. To stick it out in this confusing babel meant to become confused myself, to cultivate unsafe associations and to jeopardize the ethical foundation of my convictions. So I withdrew. The truth is that not one of those café-conspirators ever dared a conspiracy, not one of those improvised cosmic thinkers ever was able to formulate a policy when the need was present. When the time came for a positive note, with the reconstruction after the war, they were stuck fast in their carping, nagging negativism, much the same as all but a very few of the anti-war poets succeeded in producing anything of consequence after the war. It was the fever of the time that manifested itself in poetry, argument, and debate, using them as a medium and, as with all groups which owe their union to a momentary conjuncture and not to a living experience, this whole circle of interesting gifted people went up in smoke as soon as the object of their resistance—the war—was gone.

I picked a little inn in Rüschlikon, about half an hour from Zurich, as a good place to settle in; from its hills I could survey the whole lake and just see the distant towers of the city. I was under no obligation to see any but those whom I invited, my real friends; and they came, Rolland and Masereel. Here I was able to work and to make good use of time which took its inexorable course. America's entry into the war made it plain to all who were not dazzled and deafened by patriotic patter that German defeat was inevitable: when the German Kaiser came out plump with the announcement that he intended to rule "democrat-ically," we knew that the jig was up. I frankly admit that we Austrians and Germans, in spite of allegiance to spirit and language, were impatient for the inevitable, once it had become inevitable, to hasten its course, and the day when Kaiser Wilhelm, sworn to fight to the last breath of man and horse, fled across the border and General Luden-dorff, who had sacrificed millions of men for his "Vic-torious Peace," made for Denmark with a pair of blue spectacles, brought us much comfort. For we were con-fident—as was the whole world—that this war had done for all war, that the beast which had devastated our world had been overcome and killed. We believed in Wilson's magnificent program which was quite our own; in the East, during the honeymoon of the Russian revolution and its humane idealistic pattern, we perceived a vaguely spreading illumination. We were foolish, I know it. But we were not the only ones. Those whose lives spanned that time remem-ber that the streets of every city resounded with cheers to acclaim Wilson as the savior of the world, that the hostile soldiers embraced and kissed each other; never was Europe so filled with faith as in the first days of peace. At last the earth was yielding place to the long promised empire of justice and brotherhood; now or never was the hour for the united Europe of our dreams. Hell lay behind us; what was there to frighten us after that! Another world was about to begin. We were young, and said to ourselves: it will be the world of our dreams, a better, a humaner world.

XII

Homecoming to Austria

FROM the standpoint of reason the most foolish thing I could do after the collapse of the German and Austrian arms was to go back to Austria, that Austria which showed faintly on the map of Europe as the vague, gray and inert shadow of the former Imperial monarchy. The Czechs, Poles, Italians, and Slovenes had snatched away their countries; what remained was a mutilated trunk that bled from every vein. Of the six or seven millions who were forced to call themselves "German-Austrians," two starving and freezing millions crowded the capital alone; the industries which had formerly enriched the land were on foreign soil, the railroads had become wrecked stumps, the State Bank received in place of its gold the gigantic burden of the war debt. Boundary lines were still unsettled, the Peace Conference having scarcely begun; reparations had not been fixed, there was no flour, bread, or oil; there appeared to be no solution other than a revolution or some other catastrophe. According to all human prevision it was impossible for the country—an entity artificially created by the victors—to exist independently and, in the unanimous opinion of all parties, Socialsit, Clerical, and Nationalist, it had no wish to exist independently. It was the first instance in history, as far as I know, in which a country was saddled with an independence which it exasperatedly resisted. Austria wished, either to be united with its former neighbor states or with its kindred Germany, but not to lead the humiliated life of a beggar in this mutilated form. But the neighbor states wanted no economic union, partly because they thought Austria too poor and partly for fear of a return of the Habsburgs; *Anschluss* with Germany was forbidden by the Allies because it might strengthen that defeated nation. Hence the decree that the Austrian Republic was to persist. A country that did not wish to be got its orders: You must exist!

As I look back I can hardly explain what moved me to return voluntarily in those direst days that ever afflicted a country. Yet, when all is said and done, we of the prewar era had grown up with a pronounced sense of duty and it seemed, particularly in an hour of distress, as if family and home ties were calling. There was something like cowardice in smoothly evading the oncoming tragedy and, especially as the author of *Jeremiah*, I felt the responsibility of helping to surmount the defeat by means of my art. Superfluous in time of war, I considered my present stand to be the correct one after the defeat, just because my opposition to the prolongation of the conflict had given me a certain moral position, especially with young people. And even if nothing were to come of it there was at least the satisfaction of sharing in the predicted common suffering.

At that time a visit to Austria called for preparations similar to those for an Arctic expedition. Warm clothes and woolen underwear were needed because it was known that across the border there was no coal with winter at the door. Shoes had to be soled for there were none but wooden soles over there. Provisions and chocolate in such quantities as Switzerland permitted were taken so that the traveler could keep going until he received bread and fat ration cards. It was the practice to insure luggage for the maximum amount allowed since most baggage cars were looted and shoes and clothing were irreplaceable; the only time that I prepared myself similarly was when I traveled to Russia ten years later. I hesitated a moment at Buchs, the frontier station at which I had experienced so much joy upon arrival a year before, and cogitated whether it might not yet be wiser to go back. I felt that it was a turning point in my life. I concluded in favor of the difficult way and boarded the train again.

~~~

Buchs had afforded me an exciting moment a year earlier; now, upon my return, a no less memorable one awaited me at Feldkirch, the Austrian border station. Upon alighting I became aware of an odd restlessness among the customs officers and police. They paid small attention to us and made their inspection in a most negligent manner; plainly something important was to happen. At last came the bell that announced the approach of a train from the Austrian side. The police lined up, the officials piled out of their offices, their womenfolk, evidently in the know, crowded together on the platform. I was particularly struck by an old lady in black with her two daughters, from her carriage and clothes presumably an aristocrat. She was visibly excited and constantly pressed her handkerchief to her eyes.

Slowly, almost majestically, it seemed, the train rolled near, a special sort of train, not the customary, shabby, weather-beaten kind, but with spacious black cars, a train de luxe. The locomotive stopped. There was a perceptible stir among the lines of those waiting but I was still in the dark. Then I recognized behind the plate glass window of the car Emperor Karl, the last emperor of Austria standing with his black-clad wife, Empress Zita. I was startled; the last emperor of Austria, heir of the Habsburg dynasty which had ruled for seven hundred years, was forsaking his realm! He had refused to abdicate formally, yet the Republic granted every honor on the departure which it compelled rather than submitted. The tall serious man at the window was having a last look at the hills and homes, at the people of his land. The historic moment was doubly shocking to me who had grown up in the tradition of the Empire, whose first song at school had been the *Kaiserlied* and who had taken the military oath to obey "on land, at sea, and in the air" this serious and thoughtful looking man in mufti. Innumerable times had I seen the old emperor in the long since legendary splendor of elaborate celebrations; I had seen him on the great staircase of Schönbrunn, surrounded by his family and brilliantly uniformed generals, receiving the homage of the eighty thousand Viennese school children, massed on the broad green plain, singing, their thin voices united in touching chorus, Haydn's *Gott erhalte*. I had seen him at the Court ball, at the *Théâtre Paré* performances in glittering array, and again in Ischl, riding to the hunt in a green Tyrolean hat; I had seen him marching devoutly, with bowed head, in the Corpus Christi procession to the Cathedral of St. Stephen, and then the catafalque, on that foggy, wet winter day in the midst of war, which bore the aged man to his last rest in the Capuchin crypt. "The Kaiser!" From earliest childhood we had learned to pronounce those words reverently for they embodied all of power and wealth and symbolized Austria's imperishability. And now I saw his heir, the last emperor, banished from his country. From century to century the glorious line of Habsburg had passed the Imperial globe and crown from hand to hand, and this was the minute of its end. All of those who stood about sensed history, world history, in this tragic sight. The gendarmes, the police, the soldiery were embarrassed and looked abashed because uncertain whether the traditional recognition was still in order, the women hardly dared to look up, all were silent and thus the faint sobbing of the old lady in mourning who had come heaven knows what distance, only to see "her" emperor once more, was plainly audible. At last the conductor gave the signal. Everybody stared up mechanically, the irrevocable instant had come. The locomotive started with a violent jerk as if it too had to overcome a disinclination, and slowly the train withdrew. The officials followed it with a respectful gaze, after which, with that air of embarrassment which is observable at funerals, they returned to their respective stations. It was the moment in which the almost millenary monarchy really ended. I knew it was a different Austria, a different world, to which I was returning.

~~~

Hardly was the train out of sight when we were obliged to change from the spruce, clean Swiss cars into the Austrian. One had but to enter them to become aware beforehand of what had happened to the country. The guards who showed us our seats were haggard, starved and tatterdemalion; they crawled about with torn and shabby uniforms hanging loosely over their stooped shoulders. The leather straps for opening and closing windows had been cut off, for every piece of that material was precious. Predatory knives or bayonets had had their will of the seats, whole sections of the covering having been rudely removed by such as needed to have their shoes repaired and obtained their leather wherever it was to be had. Likewise the ashtrays were missing, stolen for the sake of their mite of nickel or copper. Through the broken windows the late fall wind blew the soot and cinders of the miserable lignite with which the locomotives were fueled. It smudged the floor and walls, but its odor at least tempered the smell of iodoform, a reminder of the sick and wounded who had been transported in these skeleton cars during the war. That the train moved at all was a miracle, even if a wearisome one; every time the unlubricated wheels shrieked a little less shrilly we were afraid that the work-worn engine had given up the ghost. Distances which used to take an hour now required four or five, and when dusk set in we remained in darkness. The electric bulbs had either been smashed or stolen so that whoever searched for anything had to feel his way about with matches; and if we did not freeze, it was only because we had been crowded together throughout, with six or eight people in each compartment. New passengers had been crowding in from our very first stop, and more continued to come, all of them already weary with hours of waiting. The corridors were jammed and some people even spent the semi-wintry night on the steps of the cars. Everyone held on to his baggage anxiously and hugged his package of provisions close; no one dared separate himself from a possession for a single minute in the darkness. From the midst of peace I was riding back into the horror of war which I had thought to be over.

Just before reaching Innsbruck the locomotive suddenly began to rattle and in spite of much puffing and whistling failed to master a small hill. The railway men ran to and fro excitedly with their smoking lanterns. An hour passed before an emergency engine came panting and it took us seventeen instead of seven hours to get to Salzburg. There was no porter in sight and eventually some ragged soldiers offered to carry our baggage. My cab horse was so old and undernourished that it seemed as if the shafts were there to sustain him rather than he to draw the vehicle. The spectral beast did not inspire me with belief, that he could pull the luggage-filled cab so, though I feared I would never see them again, I deposited my bags at the station. During the war I had bought myself a house in Salzburg because the estrangement from my former friends as a result of our opposite attitude to the war had aroused my desire to live away from big cities and masses of people; this withdrawal did indeed prove of advantage to my work later.

Of all Austrian towns Salzburg seemed to me the most ideal, not merely scenically but also because of its geographical position for, at Austria's edge, I could get to Munich in two and one half hours by train, to Vienna in five, to Zurich or Venice in ten and to Paris in twenty, thus the right springboard to Europe. To be sure, it was then not yet the meeting place for the "prominent" of the earth (or I should not have chosen it to work in) or famous for its festival plays, but an old-time, sleepy, romantic little town on that last slope of the Alps where the hills gently resigned themselves to the German plain. The little wooded hill on which I lived was the dying wave, so to speak, of the mighty mountain chain; inaccessible to automobiles and attainable only by a hundred or more stairs up a way of the Cross that was over three centuries old, the effort was rewarded by an enchanting view over the roofs and gables of the many-steepled city. Beyond it the panorama opened into the glorious chain of the Alps (including, too, the Salzberg at Berchtesgaden where, before long, the then obscure Adolf Hitler was to live across from me). The house itself proved as romantic as it was impracticable. A seventeenth-century archbishop's hunting lodge, it rested against a great fortress wall; late in the eighteenth century it had been enlarged by a room at either side. A splendid old tapestry and a decorated bowling ball which Emperor Franz himself, upon a visit to Salzburg in 1807, had rolled down the long corridor of our house, besides some ancient parchment attesting the chain of ownership were tangible evidence of a rather impressive past.

The fact that this diminutive manor house whose broad front made an impression of magnificence—it had little depth and contained but nine rooms—was an antique curio, tended to charm our visitors, but at the time its historic past manifested itself unhappily. We found our home in almost uninhabitable condition. The rain dripped merrily into the rooms, after every snowfall the halls were flooded. A thorough repair of the roof was impossible because the carpenters had no lumber for rafters, the tinsmith no lead for gutters; the worst leaks were painstakingly covered with tar-paper and when fresh snow fell there was no alternative to a personal clambering on the roof so as to remove the load in good time. The telephone mutinied, iron having been used for the wire instead of copper; every little item had to be lugged up the hill since nobody made deliveries. Worst of all was the cold for there was no coal for miles around; the wood cut on the place was too green and hissed like a snake instead of heating, and sputtered instead of burning. In our need we utilized peat which at least gave the semblance of warmth, but for three months I did my writing almost exclusively in bed with blue, frozen fingers which I would warm under the blanket after every finished page. But even this meager accommodation was not to be disparaged because, in this year of catastrophe, besides the dearth of provisions there was a housing famine too. There had been no building construction in Austria for four years; many houses had crumbled, and now, suddenly, countless discharged soldiers and prisoners flowed back, homeless, so that, under compulsion, each available room was allotted to a family. Commissions visited us four times, but we had long since yielded two rooms voluntarily, and now the insufficiency of our house which had been a trial to us at first turned out to be beneficent; nobody else cared to climb that hundred steps only to freeze after getting up.

Every descent into the town at that period was a moving experience; it was my first sight of the yellow and dangerous eyes of famine. The bread crumbled into black particles and tasted like pitch and glue, coffee was a brew of roasted barley, beer like yellow water, chocolate like colored sand and the potatoes were frozen. Most people raised rabbits, in order not wholly to forget the taste of meat; a young lad shot squirrels in our garden for his Sunday dinner and well nourished dogs or cats returned only seldom from lengthy prowls. Such textiles as were for sale were no more than specially treated paper, *ersatz* for an *ersatz*; men crept about almost always dressed in old uniforms—even Russian uniforms—which they had obtained from some depot or hospital and in which more than one had already died; trousers tailored from old sacks were not uncommon. Every step through the street, where show-windows had a plundered look, where decaying houses shed crumbling mortar like scurf, where visibly undernourished people painfully dragged themselves to their work, served to trouble one's soul. Out in the country the food situation was better; no peasant-farmer allowed himself to be influenced by the general breakdown of morale to sell his butter, eggs, or milk at the legally prescribed "maximum prices." He concealed his goods wherever he could and waited at home for the highest bidder. This procedure gave rise to the "black market." A man would set off with an empty bag or two and go from farm to farm, sometimes even taking the train to particularly productive illicit sources of provisions which he would then peddle in town at four and five times the cost price. In the beginning the peasants gloated over the shower of paper money for which they had sold their butter and eggs, and which made them profiteers. However, when they brought their bursting wallets to town to make purchases, they discovered to their exasperation that while they had merely quintupled normal prices, the scythe, the hammer, the kettle which they had come to buy had meanwhile risen twenty or fifty times in price. Thereafter they sought to exchange only for manufactured goods and demanded substance for substance, merchandise for merchandise; mankind with its trenches having been content to retrogress to cave-dweller times, it now dissolved the thousand-year-old convention of money and reverted to primitive barter. The whole country was seized with a grotesque traffic. The city dwellers hauled out to the farms whatever they could get along without— Chinese porcelain vases and rugs, sabers and rifles, cameras and books, lamps and ornaments—thus, entering a Salzburg peasant's home, one might be surprised by a staring Indian Buddha or a rococo book case with French leather-bound books of which the new owners were particularly proud. "Genuine Leather! France!" they bragged impressively. Substance, anything but money, became the watchword. There were those who had to take their wedding ring from their finger or the leather belt from around their body merely to keep that body alive.

Finally the authorities interfered to stop the subversive trade in the execution of which none but the well-to-do derived benefit; in every province cordons were thrown around key points and illicit goods arriving by train or bicycle were confiscated for the benefit of the municipal food offices. The hoarders responded by organizing nightly deliveries by lorry with Western desperado accompaniment or by bribing inspectors, themselves the fathers of hungry children; sometimes there were real battles with revolvers and knives which these youths, after four years of practice at the front, knew how to use just as well as they knew the approved military way of finding cover when in flight. The chaos grew from week to week, the population became more excited. The progressive devaluation of money became increasingly manifest. The neighboring states had substituted their new currency for the old Austro-Hungarian notes, thus saddling tiny Austria with the main burden, more or less, of redeeming the old krone. The first sign of distrust was the disappearance of hard money, for people tended to value a bit of copper or nickel more highly than mere printed paper. The government did its best to get maximum note production from the printing presses, following Mephistopheles' prescription, but it could not keep pace with the inflation; then every city and town, eventually every village, began to print its own "emergency money" which neighboring villages could reject and which, for the most part, was recognized to be worthless and was thrown away. An economist who knew how to describe graphically all the phases of the inflation which spread from Austria to Germany, would find it unsurpassed material for an exciting novel, for the chaos took on ever more fantastic forms. Soon nobody knew what any article was worth. Prices jumped arbitrarily; a thrifty merchant would raise the price of a box of matches to twenty times the amount charged by his upright competitor who was innocently holding to yesterday's quotation; the reward for his honesty was the sale of his stock within an hour, because the news got around quickly and everybody rushed to buy whatever was for sale whether it was something they needed or not. Even a goldfish or an old telescope was "goods" and what people wanted was goods instead of paper. The most grotesque discrepancy developed with respect to rents, the government having forbidden any rise; thus tenants, the great majority, were protected but property owners were the losers. Before long, a medium-size apartment in Austria cost its tenant less for the whole year than a single dinner; during five or ten years (for the cancellation of leases was forbidden even afterwards) the population of Austria enjoyed more or less free lodgings. In consequence of this mad disorder the situation became more paradoxical and unmoral from week to week. A man who had been saving for forty years and who, furthermore, had patriotically invested his all in war bonds, became a beggar. A man who had debts became free of them. A man who respected the food rationing system starved; only one who disregarded it brazenly could eat his fill. A man schooled in bribery got ahead, if he speculated he profited. If a man sold at cost price, he was robbed, if he made careful calculation he yet cheated. Standards and values disappeared during this melting and evaporation of money; there was but one merit: to be clever, shrewd, unscrupulous, and to mount the racing horse instead of being trampled by it.

To top it all, during the financial whirlwind when Austrians were deprived of every economic yardstick, certain foreigners recognized how our misery might be made to serve their purposes. The only thing that remained stable within the land during the three years in which the inflation progressed at accelerating tempo was foreign currency. Because Austrian money melted like snow in one's hand everyone wanted Swiss francs or American dollars and foreigners in substantial numbers availed themselves of the chance to fatten on the quivering cadaver of the Austrian krone. Austria was "discovered" and suffered a calamitous "tourist season." Every hotel in Vienna was filled with these vultures; they bought everything from toothbrushes to landed estates, they mopped up private collections and antique shop stocks before their owners, in their distress, woke to how they had been plundered.

Humble hotel clerks from Switzerland, stenographers from Holland, would put up in the de luxe suites of the Ringstrasse hotels. Incredible as it may seem, I can vouch for it as an eyewitness that Salzburg's first-rate Hotel de l'Europe was occupied for a period by English unemployed, who, because of Britain's generous dole were able to live more cheaply at that distinguished hostelry than in their slums at home. Whatever was not nailed down, disappeared. The tidings of cheap living and cheap goods in Austria spread far and wide; greedy visitors came from Sweden, from France; more Italian, French, Turkish and Rumanian was spoken than German in Vienna's business district. Even Germany, where the inflation started at a much slower pace even if eventually to become a hundred thousand times greater than Austria's, exploited our shrinking krone to the advantage of her mark. Salzburg, a border town, afforded me an opportunity to observe these daily raids. Bavarians from neighboring villages and cities poured into the little town by hundreds and by thousands. They patronized the tailor, they had their cars repaired, they consulted physicians and bought their drugs. Munich business men mailed their foreign letters and filed their cables from Austria so as to pocket the saving in the rates. Then, at the instigation of the German Government, a border control was established to stop Germans from buying their supplies in Salzburg where a mark fetched seventy Austrian crowns. Merchandise coming from Austria was strictly confiscated at the custom house. One article, however, that could not be confiscated remained free of duty: the beer in one's stomach. And the beer-drinking Bavarians would watch the daily rate of exchange to determine whether the falling krone would allow them five or six or ten liters of beer in Salzburg for the price of a single liter at home. No more superb enticement could be imagined, and so they would come in hordes with their wives and children from nearby Freilassing and Reichenhall to enjoy the luxury of gulping down as much beer as belly and stomach would hold. Every night the railway station was a veritable pandemonium of drunken, bawling, belching humanity; some of them, helpless from overindulgence, had to be carried to the train on hand-trucks and then, with bacchanalian yelling and singing, they were transported back to their own country. The merry Bavarians did not, to be sure, suspect how terrible a revenge was in store for them. For, when the krone was stabilized and the mark in turn plunged down in astronomic proportions, it was the Austrians who traversed the same stretch of track to get drunk cheaply, and the spectacle was duplicated but this time in the opposite direction. This beer war between two inflations remains one of my oddest recollections because it was a precise reflection, in grotesque graphic miniature, of the whole insane character of those years.

~

The strangest thing is that I cannot recall, however I may try, how we kept house during that era, or in what manner the Austrians kept on raising the thousands and tens of thousands of kronen and the Germans, in their turn, the millions which were daily needed to keep body and soul together. Mysteriously enough, they did raise them. Habits are acquired and the chaos became normal to life. It stands to reason that one who was not a witness would imagine that, at a time when an egg cost what a fine motor-car used to cost, (in Germany eggs went up to four billion marks, the approximate past value of all the real estate in Greater Berlin, women must have been running wildly through the streets with tousled hair, that shops were deserted for lack of purchasing power and that theaters and amusement places were surely empty. Astonishingly enough, just the opposite was the case. The will to pursue life was great enough to overcome the instability of the currency. Financial chaos prevailed yet the daily round seemed little affected. There were widespread individual changes, such as those who had wealth in the form of cash in bank or government bonds became impoverished, speculators became rich. But the balance-wheel maintained its rhythm unconcerned with single fates, there was no standstill; bakers baked bread, cobblers made boots, authors wrote books, peasants sowed and reaped, trains ran on schedule, the morning newspaper never failed, and it was just the places of entertainment, bars, and theaters, that were filled to capacity. The very fact that what once represented the greatest stability—money—was dwindling in value daily caused people to assess the true values of life-work, love, friendships, art and Nature the more highly, and the whole nation lived more intensively and more buoyantly than ever despite the catastrophe; young people went on mountain tramps and returned healthily tanned, dance halls kept going until late at night, new factories and business enterprises sprang up. I don't think that I ever lived and worked with greater zest than in those years. Whatever had meant much to us in days gone by meant even more now; at no time had we ever been so devoted to art in Austria as in those years of chaos, because the collapse of money made us feel that nothing was enduring except the eternal within ourselves.

I shall never forget what an opera performance meant in those days of direst need. For lack of coal the streets were only dimly lit and people had to grope their way through; gallery seats were paid for with a bundle of notes in such denominations as would once have been sufficient for a season's subscription to the best box. The theater was not heated, thus the audience kept their overcoats on and huddled together, and how melancholy and gray this house was that used to glitter with uniforms and costly gowns! There never was any certainty that the opera would last into the next week, what with the sinking value of money and the doubts about coal deliveries; the desperation seemed doubly great in this abode of luxury and imperial abundance. The Philharmonic players were like gray shadows in their shabby dress suits, undernourished and exhausted by many privations, and the audience, too, seemed to be ghosts in a theater which had become ghostly. Then, however, the conductor lifted his baton, the curtain parted and it was as glorious as ever. Every singer, every musician did his best, his utmost, for each had in mind that perhaps it might be his last time in this beloved house. And we strained and listened, receptive as never before, because perhaps it was really the last time. That was the spirit in which we lived, thousands of us, multitudes, giving forth to the limit of our capacity in those weeks and months and years, on the brink of destruction. Never have I experienced in a people and in myself so powerful a surge of life as at that period when our very existence and survival were at stake.

～～

I would be hard put to it to explain how Austria pillaged and desolate, managed to escape disintegration. In Bavaria, to our right, a Communist Workers' Republic had been established, Hungary, on our left, had gone bolshevik under Bela Kun; and to this day I cannot comprehend how it was that the revolution did not seize Austria. There was certainly no lack of explosive material. Underfed, tattered, returned soldiers lounged about observing resentfully the scandalous profligacy of those who profited by the war and the inflation; a "Red Guard" battalion was already on the alert in the barracks and there was no sort of counter-organization. A couple of hundred determined men could have gained mastery over Vienna and the whole of Austria then. But nothing of any consequence happened. There was one time when a raw gang attempted a *Putsch* but fifty or sixty armed policemen put it down easily. And then the miracle occurred: cut off from its sources of power, its factories, its coal mines, its oil fields, with an avalanche of worthless paper currency, the thoroughly looted nation maintained and asserted itself; it may have been because of its weakness, for the people were too exhausted and hungry to struggle for anything, but perhaps it was through the mysterious strength peculiar to Austria: its innate conciliatoriness. For in the critical hour the two largest parties, Social Democrats and Christian Socialists, despite their fundamental differences formed a coalition government. There were mutual concessions in order to prevent a catastrophe which might have swept all of Europe with it. In due time life became ordered and integrated and, surprisingly enough, the incredible came to pass: the crippled state persisted and was even ready to defend its independence when Hitler came to rob this folk—faithful and magnificently brave in suffering—of its soul.

But it was only outwardly and in a political sense that radical change was averted; a tremendous inner revolution occurred during those first post-war years. Something besides the army had been crushed: faith in the infallibility of the authority to which we had been trained to over-submissiveness in our own youth. But would it have been expected of the Germans to keep on admiring their Kaiser who first swore to fight "to the last breath of horse and man" and then fled across the border under cover of night and mist? Of their military leaders, their politicians, and their old poets who ground out commonplace patriotic rhymes? It was only after the smoke of war had lifted that the terrible destruction that resulted became visible. How could an ethical commandment still count as holy which sanctioned murder and robbery under the cloak of heroism and requisition for four long years? How could a people rely on the promises of a state which had annulled all those obligations, to its citizens which it could not conveniently fulfill? It was the same old clique, the so-called men of experience who now surpassed the folly of the war with their bungling of the peace. It is common knowledge today, and a few of us knew it then, that the peace offered one of the greatest, if not the greatest, moral potentialities of history. Wilson knew it. In his comprehensive vision he sketched the plan for a veritable and enduring world agreement. But the old generals, the old statesmen, the old captains of industry had snipped that great concept to bits and reduced it to worthless paper. The sacred promise to the world that this war would be the last war alone served to buoy up the already half-disappointed, half-exhausted and despairing soldiers, but it was cynically sacrificed to the interests of the merchants of death and to the gambling passion of the politicians who successfully played their old, fateful game of negotiations and secret treaties behind the screen of Wilson's wise and humane demands. To the extent that it was wide-awake the world knew that it had been cheated. Cheated the mothers who had sacrificed their children, cheated the soldiers who came home as beggars, cheated those who had subscribed patriotically to war loans, cheated all who had placed faith in any promise of the state, cheated those of us who had dreamed of a new and better ordered world and who perceived that the same old gamblers were turning the same old trick in which our existence, our happiness, our time, our fortunes were at stake. Small wonder, then, that the entire youthful generation looked with exasperation and contempt at their fathers who had permitted first victory, then the peace to be taken away from them; who had done everything wrong, had been without prescience and had everywhere miscalculated. Was it not intelligible that the new generation lost every trace of respect? It doubted parents, politicians, teachers; every decree, every proclamation of the state was read with a dubious eye. The post-war generation emancipated itself with a violent wrench from the established order and revolted against every tradition, determined to mold its own fate, to abandon bygones and to soar into the future. It was to be a quite new world in which fresh regulations were to govern every phase of life; and, as was to be expected, the new life began with gross excesses. Anybody or anything older than they were was put on the shelf. Children as young as eleven or twelve went off in organized *Wandervögel* troops which were well instructed in matters of sex, and traveled about the country as far as Italy and the North Sea. Following the Russian pattern "pupils' councils" were set up in the schools and these supervised the teachers and upset the curriculum, for it was the intention as well as their will to study only what pleased them. They revolted against every legitimated form for the mere pleasure of revolting, even against the order of nature, against the eternal polarity of the sexes. The girls adopted "boyish bobs" so that they were indistinguishable from boys; the young men for their part shaved in an effort to seem girlish; homosexuality and lesbianism became the fashion, not from an inner instinct but by way of protest against the traditional and normal expressions of love. The general impulse to radical and revolutionary excess manifested itself in art, too, of course. The new painting declared all that Rembrandt, Holbein, and Velasquez had created as finished and done for, and set off on the most fantastic cubistic and surrealistic experiments. The comprehensible element in everything was proscribed, melody in music, resemblance in portraits, intelligibility in language. Every sort of liberty was taken with grammar, sentence structure was wrecked, prose read like a telegram with peppery interjections; besides which, such literature as was not activistic, that is, not saturated with political theorizing, went on the dust heap. Music stubbornly sought a new tonality and did violence to the rules, architecture twisted houses inside out, the dance saw the waltz replaced by Cuban and Negro forms; fashion in dress, heavily accenting nudity, invented multiform absurdities, the theater disclosed *Hamlet* in evening dress and essayed fulminating dramatics. In that epoch of wild experiment in every field everybody desired to surpass at a single impetuous leap, whatever had been achieved in the past; the younger one was, the less he knew, the better he suited the situation because of his freedom from all tradition: at last youth's vengeance against the world of parents raged itself out triumphantly.

Nothing was more tragi-comic in this riotous carnival than the attitude of the elder intellectuals who, in a panic of fear of being considered behind the times, rushed desperately to the cover of an artificial egregiousness and dragged themselves through devious paths in the hope of keeping up with the procession. Respectable, proper, gray-bearded academicians painted over their now unsalable still life with symbolic cubes and dice, because the young curators—they had to be young, and the younger the better —regarded all other pictures as too "classic" and were removing them from the galleries to the basements. Writers who had used plain, direct language for decades obediently hacked their sentences apart and excelled in "activism," complacent Prussian Privy Councillors expounded Karl Marx from their lofty university seats, old-time ballerinas in a state of undress performed stylized gyrations to Beethoven's *Appassionata* and Schönberg's *Verklärte Nacht.* Bewildered old age everywhere pursued the latest fashion; the paramount ambition was to be "young" to discover in some new, and unheard of and more radical tendency a substitute for the outmoded tendency of yesterday.

How wild, anarchic and unreal were those years, years in which, with the dwindling value of money all other values in Austria and Germany began to slip! It was an epoch of high ecstasy and ugly scheming, a singular mixture of unrest and fanaticism. Every extravagant idea that was not subject to regulation reaped a golden harvest: theosophy, occultism, spiritualism, somnambulism, anthroposophy, palm-reading, graphology, yoga and Paracelsism. Anything that gave hope of newer and greater thrills, anything in the way of narcotics, morphine, cocaine, heroin found a tremendous market; on the stage, incest and parricide, in politics, communism and fascism, constituted the most favored themes; unconditionally proscribed, however, was any representation of normality and moderation. But I would not for anything wipe out that era of chaos, neither from my own life nor from art in its onward movement. Thrusting forward in the orgy of its first impulse it had, like every spiritual revolution, swept the air clean of all stuffy tradition, and relieved the strains of many years; for all that may be said its daring experiments have left a residuum of valuable stimuli. Much as some of its excesses amazed us, we did not feel justified in any arrogant censure or rejection for, in essence, this youth of the new day was seeking to correct—though perhaps with too great fire and impatience—what our cautious and aloof generation had failed in. Their instinct that the post-war period had to be different from the one before the war was fundamentally correct. Had not we oldsters also longed for a new and better world before and during the war? Admittedly the elders had again disclosed, after the war, their inability to erect opportunely any supernational defense against the new political orientation that menaced the world. While peace negotiations were still in progress Henri Barbusse, known throughout the world for his novel *Le Feu*, attempted to unite all European intellectuals in the spirit of conciliation. "Clarté" was to be the name of this group—the clear-thinking—and its purpose was to unite writers and artists of all nations in a pledge to oppose future mischief-making among the nations. Barbusse invited me and René Schickele to undertake leadership of the German group, a task of no small difficulty, for irritation over the Treaty of Versailles still smoldered in Germany. The prospect of gaining Germans of rank for intellectual internationalism while the Rhineland, the Saar, the bridgehead at Mainz, were occupied by foreign troops was meager. And yet such an organization would have been possible, just as Galsworthy realized one later in the P.E.N. Club, if Barbusse had not let us down. Unfortunately, as the result of a visit to Russia where great masses had demonstrated their enthusiasm for his person, he became convinced that bourgeois states and democracies were incapable of bringing about a genuine fraternity of peoples and that such world brotherhood was feasible only in Communism. Unnoticeably he sought to make of "Clarté" an instrument of class struggle but we objected to a radicalization which, of necessity, would have weakened our ranks. Thus the project, in itself a distinguished thing, collapsed prematurely. Once more we had failed in the struggle for intellectual freedom for too great love of individual freedom and independence.

There remained but to withdraw in work, quietly, and in retirement. From the point of view of the expressionists and, may I say, the excessivists, my thirty-six years made me eligible for the elder generation that was already disposed of, because I declined any ape-like adherence. My earlier works now failed to please even me and I refused to have any books of my "aesthetic" period reprinted. That meant beginning afresh and waiting for the impatient tide of the many "isms" to ebb, and in this lot of my own choosing my indifference to personal preferment proved helpful. I began my large *Master Builders* series just because of the certainty that it would occupy me for years, I wrote such stories as *Amok* and *Letter from an Unknown Woman* in quite "unactivistic" unconcern. The land in which I lived, the world about me, began to assume form and order, and my day of hesitation was past, too; gone was the time when I could pretend to myself that whatever I essayed was solely for the time being. The middle of life had been reached, the age of mere promises had gone by, the time had come to confirm promises, to stand the test, or to give up for good.

XIII

Into the World Again

For three years, 1919, 1920, 1921, Austria's three hardest post-war years, I lived buried in Salzburg, practically giving up hope of ever seeing the world again. The collapse after the war, the hate abroad against every German and all German writing, and the devaluation of our currency were so catastrophic that one was already resigned from the start to stay put for life in one's narrow sphere at home. But everything turned out much better. We ate our fill again. We sat undisturbed at our desks. There had been no plundering, there was no revolution. We lived, we sensed our powers. Why not once more test the pleasure of one's youth and travel?

Long journeys were out of the question. But Italy lay near, no more than eight or ten hours distant. Should one try it out? Although Austrians were considered the "arch-enemy" over there, they had never considered themselves to be so. Would one have to let oneself be snubbed, pass by old friends so as not to embarrass them? I took a chance and, one day at noon, crossed the frontier.

I arrived at Verona in the evening and went to a hotel. I was given a form and registered. The clerk glanced at the paper and looked up startled when, under "nationality," he read the word *Austriaco.*

"Lei è Austriaco?" he asked. I wondered whether I would be rejected. But when I said "yes" he was almost jubilant. *"Ah, che piacere! Finalmente!"* This was the first greeting and a renewed confirmation of a sense, already felt during

the war; that the entire hate propaganda and agitation had produced but a brief intellectual fever without fundamentally affecting the real masses of Europe. A quarter of an hour later the friendly clerk even came to my room to make sure that I was comfortable. He praised my Italian enthusiastically and we parted with a cordial handshake.

The next day I was in Milan. I saw the cathedral again, strolled through the Galleria. It was pleasant to hear again the beloved musical Italian language, to be confident of finding one's way about and to enjoy the strangeness as something familiar. Passing a large building the sign *Corriere de la Sera* caught my eye. At once I remembered that my old friend G. A. Borgese was an important member of the editorial staff there, Borgese with whom, together with Count Keyserling and Benno Geiger, I had spent many an intellectually elevating evening in Berlin and Vienna. One of Italy's best and most earnest writers, especially influential with the youth of the land, he had, although the translator of *Werthers Leiden* and a fanatic on German philosophy, aligned himself sharply against Germany and Austria and, shoulder to shoulder with Mussolini (with whom he broke later on), pressed for war. Throughout the war it had been a strange thought for me that an old comrade was an active participant on the other side; the more now I felt a desire to see such an "enemy." Just the same, I did not wish to chance being turned away. So I left my card for him with the address of my hotel. But I was not even down the stairs when someone ran after me, his highly animated face aglow with pleasure. It was Borgese; in five minutes we were talking as cordially as always, perhaps even more so. He too was the wiser for the war and, approaching each other from opposite banks, we came closer together than ever.

And it occurred thus everywhere. In Florence, my old friend Albert Stringa, a painter, rushed up to me on the street and embraced me so vehemently and unexpectedly that my wife, who was with me and did not know him thought this strange bearded man intended to attack me. Everything was the same as of old, no, even more cordial. I sighed with relief. The war was buried. The war was over.

But it was not over. We merely did not know it. We all deceived ourselves in our credulity and mistook our personal readiness for that of the world. But we need not be ashamed of this error, for no less than ourselves, the statesmen, the economists, and the bankers were also mistaken and during those years also thought that the deceptive boom meant recovery, and weariness contentment. Actually the struggle had only transposed itself, from the national into the social; and in those very first days I witnessed a scene the far-reaching implications of which did not become clear to me until later. In Austria, we knew no more about the Italian internal situation than that together with the post-war disappointment, definite socialistic and even bolshevistic tendencies had gained foothold. Many walls bore, crudely traced in charcoal or chalk, *Viva Lenin.* Furthermore, one had heard that a socialist leader, by name Mussolini, had separated from his party during the war and had organized a counter-group. But one received news of that sort with indifference. What significance could one attach to just another little bloc! Petty conspiracies of the kind lodged in all lands; there were "free corps" marching about in the Baltic provinces, separatist groups constituted themselves in Bavaria and the Rhineland, demonstrations and riots occurred everywhere but were nearly always suppressed. Nobody thought of regarding these "Fascists" who wore black shirts instead of the Garibaldi red, as an important factor in the future development of Europe.

But in Venice the mere word became suddenly invested with meaning. From Milan I arrived in the beloved city of the lagoons, in the afternoon. There were no porters, no gondolas; workers and railroad employees stood around idly, their hands almost conspicuously in their pockets. Since I was lugging two pretty heavy bags around with me, I looked about for help and asked an elderly gentleman where one could find a porter. "You arrived on a bad day," he answered regretfully. "But we have many such days now. There is a general strike again." I did not know why there was a strike and I didn't trouble to inquire further. We were too accustomed to such things in Austria where the Social Democrats, much to their undoing, too frequently used this most potent of weapons without ever following through. So I toiled on painfully with my bags, until finally, from a side canal I saw a gondolier beckoning to me furtively and he took me and my suitcases in. After half an hour, passing by many a clenched fist raised against the strike-breaker, we arrived at the hotel. With the spontaneity of habit I immediately went to the Piazza San Marco. It looked strikingly deserted. The shutters of most of the stores were closed, nobody sat in the cafés, only a large number of workers stood around under the arcades in small groups, like people waiting for a particular thing to happen. I waited with them and, suddenly, it came. From a side alley a company of young people, in regular formation approached in a rapid march step, confidently singing a song, the words of which were unfamiliar to me—later I knew it to be the *Giovanezza*. They had already passed in their running step, swinging their sticks, before the crowd, a hundred times greater in numbers, had had time to pounce upon its adversary. This bold and really audacious demonstration on the part of this small organized group had happened so quickly that by the time the crowd became aware of the provocation it was too late for them to catch up with their adversaries. Angrily they pressed together and shook their fists, but it was too late. The little storm troop was beyond reach.

Visual impressions always have something convincing about them. Now, for the first time, I knew that this hazy Fascism, until then almost unknown to me, was something real, something well directed and that it made fanatics of decided, bold, young people. No longer could I agree with my older friends in Florence and Rome who disposed of these young people with a contemptuous shrug of their shoulders as a "paid gang" and made fun of their *Fra Diavolo*. Out of curiosity I bought a few copies of the *Popolo d'Italia* and perceived in the sharp, concise, plastic, Latin style of Mussolini the same resoluteness as in the double-quick march of those young men across the Piazza San Marco. Naturally I could not dream of the dimensions which this struggle would acquire in not more than a year. But from that hour I was conscious that a struggle was imminent here and everywhere, and that *our* peace was not yet *the* peace.

~~~

For me this was the first warning that under the apparently quiet surface our Europe was full of dangerous subterranean currents. I did not have to wait long for the second. I had decided, again lured by the pleasure of traveling, to go to Westerland, on the German North Sea. For an Austrian a visit to Germany still had something encouraging about it. The mark, compared with our miserable krone, had held up beautifully thus far and the process of recovery seemed to be in full swing. The trains ran on time, the hotels were clean and shining; everywhere on the right and the left of the tracks there were new houses and new factories, everywhere the perfect, quiet order which one had hated before the war and which one had learned to appreciate again during the chaos. A certain tension, to be sure, was in the air; for the whole country was waiting to learn whether the negotiations at Genoa and Rapallo (the first at which Germany had a seat as an equal with the formerly hostile powers) would bring the hoped for alleviations of the war burdens, or at least a faint gesture of real understanding. The leader of these negotiations, so memorable in the history of Europe, was no other than my old friend Rathenau. His genial instinct for organization had already proven itself excellently during the war; from the start he had recognized the weakest spot in the German economy where, later on, it also received its mortal blow: the procurement of raw materials, and early (here too anticipating time), he centralized the whole economic system. When the war was over and a German Foreign Minister was needed who could meet the shrewdest and most experienced diplomats among the former opponents on their own ground, naturally the choice fell on him.

Hesitatingly I telephoned him in Berlin. Why break in on a man absorbed in shaping our destiny? "Yes, it's difficult," he said to me over the telephone, "Even friendship must now be sacrificed to my duty." But with his extraordinary facility for employing every minute he immediately devised a meeting. He had to leave his card at certain embassies and as it was a half-hour's drive from Grunewald the simplest thing was for me to go there and have a chat in his car while he was on his way. It is a fact that his capacity for mental concentration, his stupendous facility for switching from one subject to another was so perfect, that he could talk at any time, in the car or on a train, as precisely and profoundly as in his own room. I did not wish to miss this opportunity and I believe that it afforded him satisfaction to talk with someone who was politically disinterested and bound to him personally by years of friendship. It became a long talk and I can vouch that Rathenau, who personally was not free of vanity, had not accepted the position of German Foreign Minister with a light heart, let alone eagerly and impatiently. He knew from the start that for the time being the problem still was insoluble; and that at best he could return with some slight success, a few unimportant concessions, and that it was too early to hope for a real peace, for a generous understanding. "Perhaps ten years from now," he said to me, "provided that things go badly with everybody and not only with us alone. First, the old generation will have to be swept out of diplomacy and the generals will have to become silent monuments on the public squares." He was fully cognizant of his doubled responsibility through the burden of his being a Jew. Seldom perhaps in history has a man entered with so much scepticism and so many inner scruples on a task which he knew that not he but only time alone could solve—and he knew also its personal danger. Since the murder of Erzberger who had taken on the unpleasant duty of the armistice which Ludendorff had carefully shirked by going abroad, he could not doubt that a similar fate might await him also as a pioneer for mutual understanding. But, being unmarried, without children and fundamentally deeply lonesome, he felt that he should not avoid the danger; nor was I bold enough to warn him to take precautions. That Rathenau accomplished his task at Rapallo as excellently as it was possible under the then prevailing circumstances is now a historical fact. His splendid gift of quickly grasping any favorable situation, his cosmopolitan and his personal prestige never proved themselves more brilliantly. But already there were groups strong in the land that knew that they would secure followers only by assuring the vanquished people again and again that they really were not vanquished and that negotiations or compromises were treason to the nation. Already the secret organizations—strongly under homosexual influence—were far more powerful than the then leaders of the republic suspected and the latter, in their conception of freedom gave free rein to those who sought to do away with freedom in Germany for good.

It was in the city then that I said good-by to him in front of the Ministry, without having any premonition that this would be the last good-by. And later I saw by photographs that the road through which we had driven together was the same where, shortly thereafter, the murderers waylaid the same automobile; it was no more than chance that I did not witness the historically fateful scene. Thus, I was the better able to appreciate fully, because of the lively impression on my senses, the tragic episode with which the disaster of Germany, the disaster of Europe began.

On that day, I was already in Westerland. Hundreds of vacationists were bathing gaily in the surf. Again, as on the day when the assassination of Franz Ferdinand was announced, a band played to carefree people when, like white petrels, the newsboys stormed over the boardwalk. "Walter Rathenau assassinated." A panic broke out and the tremor spread through the whole Reich. Abruptly the mark plunged down, never to stop until it had reached the fantastic figures of madness, the millions, the billions and trillions. Now the real witches' sabbath of inflation started, against which our Austrian inflation with its absurd enough ratio of 15,000 old to 1 of new currency had been shabby child's play. To describe it in detail, with its incredibilities, would take a whole book and to readers of today it would seem like a fairy tale. I have known days when I had to pay fifty thousand marks for a newspaper in the morning and a hundred thousand in the evening; whoever had foreign currency to exchange did so from hour to hour, because at four o'clock he would get a better rate than at three, and at five o'clock he would get much more than he had got an hour earlier. For instance, I sent a manuscript to my publisher on which I had worked for a year; to be on the safe side I asked for an advance payment of royalties on ten thousand copies. By the time the check was deposited, it hardly paid the postage I had put on the parcel a week before; on street cars one paid in millions, trucks carried the paper money from the Reichsbank to the other banks, and a fortnight later one found hundred thousand mark notes in the gutter; a beggar had thrown them away contemptuously. A pair of shoe laces cost more than a shoe had once cost, no, more than a fashionable store with two thousand pairs of shoes had cost before; to repair a broken window more than the whole house had formerly cost, a book more than the printer's shop with a hundred presses. For a hundred dollars one could buy rows of six-story houses on Kurfürstendamm, and factories were to be had for the old equivalent of a wheelbarrow. Some adolescent boys who had found a case of soap forgotten in the harbor disported themselves for months in cars and lived like kings, selling a cake every day, while their parents, formerly well-to-do, slunk about like beggars. Messenger boys established foreign exchange businesses and speculated in currencies of all lands. Towering over all of them was the gigantic figure of the superprofiteer Stinnes. Expanding his credit and in thus exploiting the mark he bought whatever was for sale, coal mines and ships, factories and stocks, castles and country estates, actually for nothing because every payment, every promise became equal to naught. Soon a quarter of Germany was in his hands and, perversely, the masses, who in Germany always become intoxicated at a success that they can see with their eyes, cheered him as a genius. The unemployed stood around by the thousands and shook their fists at the profiteers and foreigners in their luxurious cars who bought whole rows of streets like a box of matches; everyone who could read and write traded, speculated and profited and had a secret sense that they were deceiving themselves and were being deceived by a hidden force which brought about this chaos deliberately in order to liberate the State from its debts and obligations. I have a pretty thorough knowledge of history, but never, to my recollection, has it produced such madness in such gigantic proportions. All values were changed, and not only material ones; the laws of the State were flouted, no tradition, no moral code was respected, Berlin was transformed into the Babylon of the world. Bars, amusement parks, honky-tonks sprang up like mushrooms. What we had seen in Austria proved to be just a mild and shy prologue to this witches' sabbath; for the Germans introduced all their vehemence and methodical organization into the perversion. Along the entire Kurfürstendamm powdered and rouged young men sauntered and they were not all professionals; every high school boy wanted to earn some money and in the dimly lit bars one might see government officials and men of the world of finance tenderly courting drunken sailors without any shame. Even the Rome of Suetonius had never known such orgies as the pervert balls of Berlin, where hundreds of men costumed as women and hundreds of women as men danced under the benevolent eyes of the police. In the collapse of all values a kind of madness gained hold particularly in the bourgeois circles which until then had been unshakeable in their probity. Young girls bragged proudly of their perversion, to be sixteen and still under suspicion of virginity would have been considered a disgrace in any school of Berlin at that time, every girl wanted to be able to tell of her adventures and the more exotic, the better. But the most revolting thing about this pathetic eroticism was its spuriousness. At bottom the orgiastic period which broke out in Germany simultaneously with the inflation was nothing more than feverish imitation; one could see that these girls of the decent middle class families much rather would have worn their hair in a simple arrangement than in a sleek man's haircut, that they would much rather have eaten apple pie with whipped cream than drink strong liquor; everywhere it was unmistakable that this over-excitation was unbearable for the people, this being stretched daily on the rack of inflation and that the whole nation, tired of war, actually only longed for order, quiet, and a little security and bourgeois life. And, secretly it hated the republic, not because it suppressed this wild freedom, but on the contrary, because it held the reins too loosely.

Whoever lived through these apocalyptic months, these years, disgusted and embittered, sensed the coming of a counterblow, a horrible reaction. And behind the scenes, smiling, there waited, watch in hand, those same people who had driven the German nation into the chaos: "The worse it is for the country, the better for us." They knew that their hour was at hand. Around Ludendorff, more than around the then still powerless Hitler, the counterrevolution was already crystallizing openly; the officers whose epaulettes had been torn off their shoulders organized in secret, the small tradesmen who had been cheated out of their savings silently closed ranks and aligned themselves in readiness for any slogan that promised order. Nothing was as fateful to the German Republic as the idealistic attempt to give liberty not only to the people but even to its enemies. For the German people, a disciplined folk, did not know what to do with their freedom and already looked impatiently toward those who were to take it from them.

～～

The day the German inflation ended (1924) could have become a turning point in history. When, as if at the sound of a gong, each billion of artificially inflated marks was exchanged for a single new mark, a norm had been created. And, truly, the muddy tide with all its filth and slime flowed back soon, the bars, the honky-tonks disappeared, conditions became normal again, everybody could now figure clearly how much he had won, how much he had lost. The great majority, the mighty masses, had lost. But the blame was laid not on those who had caused the war but on those who with sacrifice and without thanks had undertaken the burden of reconstruction. Nothing ever embittered the German people so much—it is important to remember this— nothing made them so furious with hate and so ripe for Hitler as the inflation. For the war, murderous as it was, had yet yielded hours of jubilation, with ringing of bells and fanfares of victory. And, being an incurably militaristic nation, Germany felt lifted in her pride by her temporary victories; while the inflation served only to make it feel soiled, cheated, and humiliated; a whole generation never forgot or forgave the German Republic for those years and preferred to reinstate its butchers. But all of that was still far away. On the surface, in 1924 the wild phantasmagoria seemed to have passed like a dance of will-o'-the-wisps. It was day again, one saw one's way in and out. And already we greeted the ascendance of order as the beginning of lasting peace. Again, once more, we thought we had risen above war, chronic fools as we always had been. But at least this deceptive delusion bestowed on us a decade of work, of hope and even of security.

~

Viewed from today, the short decade between 1924 and 1933, from the end of the German inflation to Hitler's seizure of power, represents—in spite of all—an intermission in the catastrophic sequence of events whose witnesses and victims our generation has been since 1914. Not that the period was free of tension, excitement or crises—there was the economic collapse of 1929—but during this decade, peace at least seemed guaranteed in Europe and that in itself meant much. Germany had been taken into the League of Nations with all honors, had received loans to facilitate her economic reconstruction—actually her secret rearmament—England had disarmed, in Italy Mussolini had taken over the protection of Austria. The world seemed dedicated to reconstruction, Paris, Vienna, Berlin, New York, Rome, the victor's cities as well as those of the vanquished became more beautiful than ever, the airplane gave wings to travel, passport and visa restrictions were relaxed. The fluctuations of currencies had ceased; one knew how much one earned and how much one could spend, attention was no longer centered so feverishly on such externals. Once more one could work, concentrate inwardly, apply oneself to things of the spirit. One might even dream again and hope for a united Europe. For a world-moment—those ten years—it seemed as if a normal life was again in store for our much-tried generation.

In my personal life the most notable happening of those years was the presence of a guest who settled himself most benevolently, a guest whom I had never expected: success. It is understandable that I do not feel at ease in mentioning the public success of my books, and in normal times I would have avoided even the most casual reference which might be interpreted as vanity or bragging. But I have a particular right and am even compelled not to pass over this fact in the story of my life, because this success, upon Hitler's advent nine years ago passed into history. Of the hundreds of thousands and even millions of my books which had their secure place in the book shops and in innumerable homes in Germany, not a single one is obtainable today; whoever still has a copy keeps it carefully hidden and in the public libraries they remain locked away in the so-called "poison cabinet" for those few who with a special permit from the authorities want to use them "scientifically"—mostly for purposes of defamation. Of my readers, the friends who used to write me, it is long since any dared to write my infamous name on an envelope. Nor is this all: in France also, in Italy, in all the countries now enslaved and in which my books in translation were among those most widely read, they have been similarly banned by Hitler's command. Today, as a writer I am, in Grillparzer's words, one "who living follows his own corpse"; everything, or almost everything that represents my work in the world during forty years has been destroyed by one and the same fist. So, if I allude to my "success" I do not refer to something that belongs to me but something that formerly was mine, like my house, my home, my security, my freedom, my ease of manner; I could not adequately describe the fall into the abyss which I with countless others equally innocent suffered, if I did not indicate the height from which it occurred, and the singularity and consequences of this destruction of our whole literary generation, an occurrence unique in history.

This success had not stormed my house suddenly; it came slowly, consideredly, but it stayed constantly and faithfully until the hour when Hitler chased it away from me with the whip of his decrees. Its influence grew from year to year. The very first book which I published after *Jeremiah*, the first volume of my *Master Builders,* the trilogy *Three Masters* evened the way for me; the expressionists, the activists, the experimentalists had played out, the way to the people was again open to the patient and the persistent. My stories, *Amok* and *Letter from an Unknown Woman* achieved the popularity usually reserved to full-length novels, they were dramatized, publicly read, made into films; a small book was adopted by the schools and in a short time achieved 250,000 copies in the *Inselbücherei*. In a few years I had created what to my way of thinking is the most valuable kind of success for an author: a community, a dependable group of people which looked forward to each new book, which bought each new book, which trusted in one and which trust one dared not disappoint. As time went on it became bigger and bigger; on the day each of my books was published, twenty thousand copies were sold in Germany before even a single advertisement appeared in the newspapers. Sometimes, I tried consciously to avoid success, but it followed me in a surprisingly insistent manner. Thus I wrote for my own private pleasure the biography of Fouché; when I sent it to my publisher, he wrote that he would make a first printing of ten thousand copies. I promptly implored him not to print so many, urging that Fouché was an unsympathetic personality, that the book contained no single episode with women and could not possibly attract a great circle of readers; better try five thousand at first. Within a year fifty thousand copies had been sold in Germany, the same Germany that today is not allowed to read a single line of mine. Something similar happened to me, in my almost pathological self-distrust, with my version of *Volpone*. I had intended to write it in verse and in nine days in Marseilles I had loosely sketched out the various scenes in prose. The Court Theater in Dresden to which I felt morally obligated because of their production of my first work, *Thersites,* chancing to ask about my current plans, I sent them the prose version, apologizing for presenting only a first sketch of the work which was to take final form in verse. But the theater telegraphed back immediately, saying for the love of heaven not to change a thing; and surely enough that version of the play has been produced all over the world (in New York by the Theater Guild with Alfred Lunt). Whatever I undertook in those years, success and a steadily increasing body of German readers remained faithful to me.

As a biographer and essayist I had always felt it incumbent on me to study the causes of the influence or lack of influence of books or personages within their own time, and I could not but ask myself in hours of reflection to what particular characteristics my books owed their, to me, unexpected success. In the final analysis, I believe it sprang from a personal bad habit of mine, namely, that I myself am an impatient and temperamental reader. Every redundance, all embellishment and anything vaguely rapturous, everything nebulous and unclear, whatever tends to retard a novel, a biography, an intellectual discussion, irritates me. Only a book that steadily, page after page, maintains its level and that seizes and carries one breathlessly to the last line, gives me perfect enjoyment. Nine-tenths of the books that happen into my hands are too greatly expanded by superfluous description, talky dialogue, and unnecessary minor characters, hence fail in magnetism and dynamic power. Even in the most celebrated classics the many sandy and dragging passages disturb me, and often I have laid before publishers the bold notion of a comprehensive series of the literature of the world from Homer through Balzac and Dostoievsky to *The Magic Mountain* thoroughly curtailing the superfluous in each; then all of those works whose timeless value is undoubted could acquire new life and influence in our day.

This distaste for everything redundant and long-winded necessarily had to transfer itself from the reading of other peoples' works to my own writing and had to train me to a special caution. Usually I produce very easily and fluently, and in the first draft of a book I let my fancy run away with me and put no brake in my pen. Similarly, in a biography, in the beginning I use all available documentary details of every kind; preparing for my *Marie Antoinette* I actually checked every single account in order to determine her personal expenditures, I pored over contemporary newspapers and pamphlets, ploughed through legal documents to the last dot. But in the printed book not a single line of that remains because, hardly is there a fair copy of the first approximate version of a book than my real work begins, that of condensing and composing, a task I cannot do too thoroughly from version to version. It is an unrelenting throwing overboard of ballast, an ever tightening and clarifying of the inner structure; where many others cannot bring themselves to withhold something that they know and, with a sort of infatuation for every rounded period seek to display a greater breadth and depth than they possess, it is my ambition always to know more than the surface discloses.

This process of condensation and dramatization repeats itself once, twice and three times in the proof sheets; in the end it becomes a kind of joyful hunt for another sentence or even merely a word the absence of which would not lessen the precision and yet at the same time accelerate the tempo. The task of cutting is the one that really affords me the most enjoyment. And I remember that one day, when I got up from my work particularly pleased and my wife remarked that I must have hit something off very well today, I answered proudly, "Yes, I was able to kill another whole paragraph and consequently to achieve a much more rapid continuity." If, then, the sweeping pace of my books is sometimes lauded, this characteristic owes nothing to a native heat or an inner excitation, but only to that systematic method of steady elimination of all superfluous stops and starts, and if I am aware of any art of my own it is that of being able to forego, for I make no complaint if of a thousand manuscript pages eight hundred make their way into the waste basket and only two hundred—the essence— survive the sifting. If anything, the strict discipline of restricting myself rather to the more limited forms of expression and always to the absolutely essential partially accounts for the effect of my books. It made me extremely happy, who had always thought in terms of the Continent, of the super-national, when publishers from abroad announced their interest, French, Bulgarian, Armenian, Portuguese, Argentinian, Norwegian, Latvian, Finnish, Chinese. Soon I had to buy a large cabinet in which to stow copies of the various translations, and one day I read in the statistics of the *Coopération Intellectuelle* of the League of Nations at Geneva that I was then the most-translated author in the world (but true to my disposition I doubted the correctness of the report). And on another day a letter came from my Russian publisher at Leningrad, stating that he wished to publish a complete edition of my works in Russian and asking whether it would be agreeable to me if Maxim Gorky were to write the introduction to it. Would it be agreeable to me! As a boy at school I had read Gorky's stories hidden under the desk, for years I had loved and admired him. But I had never flattered myself that he had ever heard my name, let alone that he had read anything of mine, and certainly not that it might appear important enough to such a master to write an introduction to my work. Still another time an American publisher appeared in my house in Salzburg with a letter of introduction—as if such would have been necessary—with the proposal to take over my work in its entirety and publish it regularly in the future. It was Benjamin Huebsch of the Viking Press, who has remained the most reliable friend and adviser and who—all and everything having been crushed under Hitler's hob-nailed boots—has conserved a last homeland of expression for me, now that I have lost the old one, the one that was my own, the German, the European.

Such apparent success was apt to confuse one whose faith, hitherto, had been in his good intentions rather than in his ability and the efficacy of his work. Publicity in itself, of whatever nature, connotes a disturbance of the natural equilibrium of a man. Under normal circumstances, the name a human being bears is no more than the band is to a cigar: a means of identification, a superficial, almost unimportant thing that is only loosely related to the real subject, the true ego. In the event of a success the name begins to swell, so to say. It loosens itself from the human being that bears it and becomes a power in itself, a force, an independent thing, an article of commerce, a capital asset; and psychologically again with strong reaction it becomes a force which tends to influence, to dominate, to transform the person who bears it. Happy, self-confident people usually identify themselves unconsciously with the effect they produce. A title, a post, a decoration, let alone a name become well-known, have a tendency to create in them a greater measure of self-assurance, a heightened self-confidence and to seduce them into the conviction that special importance is their due in society, the State and the age, and involuntarily they inflate themselves in order to attain in their person the volume of their external achievement. But whoever is naturally distrustful of himself regards every kind of outward success as just so much more of an obligation to preserve himself as unchanged as possible in such difficult case.

I do not mean to intimate thereby that I was not happy about my success. On the contrary, it made me extremely happy, but only in so far as it applied to what I produced, to my books with which the shadow of my name was linked. Chancing to be in a book shop in Germany, I was touched on observing—unrecognized—a very young Gymnasium student enter and ask for *The Tide of Fortune*, paying for it out of his meager allowance. It tickled one's vanity when a sleeping-car conductor reacted respectfully to the sight of my name on my passport, or an Italian customs officer, in recognition of some book that he had read, would magnanimously forego mussing my baggage. There is something fascinating, too, in the purely quantitative aspect of authorship. I happened to arrive at Leipzig on the day when a new book of mine began to be shipped out. It thrilled me strangely to see how much human labor one sets into motion unconsciously by means of something set down on three hundred pages of paper in the course of three or four months. Workers packed books into large cases, others lugged them pantingly to trucks which took them to freight cars thence to the four corners of the world. Dozens of girls gathered the folded sheets in the bindery, type setters, printers, shipping clerks, salesmen worked from morning until night; one could conjure up these books, laid side by side like bricks, as paving a street of impressive dimensions. Nor did I ever haughtily disdain the material aspect. During the first years I was never bold enough to think of earning money with my books, let alone to be able to make a living out of their proceeds. Now, suddenly they brought in considerable and ever-increasing amounts which seemed—who could have foreseen times like the present?—to lift me above financial worries for all time. I was able to give free rein to the passion of my youth, manuscript collecting, and some of the most beautiful, most valuable of those marvelous relics became the objects of my tender care. For those relatively ephemeral works which I had written I was able to acquire manuscripts of everlasting works, manuscripts by Mozart and Bach and Beethoven, Goethe and Balzac. So it would be a ridiculous pose for me to declare that the unexpected public success left me indifferent or even inwardly averse.

But I am honest when I say that I enjoyed my success only

as it applied to my books and my name as an author; but that it irked me, rather, when inquisitive interest directed itself to my person. From my earliest youth my strongest instinct was to remain free and independent. And I sensed that much of the best part of any human being's personal freedom becomes inhibited and deformed by photographic publicity. Besides, what I had commenced as inclination, threatened to take the shape of a profession, even of a business. Every mail brought piles of letters, invitations, requests, inquiries that required answers, and upon my return from an occasional month's absence it always took two or three days afterwards to clear away the accumulation and get the "business" going again. Unintentionally and because of the currency of my books I found myself in something that was like a business which demanded order, clarity, punctuality and skill if it were to be handled correctly—all very respectable virtues which alas by no means correspond to my nature and which seriously threatened to disturb my innocent, simple musings and dreaming. Thus the more frequently I was invited to lecture, to attend public affairs, the more I withdrew, and I have never been able to surmount this almost pathological aversion to appearing publicly as a substitute for my name. Even today, in any public gathering, at a concert or theater, my instinct is to take an inconspicuous back seat and nothing is more unbearable than to have to expose my face in the center of a platform or some other dangerous place. Anonymity in every aspect of life is a necessity to me. Even as a boy I could never understand those writers and artists of an earlier generation who, by means of velvet coats and waving hair, by means of unruly locks falling over their brow, as with my esteemed friends Arthur Schnitzler and Hermann Bahr, by means of showily trimmed beards or clothing in extreme style, sought easy recognition on the street. I am convinced that when the physical appearance of a man becomes familiar, he is unconsciously tempted to live like—to use Werfel's title—a "Mirror-man" of his own ego; to assume with each and every gesture a particular manner, and with this external alteration cordiality, freedom and carefreeness of the inner self are usually effaced. Therefore, if I could start all over again today, I should try to derive double enjoyment, as it were, from those two happy states, those of literary success and of personal anonymity, by publishing my works under another, an invented name, a pseudonym; because if life itself is exciting and full of surprises, how much more so is a double life!

XIV

Sunset

It was a comparatively peaceful time for Europe—I shall recall it often in gratitude—this decade from 1924 to 1933, until that one man confused our world. Just because our generation had suffered so much from the disturbances it accepted the relative peace as an unhoped for gift. We all had the feeling that one had to catch up with what the terrible war and post-war years had stolen out of our life, happiness, freedom, mental concentration; one did more work but felt less burdened, one experimented, one again discovered Europe, the world. Never did people travel as much as in those years—was it the impatience of the young to absorb quickly what they had missed during their forced separation from each other? Or was it, perhaps, some dark premonition that one had to escape in time before the barriers closed down anew?

I, too, traveled much during that time, only it was a different sort of traveling than in the days of my youth. For now I was no longer a stranger in the world, I had friends everywhere, publishers, a public. I entered as the author of my books and not as the unknown inquisitive of former days. This had various advantages. I was able to agitate with greater sweep and better effect for the idea which, over the years, had become central to my life: the intellectual unification of Europe. In this spirit I lectured in Switzerland and in Holland, I spoke in French in the Palais des Arts at Brussels, in Italian at Florence in the historic Sala dei Duecenti where once Michelangelo and Leonardo had sat, in English in America on a lecture tour from the Atlantic to the Pacific. It was a different kind of traveling; everywhere I now had access to the best minds on terms of fraternity; men to whom I had looked up in awe in my youth and to whom I would have never dared to address a line, had become my friends. I entered into circles which commonly were stiffly closed to the stranger, I saw the *palais* of the Faubourg St. Germain, the *palazzi* of Italy, the private collections; in public libraries I no longer stood a suppliant at the counter where the books were handed out, but the directors in person showed me their hidden treasures and at the rare book sellers to the rich, such as Dr. Rosenbach in Philadelphia, whose shops the modest collector had once passed with furtive gaze, I was a guest. For the first time I had a view of the "upper" world and under such circumstances of comfort and convenience as to make advances on my part unnecessary; everything came to me unbidden. But did I see the world the better for this? Many times I yearned for the travels of my youth when my movements were unnoticed and when my solitude contributed to make everything seem more mystical; so I had no desire to abandon my old way of wandering. When I came to Paris I refrained from notifying even my best friends like Roger Martin du Gard, Jules Romains, Duhamel. Masereel immediately on the day of my arrival. First, as when a student, I wanted again to ramble unhampered and unawaited through the streets. I looked up the old cafés and the small taverns, I pretended a return to my youth; similarly, when I wanted to work, I chose the most absurd places, small provincial spots like Boulogne, or Tirano or Dijon; it was wonderful to be unknown, to live in little hotels after the disgustingly luxurious ones, to advance or to recede, to choose light or shade entirely of one's discretion. And much as Hitler later took from me, the satisfaction of having lived the life of a European for at least one decade according to one's own free will and with complete interior freedom, this satisfaction not even he was able to confiscate or destroy.

~

Of all those journeys one was particularly exciting and instructive to me: a trip into the new Russia. In 1914, just before the war, when I was working on my book about Dostoievsky, I had prepared for this trip; then the bloody scythe of war had intervened and since then a scruple had deterred me. Russia, by reason of her bolshevist experiment, had become the most fascinating country of the post-war period for all thinking people; precise information being lacking she was as enthusiastically admired as fanatically attacked. Thanks to the propaganda and the equally unscrupulous counter-propaganda no one knew exactly what was happening. But one did know that something absolutely new was being tried there, something that—for better or for worse—might have a determining influence on the future form of our world. Shaw, Wells, Barbusse, Istrati, Gide and many others had gone there, some returning as enthusiasts, others disappointed. And I would have been wanting in spiritual affinity with progress if I had not also been tempted to see with my own eyes. My books gained unusual circulation there, not only the complete edition with Maxim Gorky's introduction, but also small cheap editions at but a few kopeks, which seeped through to the widest possible public; so, I could be confident of a pleasant reception. But what gave me pause was that any trip to Russia in itself implied some kind of partisanship which forced one into either a public acceptance or repudiation; while I, who deeply loathed anything political and dogmatic, did not want to declare a compulsory judgment of an endless country and a still unsolved problem after a few weeks' survey. So, in spite of my burning curiosity, I could never make up my mind to travel to Russia.

But in the early spring of 1928 I was invited to take part in the celebration of the hundredth birthday of Leo Tolstoy in Moscow as the delegate of the Austrian authors and to make a speech in his honor on the festive night. There was no ground to evade such an occasion, for because of the non-partisan subject matter the visit was removed from the political sphere. Tolstoy, the apostle of non-violence was not to be interpreted as a bolshevik, and to discuss him as a creative writer was my obvious right for my book about him had been widely disseminated; also, it seemed to me in terms of Europeanism, that it would be a significant demonstration for the writers of all countries to unite to pay homage in common to the greatest among them. Hence I accepted and I had no reason to regret my quick decision. The trip through Poland in itself was an experience. I saw how quickly our time heals wounds which it itself had inflicted. The same towns of Galicia, which, in 1915, I had seen in ruins, stood there bright and new; again I realized that ten years, which in a man's life means a good bit of his existence are only the blink of an eye in the life of a nation. In Warsaw there was nothing to indicate that twice, three and four times victorious and vanquished armies had stormed through the city. The cafés shone with elegant women. The trim and slender officers promenading through the streets seemed more like practiced actors impersonating soldiers than like fighters. Everywhere one sensed activity, confidence and a justifiable pride in the new Republic of Poland which rose so vigorously from the ashes of the centuries. From Warsaw we went on towards the Russian frontier. The country became flatter and sandier; at every stop the whole village population assembled at the station in their colorful rustic costumes, for then only one passenger train a day crossed into the forbidden and sealed land and it was a great event to look at the bright cars of this one express train that connected the world of the East with the world of the West. Finally, the border station was reached, Negoreloe, above the tracks a blood-red banner was stretched with an inscription in Cyrillic letters which I could not read. It was translated for me: "Workers of the world, unite!" Passing under this flaming red band one had entered the empire of the proletariat, the Soviet Republic, a new world.

The train in which we traveled was, however, by no means proletarian. It turned out to be a sleeper-train of the czarist era, more comfortable and more convenient than the European trains, because it was wider and slower in tempo. For the first time I rode through the Russian land and, peculiarly enough, it did not strike me as being strange. All seemed remarkably familiar to me, the vast empty steppes with their quiet melancholy, the little huts and villages with their onion-shaped towers, the long-bearded men, half peasants, half-prophets with their amiable, broad welcoming smile, the women with their colored kerchiefs and white smocks who offered kvass, eggs and cucumbers for sale. How did I come to know all this? Only through the masters of Russian literature, through Tolstoy, Dostoievsky, Aksahov, and Gorky who had painted for us with such magnificent realism the life of the people. Although I did not know the language it seemed to me as though I understood the people when they spoke, these touchingly simple men in their white blouses, broad and stocky, or the young workers in the train who played chess or read or debated, this restless and intractable intellectualism of youth which had been accelerated by the appeal for every possible effort. Was it the memory of Tolstoy's and Dostoievsky's love for the "people," which operated?—anyway, already in the train a feeling of sympathy overcame me for that which was childlike and mov-

ing, that which was at once wise and yet uninstructed, in
these people.

The fortnight I spent in Soviet Russia passed in a state of
continuous high tension. One saw, one heard, one admired,
one was repelled, fascinated, annoyed, the current always
alternating between hot and cold. Moscow itself was of a
dual aspect—there the beautiful Red Square with its walls,
its onion-shaped towers, something wonderfully Tartar,
Oriental, Byzantine, and thus Russian to the core—and
alongside it, like a strange horde of American giants,
modern, supermodern skyscrapers. There was no congruity;
in the churches the old smoke-blackened icons and the jewel-
studded altars to the saints still glimmered duskily, and a
hundred paces beyond, in its glass coffin, lay Lenin's corpse
just freshly rouged (I don't know whether in our honor),
garbed in black. Next to some shiny automobiles, were
bearded, dirty, *izvoschiki* whipping their little lean horses
with smacking endearments; the big opera house, in which
we held forth, glowed magnificently and czaristically in
pompous splendor before the proletarian audience; and in
the outskirts stood, like dirty neglected old men, the old
crumbling houses which had to lean one against the other
so as not to collapse. Everything had been old for too long,
lazy and rusty and now, it wanted, at a single jolt, to become
modern, ultramodern, supertechnical. Because of this haste
Moscow looked overcrowded, overpopulated, and messed
up in wild confusion. Everywhere there were crowds, in the
stores, in front of the theaters, and everywhere they were
made to wait, everything was overorganized and thus failed
to function properly. The new bureaucracy created to bring
about "order" was still reveling in the emission of mem-
oranda, permits, etc., which resulted in every sort of delay.
The principal event which was announced for six o'clock
began at 9:30; when I left the opera house exhausted at

three in the morning, the speakers were still hard at it. A
European who came on time was always an hour early for
every reception, every appointment. Time dissolved rapidly
yet every second was filled to the brim with searching,
observing and debating; some kind of fever was in all this
and one felt that it seized one insensibly, this mysterious
Russian firing of the emotions and the irrepressible
impulse to expel feelings and ideas at white heat. A state of
exaltation was easily attained, and without why or wherefore, its cause lay in the climate of unrest and novelty;
who knows, it may have been intimidations of a Russian
soul developing within one.

There was much of magnificence, above all, Leningrad,
this city genially conceived by daring princes, with its wide
avenues, its mighty palaces, and yet at the same time the
depressing Petersburg of the "white nights" and Raskolnikov. Impressive the Hermitage and unforgettable the
sight of the crowd, hat in hand as once they stood reverently
before their icons, of workers, soldiers, peasants with their
heavy boots, trudging through the former imperial halls and
gazing at the paintings with a secret pride: this belongs to us
now and we shall learn to understand such things. Teachers
lead round-cheeked children through the galleries, art comis-
sars explained Rembrandt and Titian to farmers who would
listen somewhat embarrassedly and raise their eyes timidly
under the heavy lids when some detail was pointed out.
Here also, like everywhere there was a slight ludicrousness in
this honest and well-meant attempt to elevate the "people"
over night from illiteracy to an understanding of Beethoven
and Vermeer; but this endeavor, on the one hand to make
the highest values intelligible at the first attempt, and, on
the other, to understand them, tried the patience of both
parties. In the schools, children would paint the wildest and
most extravagant subjects, the works of Hegel, and Sorel

(whom I myself did not know at that time); lay on the desks of twelve-year-old girls; cabdrivers who could hardly read would hold a book in their hands just because it was a book and a book meant "education," hence honor, the duty of the new proletariat. Often one had to smile when they showed us middling factories and expected startled amazement as if we had never seen such things in Europe or America; "electric," said a worker, quite proud, pointing to a sewing machine and looking at me in expectation of wonderment and admiration. Because the people had never before seen these technical contrivances they humbly believed the revolution and the little fathers Lenin and Trotsky had thought up and invented them all. So, one smiled in admiration and admired while being inwardly amused; what a wonderful, big, gifted and kindly child, this Russia, was the constant thought, and one asked oneself: will it really learn its enormous lesson as quickly as it proposes to do? Will this plan continue to unfold itself magnificently or will it break up on the reef of the traditional Russian Oblomovism. At one moment I was filled with confidence, at the next with doubt. The more I saw the less I could make up my mind.

But this duality, was it in me or was it not rather founded in the very nature of the Russian, did it not lie in the very soul of Tolstoy whom we had come to celebrate? On the train ride to Yasnaya Polyana I discussed this with Lunacharsky. "Which was he really," Lunacharsky said to me, "revolutionary or reactionary? Did he know which himself? As an ingrained Russian he was too eager for results to change the whole world in a twist of the wrist, after thousands of years just as we do," he added smiling, "and with a single formula, exactly like us. They misunderstand us, us Russians, if they call us patient. We are patient with our bodies and even with our soul. But in our thinking we are more impatient than any other folk, we want to know all truths, 'the' truth, instanter. And how he tortured himself about it, the great old man!" And really, as I walked through Tolstoy's house in Yasnaya Polyana, I felt ever this "how he tortured himself, the great old man." There was the table at which he had written his everlasting works and which he had left to cobble shoes in a shabby room next to it, bad shoes; there was the door, this was the stair through which he wanted to escape the house and the duality of his existence. There was the rifle with which he had killed enemies during the war, he, who was the enemy of all war. The whole problem of his life stood out before me clearly, in this low white manor house; but all that was tragic was beautifully alleviated by the visit to his last resting place.

For I saw nothing more magnificent, nothing more moving in Russia than Tolstoy's grave. Away from the road and lonely, this noble shrine lies shaded in the forest. A small footpath leads to the mound which is no more than a built-up rectangle of earth, guarded by none and watched by none, merely shaded by a few big trees. These towering trees, as his granddaughter told me at the grave, Leo Tolstoy had planted himself. His brother Nicolai and he as boys had once heard from some village crone a proverb, that happiness would prevail where trees were planted. So half in play, they had planted a few shoots. Long afterward when the old man remembered this beautiful prophecy he expressed the wish to be buried under the trees he had planted. That was done, according to his desire, and it proves the most impressive grave in the world, through its overpowering simplicity. A small rectangular mound amidst the forest, overarched by trees—*nulla crux, nulla corona*—no cross, no tombstone, no inscription. Nameless the great man lies buried who like none other suffered from his name and his fame, just like some wayside vagrant, like an unknown soldier. Anyone may approach his last resting place, the light wooden fence around it is not locked. Nothing guards the last rest of the restless but the respect of mankind which usually throngs curiously around the splendor of a grave. But here the compelling simplicity banishes mere curiosity. The wind tones like God's word over the grave of the nameless; no other voice; one might pass it unsuspectingly without knowing more than that a body lies there, that of any Russian man in Russian earth. Not Napoleon's crypt under the marble arches of the Invalides, not Goethe's coffin in the Fürstengruft, not the sepulchers in Westminster Abbey evoke such profound emotion as this gloriously silent, touchingly unmarked grave somewhere in the forest, that hears only whispers of the wind and itself offers no word or message.

~~

I had spent two weeks in Russia and still felt this inner tension, this warm haze of spiritual intoxication. What was it exactly that so aroused one? Soon, I hit on it: it was the people and the impulsive cordiality that welled from them. All of them, from the first to the last, were convinced that they were participants in a momentous matter which concerned all mankind; all were imbued with the thought that the privations and restrictions which they had to take upon themselves were for the sake of a higher mission. The old sense of inferiority to Europe had converted itself into a drunken pride of leadership, a desire to be ahead of everybody. *"Ex oriente lux"*—that salvation would come from them was their honest and sincere belief. It was they who had recognized *the* truth, it was given them to fulfill what others had only dreamed of. They would display a quite insignificant thing with glowing eyes. "This *we* have done," and that "we" permeated all of life. The coachman who drove one around would point with his whip to any sort of new structure his face widening to a smile: *we* built this. The Tartars, the Mongols in classrooms revealed their books full of pride: "Darwin!" one would say; "Marx!" the other, with the same air as if they themselves had written the books. Incessantly they pressed to exhibit, to explain; they were so thankful that somebody had come to see "their" work. Everybody had—years before Stalin!—boundless confidence in Europeans, they looked at one with kindly, trusting eyes and shook one's hand mightily. But the least of them showed that though they loved one, they did not feel "respect," for was one not a brother, a tovarisch, a comrade? It was no different amongst writers. We were sitting together in a house that once was Alexander Herzen's, not only Europeans and Russians, but Tungus, Georgians and Caucasians as well, for every Soviet republic had sent its delegate for Tolstoy. None could make himself understood to most of them, nevertheless there was mutual understanding. Occasionally one would rise, approach, name the title of a book one had written and, pointing to his heart as if to say, "I like it very much," would grip one's hand and shake it as if he wanted to break all its bones for love. And what was even more touching, each one brought a gift. Times were still bad; they did not own anything of value yet each had found something, an old worthless etching, a book one could not read, a rustic wood carving. I had the advantage over them of being able to reciprocate with treasures unknown in Russia for years, with a Gillette razor blade, a fountain pen, a few sheets of good white writing paper, a pair of soft leather slippers, so that I came home with meager baggage. But just this silent and yet impulsive cordiality was overwhelming with its heartiness and warmth —new to us—that affected every sense, for in our own homes one never reached the underlying population. Each contact with these people became a dangerous temptation to which not a few foreign writers succumbed during their visits in Russia. They saw themselves celebrated as never before and loved by the real masses, thus considered it incumbent on them to applaud the régime under which they were so fervently read and loved; it is no more than natural to wish to reciprocate generosity with generosity, rapture with rapture. I must admit that I myself in many a moment in Russia came near to crying hosanna and to becoming exalted from the exaltation.

That I did not succumb to this magic intoxication was due less to any force within myself than to an unknown whose name I do not know and never shall find out. It was after a celebration with some students. They had pressed about me, there were embraces and hearty handshakes. I was still warm from their enthusiasm, still saw their joyous vivid faces. Four or five of them escorted me home, a whole troop, while the interpretress allotted to me, also a student, translated all that was said. Only after I had closed the door of my hotel room behind me, was I really alone, alone indeed for the first time in twelve days, for one was always accompanied, always guarded, carried on waves of warmth. I started undressing and took off my coat. I heard something crackle. I reached into the pocket. It was a letter. A letter in French but not a letter that had come to me by mail, but one which someone during these embracings or jostlings must have cleverly slipped into my pocket.

It was a letter without signature, a very wise, human letter, not one from a White Russian but full of bitterness against the ever growing restriction of freedom during recent years. "Don't believe everything one tells you," this unknown said. "Don't forget that with all that they show you, there is much that is not shown you. Remember that most of the people who talk to you, do not say what they wish

to say but only what they may tell you. We all are watched
and you yourself no less. Your interpreter reports every
word, your telephone is tapped, every step is observed."
He cited instances and details which I was unable to check.
But I burned the letter as he directed—"don't just tear it up
because they will piece it together from your wastebasket"—
and began, for the first time, to think it all over. Was it not
really a fact that amidst all this hearty warmth, this wonderful comradeship, I had not had a single opportunity to talk
with anybody privately, face to face? My ignorance of the
language had prevented close touch with the man in the
street. And furthermore: how small a part of this endless
country I had seen in these two weeks. If I wanted to be
honest with myself and to others, I could not but admit that
my impression, exciting and stimulating in many a detail as
it was, could yet have no objective validity. This was the
reason why, though almost all other European authors who
returned from Russia promptly published a book of either
enthusiastic affirmation or incensed negation, I wrote no
more than a few articles. And I did well with this restraint;
for already after three months, much was different from
what I had seen, and after a year, due to the rapid transformations, every word would have been given the lie by the
facts. In any event I felt the underlying currents of our time
as keenly in Russia as ever in my life.

~~

My suitcases were fairly empty when I departed from
Moscow. Whatever I could give away I had distributed
and for my part, I took only two icons with me, which
graced my room for a long time. But the most valuable
thing I brought home with me was the friendship of Maxim
Gorky whom I had met personally for the first time in
Moscow. I saw him again one or two years later in Sorrento,

where he had gone because of poor health, and spent three
unforgettable days as a guest in his house.

This occasion had its odd aspect. Gorky did not know any
foreign language nor, again, did I know any Russian.
According to all rules of logic we would consequently have
had to face each other silently or would only have been
able to converse through the interpretership of our valued
friend, Marie, Baroness Budberg. But it was not by mere
chance that Gorky was one of the most genial narrators
in world literature; storytelling to him meant not only an
artistic form of expression, it was a functional emanation
of his whole being. He was alive, he became one with the
stuff of his narrative, and from the outset I understood him,
without understanding his language, through the mobility
of his face. He looked just "Russian," there is no other
expression for it. There was nothing striking about his
features; one could have imagined the tall lank man with
the straw-yellow hair and the broad cheekbones a peasant
in the fields, a cab driver, an insignificant cobbler, an
unkempt vagabond—he was no more than "folk," the concentrated prototype of the Russian people. On the street,
one would have passed by him indifferently, without per-
ceiving anything extraordinary. Only when seated opposite
him and he began to talk did one recognize what he was.
For involuntarily he became the character which he por-
trayed. I remember how he described—and I grasped it
before it was translated—an old, hunchbacked tired man
whom he had encountered in his travels. Without exercise
of the will, his head sank in, the shoulders pressed themselves
down, his eyes, radiant blue and shining when he started,
became clouded and weary, his voice broke; unknown to
himself he had been transformed into the old hunchback.
And promptly, when he related something humorous, he
would break into wide laughter, lean back relaxed with

face aglow; it was an indescribable joy to listen to him as he recreated countryside and people to the accompaniment of almost sculptural gestures. Everything about him was simple, natural: his gait, his sitting posture, his attentiveness, his merriment. One evening he dressed up as a boyar, girded himself with a saber and at once his eye took on something lofty. His eyebrows tightened imperiously, he paced the floor energetically as if contemplating some stern ukase and a moment later, after removing the disguise, he laughed childlike as if he were a country boy. His vitality was a miracle, he lived with his wasted lung against every law of medicine, but a prodigious will to live, an iron sense of duty kept him going; every morning he wrote in his clear, calligraphic handwriting at his current novel, answered hundreds of questions which young writers and workers addressed to him from the homeland. To be with him meant for me to experience Russia, not the bolshevik, neither the erstwhile Russia, nor that of today, but the broad, strong, dark soul of the whole people. Inwardly, in these years, he had not yet quite come to a decision. As an old revolutionary he had desired the revolution, had been a personal friend of Lenin, but he still hesitated to align himself fully with the party, "to become priest or pope," as he said, and yet his conscience bothered him at being away from his people in those years when no week was without its crisis.

By chance I witnessed a scene which was very characteristic and thoroughly new-Russian, one which revealed his whole inner duality to me. For the first time a Russian warship on a training cruise had anchored in Naples. The young sailors who had never seen the Western world sauntered through the Via Toledo in their trim uniforms and could not see enough of all the novelty with their big, hungry peasant eyes. The next day, a group of them decided

to go to Sorrènto to visit "their" author. They did not
announce their coming; in their Russian idea of fraternity
it seemed quite a matter of course that "their" author should
receive them whenever they came. There they were, then,
and they had guessed correctly: Gorky welcomed them at
once and invited them in. But—Gorky related it laughingly the following day—these young men to whom the
"cause" rose above all else, began by taking him sternly to
task. "What sort of life is this that you live here?" they said,
having barely entered the nice, comfortable villa. "You live
exactly like a bourgeois. And anyway, why don't you come
back to Russia?" Gorky was obliged to explain in detail
as best he could. But at bottom, these good lads were not as
strict as they sounded. They had merely wanted to demonstrate that they had no "respect" for fame and that their
primary consideration was for party convictions. They made
themselves comfortable, took tea, chatted and at parting one
after the other embraced him to say good-by. It was wonderful, how Gorky related the whole scene, completely enchanted with the easygoingness of this new generation and
without being in the least offended by their unceremonious-
ness. "How different we were," he repeated again and again,
"either timid or very impetuous, but never with self-
confidence." His eyes glowed throughout the evening. And
when I said to him: "I think the thing you wanted most was
to sail home with them," he stopped short and looked at me
sharply. "How did you know that? Actually, up to the last
moment I was cogitating whether I shouldn't drop everything, books, papers and work, and go off with these young
lads for a fortnight's sail into the blue on their boat. That
would have taught me again what Russia is. Away, one forgets the best, none of us has ever produced anything of value
in exile."

But Gorky was mistaken in calling Sorrento exile. He could have returned home any day and as a matter of fact did go home. He had not been banned, nor his books, like Merejkovsky whom I had met in Paris, tragically embittered; not as we today who, as Grillparzer put it, "have two abroads but not a home," homeless in borrowed languages, tossed about by the wind. As against that I found myself looking up a real exile, one of an unusual sort, a few days later in Naples, Benedetto Croce. For decades the youth of the land had looked up to him as its intellectual leader, as a senator and minister he had enjoyed every public honor, until his opposition to fascism brought him into conflict with Mussolini. He resigned his offices and retired, which did not satisfy the intransigents who wanted to break his resistance and, if necessary, even to punish him. The students, in contrast with former times, in these days the storm troops of reaction, attacked his house and broke his windows. But the short, thickset man, whose little, knowing eyes and small pointed beard suggested the comfortable burgher, would not be intimidated. He did not leave the country, he stayed right in his house behind the ramparts of his books despite the many calls from American and other foreign universities. He kept on publishing his periodical *Critica* in unaltered tone, continued producing his books and, so powerful was his authority that the otherwise inexorable censor stopped short of him upon Mussolini's orders while his students and like-minded colleagues were completely liquidated. For an Italian or even a foreigner to look him up took a good deal of boldness, for the authorities knew well enough that in the citadel of his book-crowded rooms he made no bones about his views. So he lived in an airtight sealed room, as it were, in a sort of glass bottle in the midst of the forty millions of his countrymen. This hermetic isolation of a single individual in a city of millions, a country of millions was at once weird and magnificent. Although I could not then realize that this yet constituted a much milder form of intellectual devitalization than the one which we were to experience, I could not but admire the freshness and mental elasticity which the old man preserved in the daily struggle. But he merely laughed: "It's just opposition that rejuvenates. Had I remained a senator, it would have been too easy for me; I would long since have become intellectually lazy and inconsistent. Nothing harms a thinking man more than lack of opposition; it is only since I found myself alone and no longer surrounded by youth that I was forced to become young again myself."

Some years had to pass before I understood that trials challenge, persecution strengthens, and isolation exalts, provided they do not break one. Like all important things in life one never derives such knowledge from other peoples' experience but only from one's own fate.

～～

That I have never seen the most important man of Italy, Mussolini, is ascribable to my reluctance to approach political dignitaries; even in my fatherland, modest Austria, where it was almost an achievement not to do so, I never met any of the leading statesmen, neither Seipel nor Dollfuss nor Schuschnigg. It would seem to have been my duty to thank Mussolini personally—friends whom we had in common told me that he was one of the first and most appreciative of my readers in Italy—for the spontaneous way in which he granted the first request I ever addressed to a statesman.

This is what happened. One day I received a special delivery letter from a friend in Paris saying that an Italian lady wanted to see me in Salzburg on a matter of great importance and asking me to receive her at once. She called the next day and her story was truly affecting. Her husband, an outstanding physician had come from a poor family and had been educated at the expense of Mateotti, the socialist leader who had been so brutally murdered by the fascists; that was the last occasion on which the already overfatigued world-conscience once more reacted in rage against a single crime. All Europe had risen in indignation. The faithful friend was one of the six courageous men who had dared to carry the coffin of the murdered man publicly through the streets of Rome; shortly afterwards, boycotted and threatened, he had gone into exile. But the fate of Mateotti's family left him no peace, and in memory of his benefactor he wanted to smuggle his children out of Italy. In his attempt to do so he had fallen into the hands of spies or *agents provocateurs* and had been arrested. Since every reminder of Mateotti was very embarrassing to Italy, a trial might not have turned out very badly for him; but the prosecutor cleverly implicated the man in another trial, which dealt with a planned attempt on Mussolini's life. So the young physician who had earned the highest war decorations in combat, was sentenced to ten years at hard labor.

The young woman was naturally very excited. Something had to be done about the sentence, her husband would not survive it; the thing to do was to unite the big literary names of Europe in a great protest, and she wanted my help to this end. I promptly advised her against attempting anything with protests. I knew how threadbare such manifestations had become since the war. I reminded her that national pride alone would prevent a country from permitting its justice to be corrected from abroad and that the European protest in the case of Sacco and Vanzetti had operated badly rather than favorably in America. I begged her earnestly not to do anything of that kind. She would make her husband's situation only more bitter and acute for Mussolini never would, never could, even if he wanted to, order any reduction of the sentence if outside pressure were exerted to force him to do so. Being genuinely moved, I promised to do the best I could. It happened that I was going to Italy the next week, where I had kindly friends in influential positions. Perhaps they could privately do something in his favor.

I made an attempt on the first day. But I saw how greatly fear had already eaten its way into men's souls. Hardly had I mentioned the name when people became embarrassed. Sorry, but I can't help you there. It's quite out of the question. I got that from one after another. I returned shamed, for might not the unhappy woman doubt that I had done my utmost? Nor had I. One possibility remained: the straight, frank way, to write to the man in whose hands the decision lay, to Mussolini himself.

I did that. I wrote a straightforward letter. I did not wish to open with flattering phrases, I said, and I wished to make plain at the outset that I knew neither the man nor the measure of his guilt. But I had seen his wife who was undoubtedly innocent and on whom the full impact of the sentence would also fall if her husband had to spend ten years in prison. It was not my purpose to criticize the sentence in any way, but I imagined that it might mean saving the woman's life if her husband were to be consigned to one of the penal islands where women and children were permitted to live with the exiled, instead of the penitentiary.

I took the letter, addressed to His Excellency Benito Mussolini, and dropped it into the usual Salzburg mail box. Four days later, the Italian legation in Vienna wrote me that His Excellency wished them to thank me and to inform me that he had granted my wish and also had ordered a reduction in the sentence. At the same time a telegram came from Italy confirming the requested transfer. With a single stroke of the pen Mussolini personally had granted my request and, as a matter of fact, the prisoner was soon there-after fully pardoned. No letter in my life has ever given me more joy and satisfaction, and if I think of any literary success, it is this one that I recall with particular gratitude.

~~

It was pleasant to travel in those years of the last period of calm, but homecoming, too, was agreeable. A remarkable thing had come about quite silently. The little town of Salzburg with its forty thousand inhabitants, which I had selected just for its romantic remoteness, had become amaz-ingly transformed: it had become the summer artistic capital not only of Europe but of the whole world. Max Reinhardt and Hugo von Hofmannsthal, in order to allevi-ate the plight of actors and musicians who were unem-ployed during the summer months of the hard post-war years had arranged a few performances, notably that famous outdoor production of *Everyman* on the Domplatz, which first had attracted visitors from the immediate vicinity; subsequently they added operatic performances which grew constantly toward perfection. Little by little the world began to take notice. The best conductors, singers, actors competed ambitiously for the opportunity to disclose their talents not only in the limits of their home but before an international audience. All at once the Salzburg Festival plays became a world attraction, a modern olympic of art at which all nations contended to exhibit their best, as it were. These extraordinary performances became something that none wanted to miss. Kings and princes, American millionaires and film stars, music lovers, artists, poets and snobs would assemble in Salzburg; never had there been a similar concentration of theatrical and musical perfection in Europe as in this little town of little, long neglected

Austria. Salzburg blossomed out. In summer one encountered on its streets everybody from America and Europe
who sought the highest manifestations of art, in Salzburg
costumes; white linen shorts and jackets for the men, the
gay *Dirndls* for the women. Diminutive Salzburg suddenly set the world's fashions! One battled for rooms in the
hotels, the line-up of automobiles at the Festspielhaus was
as ostentatious as once at the Imperial court ball; the railroad station was uninterruptedly overcrowded. Other towns
tried to divert this gold-laden stream to themselves, none
succeeded. Salzburg was and remained for a decade the
artistic Mecca of Europe.

Thus I found myself in my own town in the center of
Europe. Fate had again granted a wish of mine which I had
hardly dared dream, and our house on the Kapuzinerberg
had become a European house. What a variety of visitors
we had! Our guestbook would bear witness more reliably
than mere memory but it, together with the house and much
else, fell to the National Socialists. What cordial hours we
spent with our guests there, looking out from the terrace
into the beautiful and peaceful countryside without suspecting that on the Berchtesgaden mountain directly opposite
sat the one man who was to destroy all this! Romain Rolland
stayed with us and Thomas Mann; among writers H. G.
Wells, Hofmannsthal, Jacob Wassermann, Van Loon, James
Joyce, Emil Ludwig, Franz Werfel, Georg Brandes, Paul
Valéry, Jane Addams, Shalom Asch, Arthur Schnitzler were
welcome guests; among the musicians, Ravel and Richard
Strauss, Alban Berg, Bruno Walter, Bartok, and many
others among painters, actors, scientists, and scholars from
the four corners of the world. The many lucid hours of
intellectual conversation that each summer wafted into
our house! One day Arturo Toscanini climbed the steep
way to us and in that hour a friendship began which enabled

me to love and enjoy music even more and more under-
standingly than ever before. For years thereafter, I was a
faithful attendant at his rehearsals and experienced repeatedly the passionate struggle with which he compels this
faultless perfection which in the subsequent public concerts
seems a miracle while merely fulfilling expectation. (In an
essay I once tried to describe these rehearsals which, for the
artist, constitute the most exemplary motive never to desist
until final perfection has been attained.) Shakespeare's
"music be the food of love" was gloriously confirmed for
me; and, observing the contest of the arts I blessed the fate
that had given me lasting union with them. How rich, how
colorful were these summer days when art and the blessed
countryside enhanced each other! And always when, in
retrospect, I remembered the little town, shabby, neglected,
gray, depressing as it had been immediately after the war,
our own house where, freezing, we had contended with the
rain that came through our roof, I sensed what those blessed
years of peace had meant to my life. Faith in the world, in
humanity, had again become possible.

～

Many desired and famous guests came into our house in
those years, but in the hours of solitude, too, a magic circle
of exalted figures whose shadow and trace I had slowly
succeeded in conjuring up, gathered around me: in the
manuscript collection, which I have already mentioned,
the greatest masters of all times had assembled in their
handwriting. That which I had begun amateurishly at the
age of fifteen had, in the course of years—thanks to much
experience, larger means, and an even augmented passion—
developed from a mere accumulation into an organic structure and, I feel free to say, into a real work of art. At first,
like every beginner, I had striven merely to collect names,

famous names; later, out of psychological curiosity I sought only manuscripts—the originals of works or fragments of works—which served also to give me a glimpse into the creative method of some beloved master. For, if we look at the whole world with its countless insoluble riddles, the secret of creation remains still the deepest and the most mysterious one. Here Nature permits no eavesdroppers, never will she permit anyone to detect the ultimate trick, how the earth originated and how a little flower is created, how a poem, how man is made. At this, merciless and inexorable, she draws the veil. Even the poet, even he who achieves poetical creation, even the musician cannot describe and explain the moment of his inspiration. Once his creation is perfectly shaped, the artist is no longer cognizant of its origin, of its growing and becoming. Never, or almost never, is he able to explain how in his exalted state words joined themselves into a verse, single tones into melodies, which then resound through the centuries. The one thing that can grant a slight inkling of this incomprehensible process of creation is the handwritten pages and particularly those not yet intended for the press, those sprinkled with corrections, the tentative first outlines, from which gradually the future valid form crystallizes. The assembling of such pages of the great poets, such proof sheets with the testimony to struggle that they bear, was the second, more knowing period of my autograph collecting. It was a pleasure to me to hunt them down at auctions, a joyous effort, to follow a scent to the most hidden places, and at the same time a kind of science. For slowly, in addition to my collection of manuscripts, a second had developed which comprised all the books that were ever written about autographs, all the catalogues that had ever been printed, more than four thousand in number, an unequaled reference library without a single rival, because even dealers could not devote so much time and love to their specialty. I may well say—what I would never dare to say in reference to literature or any other field of life—that in these thirty or forty years of collecting I had become an authority in the field of manuscripts and that I knew about every important handwriting, where it was, to whom it belonged, and how it had come to its possessor; thus a real connoisseur who could judge authenticity at the first glance and who, in appraisal, was more experienced than most professionals.

But, gradually my collector's ambition went even further. I was not satisfied with having a mere manuscript gallery of the world's literature and music, a mirror of the thousand kinds of creative methods; the mere amplification of the collection no longer tempted me, but what I undertook in the last ten years of my collecting was a systematic refinement. If at first I was satisfied to have manuscript pages of a poet or composer which disclosed him in a creative moment, my efforts gradually led to represent each one in his happiest creative moment, the one of highest achievement. So I searched not only for the manuscript of one of a poet's poems, but of one of his most beautiful poems, and if possible, one of those poems which from the minute that the inspiration found its first earthly realization started on its way to eternity. I wanted from the immortals—bold presumption!—in the relic of their autograph precisely that which had made them immortal for the world.

In consequence the collection was in a state of continuous flux; any leaf not adequate to the goal which I had set was eliminated, sold or traded in, as soon as I succeeded in finding a more essential, more characteristic, a more—if I may use the word—eternity-containing one. And miraculously, I succeeded in many instances because there were very few besides me, who collected the most significant works of art with such experience, such tenacity, and at the same time

such knowledge. So finally it was first a portfolio and then
a whole box, with metal and asbestos protecting them against
destruction that united manuscripts of works or parts of
works which belong to the most durable manifestations of
creative humanity. I do not have at hand here—in my
enforced nomadic existence—the catalogue of this long-since
dispersed collection and can enumerate only haphazardly
some of the things to illustrate how earthly genius was
embodied in a moment of eternity.

There was a leaf from Leonardo's workbook, notes in
mirror writing for sketches; dashed in scarcely legible writing on four pages, Napoleon's order of the day to his
soldiers at Rivoli; there was a complete novel in proof
sheets by Balzac, every page a battlefield with a thousand
corrections and representing with indescribable clarity his
titanic struggle from proof to proof (a photostat copy was
luckily saved for an American university). There was
Nietzsche's *Birth of Tragedy* in a first, unknown version,
which long before publication he had written for the
beloved Cosima Wagner, a cantata by Bach and the aria of
Alceste by Gluck and one by Handel, whose music manuscripts are the rarest of all. Always the most characteristic
was sought and for the most part found. Brahms's *Zigeun-
erlieder*; Chopin's *Barcarolle*; Schubert's immortal *An
die Musik*, no more and no less than the undying melody
of *Gott erhalte* from the Kaiser Quartet by Haydn. In
some cases I even succeeded in expanding the unique
manifestation of the creative into a complete life picture
of the creative individuality. So of Mozart I had not only
a crude page written by the eleven-year-old boy, but also as
a token of his art in song, the immortal *Veilchen*, of his
dance music the minuets which paraphrase Figaro's *Non piu
andrai*, and from *Figaro* itself the aria of Cherubino; besides
which the charmingly improper letters (never yet published

unabridged) to *"das Bäsle,"* a scabrous canon, and finally a page written just before his death, an aria from *Titus.* Just as full was the arc of Goethe's life, the first leaf a translation from the Latin by the nine-year-old boy, the last a poem written in his eighty-second year, shortly before he died, and in between a mighty page from his crowning work, a double folio from *Faust,* a manuscript on the natural sciences, a number of poems and besides drawings from the widely varying stages of his career; in these fifteen leaves one surveyed Goethe's entire life. But in the matter of Beethoven, revered above all, I was unable to achieve so rounded a picture. As my publisher Professor Kippenberg competed with me in the field of Goethe, so one of the richest men of Switzerland, owner of an incomparable Beethoven collection, opposed and outbid me. But, apart from the early notebook, the song *Der Kuss* and fragments from the *Egmont* music, I was successful in presenting visually in its entirety one moment, the most tragic of his life, in a fullness impossible to any museum. By a first stroke of luck I was able to acquire all the remaining pieces of furniture from his room which had been auctioned off after his death and bought by Privy Councilor Breuning; the great desk above all, in whose drawers were concealed pictures of two loves, Countess Giulietta Guicciardi and Countess Erdödy; the strongbox which stood next to his bed up to the last moment, the little portable desk on which he had written in bed, his last compositions and letters, a white lock of his hair cut off on his death-bed, the invitation to his funeral, the last laundry list written in a trembling hand, the inventory of Beethoven's goods for the auction, and the subscription list of all his friends for the benefit of his cook Sali who was left impecunious. As if to demonstrate to me that chance always deals good cards to the true collector, I had an opportunity, shortly after I had purchased all these objects from his death chamber, to acquire the three drawings of his deathbed. According to contemporary reports a young painter, friend of Schubert's, Josef Teltscher, had tried to sketch the dying man on that 27th of November when Beethoven lay in his death struggle, but had been ordered out of the room by Privy Councilor Breuning who considered the act irreverent. For a hundred years the sketches were gone until at a small auction at Brünn some dozens of this minor painter's sketchbooks were sold for a song and among them were revealed the present drawings. And as chance follows chance, a dealer rang me up one day to ask whether I was interested in the original of the drawing of Beethoven's deathbed. I told him that I owned these myself, but it turned out that what he was offering was the original of Dannhäuser's famous lithograph of that subject. Thus it came about that I assembled all the visible evidences that remained to recall this last memorable and truly immortal moment.

That I never considered myself as owner of these things but only their temporary custodian, went without saying. Not the sense of possession, of having them for my very own, enticed me but the allurement of unifying, of molding a collection into a work of art. I was aware that in this collection I had created something which, as an entity, was worthier of survival than my own works. In spite of many proposals I was reluctant to make a catalogue because the structure was still in the building and lacked some names and many specimens in their most desirable forms. My carefully considered purpose was to bequeath this unique collection to such institution as would fulfill my particular condition: namely, to spend a certain sum annually to further the collection in the spirit that had animated me. Thus it would not have remained a rigid thing but a living organism which, for fifty or a hundred years after my own life would improve and perfect itself toward a fuller beauty.

But to our tried generation it is denied to think beyond itself. When Hitler's day set in and I left my home, the pleasure of collecting was gone and also the certainty of being able to preserve anything lastingly. For a while I still kept parts of it in safes and with friends, but then I decided, remembering Goethe's admonition, that museums, collections and arsenals grow numb if they be not constantly developed, rather to say good-by to a collection to which I could no longer devote creative effort. One section I gave by way of farewell to the National Library of Vienna, mainly those items which had been gifts to me from friends among contemporaries; another part I sold, and what has happened or is happening to the rest no longer burdens my thoughts. My joy always lay in the act of creating, never in what had been created. So I do not lament for what I once owned; for, if we, driven and hunted in these times which are inimical to every art and every collection, were put to it to learn a new art it would be that of parting from all that once had been our pride and our love.

～

And so the years passed with work and travel, with study, reading, collecting, and enjoying life. One morning in November 1931 I woke to find myself fifty years old. For the good white-haired Salzburg postman this date marked a bad day for, as it was an established tradition in Germany to celebrate an author's fiftieth birthday widely in the newspapers, the old man had a goodly freight of letters and telegrams to lug up the steep stairs. Before I opened and read them, I paused to reflect on what this day signified to me. The fiftieth year means a turning point; disturbed, one looks back to see how much of the way has already been covered and silently asks oneself whether it leads further upward. I reviewed the time I had lived. In the same way as I looked from my house at the range of the Alps and the gently sloping valley, I looked back at those fifty years and had to admit that it would be wicked not to feel grateful. After all, more, immeasurably more had been given me than I had expected or had thought myself capable of. The medium through which I had wanted to develop and to express my being, that of literature, had operated with an efficacy beyond the boldest dreams of my boyhood. There lay, as a present from the Insel-Verlag, printed for my birthday, a bibliography of my books as published in all languages, a book in itself; no language was absent, not Bulgarian or Finnish, not Portuguese or Armenian, not Chinese or Marathi. In Braille, in shorthand, in all exotic alphabets and idioms, thoughts and words of mine had gone out to people; I had expanded my existence immeasurably beyond the space of my being, I had established personal friendship with many of the best people of our time, had enjoyed the most perfect performances; it was given me to see and to enjoy the eternal cities, the eternal paintings, the most beautiful prospects on earth. I had retained my freedom, was not dependent on office or profession, my work was my joy and furthermore, it had brought joy to others. What evil could possibly happen? There were my books: could they be destroyed? (So I mused, unsuspectingly, at that hour.) My house—could I be dispossessed of it? There were my friends —could I ever lose them? I thought without fear of death, of illness, but not the remotest picture came into my mind of what I was still to live through. That homeless, pursued, hunted, as a refugee I would again have to wander from land to land, across oceans and oceans, that my books would be burned, forbidden, proscribed, that my name would be posted in Germany like a criminal's and that those friends whose letters and telegrams lay before me on the table, would pale if by chance they encountered me. That the achievements of thirty or forty years of perseverance could be extinguished without trace; that the structure of a life seemingly firm and secure as I surveyed it could collapse; and that, close to its summit, I would be compelled, with powers already slightly on the wane and troubled soul, to start all over again. Truly, this was no day to conjure up anything so irrational and absurd. I had reason to be satisfied. I loved my work, hence loved life. I was protected from material worry; even if I never wrote another line my books would take care of me. It seemed as if there were nothing further to be achieved, destiny seemed to be tamed. The security which I had known of old in my parents' home and which had disappeared during the war, had been recaptured by my own efforts. What more could one wish?

But strangely enough, the very fact that I had no desire in this hour caused me private discomfort. Something in me—not I, myself—asked me whether it was really desirable that life go on like this, so calmly, orderly, lucratively, comfortably, quite without fresh exertions or trials? Were not the privileges and complete security of my existence foreign to my essential self? Thoughtfully I walked through the house. It had taken on beauty in these years and had become just as I had wanted it. But yet, was I always to live here, always sit at this same desk and write books, one book then another book, receive royalties and then more royalties, eventually becoming a dignified gentleman required to live up to his name and his work with grace and propriety, absent from the play of chance, all dangers and suspense? Was it always to go on like this, until sixty, until seventy on an even keel? Would I not be better off—my dream continued —if something were to enter my life that would make me more restless, more eager, younger by challenging me to new and perhaps more dangerous struggle? Every artist harbors a mysterious duality: if life tosses him about stormily he yearns for peace; but no sooner is peace given him than he longs for the old agitation. So, on this fiftieth birthday, deep within myself I had but one wicked wish— for something that would once more tear me away from all these guarantees and comforts, that would necessitate my not merely continuing, but my starting anew. Was it the fear of growing old, of weariness, of becoming lazy? Or was it a mysterious premonition which made me desire a different, a harder life for my soul's sake? I do not know.

I do not know. For that which emerged from the twilight of the unconscious in this strange hour was not a clearly formed wish and surely nothing that was related to my conscious will. It was no more than a passing thought that blew my way, perhaps not even my own thought but rather one which came from depths I knew nothing of. But the obscure, incomprehensible power over my life which had fulfilled so much more for me than I had ever presumed to wish, must have made it out. And, obediently, its hand was already raised to destroy my life to its very foundation and to make me build out of its ruins a completely different, harder and more difficult one, anew from the ground up.

XV

Incipit Hitler

It REMAINS an irrefragable law of history that contemporaries are denied a recognition of the early beginnings of the great movements which determine their times. So I am frankly unable to recall when I first heard the name of Adolf Hitler, that name which for years we have been forced to think of or to pronounce every day, yes, almost every second, in one connection or another; the name of the man who has brought more evil to our world than any other through the ages. However, it must have been fairly early, because Salzburg, within two and a half hours by train, was so much of a neighbor to Munich that even its local concerns became our familiar talk. I only remember that one day—I can not remember the date—an acquaintance dropped in and bemoaned that Munich was again becoming restless. In particular, a wild agitator named Hitler, who held meetings at which fights occurred and who agitated most vulgarly against the Republic and the Jews.

The name made no impression upon me. I gave it no thought. There were so many, now long forgotten, names of agitators and *Putschists* in the confused Germany of that day which rose only to disappear. Those of Captain Ehrhardt with his Baltic troops, of General Kapp, of the Vehmic murderers, of the Bavarian, the Rhenish Separatists, the Freecorps leaders. Hundreds of such small bubbles floated about in the general fermentation which bursting, left nothing but a foul odor that clearly betrayed the inner decomposition in Germany's still open wound. The little organ of the new National-Socialist movement happened into my hands, the *Miesbacher Anzeiger* (which was to evolve into the *Völkische Beobachter*.) But Miesbach was nothing more than a tiny village and the newspaper was a common performance. Who cared?

Then, however, in the neighboring frontier towns of Reichenhall and Berchtesgaden, which I visited almost weekly, there bobbed up small but ever-growing squads of young fellows in riding boots and brown shirts, each with a loud-colored swastika on his sleeve. They arranged rallies and marches, paraded through the streets singing and shouting in unison, plastered the walls with large posters and besmeared them with swastikas; only then I sensed that financial and otherwise influential forces must be behind these mobs which disclosed themselves so unexpectedly. Hitler alone, whose speeches then were limited to Bavarian beer cellars, could not have manipulated these thousands of lads into so expensive an apparatus. There must have been mightier hands which used this new "movement" as a front.

For the uniforms were brand new and the "storm-troops" which were sent from town to town in a time of such poverty that the real army veterans had only their tattered uniforms, commanded a remarkable fleet of fine new automobiles, motorcycles and lorries. Furthermore, it was notorious that these young men were learning tactics from army men and were receiving what was then known as "paramilitary" discipline, and that it must have been the Reichswehr itself, in whose secret service Hitler had been a spy from the outset, which here undertook the systematic technical training of manpower that was answerable to him. By chance, I had an early opportunity of observing one of these well-rehearsed combat maneuvers. In a border village, where a Social-Democrat meeting was being conducted in perfect peace, four lorries suddenly whizzed up, each one filled with young National Socialists armed with rubber truncheons and, exactly as I had once seen it before at St. Mark's in Venice, their adversaries succumbed to rapid surprise tactics. It was the same method copied from the fascists, only drilled in with greater military precision and systematically prepared down to the smallest detail in the German way. Like a flash the S. A. men were out of their autos at the sound of a whistle and beat aside all who stood in their way with their clubs; and before the police could interfere or the workers could collect themselves, they were already back on their trucks and off at top speed. What dumbfounded me, was the exact technique of this jumping-off and jumping-on which followed the single shrill whistle of the file-leader. It was apparent that each fellow knew, and felt in every muscle and nerve, just which handle he had to grasp, at which wheel of the truck and where he had to jump in order not to obstruct the next one so as not to lose a second. It was not individual skill, rather every one of these manipulations must have been practiced in advance dozens and perhaps hundreds of times in barracks and on drill grounds: from the start—it was plain at a glance—these troops had been trained to attack, force, and terror.

Soon one heard more about these undercover maneuvers in Bavaria. In the dead of night the young men sneaked out of their homes and assembled for such nightly "terrain exercises"; officers of the Reichswehr on active duty or retired, paid by the State or the Party's mysterious financial backers, drilled these troops, and the authorities paid little attention to these strange nocturnal goings on. Were they really asleep or did they just shut their eyes? Did they think the movement was unimportant or did they secretly further its expansion? In any event, even those who covertly supported the movement, eventually became terrified by the brutality and rapidity with which it suddenly matured. One morning, in 1923, the authorities woke up to find Munich in Hitler's hands, all official buildings occupied, the newspapers forced at the point of a gun to announce triumphantly the successfully accomplished revolution. As from the clouds, to which the unsuspecting republic had only looked up dreamily, appeared the *deus ex machina*, General Ludendorff, the first of the many who thought they could beat Hitler at his own game but who lived to be fooled by him instead. In the morning this famous *Putsch* that was intended to conquer Germany started; at noon (this is no place to recount world history) as is known, it was already over. Hitler fled and was soon arrested and therewith the movement seemed to be snuffed out. During 1923 the swastikas disappeared, the storm troops and the name of Adolf Hitler all but fell into oblivion. Nobody thought of him any more as a possible political factor.

A few years elapsed before he again rose to the surface, this time on a rising wave of dissatisfaction that quickly lifted him high. Inflation, unemployment, the political crises and, not least, the folly of lands abroad, had made the German people restless; a tremendous desire for order animated all circles of the German people, to whom order had always been more important than freedom and justice. And anyone who promised order—even Goethe said that disorder was more distasteful to him than even an injustice —could count on hundreds of thousands of supporters from the start.

Even then we did not note the danger. The few among writers who had taken the trouble to read Hitler's book, ridiculed the bombast of his stilted prose instead of occupying themselves with his program. The big democratic newspapers, instead of warning their readers reassured them day by day, that the movement, which in truth found diffi-

culty in financing its enormous activities with no more than
the contributions of big business and audacious borrowing,
would inevitably collapse in no time. But perhaps to the
outside world the real reason why Germany in all these
years had so greatly underestimated and belittled the person
and growing power of Hitler has never been intelligible.
Germany has not only always been a class-conscious country,
but within these class ideals she has, besides, always borne
the burden of a blind over-estimation and deification of
"education." Except for a few generals, the high government
positions were always the exclusive preserves of the so-called
"academically educated;" while in England a Lloyd George,
in Italy a Mussolini and a Garibaldi, in France a Briand had
truly risen from the people to the highest posts in the gift of
the state, it was unthinkable to Germans that a man who
had not even finished high school, to say nothing of college,
who had lodged in flop-houses and whose mode of life for
years is a mystery to this day, should even make a pass
toward a position once held by a Bismarck, a Baron vom
Stein, a Prince Bülow. Nothing misled the German intellectuals as much as this education-vainglory into believing that
Hitler was still only the beer-hall agitator who never could
become a real danger, at a time when, thanks to his invisible
wirepullers, he already had won to himself powerful supporters in the most varied circles. And even when he had
become chancellor on that day in January 1933 the masses,
as well as those who had backed him for the post, regarded
him as no more than a temporary incumbent and the
National Socialist mastery as an episode.

Then it was that the technique of Hitler's cynical genius
revealed itself for the first time on a grand scale. For years he
had made promises right and left and in all parties he had
gained important adherents, each of whom thought he
could make use of the mystical powers of the "unknown

soldier" for his own ends. But the technique which Hitler later used on a world scale when he made pacts under oath and with German candor with those whom he intended to destroy and emasculate, now celebrated its first triumph. So well had he distributed his promises that on the day of his coming to power there was jubilation in the most diverse camps. The monarchists in Doorn thought he was the Kaiser's most faithful advance agent, and the Bavarians, the Wittelsbach monarchists rejoiced similarly in Munich for they regarded him as "their" man. The German Nationalists were in hopes that he would fill their crib, their leader, Hugenberg, having contracted for the most important place in Hitler's cabinet thus had a foot in the stirrup, naturally, in spite of a sworn agreement, he was thrown out in the first few weeks. Heavy industry felt relieved of the bolshevik menace; it saw in power the man whom it had financed secretly for years; and simultaneously the impoverished petty citizen to whom in hundreds of meetings had been promised emancipation from "interest-slavery" breathed a joyous sigh. The small shopkeepers remembered his promise to abolish the big department stores, their greatest competitors (a promise that was never fulfilled) and Hitler was particularly welcome to the military because his outlook was militaristic and he vilified pacifism. Even the Social Democrats were not as unfriendly to his ascent as one might have expected because they hoped he would do away with their arch-enemies, the communists who were crowding them so uncomfortably. The most varied, most contrary parties considered this "unknown soldier" who had promised and confirmed by oath everything to every class, every party, every movement, as their friend—even the German Jews were not very worried. They flattered themselves that a *ministre Jacobin* was no longer a Jacobin, an anti-semitic agitator become chancellor would as a matter of course throw off such

vulgarities. And finally, what could he put through by force
in a State where law was securely anchored, where the
majority in parliament was against him, and where every
citizen believed his liberty and equal rights secured by the
solemnly affirmed constitution?

Then came the Reichstag fire, parliament disappeared,
Goering let loose his hordes, and at one blow all of justice
in Germany was smashed. Shudderingly one learned of
peace-time concentration camps and of secret chambers built
into barracks where innocent people were done away with
without trial or formality. This could only be an eruption
of an initial, senseless rage, one told oneself. That sort of
thing could not last in the twentieth century. But it was
only the beginning. The world was startled and at first
refused to believe the unbelievable. But already in those
days I saw the first refugees. At night they had climbed over
the Salzburg mountains or swum across the frontier-stream.
Starved, shabby, agitated they stared at one; they were the
leaders in the panic flight from inhumanity which was to
spread over the whole earth. But even then I did not suspect
when I looked at these fugitives that I ought to perceive in
their pale faces, as in a mirror, my own life and that we all,
we all, we all would become victims of the lust for power of
this one man.

～

One cannot easily dispose of thirty or forty years of deep
faith in the world inside of a few brief weeks. In the clutch
of our conception of justice we believed that there was a
German, a European, a world conscience and were convinced
that there existed a measure of barbarousness that would
make its own quietus, once and for all, because of mankind.
Since I am trying here to stick to the truth as much as possible I have to admit that none of us in Germany and in

Austria in 1933 and even in 1934 thought that even a hundredth, a thousandth part of what was to break upon us within a few weeks could be possible. However, it was clear from the beginning that we free and independent writers had to expect certain difficulties, troubles, hostility. Immediately after the Reichstag fire I warned my publisher that the end of my books in Germany was in sight. I shall not forget his astonishment. "Who is there to forbid your books?" he said then, in 1933, still nonplussed. "You haven't ever written a word against Germany or interfered in politics." Note that such monstrous things as book burnings and pilloryings which but a few months later were to be facts seemed, a month after Hitler's seizure of power still beyond the comprehension of even rather ample minds. For National Socialism in its unscrupulous technique of deceit was wary about disclosing the full extent of its aims before the world had become inured. Thus they practised their method carefully: only a small dose to begin with, then a brief pause. Only a single pill at a time and then a moment of waiting to observe the effect of its strength, to see whether the world conscience would still digest this dose. And since the European conscience—to the hurt and shame of our civilization—eagerly accented its unconcern because, after all, these atrocities occurred "beyond the border," the doses became progressively stronger until all of Europe finally perished from them. Hitler has achieved nothing more ingenious than this technique of slowly feeling his way and increasing pressure with accelerating force against a Europe that was waning morally and soon also militarily. The long-planned project to destroy all free speech and every independent book in Germany was effected according to this method, too. By no means was an order issued immediately—that followed only after two years—to shut down on our books; instead they first felt their way to see how far they could go in that the first attack on our books was assigned to an officially non-responsible group, the National Socialist students. Using the same system with which they staged "public wrath" to put over the long-decided boycott of the Jews, they quietly tipped the students off to display their "indignation" against our books publicly. And the German students, glad of any opportunity of manifesting their reactionary sentiments, obediently assembled in every university, possessed themselves of copies of our books from book shops and marched with their booty, banners waving, to a public square. There they would either nail the books to a pillory according to the ancient German custom—mediaevalism having suddenly become their strong card—I myself once had a nail-perforated copy of one of my books, the gift of a student friend who had retrieved it after the execution—or, permission to burn human beings not being accorded,—they were reduced to ashes in huge bonfires to the accompaniment of patriotic sentiments. Although propaganda minister Goebbels had decided after long hesitation and at the last moment, to bless the burning of books, it yet remained a semi-official proceeding; and nothing more clearly indicated Germany's unconcern with such acts than that the public failed to react to these undergraduate burnings and proscriptions. Book dealers were warned not to display any of our books and newspapers ignored them, nevertheless the general public remained indifferent. While yet there was no threat of punishment in prison or concentration camp my books sold almost as well in 1933 and 1934 in spite of all difficulties and chicaneries as they had before. Only after the grandiose order "for the protection of the German people" by which the printing, sale, and distribution of our books were declared criminal had become law, were we forcibly estranged from the millions of Germans who even today would rather read our works than all the mushroom growth "blood and soil" writers and would endorse what we represent.

I regarded it more as an honor than a disgrace to be permitted to share this fate of the complete destruction of literary existence in Germany with such eminent contemporaries as Thomas Mann, Heinrich Mann, Werfel, Freud, Einstein, and many others whose work I consider incomparably more important than my own, and as any gesture of martyrdom is so repugnant to me I mention my personal inclusion in the common fate only reluctantly. But by strange chance it was just my lot to get the National Socialists and even Adolf Hitler in person into a very embarrassing situation. It was allotted to me, among the literary outlaws, to become repeatedly the object of heated and long debate in the high circles of the Berchtesgaden villa with the result that I am able to record among the pleasant things in my life the modest satisfaction of having annoyed Adolf Hitler, the most powerful man of modern times.

In the very first days of the new regime I had innocently been the cause of something like tumult. A motion picture based on my short story "The Burning Secret" and bearing that title was being shown all over Germany. Nobody made the slightest objection to that. But the day after the Reichstag fire, responsibility for which the National Socialists vainly tried to put on the communists, it was noted that people gathered in front of the theater placards nudging each other, winking and laughing. It was not long before the Gestapo understood what was funny about the title, for by evening, motorcycle policemen had made the rounds, the performances were forbidden and the next day the title of my story "The Burning Secret" had disappeared without trace from all the newspaper advertisements and from all of

the posters. It was easy enough for them to forbid a word
that annoyed them or even to burn and destroy all the books
whose authors they did not like. In one particular case however, they could not touch me without at the same time
hurting a man, whom they needed more than anyone else in
this critical moment for their prestige before the world,
the greatest, the most famous living composer of the German nation, Richard Strauss, together with whom I had just
finished an opera.

This had been my first collaboration with Richard Strauss.
Ever since *Elektra* and the *Rosenkavalier* Hugo von Hofmannsthal had written all of his opera books and I had never
personally met Richard Strauss. After Hofmannstahl's death
he notified my publisher that he wished to start on a new
work and inquired whether I would be willing to write an
opera libretto for him. I was fully conscious of the honor
of such a request. Since Max Reger had set my first poems
to music. I had always lived in music and with musicians. I
had ties of close friendship with Busoni, Toscanini, Bruno
Walter, and Alban Berg. But there was no productive
musician of our time whom I would more willingly have
served than Richard Strauss, last of the great line of
thoroughbred musicians that reaches from Handel and Bach
by way of Beethoven and Brahms to our day. I consented at
once and at our first meeting suggested using *The Silent
Woman* by Ben Jonson as the theme for an opera, and it was
a pleasant surprise to see how quickly, how clearsightedly
Strauss responded to my suggestions. I had not suspected
in him so alert an understanding of art, so astounding a
knowledge of dramaturgy. While the nature of the material
was being explained to him he was already shaping it dramatically and adjusting it astonishingly to the limits of his own
abilities of which he was uncannily cognizant. I have met
many great artists in my life but never one who knew how

to maintain such abstract and unerring objectivity towards himself. Thus Strauss frankly admitted to me in the first hour of our meeting that he well knew, that at seventy the composer's musical inspiration no longer possesses its pristine power. He could hardly succeed in composing symphonics works like *Till Eulenspiegel* and *Death and Transfiguration* because just pure music requires an extreme measure of creative freshness. But the word could still inspire him. Something tangible, a substance already scaffolded appealed to him for full dramatic realization, because musical themes sprang to him spontaneously out of situations and words, hence he had been devoting himself exclusively to the opera in his later years. He knew well indeed, he said, that as an art form opera was dead. Wagner was so gigantic a peak that nobody could rise higher. "But," he added, with a broad, Bavarian grin. "I solved the problem by making a detour around it."

After we had agreed on outlines, he gave me a few minor instructions. He wished me to write unrestrictedly because he never was inspired by a ready-made book after the manner of a Verdi libretto, but only by a work conceived poetically. But it would suit him well if I were able to work in some complicated effects which would afford special possibilities for the employment of color. "I am not one to compare long melodies as did Mozart. I can't get beyond short themes. But what I can do, is to utilize such a theme, paraphrase it and extract everything that is in it, and I don't think there's anybody today who can match me at that." Again I was dumbfounded by this frankness, for it is true enough that there is hardly a Strauss melody that is longer than a few bars; but how these few bars—take the *Rosenkavalier* waltz—are enhanced and fugued into a rich fulfillment!

Subsequent meetings confirmed my admiration of the

surety and objectivity with which the old master evaluated his own work. Once I sat alone with him at a private rehearsal of his *Egyptian Helena* in the Salzburg Festival Theater. Nobody else was there, the place was completely dark. Strauss listened intently. All at once he began to drum inaudibly and impatiently with his fingers upon the arm of the chair. Then he whispered to me: "Bad, very bad! That spot is a blank." And again, after a few minutes: "If I could cut that out! O Lord, Lord, that's just hollow, and too long, much too, long!" A little later: "Look you, that's good!" He appraised his own work as objectively and unconcernedly as if he were hearing the music for the first time and as if it were written by a composer unknown to him; and this astounding sense of his own dimensions never deserted him. He was always exactly aware of his significance and of his capacity. How little or how much others registered in comparison to him interested him but little and just as little how he registered on others. What gave him pleasure was work in itself.

Work, as he practiced it, was a quite remarkable procedure with Strauss. Nothing of the daemonic, nothing of the artist's mad exaltation, nothing of those depressions and desperations which we know from accounts of Beethoven and Wagner. Strauss works to the point and composes like Johann Sebastian Bach, like all those sublime craftsmen of their art, quietly and systematically. At nine in the morning he sits down to resume his work just where he left off the day before, always writing the first sketch of his composition with pencil, the piano score in ink, and continues thus without pause until twelve or one o'clock. In the afternoon he plays *Skat*, a German card game, transfers two or three pages to the final score and possibly conducts an opera in the evening. He does not know what nervousness is, by day and night his artistic mind is equally alert and lucid. When

his valet knocks at the door to bring his evening clothes, he
gets up from his work, dresses, rides to the theater and conducts with the same assurance and calm with which he plays
Skat in the afternoon, and the next morning inspiration
again falls into its proper place. For, as Goethe says, Strauss
"commands" his fancies; art means to him knowing and
even knowing everything, as his jest implies: "Anybody who
wants to be a real musician must be able to set even a menu
to music." Difficulties do not menace him but rather serve
to amuse his creative mastery. I recall with pleasure how
his little blue eyes glistened when he said to me triumphantly about a certain passage: "I've given the singer a hard
nut to crack there. Let her struggle like hell to get what's
in it." In such rare seconds, when his eyes light up, one feels
that something daemonic lies deep down in this extraordinary person who at first arouses something like distrust,
by his punctuality, by his methodical ways, his respectability,
his artisanship, his seeming nervelessness at work, just as his
face first impresses as almost banal with its fat, child-like
cheeks, the rather ordinary roundness of features and the
hesitantly retreating brow. But only one glance into his
eyes, these bright, blue, highly radiant eyes, and one instantly feels some particular magic power behind this bourgeois mask. They are perhaps the most wide-awake eyes I
have ever seen in a musician, not daemonic but in some way
clairvoyant, the eyes of a man cognizant of the full significance of his task.

Back in Salzburg after so stimulating an encounter I
immediately started to work. Curious myself whether my
verses met his views I sent him the first act within two weeks.
Promptly he wrote me on a postcard a quotation from *Die
Meistersinger*: "The first stanza is successful." His response
to the second act was even more heartfelt, the opening bars
of his song "Oh, that I have found you, my dear beloved

child!" and this joy of his, his enthusiasm, invested my
continued work with an indescribable pleasure. Strauss did
not change a single line in my whole libretto and asked
only that I add three or four lines for the sake of a counterpart. Thus developed between us the most cordial relation
imaginable; he came to our house and I would visit him
at Garmisch where, with his long thin fingers he played for
me on the piano little by little, from his sketch, the whole
opera. And without contract or obligation it was taken for
granted and accepted that, after finishing this opera, I
should outline a second one, the plan for which he had
already fully approved in advance.

~~~

In January 1933, when Hitler came into power, the piano
score of our opera the *The Silent Woman* was as good as
finished and the first act practically orchestrated. A few
weeks later a strict order was issued to German theaters not
to produce any works by non-aryans or even such in which
a Jew had merely participated. This comprehensive ban
reached even to the dead and to the indignation of music
lovers everywhere the statue of Mendelssohn in front of the
Gewandhaus in Leipzig was removed. For me this order
seemed to seal the fate of our opera. It went without saying
that Richard Strauss would abandon further work on it and
begin another with someone else. Instead, he wrote me letter
after letter asking what had got into me; quite the contrary,
he said, for as he was already at the orchestration he wanted
me to work on the text of his next opera. He would not
think of letting anybody forbid his collaboration with me,
and I have to admit that he kept faith with me throughout
this whole affair as long as it was possible for him to do so.
To be sure, simultaneously he took steps which I liked less,
he approached the men in power, met frequently with Hit-

ler, Goering, and Goebbels and at a time when even Furtwängler was still in mutiny, allowed himself be made president of the Nazi Chamber of Music.

Strauss's open participation was of tremendous importance to the National Socialists at that moment. For annoy-
ingly enough, not only the best writers but the most important musicians as well had openly snubbed them, and the
few who held with them or came over to the reservation were
unknown to the wide public. To have the most famous
musician of Germany align himself with them at so
embarrassing a moment meant, in its mere decorative aspect,
an immeasurable gain to Goebbels and Hitler. Hitler who
had, as Strauss told me, during his Viennese vagabond years
scraped up enough money to travel to Graz to attend the
première of *Salome,* was honoring him demonstratively; at
all festive evenings at Berchtesgaden besides Wagner, Strauss
songs were sung almost exclusively. Strauss's cooperation
however, was much more purposeful. Through his art-
egoism which he always acknowledged openly and coolly, he
was inwardly indifferent whatever the regime. He had served
the German Kaiser as a conductor and had arranged military
marches for him, later he had served the Emperor of Austria
as court-conductor in Vienna, and had been *persona gratis-
sima* likewise in the Austrian and German Republics. To be
particularly cooperative with the National Socialists was
furthermore of vital interest to him, because in the National
Socialist sense he was very much in the red. His son had
married a Jewess and thus he feared that his grandchildren
whom he loved above everything else would be excluded
as scum from the schools; his new opera was tainted
through me, his earlier operas through the half-Jew Hugo
von Hofmannsthal, his publisher was a Jew. Therefore it
seemed to him more and more imperative to create some
support and security for himself and he did it most persever-

ingly. He conducted wherever the new masters wanted him to, he set a hymn to music for the Olympic games, at the same time writing me with little enthusiasm in his shockingly frank letters about this commission. In truth, in the *sacro egoismo* of the artist he cared only about one thing: to keep his work alive and above all for a production of the new opera, which lay particularly close to his heart.

That such concessions to National Socialism were extremely embarrassing to me, goes without saying. For how easily might the impression develop that I collaborated secretly or even agreed that in my person a single exception to such a shameful boycott should be made. From all quarters friends urged me to protest publicly against a performance in National Socialist Germany. But fundamentally I loathe public and pathetic gestures; besides, I was reluctant to cause difficulties for a genius of his rank. After all, Strauss was the greatest living musician and seventy years old, he had spent three years at this work, and during the entire time had always given evidence of the most friendly sentiments, propriety and even courage. Hence I considered that my course was to wait silently and to let matters develop as they might. Besides, I knew that I caused the new guardians of German culture more difficulties by complete passivity than by doing anything else. For the National Socialist Chamber of Writers and the propaganda ministry were just looking for a welcome reason or pretext to be able to cloak an injunction against their greatest composer in an unquestionable manner. So, for instance, the libretto was demanded by every imaginable office and person in the secret hope of finding a pretext. How convenient would it have been, had the *Silent Woman* contained a situation something like the one in the *Rosenkavalier* where a young man emerges from the bedroom of a married woman! Then they could have pretended the protection of German morals.

But to their disappointment my book held nothing immoral.
Then all imaginable files of the Gestapo and all my earlier
books were combed through. But here also nothing could
be found to show that I ever had said a detrimental word
about Germany (or about any other nation of the earth)
or that I had been politically active. However they maneu-
vered, the decision immutably fell back into their hands:
should they, in the sight of the whole world, deny to the
senior master of National Socialist music in whose hands
they themselves had placed the banner, the right to have
his opera performed or—oh, day of national shame—should
the name Stefan Zweig on the appearance of which on the
libretto Richard Strauss had expressly insisted, once again
as so often before sully a German theater program? How
I secretly enjoyed their great worry and painful headache;
I sensed that, even without my doing anything or just
because of my doing nothing for and nothing against it,
my musical comedy would inevitably develop into a cater-
wauling of party politics. The party evaded deciding as long
as it could possibly do so. But in the beginning of 1934 it
had to determine whether to take its stand against its own
law or against the greatest musician of the day. The date
could not longer be delayed. The score, the piano version,
the librettos had long since been printed, the costumes had
been ordered by the Dresden Court Theater, the rôles
allotted and even studied and still the various authorities,
Goering and Goebbels, Chamber of Writers, Council of Culture, Ministry of Education, and the Streicher Guard had
not been able to agree.* Of all these authorities none
dared to take the full responsibility for saying yes or no,
thus nothing remained but to leave the matter to the personal decision of the master of Germany and master of the

---

* Silly as all this may sound, the matter of *The Silent Woman* eventually developed into an exciting affair of State.

party, Adolf Hitler. My books had already enjoyed the honor of being widely read by the National Socialists; it had been the *Fouché* in particular which as an example of political unscrupulousness they had studied and discussed repeatedly. But, I had truly never expected that after Goebbels and Göring I would have to trouble Adolf Hitler personally to study the three acts of my lyric libretto. The decision was not easy for him. There were many conferences and meetings, as I learned later in round-about ways. Finally Richard Strauss was summoned before the all powerful and Hitler in person told him that he would permit the performance as an exception although it was an offense against all laws of the new Germany; a decision which probably was given just as unwillingly and dishonestly as the signing of the treaty with Stalin and Molotov.

Thus the black day broke over National Socialist Germany when once again an opera was to be performed where the proscribed name of Stefan Zweig showed up on every poster. Of course I did not attend the performance because I knew that the audience would be full of brown uniforms and that Hitler himself was expected at one of the performances. The opera was a great success and I must say to their credit that nine-tenths of the music critics enthusiastically used the favorable opportunity, once more and for the last time, to give evidence of their inner resistance to the race theory by writing the friendliest possible words about my libretto. All of the German theaters, Berlin, Hamburg, Frankfort, Munich, immediately announced the production of the opera for the next season.

Suddenly after the second performance, lightning struck from the high heavens. Overnight everything was cancelled, the opera was forbidden in Dresden and throughout all of Germany. And even more: one read in astonishment that Richard Strauss had submitted his resignation as president of the Reich Chamber of Music. Everyone knew that something extraordinary must have had happened. But it took a while before I learned the whole truth. Strauss had once more written a letter to me urging that I begin the libretto of a new opera, and in which he expressed himself with too much frankness about his personal attitude. This letter had fallen into the hands of the Gestapo. Strauss was confronted with it, he was required immediately to submit his resignation and the opera was forbidden. In the German language it has been produced only in free Switzerland and in Prague; later on also in Italian at the Scala in Milan with the special permission of Mussolini who had then not yet been required to subject himself to Hitler's racial notions. The German people, however, have never again been allowed to hear a single note of this in part enchanting opera of the old age of their greatest living composer; it is not my fault.

~

I lived abroad while this rather noisy affair took place, because I felt that the unrest in Austria would make tranquil work impossible for me. My house in Salzburg lay so close to the border that with the naked eye I could view the Berchtesgaden mountain on which Adolf Hitler's house stood, an uninviting and very disturbing neighborhood. This proximity to the German border, however, gave me an opporunity to judge the threat to the Austrian situation better than my friends in Vienna. In that city the café observers and even men in the Government regarded National Socialism as something that was happening "over there" and that could in no way affect Austria. Was not the Social Democratic party with its tight organization comprising practically half of the population firmly placed? Was not the Clerical party united with them in hot defense since Hitler's "German Christians" had publicly persecuted Christianity and proclaimed their leader frankly and literally "greater than Christ"? Were not France, England, and the League of Nations Austria's protectors? Had not Mussolini explicitly undertaken the protection and even the guarantee of Austrian independence? Not even the Jews worried, and they acted as if the cancelling of all the rights of physicians, lawyers, scholars, and actors was happening in China instead of across the border three hours away where their own language was spoken. They rested comfortably in their homes, rode about in their cars. Moreover, everybody had a ready-made phrase: "That cannot last long." But I remembered a conversation with my publisher in Leningrad on my short trip to Russia. He had been telling me how rich he had once been, what beautiful paintings he had owned and I asked him why he had not left Russia immediately on the outbreak of the revolution as so many others had done. "Ah," he answered, "who would have believed that such a thing as a Workers' and Soldiers' Republic could last longer than a fortnight?" It was the self deception that we practice because of reluctance to abandon our accustomed life.

In Salzburg, to be sure, close to the border, one saw things clearer. A constant traffic across the narrow border stream had set in, young men would slink across at night to be drilled, agitators would arrive over the border in automobiles or on foot with mountain sticks as simple "tourists" and organize their "cells" among all classes. They preached their gospel to the accompaniment of threats that whoever did not join promptly, would have to pay for it later. Such intimidation was effective with the police and civil servants. Increasingly I perceived, from a certain uneasiness in their behavior, how the public vacillated. It is the petty, personal experiences in life that are the most convincing. I had a boyhood friend in Salzburg, a rather well-known writer with whom I had been on the most intimate and cordial terms for thirty years; we had dedicated books to one another, we saw each other every week. One day, I saw this old friend on the street with a stranger and noticed that he stopped abruptly before a show-window that could have meant nothing to him and, with his back to me, pointed out something to his companion with conspicuous eagerness. "How odd," I thought, "surely he must have seen me. But perhaps it just happened that way." The next day he telephoned to ask whether he could come over in the afternoon for a little chat. I agreed, somewhat astonished, because we usually met in a café. It turned out that he had nothing in particular to say in spite of the seeming urgency of his visit. And immediately I became aware that while he was desirous of keeping up his friendship with me he did not want to make a show of intimacy with me in the little town in order not to be suspected of friendship with Jews. That made me attentive. And soon it became apparent that a number of my friends who used to visit me frequently were staying away. The situation was dangerous.

At this time I had not yet considered leaving Salzburg for good, but I decided more readily than usual to spend the winter abroad so as not to be occupied by all these petty discords. I did not suspect, though, that when I left my beautiful home in October 1933 it was already a kind of farewell.

~~~

My plan had been to spend January and February at work in France. I loved that beautiful intellectual country as a second homeland and had no sense of being a foreigner there. Valéry, Romain Rolland, André Gide, Roger Martin du Gard, Duhamel, Vildrac, and Jean-Richard Bloch, the leaders of literature, were all old friends. My circle of readers was almost as large as in Germany, I was not regarded as a foreign writer, a stranger. I loved the people, I loved the country, I loved the city of Paris and felt so much at home there that every time my train pulled into the Gare du Nord it was like "coming back." But this time, because of the particular circumstances, I had left sooner than was my habit and it was not my purpose to go to Paris until after Christmas. Whereto in the meantime? Then it occurred to me that I had not been to England since my student days, more than a quarter of a century. "Why always only Paris?" I asked myself. "Why not once again spend a week or two in London, to study the museums with different eyes after these many years, to see the city and the country?" So, instead of the express train to Paris I took the one to Calais. And in the prescribed fog of a November day I once more alighted after thirty years at Victoria Station and my only surprise was that it was not a cab that took me to my hotel but an automobile. The fog, that cool soft grayness, was unchanged. Before even looking at the city my sense of smell after three decades, had recognized this singular acerb, dense, moist, almost enveloping air.

The baggage that I brought along was meager and so were my expectations. In London I had as good as no ties of friendship; professionally, too, there was but little contact between Continental and English writers. They lived a bounded life peculiarly their own in their own sphere of activity within their tradition which was never fully accessible to us. Among the many books which arrived on my library table from all over the world I cannot remember ever having found one from an English writer as a fraternal gift. I had met Shaw once in Hellerau and Wells had visited me at my house in Salzburg. All of my books had been translated but they were not widely known; always England was the country in which they were the least effective. And, too, while my American, my French, my Russian, and my Italian publishers were my personal friends I had never seen anybody from the firm which published me in England. I was thus prepared to feel no more at home than I had felt thirty years before.

But it worked out differently. After a few days I felt indescribably satisfied in London. Not that London had materially changed. But I myself had changed. I had grown thirty years older and filled with longing, after the war and post-war years of strain and overstrain, to live the quiet life and get away from political talk. Of course there were parties in England, a Conservative, Liberal, Labour, but their arguments did not concern me. Doubtless in literature, too, there were controversies and currents, strife and covert rivalries, but here I stood completely outside. What was really salutary was the sense of again being in a civil, courteous, unexcited, hateless atmosphere. Nothing poisoned my life more during the preceding years than the consciousness of being surrounded by hate and stress, in the country, in the city; of always having to ward off embroilment in these discussions. Here the population was not confused in the same degree, a higher measure of justice and decency obtained in public life than in our countries which through the fraud of inflation alone had become immoral. They lived more peacefully, more contentedly and were more interested in their gardens and little hobbies than in their neighbors. Here one could breathe, reflect, and think things over. But the real thing that held me was a new task.

This is how it came about. My *Marie Antoinette* had just been published and I was reading the proof of my book about Erasmus in which I attempted a spiritual portrait of the humanist who, though he understood the madness of the time more clearly than the professional world-reformers, for all his sound reason was, tragically enough, unable to oppose unreason. After the completion of this veiled self-portrait it had been my intention to write a long-planned novel. I had had enough of biographies. But it happened that on my third day, attracted by my old passion for autographs, I was looking at the public exhibit in the British Museum. Among them was the hand-written report of the execution of Mary Stuart. Involuntarily I asked myself: "What was the truth about Mary Stuart? Was she really involved in the murder of her second husband or was she not?" Not having anything to read that night I bought a book about her. It was a laudation that defended her as a saint, a flat and silly book. In my incurable curiosity I purchased another the next day that expressed a point of view approximately the exact opposite. And now the case began to interest me. I asked for a truly reliable book. Nobody was able to name one and thus, through searching and inquiring, without consciously willing it, I found myself working on a book about Mary Stuart which then kept me in the libraries for weeks. Returning to Austria early in 1934 I was determined to come back to London which had gained my affection, in order to complete the book there in quietude.

~~~

Two or three days in Austria were enough to see how much worse the situation had become within the few months of the new year, 1934. Coming from the serene and secure atmosphere of England into this fever-and struggle-shaken Austria was like suddenly, on a stifling hot July day in New York changing from an air-conditioned room to the steaming street. The National Socialist pressure began slowly to undermine the nerves of the Clerical and middle-class population; the severity of the economic, the subversive thumbscrews of impatient Germany was increasingly felt. The Dollfuss administration, which sought to keep Austria independent and to save her from Hitler, looked about with growing desperation for firm support. France and England were too remote besides feeling no real concern, Czechoslovakia still remembered her old rancor and rivalry toward Vienna, so there was only Italy which then aspired to an economic and political protectorate over Austria so as to make secure the Alpine passes to its own territory, and Trieste. For this protection Mussolini, however, demanded a stiff price. Austria was to be adapted to fascist principles, parliament was to pass out and with it democracy. This was impossible without either the collaboration of or the emasculation of the Social Democratic Party, the strongest and best-organized of Austria. There was no other way to break it than by brute force.

For such terrorism an organization already existed, the Heimwehr, the creation of Ignaz Seipel, Dollfuss's predecessor. Superficially viewed it was about as shabby an affair as one could imagine; petty provincial lawyers, disbanded officers, black sheep, unemployed engineers, each one a frustrated mediocrity, all hating one another bitterly. Finally a leader was found in the young Prince Starhemberg, who although he once had sat at Hitler's feet and had fulminated against the republic and democracy, paraded about with his hired soldiers and promised "to make heads roll." What the Heimwehr actually wanted was quite obscure. The truth is that the Heimwehr had no other aim than somehow to get to the public crib and its power consisted of Mussolini's fist which pushed it forward. Those allegedly patriotic Austrians never noticed that they were sawing off the limb on which they were sitting, with their "made in Italy" bayonets.

The Social Democratic Party understood better where the real danger lay. They had no need to fear an open fight. They had their weapons and could, by means of a general strike, paralyze the railroads, the water-works and all the

power works. But they also knew that Hitler was only waiting for such a so-called "red revolution" in order to have
a pretext to march in as Austria's "savior." So it seemed
better to them to sacrifice their rights in large part and even
their parliament in order to reach a bearable compromise.
All sensible people advocated such a settlement in view of
the precarious position in which Austria found herself under
the menacing shadow of Hitlerism. Even Dollfuss himself,
a shrewd, ambitious but quite realistic person, seemed
inclined toward an agreement. But young Starhemberg and
his compeer Major Fey, who afterward played a peculiar
role at the murder of Dollfuss, demanded that the Schutzbund should surrender its arms and that all traces of
democratic and civil liberty should be eradicated. Up to the
present the Social Democrats had resisted the demand and
threats were being exchanged by the two camps. A decision,
one felt, was imminent and in this state of general tension,
I thought forebodingly of Shakespeare's words: "So foul a
sky clears not without a storm."

~

I spent only a few days in Salzburg and soon went on to
Vienna. And just in those first days of February the storm
broke. The Heimwehr had raided the Workers' House at
Linz in order to confiscate the stock of arms which allegedly
was hidden there. The workers' response was a general strike
upon which Dollfuss ordered this ingeniously forced "revolution" to be suppressed by armed force. Thereupon the
regular army advanced with machine guns and artillery
against the Viennese workers' houses. For three days there
was severe fighting from house to house; it was to be the last
time, until Spain, that democracy defended itself against
fascism in Europe. The workers held out for three days
before they succumbed to technical superiority.

I was in Vienna during these three days and thus can testify to this decisive battle which was no less than the suicide
of Austrian independence. But as I have to testify honestly
I must admit the seemingly paradoxical fact that I saw not
the least bit of this revolution that actually took place during
my presence there. One who aims to depict his time as
honestly and clearly as possible must also have the courage
to disappoint romantic conceptions. And nothing seems to
me more characteristic of the technique and peculiarity of
modern revolutions than that in the great area of a modern
capital they unfold in only a very few spots and hence remain
completely out of sight of most of the inhabitants. Singular
as it may seem I was in Vienna during these historic February days of 1934 without seeing anything of the historic
events which were then occurring and without the slightest
inkling that they were happening. Cannon were thundering, buildings were being occupied, hundreds of corpses were
being carried off—I saw not a single one. Every newspaper
reader in New York, London, or Paris knew more of what
was really going on than those of us who seemingly were
witnesses. Later I had frequent confirmations of the phenomenon that people thousands of miles away are better informed than those who live ten blocks from the scene of
momentous decisions. When, a few months thereafter, Dollfuss was murdered in Vienna one day at noon, I saw the news
placards in the streets of London at five-thirty in the afternoon. I put in a call to Vienna and, to my astonishment, was
connected at once and discovered to my still greater astonishment, that five streets away from the Foreign Office in Vienna
they knew less than was known in London on every street corner. My experience of the Viennese revolution, therefore,
has only the value of demonstrating how little a contemporary, unless he chances to stand at the crucial spot, sees of
events which alter the face of the earth and his own destiny

as well. All that I knew of it was this: I had an appointment
on that evening with the choreographer of the opera, Margarete Wallmann, in a café on the Ringstrasse. I walked
along and was about to cross that street mechanically. Suddenly a few armed men in worn, sketchy uniforms interrupted me and asked where I was bound for and upon my
explanation that I was going to the Café J., they quietly
made way. I knew neither why soldiers were abruptly posted
in the streets, nor what purpose was sought. In reality, shooting and hard fighting had been going on at the outer edge
for hours but in the inner city it went quite unknown. It was
only that night, when I returned to my hotel and offered to
pay my bill because I was leaving for Salzburg the next morning that the clerk said that he was afraid that would be impossible since no trains were running. There was a railroad
workers' strike on and, besides, something was doing in the
suburbs.

The next day's newspapers published rather nebulous
reports about an uprising of the Social Democrats which
however, had already been more or less suppressed. The
fact is that the struggle only reached its full force on this
day and the Government decided to follow up the use of
machine guns on the workers' houses with artillery. But I
did not know anything about that either. If all of Austria had
been seized then, be it by the Socialists, National Socialists,
or Communists I would have known it as little as did the
citizens of Munich who woke up one morning only to learn
from the *Münchener Neueste Nachrichten* that their city was
in Hitler's hands. In the center of the town life pursued the
even tenor of its way while in the outer districts the battle
was raging and we stupidly believed the official communiqués that the trouble was over and done with. In the
National Library where I had gone to look up something,
the students were at their books as always, the stores were

open, nobody was excited. Only on the third day, when all was over, one began to get the truth piecemeal. By the fourth day the trains were running again, and in the morning I went back to Salzburg, where two or three acquaintances whom I met in the street plied me with questions as to what had really happened in Vienna. And I who chronologically had been the eye witness of the revolution had to tell them honestly: "Don't ask me. Better buy a foreign newspaper."

~~~

Oddly enough the next day marked a critical point in my own life in connection with these events. I had arrived in Salzburg from Vienna in the afternoon, had found waiting piles of proof-sheets and letters and had worked late into the night in order to settle arrears. The next morning while I was still in bed there was a knock at the door; our loyal old servant who never woke me unless I expressly set a definite hour appeared with a worried look. Would I come down, there were several gentlemen from the police who asked to see me. I was somewhat surprised, put on a dressing-gown and went downstairs. There stood four policemen in mufti who said that they had orders to search the house and to seize immediately whatever arms belonging to the Republican Schutzbund were hidden there.

I have to admit that in the first moment I was too dumbfounded to make any reply. Arms of the Republican Schutzbund in my house? It was too absurd. I never had belonged to any party, never bothered with politics. I had not been in Salzburg for many months and besides, it would have been the most ridiculous thing in the world to establish an arms depot in this house which lay outside the town on a hill, for anybody who carried a rifle or other weapon could have been observed on the way. So I only answered coolly:

"Please look for yourself." The men went through the house, opened a few chests, tapped on a few walls, but it became immediately apparent to me from the sluggish manner of their operations, that the search was only a matter of form and that none of them seriously believed that there were arms in my house. After half an hour they declared the investigation finished and disappeared.

My reason for being so embittered at that farce unfortunately calls for an explanatory historical annotation. For of recent decades Europe and the world have almost forgotten the old sacredness of personal rights and civil liberties. Since 1933, searches, arbitrary arrests, expropriation of property, expulsion from home and country, deportation and all other imaginable forms of humiliation have become an almost matter-of-course occurrence; I have hardly any European friends who have not experienced something of the sort. But then, at the beginning of 1934, a house search in Austria was still a tremendous affront. That somebody like myself who stood completely aloof from all politics and for years had not even exercised my right to vote, should be searched must have had a special reason and, in point of fact, it was a typically Austrian matter. The Chief of Police in Salzburg had been forced to take sharp measures against the National Socialists, who terrorized the populace night after night with bombs and explosives, and his course was risky and courageous for the party had already started its practice of terrorism. Every day the authorities received letters threatening reprisals if they kept on "persecuting" the National Socialists and, truly—where revenge was concerned the National Socialists have always kept their word one hundred per cent—on the very first day of Hitler's invasion the most faithful of Austrian officials were dragged to the concentration camps. Therefore it seemed a good idea to search my house by way of conspicuous announcement that none was exempt from such measures of security. Behind this episode, in itself unimportant, I felt how serious the situation had become in Austria, how overpowering the pressure from Germany. I did not care for my house any more after that official visit and a certain intuition told me that an episode of that nature could be no less than a timid prologue to much more far-reaching encroachments. The same evening I started to pack my most important papers, determined to live abroad permanently from now on, and this meant more than giving up house and country, for my family clung to the house as their home, they loved the land. For me, however, personal liberty was the most important thing on earth. Without notifying any of my friends or acquaintances of my intention, I went back to London two days later; the first thing I did on arrival there was to notify the authorities in Salzburg that I definitely had given up my residence there. It was the first step toward detaching me from my homeland. But since those days in Vienna I had been aware that Austria was lost, not yet suspecting, to be sure, how much I had lost thereby.

XVI

The Agony of Peace

The sun of Rome is set. Our
  day is gone.
Clouds, dews, and dangers come;
  our deeds are done.

SHAKESPEARE, *Julius Caesar*

DURING my first years in England, I felt no more an exile than Gorky did in Sorrento. Austria continued to endure even after the so-called "revolution" and the attempt, hard thereupon, of the National Socialists to seize the country by a coup d'état and the murder of Dollfuss. The agony of my native land was to last for four more years. I could have gone home at any hour, I was not banned, not proscribed. My books stood still unmolested in my house at Salzburg, I still bore my Austrian passport, the homeland was still my homeland, I was still a citizen there, a citizen with unimpaired rights. Not yet had that terrible state of homelessness begun, inexplicable to such as have not experienced it, that nerve-wracking sensation of reeling, open-eyed and wide-awake, through space knowing that wherever one might gain a foothold one might momentarily be thrust back. But as yet I was merely at the start. However it was a different sort of arrival when, late in February 1934, I got off at Victoria Station; one looks with different eyes at a city in which one intends to remain than at one which one enters merely as a visitor. I had no idea how long I would stay in London. Only one thing was important to me: to get back to my work again, to maintain my freedom of thought and action. Because property implied fresh ties, I did not take a house but rented a little flat, just big enough to accommodate the two bookcases holding the volumes which I was unwilling to do without and a writing table. Therewith I really had all that an intellectual worker needs. For social life there was no room, to be sure. But I preferred to lodge modestly so as to be free to travel at intervals: my life was already unconsciously accommodating itself to the temporary rather than to the permanent.

On the first evening, it was already getting dark with the contours of the walls fading away in the dusk, I entered the small apartment which was finally ready and experienced a shock. For in that moment I felt as if I had entered that other little apartment which I had fixed up for myself almost thirty years earlier in Vienna; the rooms quite as small, and the one welcome greeting these very books against the wall and the hallucinatory eyes of Blake's "King John" which accompanied me everywhere. It really took me a moment to collect myself, because for years and years I had not given that earlier apartment a thought. Was this a symbol that my life after long expansion was shriveling to an earlier form of being and that I was becoming my own shadow? Thirty years back when I had chosen that room in Vienna it represented a beginning. I had not yet created anything, at least nothing of importance; neither my books nor my name were yet known to my own country. Now in turn, in strange similarity, my books once more had almost vanished from their language; my recent work remained unknown to Germany. My friends were far away, the old circle was destroyed, the home with its collections and paintings and books lost; I stood alone in a strange land, exactly as in the past. Everything which I had attempted, achieved, learned, enjoyed, in the meantime seemed wafted away and now, over fifty years old, I faced a beginning, was once more a

student working at a desk or in a library, only not as cred-
ulous, not as enthusiastic, with a suspicion of gray in my
hair and a faint dawn of despair over my wearied soul.

~~~

I am reluctant to say much about the years 1934 to 1940
in England because it brings me close to our own time which
all of us have lived through in almost equal manner, with
like unrest, baited by radio and newspaper, with the same
hopes and the same worries. We reflect on it with little
pride in its political folly and with horror of whither it has
led us; whoever would wish to explain would have to make
charges and who among us all would have the right to do
so? What is more, my life in England was one long reserve.
Foolish as I knew so superfluous an inhibition to be, I spent
those years of semi-exile and exile apart from wholesome
intercourse in the delusion that it was bad form to express
myself on topics of the day in a foreign land. In Austria
I had not been able to combat the folly of influential circles,
how then could I attempt it here? Here where I considered
myself a guest of this kindly island, knowing well that if,
in our clearer, better informed judgment, I were to point
out the world danger which Hitler represented, it would
be considered a personal, prejudiced opinion. Indeed, it was
sometimes hard to keep my mouth shut in the face of notorious errors. It was painful to stand by when the greatest
virtue of the English, their loyalty, their honest desire to
believe anyone until proved a liar, was being abused by a
masterfully conducted propaganda. Ever and again there
was the cajoling intimation that Hitler wanted no more
than to absorb the Germans of the border States after which
he would be content and would, in gratitude, exterminate
bolshevism; this bait worked excellently. Hitler merely had
to utter the word "peace" in a speech to arouse the news-

papers to enthusiasm, to make them forget all his past deeds, and desist from asking why, after all, Germany was arming so madly. Tourists coming back from Berlin where they had been painstakingly escorted and flattered, praised the management of things and the new manager; gradually one began to hear quiet approval in England of the justice of his "claims" for a Greater Germany, there being none to grasp the fact that Austria was the stone whose removal from the wall would cause Europe's collapse. I, however, experienced the naïveté, the good faith in which the English and their leaders let themselves be bamboozled with the smarting eyes of one who had seen the faces of the storm troopers at close range at home and who had heard them sing: "Today we conquer Germany, tomorrow the whole world." The sharper the political tension became the more I withdrew from discussions and from any public participation. England was the only country in the old world in which I never published an opportune article in a newspaper, never spoke over the radio, never shared in a public discussion; my life in the small apartment there was more anonymous than that of the student in his Vienna thirty years before. Thus I am not qualified to describe England, the less so for having to admit to myself later on that prior to the war I had never recognized England's profound, repressed power which discloses itself only in the hour of extremest danger.

Nor did I see many of its literary men. Just those two whom I was beginning to know well, John Drinkwater and Hugh Walpole, were removed by an early death; the younger ones I met infrequently because I avoided—out of that wretched feeling of being a "foreigner"—clubs, dinners, and public occasions. However, once I had the special and truly unforgettable pleasure of hearing those two cleverest brains, Bernard Shaw and H. G. Wells, engage in a brilliant discussion which was outwardly perfectly courteous though highly charged with a concealed current. It was at an intimate luncheon at Shaw's and I found myself in the interesting yet embarrassing position of one who was not in the know concerning the cause of this underground high tension which could be deduced even from the way the two Elders greeted each other, with a familiarity slightly shot through with irony; something important must have been up between them which had only recently been settled or was to be settled at this luncheon. These two great figures, each one a part of England's glory, had, half a century ago, fought shoulder to shoulder for Socialism, then young like themselves, in the Fabian Society. Since then, in accordance with their very pronounced personalities, they had developed more and more away from each other, Wells persisting in practical idealism, indefatigably perfecting his vision of the future of mankind, Shaw on the contrary increasingly viewing the future with the same skepticism and irony as the present, as stuff for his amused, superior play of intellect. In physical appearance, too, the years had heightened the contrast between them: Shaw, the incredibly brisk octogenarian, whose lunch was only nuts and fruit, tall, slim, always intent, always a sharp smile about his mobile lips and more than ever in love with the fireworks of his paradoxes: Wells, feeling the joy of life at seventy, more epicurean, more easy-going than ever before, short, red-cheeked, and inexorably serious behind his occasional cheerfulness. Shaw, dazzling in his aggressiveness, quickly and adroitly changing the points of attack, the other employing the right tactics for defense, steadfast in belief and conviction. At once I had the impression that Wells was present not merely for a friendly luncheon chat but for some sort of fundamental discussion. And just because I was not informed about the background of the intellectual conflict, I was the more susceptible to its atmosphere. In every gesture, every glance, every word they spoke there was a flicker of high spirits but with more than a suspicion of pugnacity; it was as if two fencers, before getting down to serious business try themselves out with a series of feints. Shaw was the more rapid of mind. There was a gleam under his bushy eyebrows whenever he responded or parried, his joy in wit and play on words, which he had perfected over sixty years to an unequaled virtuosity, accelerated to a sort of arrogance. His white bushy beard sometimes trembled with a grim, quiet laughter, and with head slightly cocked and inclined, his gaze always seemed to follow his arrow to see whether it had really hit. Wells, with his little red cheeks and his quiet masked eyes was more caustic and direct; his mind also operated at extreme speed but he did not seek to make sparks fly, his thrust was limber and made with a light assurance. This flashing exchange went on so rapidly, back and forth, with its parry and thrust, thrust and parry, always within the bounds of fun, that the outsider could not but admire the play of the foils, the sparkle, and give and take. But behind this swift dialogue maintained on a high level there was some kind of intellectual irritation which in the English manner grandly disciplined itself into urbane dialectics. What made the discussion specially interesting was the serious way in which they engaged in sport and the sporting way in which they were serious in this opposition of two polar characters which only seemingly flamed up because of something pertinent but really because it was immutably fixed. In any event, I had seen the two best men of England in one of their best moments and the continuation of that polemic as printed in the London *Nation* during the weeks that followed did not give me a fraction of the pleasure that I had derived from the animated dialogue because the arguments had become abstract and the living person, the true essence, was no longer present. But seldom have I enjoyed the phosphorescence induced by mutual friction of two spirits, never before or since have I seen a play in which the art of dialogue was practiced with such virtuosity as on that occasion when it achieved itself unintentionally, untheatrically and in finest fashion.

~~

But during those years I lived in England only spatially and not with my whole soul. It was just my worry about Europe, that worry which pressed painfully upon our nerves for all those years, which made me travel so much in the years between Hitler's rise to power and the outbreak of the Second World War; I crossed the ocean twice. Perhaps some premonition told me that one should hoard against darker days as many impressions and experiences as the heart could hold while the world was still open and ships could still take their course peacefully across the seas, also it may have been the longing to know that while the old world was destroying itself through suspicion and strife another one was building itself over there; perhaps it was even a dim prescience that our, and even my personal, future lay beyond Europe. A lecture tour straight across the United States gave me welcome opportunity to see this mighty land in all its variety and yet inward unity from East to West, from North to South. But perhaps even deeper was my impression of South America where I gladly accepted an invitation to attend the convention of the International P. E. N. Club; never had it seemed more important to me than then to support the idea of intellectual solidarity over and beyond national boundaries and languages.

The last hours in Europe before my departure offered serious warning to ponder on my way. In the summer of 1936 the Spanish Civil War had begun; superficially viewed

it was no more than an internal strife of that beautiful and
tragic country, in reality, however, the preparatory maneu-
ver of the two ideological power groups for their future
encounter. I had left from Southampton on an English
boat and was under the impression that the ship would, in
order to avoid the war zone, skip its usual first stop, Vigo.
To my surprise we entered the harbor nonetheless, and the
passengers were even allowed to go ashore for a few hours.
Vigo was under Franco's control at the time and lay far
away from the scene of battle. Yet I saw things during my
brief stay which afforded justifiable reasons for depressing
thoughts. In front of the town hall, over which Franco's
banner waved, young lads, peasants to judge by their dress,
were lined up, led mostly by priests, and apparently rounded
up from the neighboring villages. At first I did not know
what they were there for. Were they workers hired for some
emergency or unemployed assembled to get food? After a
quarter of an hour I saw these same youths emerge from
the town hall quite different persons. They wore spotless
new uniforms and carried rifles with bayonets; under the
supervision of officers they were loaded into similarly spotless new automobiles and whizzed through the streets out
of the city. I was startled. Where had I seen this once before?
First in Italy and then in Germany! Here as there, these
faultless new uniforms, these new automobiles, and machine
guns, turned up unexpectedly. And again I asked myself:
who supplies, who pays for these new uniforms, who organ-
izes these impoverished young men, who whips them up
against the powers that be, against the elected parliament,
against their own legal representatives? The state treasury,
I was aware, was controlled by the duly constituted government, so were the arms depots. Thus the automobiles and
arms must have been delivered from abroad and doubtlessly
they had come across the border from Portugal. But who

had supplied them and who had paid for them? It was a new power that sought to come into power, one and the same power which was at work here, there and everywhere, a power that loved violence and stood in need of violence and to which all those concepts to which we held and for which we lived—peace, humanity, conciliation—seemed infirmities of a bygone day. It was mysterious groups, screened by offices and businesses which cynically diverted the naïve idealism of youth to their lust for power and their concerns. It was the will to violence which sought with a new and subtler technique to engulf our unfortunate Europe in the old barbarism of war. A single optical impression exerts greater power over the soul than a thousand newspaper articles and pamphlets. And in that hour, as I watched how those innocent young lads were being supplied with arms that were intended for use against just as innocent young lads of their own homeland, by mysterious concealed wire pullers I was affected as never before by a prescience of what was in store for us, for Europe. When the ship put out again, after a few hours I quickly went down into my stateroom. It was too painful for me to cast another glance at the beautiful country which had fallen prey to gruesome devastation through foreign guilt; Europe seemed to me doomed to die by its own madness; Europe, our sacred home, cradle and Parthenon of our occidental civilization.

All the more joyous, then, was the sight of Argentina. Once again there was Spain, her culture preserved and tended in a new, broader earth not yet fertilized with blood, not yet poisoned by hate. There was an abundance of food, wealth, surplus, there was endless room and hence food for the future. Immeasurable happiness and something like a new confidence animated me. Had not cultures been wandering from country to country for thousands of years, had not always, even though the tree had fallen to the axe, the seeds been saved and thus new blossoms and new fruit? Whatever generations before ours had created never disappeared entirely. It was necessary to learn to think on a grander scale, in more ample periods of time. One ought to start, I said to myself, to think no longer merely in terms of Europe, but over and beyond Europe, not bury oneself in a moribund past but participate in its rebirth. For in the warmth with which the whole population of Buenos Aires, the new city of millions, shared in our congress, I recognized that this was not foreign soil and that the belief in intellectual unity to which we had devoted the best of ourselves, was still alive, valid and effective, that in our day of new speeds even the ocean ceased to be a barrier. A new task replaced the old: to build the union of our dreams on a broader scale and in a bolder conception. If I had given Europe up for lost with that last look toward the coming war, I began to hope and believe again under the Southern Cross.

Brazil, so prodigally endowed by nature, with the most beautiful city on earth, a country whose gigantic area neither rails nor roads nor hardly even airplanes are yet able to cover, offered no less mighty and promising an impression. Here there was an even more tender feeling for the past than in Europe itself, the brutality that came in the wake of the First World War had not penetrated the customs or the spirit of the nation. People got along together more peaceably; intercourse even between the most varied races was more courteous and less hostile than in Europe. Here man was not separated from man by absurd theories of blood, race, and origin; here, one sensed with intuitive foreknowledge, one might yet live happily; here, in immeasurable abundance was the room for the smallest atom of which Europe and nations fought and statesmen wrangled. Here the land, ready for the future, still waited for man, so that he might use it and fill it with his presence. Europe's contribution to civilization could be extended and developed magnificently here in new adaptation. My vision blessed by the manifold beauty of this bountiful new Nature, I had had a glimpse into the future.

~~

But Europe and anxiety about Europe were not to be eluded by travel, not even by journeys to far-off places under other constellations and into different worlds. It almost seems like the mysterious revenge of Nature on man, that all the achievements of science by which he has harnessed her most secret powers should serve also to confuse his soul. Science has brought no worse curse on us than that it prohibits our escaping the present even for a single moment. In times of catastrophe former generations could revert to isolation and remoteness; it was reserved for us to have to know and to co-sense whatever evil happened on our globe at the moment of its occurrence. No matter how far I withdrew from Europe, its fate accompanied me. Landing one night in Pernambuco under the Southern Cross, dark-skinned people in the streets, I read on a news placard of the bombing of Barcelona and of the execution of a Spanish friend together with whom, a few months before, I had spent some pleasant hours. Once in a Pullman car between Houston and another Texas city I suddenly became aware of loud, mad shouting in German: a fellow-passenger had innocently tuned the train radio to Germany's wave length and in consequence I had to listen to one of Hitler's inflammatory speeches while the train rolled along the Texas plains. There was no escape, not by day, not by night; always I was in a torment of anxiety about Europe and of Austria within Europe. It may seem like narrow patriotism that, with the immense complex of the danger which spread from China to the Ebro and Manzanares, the fate of Austria particularly should have occupied me. But I knew that the fate of all Europe was bound up with this small country, by chance my own. Looking back, if one tries to show up the mistakes of statesmanship after the World War, it will be recognized that the greatest was that the European as well as the American politicians mutilated instead of carried out Wilson's clear and simple plan. His idea was to give the small nations freedom and independence, but he well knew that freedom and independence could endure only within an association of all States, large and small, in an authoritative entity. By not creating such a superior organization, a real and total League of Nations, but by realizing only that part of the program that called for the independence of small States, the result was constant tension instead of peace. For nothing is more dangerous than the ambition of the small to be like the great, and the first thing that the small States did, hardly had they been created, was to intrigue against one another and to dispute for insignificant tracts of land—Poles against Czechs, Hungarians against Rumanians, Bulgarians against Serbs—and weakest among all in these rivalries stood tiny Austria against overwhelming Germany. This dismembered, mutilated land whose rulers once had reigned over Europe, was—I must reiterate it— the stone in the wall. I knew, but the people amongst whom I lived in the English capital could not know, that Czechoslovakia was bound to fall with Austria upon which the Balkans would be easy prey for Hitler; that by taking Vienna, because of its peculiar structure, National Socialism would hold in its hard hand the lever with which to loosen up the whole of Europe and lift it from its hinges. We Austrians alone knew the eagerness stung to action by a grievance which was driving Hitler toward Vienna, the scene of his greatest wretchedness and which he now wished

to enter in triumph. Every time, therefore, I went to
Austria for a hasty visit and then recrossed the border, I
sighed with relief, "Not yet, this time" and looked back
as if for the last time. I saw the catastrophe coming, inevitably: on hundreds of mornings during those years, when
everybody else reached for the newspapers confidently, I
was gripped by an inner fear of the headline: *Finis Austriæ*.
Oh, how had I deceived myself when I had pretended to
myself that I had long since pried myself loose from her
fate! From afar I suffered her long and feverish agony daily,
infinitely more than my friends in the country itself, for
they deceived themselves with patriotic demonstrations and
reassured each other with "France and England cannot let
us down. And above all, Mussolini will never stand for it."
They believed in the League of Nations and in the peace
treaties as sick people do in neatly labeled medicines. They
lived on carefree and happy while I, seeing more plainly,
worried my heart out.

My last trip to Austria had no other ground than one of
those bursts of inward fear of the ever-closer catastrophe.
I had been in Vienna in the fall of 1937 to visit my aged
mother, and for some time there had been nothing of consequence to call me there. One day at noon a few weeks later,
it must have been toward the end of November, I was on
my way home through Regent Street and bought the *Evening Standard*. It was the day when Lord Halifax flew to
Berlin to try for the first time to negotiate with Hitler personally. On the front page of the *Evening Standard*—I still
see it graphically before me, the text in heavy type at the
right—were enumerated the particular points on which
Halifax was seeking an understanding with Hitler. One of
them was a paragraph on Austria. And between the lines
I read or permitted myself to infer, the surrender of Austria,
for what else could a discussion with Hitler mean? We

Austrians knew well that on this point Hitler would never yield. Significantly, that list of subjects for discussion appeared only in that noon edition of the *Evening Standard* and by the afternoon it had vanished without trace in any later edition of the same newspaper. (Afterward there was a rumor that this information had been slipped over to the paper by the Italian Legation for in 1937 there was nothing Italy feared more than an agreement between Germany and England behind her back.) How much of the article (which went unnoticed by the general public) was factually correct I cannot judge. I know only how greatly I was frightened at the thought that Hitler and England were already negotiating about Austria; I am not ashamed to say that the newspaper trembled in my hands. True or false, the story excited me as none had for years because I knew that if only a fraction of it came true it was the beginning of the end, then the stone would fall out of the wall and the wall with it. I reversed my steps immediately and made for the Imperial Airways to book passage for the next morning. I wanted to see my old mother, my family, my homeland once more. Fortunately I was able to get a ticket; I quickly threw a few things into a bag and flew to Vienna.

My friends were astonished at my quick and unexpected return. But how they ridiculed me when I indicated my concern; I was still the same old "Jeremiah," they mocked. Was I not aware that the whole population of Austria now stood one hundred per cent strong behind Schuschnigg? They praised in detail the magnificent demonstrations of the *Vaterländische Front,* of which I well knew of old from Salzburg that most of the participants wore the prescribed insignia of unity only outwardly on their jacket collar in order not to jeopardize their jobs, but that at the same time they had long since prudently registered with the National Socialists in Munich. I had learned and written too much history not to know that the great masses always and at once respond to the force of gravity in the direction of the powers that be. I knew that the same voices which yelled "Heil Schuschnigg" today would thunder "Heil Hitler" tomorrow. But everybody I spoke to in Vienna showed an honest unconcern. They invited each other to full-dress parties (little thinking that they would soon be wearing prisoner's clothes in a concentration camp), they were lavish customers at Christmas for their beautiful homes (little thinking that in a few months they would be confiscated and plundered). And this eternal gay unconcern of old Vienna which I had formerly so much loved and which, as a matter of fact, I am always redreaming, this gay unconcern which Vienna's poet laureate Anzengruber once caught concisely in *Es kann Dir nix g'schehn*—for the first time it gave me pain. In the last analysis it seems likely that they were wiser than I, all those friends in Vienna, because they suffered everything only when it really happened, whereas I had already suffered the disaster in advance in my fantasy, and then again when it became reality. In any event, I no longer understood them and could not make myself understood by them. I stopped warning people after the second day. Why disturb people who do not wish to be disturbed?

It is not a decorative afterthought but the sober truth when I say that in those last two days in Vienna I looked at all the familiar streets, every church, every park, every hidden corner of my native city, with a despairing, silent "nevermore." I embraced my mother with the secret thought, "It is the last time." I reached to everything in the city, in the land, with this "never again," knowing that it was a farewell, a farewell for ever. I passed through Salzburg where stood the house in which I had worked for twenty years without even getting off at the station. I could have seen my house on the hill from the train window, with all its memories of faded years. But I did not look. What was the use? I would never again occupy it. And the moment when the train rolled across the Austrian border I knew, as did Lot in the Bible, that all that I had left behind was dust and ashes, a past frozen to a pillar of salt.

~~

I thought that I had foreboded all the terror that would come to pass when Hitler's dream of hate would come true and he would triumphantly occupy Vienna, the city which had turned him off, poor and a failure, in his youth. But how timid, how petty, how lamentable my imagination, all human imagination, in the light of the inhumanity which discharged itself on that March 13, 1938, that day when Austria and Europe with it fell prey to sheer violence! The mask was off. The other States having plainly shown their fear, there was no further need to check moral inhibitions or to employ hypocritical pretexts about "Marxists" having to be politically liquidated. Who cared for England, France, for the whole world! Now there was no longer mere robbery and theft, but every private lust for revenge was given free rein. University professors were obliged to scrub the streets with their naked hands, pious white-bearded Jews were dragged into the synagogue by hooting youths and forced to do knee-exercises and to shout "Heil Hitler" in chorus. Innocent people in the streets were trapped like rabbits and herded off to clean the latrines in the S. A. barracks. All the sickly, unclean fantasies of hate that had been conceived in many orgiastic nights found raging expression in bright daylight. Breaking into homes and tearing earrings from trembling women may well have happened in the looting of cities, hundreds of years ago during medieval wars; what was new, however, was the shameless delight in public tortures, in spiritual martyrization, in the refinements of humiliation. All this has been recorded not by one but by thousands who suffered it; and a more peaceful day—not one already morally fatigued as ours is—will shudder to read what a single hate-crazed man perpetrated in that city of culture in the twentieth century. For amidst his military and political victories Hitler's most diabolic triumph was that he succeeded through progressive excesses in blunting every sense of law and order. Before this "New Order," the murder of a single man without legal process and without apparent reason would have shocked the world; torture was considered unthinkable in the   twentieth century, expropriations were know by the old names, theft and robbery. But now after successive Bartholomew nights the daily mortal tortures in the S. A. prisons and behind barbed wire, what did a single injustice or earthly suffering signify? In 1938, after Austria, our universe had become accustomed to inhumanity, to lawlessness, and brutality as never in centuries before. In a former day the occurrences in unhappy Vienna alone would have been sufficient to cause international proscription, but in 1938 the world conscience was silent or merely muttered surlily before it forgot and forgave.

$\sim$

Those days, marked by daily cries for help from the homeland when one knew close friends to be kidnaped and humiliated and one trembled helplessly for every loved one, were among the most terrible of my life. These times have so perverted our hearts that I am not ashamed to say that I was not shocked and did not mourn upon learning of the death of my mother in Vienna; on the contrary, I even felt something like composure in the knowledge that she was now safe from suffering and danger. Eighty-four years old, almost completely deaf, she occupied rooms in our old home and thus could not, even under the new "Aryan" code be evicted for the time being and we had hoped somehow to get her abroad after a while. One of the first Viennese ordinances had hit her hard. At her advanced age she was a little shaky on her legs and was accustomed, when on her daily laborious walk, to rest on a bench in the Ringstrasse or in the park, every five or ten minutes. Hitler had not been master of the city for a week when the bestial order forbidding Jews to sit on public benches was issued—one of those orders obviously thought up only for the sadistic purpose of malicious torture. There was logic and reason in robbing Jews for with the booty from factories, the home furnishings, the villas, and the jobs compulsorily vacated they could feather their followers' nests, reward their satellites; after all, Goering's picture-gallery owes its splendor mainly to this generously exercised practice. But to deny an aged woman or an exhausted old man a few minutes on a park bench to catch his breath—this remained reserved to the twentieth century and to the man whom millions worshiped as the greatest in our day.

Fortunately, my mother was spared suffering such brutality and humiliation for long. She died a few months after the occupation of Vienna and I cannot forbear to write about an episode in connection with her passing; it seems important to me to record just such details for a time in which such things will again seem impossible.

One morning the eighty-four year old woman suddenly lost consciousness. The doctor who was called declared that she could hardly live through the night and engaged a nurse, a woman of about forty, to attend her deathbed. Neither my brother nor I, her only children, was there nor could we have come back, because a return to the deathbed of a mother would have been counted a misdeed by the representatives of German culture. A cousin of ours undertook to

spend the night in the apartment so that at least one of the
family might be present at her death. He was then a man of
sixty, and in poor health; in fact he too died about a year
later. As he was uncovering his bed in an adjoining room
the nurse appeared and declared her regret that because of
the new National-Socialist laws it was impossible for her
to stay overnight with the dying woman. To her credit be it
said that she was rather shamefaced about it. My cousin
being a Jew and she a woman under fifty, she was not permitted to spend a night under the same roof with him, even
at a deathbed, because according to the Streicher mentality,
it must be a Jew's first thought to practice race defilement
upon her. Of course the regulation was extremely embarrassing, but she would have to obey the law. So my sixty-year-old
cousin had to leave the house in the evening so that the
nurse could stay with my dying mother; it will be intelligible, then, why I considered her almost lucky not to have
to live on among such people.

~

   The fall of Austria brought with it a change in my personal life which at first I believed to be a quite unimportant
formality: my Austrian passport became void and I had to
request an emergency white paper from the English authorities, a passport for the stateless. Often in my cosmopolitan
reveries I had imagined how beautiful it would be, how
truly in accord with my inmost thoughts, to be stateless, obligated to no one country and for that reason
undifferentiatedly attached to all. But once again I had to
recognize the shortcomings of our mortal imagination and
also that one can comprehend really significant sensations
only after one has suffered them oneself. Ten years before,
meeting Dmitri Merejkovsky in Paris, he lamented that his
books were banned in Russia and I, in my inexperience

rather thoughtlessly tried to console him by saying that this really meant little when measured by world distribution. But, when my own works disappeared from the German language I could more clearly grasp his lament at being able to produce the created word only in translation, in a diluted, altered medium. Similarly, I only understood what this exchange of my passport for an alien's certificate meant in the moment when I was admitted to the English officials after a long wait on the petitioners' bench in an anteroom. An Austrian passport was a symbol of my rights. Every Austrian consul or officer or police officer was in duty bound to issue one to me on demand as a citizen in good standing. But I had to solicit the English certificate. It was a favor that I had to ask for, and what is more, a favor that could be withdrawn at any moment. Overnight I found myself one rung lower. Only yesterday still a visitor from abroad and, so to speak, a gentleman who was spending his international income and paying his taxes, now I had become an immigrant, a "refugee." I had slipped down to a lesser, even if not dishonorable, category. Besides that every foreign visa on this travel paper had thenceforth to be specially pleaded for, because all countries were suspicious of the "sort" of people of which I had suddenly become one, of the outlaws, of the men without a country, whom one could not at a pinch pack off and deport to their own State as they could others if they became undesirable or stayed too long. Always I had to think of what an exiled Russian had said to me years ago: "Formerly man had only a body and a soul. Now he needs a passport as well for without it he will not be treated like a human being."

Indeed, nothing makes us more sensible of the immense relapse into which the world fell after the First World War than the restrictions on man's freedom of movement and the diminution of his civil rights. Before 1914 the earth had belonged to all. People went where they wished and stayed as long as they pleased. There were no permits, no visas, and it always gives me pleasure to astonish the young by telling them that before 1914 I traveled from Europe to India and to America without passport and without ever having seen one. One embarked and alighted without questioning or being questioned, one did not have to fill out a single one of the many papers which are required today. The frontiers which, with their customs officers, police and militia, have become wire barriers thanks to the pathological suspicion of everybody against everybody else, were nothing but symbolic lines which one crossed with as little thought as one crosses the Meridian of Greenwich. Nationalism emerged to agitate the world only after the war, and the first visible phenomenon which this intellectual epidemic of our century brought about was xenophobia; morbid dislike of the foreigner, or at least fear of the foreigner. The world was on the defensive against strangers, everywhere they got short shrift. The humiliations which once had been devised with criminals alone in mind now were imposed upon the traveler, before and during every journey. There had to be photographs from right and left, in profile and full face, one's hair had to be cropped sufficiently to make the ears visible; fingerprints were taken, at first only the thumb but later all ten fingers; furthermore, certificates of health, of vaccination, police certificates of good standing, had to be shown; letters of recommendation were required, invitations to visit a country had to be procured; they asked for the addresses of relatives, for moral and financial guarantees, questionnaires, and forms in triplicate and quadruplicate needed to be filled out, and if only one of this sheaf of papers was missing one was lost.

Petty details, one thinks. And at the first glance it may seem petty in me even to mention them. But our generation has foolishly wasted irretrievable, valuable time on those senseless pettinesses. If I reckon up the many forms I have filled out during these years, declarations on every trip, tax declarations, foreign exchange certificates, border passes, entrance permits, departure permits, registrations on coming and on going; the many hours I have spent in ante-rooms of consulates and officials, the many inspectors, friendly and unfriendly, bored and overworked, before whom I have sat, the many examinations and interrogations at frontiers I have been through, then I feel keenly how much human dignity has been lost in this century which, in our youth, we had credulously dreamed of as one of freedom, as of the federation of the world. The loss in creative work, in thought, as a result of those spirit-crushing procedures is incalculable. Have not many of us spent more time studying official rules and regulations than works of the intellect! The first excursion in a foreign country was no longer to a museum or to a world renowned view, but to a consulate, to a police office, to get a "permit." When those of us who had once conversed about Baudelaire's poetry and spiritedly discussed intellectual problems met together, we would catch ourselves talking about affidavits and permits and whether one should apply for an immigration visa or a tourist visa; acquaintance with a stenographer in a consulate, who could cut down one's waiting-time was more significant to one's existence than friendship with a Toscanini or a Rolland. Human beings were made to feel that they were objects and not subjects, that nothing was their right but everything merely a favor by official grace. They were codified, registered, numbered, stamped and even today I, as a case-hardened creature of an age of freedom and a citizen of the world-republic of my dreams, count every impression of a rubber-stamp in my passport a stigma, every one of those hearings and searches a humiliation. They are petty trifles, always merely trifles, I am well aware, trifles in a day when human values sink more rapidly than those of currencies. But only if one notes such insignificant symptoms will a later age be able to make a proper clinical record of the mental state and mental disturbances with which our world was seized between the two World Wars.

It may be that I had been too greatly pampered. Perhaps, too, my sensibility had gradually become unstrung through all the harsh reverses of the past years. Emigration in itself, whatever the reason, inevitably disturbs the equilibrium. On alien soil one's self-respect tends to diminish, likewise self-assurance and self-confidence; but this cannot be understood until it has been experienced. I have no compunction about admitting that since the day when I had to depend upon identity papers or passports that were indeed alien, I ceased to feel as if I quite belonged to myself. A part of the natural identity with my original and essential ego was destroyed forever. I have developed a reserve that is not consonant with my real disposition and—cosmopolite that I once thought myself—I am possessed by the feeling that I ought express particular gratitude for every breath of air of which I deprive a foreign people. On sober thought I am, of course, aware of the absurdity of such whims, but of what avail reason, against one's emotion? For all that I had been training my heart for almost half a century to beat as that of a *citoyen du monde* it was useless. On the day I lost my passport I discovered, at the age of fifty-eight, that losing one's native land implies more than parting with a circumscribed area of soil.

〜〜

I was not alone in sensing jeopardy. Little by little uneasiness began to spread over the whole of Europe. The political horizon remained obscure from the day that Hitler invaded Austria, and those people in England who had secretly paved the way for him in the hope of thus purchasing peace for their own country, now became thoughtful. From 1938 on, in London, in Paris, in Rome, in Brussels, in every town and village, there never was a conversation which— remote as its original subject might have been—did not lead up to the inevitable question: how can war be avoided, or at least be put off? Looking back on those months of constant and growing fear of war in Europe, I remember only two or three days of real confidence; two or three days when one felt, for the last time, that the clouds would blow over, and that one would again be able to breathe peacefully and freely. Perversely enough those two or three days were the very ones that now are held to be the most fateful in modern history; the days of Chamberlain's meeting with Hitler in Munich.

I know that reminders of that meeting in which Chamberlain and Daladier, impotently backing against the wall and capitulating to Hitler and Mussolini, are distasteful. But my desire to serve the literal truth calls for an admission that all who lived through those three days in England found them to be wonderful. The situation was desperate in those days of late September 1938. Chamberlain had just come back from his second flight to Hitler and a few days later all the facts were known. Chamberlain had gone to Godesberg to grant Hitler unreservedly what Hitler had previously demanded at Berchtesgaden. However, what Hitler had considered sufficient a few weeks before no longer satisfied his power-hysteria. The policy of appeasement and of "try, try again" had failed miserably and the epoch of confidence had ended in England overnight. England, France, Czechoslovakia—all of Europe—had to choose between humiliating themselves in the face of Hitler's peremptory will to power and challenging it with arms. England seemed determined to go the limit. There was no longer any concealment of armament, rather a conspicuous display. There was a sudden show of laborers digging shelters against the threatened bombings right in London's open spaces, in Hyde Park, in Regent's Park and particularly across from the German Embassy. The Fleet was mobilized, officers of the General Staff were shuttling between Paris and London in order to perfect their common arrangements, American liners were stormed by foreigners seeking safety; England had not been so wide awake since 1914. Everybody became more serious and thoughtful. Looking at buildings and at the crowded streets one could not but think of the possibility of bombs crashing down there tomorrow. Inside those buildings people stood or sat around radios avid for news. Invisible and yet perceptible in every person and in every second, the whole country was gripped in a monstrous strain.

Then came the historic session of the House in which Chamberlain announced a further attempt at an agreement with Hitler, another proposal, the third, to meet him wherever he chose in Germany, to preserve the seriously endangered peace. No answer to the proposal had yet been received. Then, in the midst of the session—rather too dramatically conceived—came the telegram with Hitler's and Mussolini's consent to a joint conference at Munich, the signal for a perhaps unique event in the history of England:—the Commons lost its self-control. The members sprang to their feet, shouted and applauded; the galleries were wild with enthusiasm. Not in many years had the dignified House been stirred to such an outbreak of jubilation. From the human point of view it was a great show, this honest burst of joy at the thought that peace might yet be preserved rising superior to the expert English practice of restraint and reserve. Politically, however, the ebullition represented a grave error for, in its wild rejoicing Parliament, the whole land, had revealed how much it loathed war, how ready it was for any sacrifice, for any surrender of its interests and even its prestige, for the sake of peace. Thus Chamberlain was marked from the beginning not as one who went to Munich to fight for peace, but as one who pleaded for peace. But none could then even suspect how great a capitulation was imminent. Everybody, (and I was one of them) thought that Chamberlain was going to Munich to negotiate, not to surrender. And then came two or three days of feverish expectancy, three days in which it seemed as if the world was holding its breath. Digging went on in the parks and labor in the munition factories, anti-aircraft guns were installed, gas masks distributed, plans for evacuating children from London were weighed and mysterious preparations took place which none understood but the intention of which was known to all. Morning, noon, evening, and night were occupied with waiting for the newspaper, listening to the radio. It was a renewal of those moments of July 1914 with their terrible nerve-wracking waiting for a yes or no.

And then suddenly, as if by a gigantic blast of wind, the oppressive clouds were dispersed, hearts were relieved and spirits freed. It was announced that Hitler, Chamberlain, Daladier, and Mussolini had come to a complete understanding and, moreover, that Chamberlain had concluded an agreement which guaranteed the peaceful settlement of all possible future conflicts between England and Germany. It looked like the triumph of the dogged will to peace of an otherwise unimportant and leathery statesman, and the immediate reaction was universal gratitude to him. Over the radio came the message "Peace in our time," an assurance to our tried generation of further opportunity to live contentedly, to be free of anxiety, to assist in building a new and better world; and any subsequent denial of our intoxication by the magic formula is an untruth. For who could conceive of a beaten general preparing for a triumphant return? If London had known the exact hour of his coming hundreds of thousands would have converged at the Croydon airport to welcome Chamberlain, to cheer the man who, as was commonly believed, had saved Europe's peace and England's honor. Then came the newspapers with a picture of Chamberlain, whose face usually bore an unfortunate similarity to the head of an irritated bird, proud and smiling at the door of his plane waving the historic document which announced "peace in our time" which he had brought home to his people as a most precious gift. By evening the scene was already being shown in the cinema; the spectators jumped up from their seats and rejoiced vociferously—they all but embraced one another in the access of fraternity that was about to possess the world. For those who were in London, indeed in England, it was an incomparable, a soul-stirring day.

I love to knock about the streets on such historic days, to get a closer and more physical sense of the atmosphere, to breathe the air of time in the full meaning of the term. The digging of shelters had ceased; people stood around them chatting good-humoredly for by "peace in our time" air-raid shelters had indeed become superfluous. I heard two lads joking in the best cockney about the hope that the shelters would be transformed into underground comfort stations of which there were too few in London. Everybody laughed with them wholeheartedly, they all seemed more refreshed, more animated, like plants after a thunder shower. They walked more erectly than on the day before, with lighter shoulders, and there was a cheerful sparkle in their

usually cool English eyes. Buildings seemed to show more
brightly since one knew they were no longer in danger of
bombs, the busses smarter, the sun warmer, the life of thousands stimulated and strengthened by this one intoxicating
word. I was conscious, myself, of acquiring fresh energy.
I found myself walking more easily and quickly, without
becoming fatigued; the new wave of confidence, was carrying me forward with fresh strength and joy. At a Piccadilly
corner I was accosted abruptly. It was an English civil
servant whom I knew only slightly, a quite unemotional,
very retiring person. Under ordinary circumstances we
would have saluted each other politely and it never would
have occurred to him to speak to me. This time he
approached me with glistening eyes: "What do you think
of Chamberlain?" he said, beaming. "Nobody believed him
yet he did just the right thing. He wouldn't yield; that's
how he saved the situation."

That is how they all felt, and so did I on that day. Even
the next day was a happy one. The newspapers rejoiced
without exception, stocks shot up wildly on the exchange,
the echoes from Germany were friendly for the first time
in years, and in France there was a proposal to build a
monument to Chamberlain. But, alas, it was only the last
flaring up of the flame before it went out for good. It took
only a few days for the evil details to trickle through, of the
completeness of the capitulation to Hitler, of the shameful
betrayal of Czechoslovakia to which solemn asurance of help
had been made and by the next week it was already notorious that even that capitulation had satisfied Hitler so little
that he had violated its provisions in all details before the
signatures on the treaty had dried. Goebbels no longer
restrained himself from shouting to heaven that England
had been held up at Munich. A beacon of hope had been

extinguished. It shone, however, for a day or two and warmed our hearts. I can not and do not wish to forget those days.

~~

After realizing what actually had happened at Munich, paradoxically enough I saw fewer Englishmen in England. The fault lay with me because I evaded them or, rather, conversation with them, although I had to admire them more than ever. They were generous to the refugees who now came over in hordes, they showed the most noble sympathy and helpful understanding. But a sort of invisible wall grew between them and us, it was hither or yon; the thing that had already happened to us had not yet happened to them. We understood what had occurred and what was to occur, but they still refused—partly against their inner conviction—to understand. In spite of all they tried to maintain the delusion that promises were promises, treaties were treaties, and that Hitler could be negotiated with if one but reasoned with him as man to man. Committed by the democratic tradition of centuries to government by law, English leaders could not or did not wish to perceive that a new technique of conscious cynical amorality was at work and that the new Germany scrapped all the rules of the game of intercourse between nations under international law, whenever it suited her purpose. It seemed too improbable to clear- and far-thinking Englishmen who long since renounced adventure that this man who had risen so high, so quickly and so easily, would hazard the extreme; they cherished the belief and hope that he would first turn elsewhere—preferably against Russia!—and that in the meantime things could be patched up with him. We, on the contrary, knew that whatever was the most monstrous was the natural thing to expect. Everyone of us had the vision of a slaiñ friend, a tortured comrade in our mind's eye, hence had harder, sharper, more pitiless eyes. The proscribed, the hunted, the expropriated knew that no pretext was too absurd or false when robbery and power were concerned. Thus those of us who had been subjected to trial and those who as yet had been spared it, the immigrants and the English, spoke different languages. It is no exaggeration to say that besides a negligible number of Englishmen we were then the only ones in England who did not delude ourselves about the full extent of the danger. Here in England, too, just as in Austria, I was destined to foresee the inevitable clearly with tortured heart and tormenting clairvoyance; with the difference that I was a stranger, a tolerated guest in England and dared not utter a warning.

That is why those of us who were already branded by fate had only each other to look to, when the bitter foretaste of the imminent corroded our lips, and when we were tormented about the fate of the country that had accepted us fraternally. However gloomy the outlook, a conversation with a great mind on a high moral plane can afford immeasurable consolation and can stiffen the spirit; this was brought home to me unforgettably by the friendly hours which I was privileged to spend with Sigmund Freud during those last months before the catastrophe. The thought of the eighty-three year old invalid in Hitler's Vienna had weighed on me for months until finally the amazing Princess Maria Bonaparte, his most faithful pupil, had succeeded in getting this pre-eminent man out of subjugated Vienna and to London. I counted it a happy day in my life when I read in the paper that he had arrived on the isle and I saw the most reveřed of my friends, whom I had believed lost, restored from Hades.

I had known Sigmund Freud, that great and austere spirit who, more than any other in our time, deepened and broadened our knowledge of the soul of man when in Vienna, he was still appraised and opposed as an obstinate and difficult intellectual hermit. A fanatic for truth while yet fully cognizant of the limits of all truths, (once he said to me, "Absolute truth is as impossible as to obtain an absolute zero temperature,") he had estranged himself from the University and its academic scruples by his imperturbable venturing into heretofore unexplored and timidly avoided zones of the upper-nether realm of instincts, the very sphere on which the epoch had set a solemn taboo. Unconsciously the optimistic-liberal world sensed that the well-spring psychology of this uncompromising mind utterly undermined its thesis of gradual suppression of the instincts by "reason" and "progress," that he menaced its method of ignoring whatever was uncomfortable by his relentless technique of disclosure. However, it was not merely the University nor the clique of old-school neurologists who resisted this inconvenient "outsider," it was the whole old world, the mind of another day, the "proprieties," it was the entire epoch that feared the unveiler in him. A medical boycott against him slowly took form and his practice dwindled; but as his theses and even the boldest of his theories were scientifically irrefutable they tried, Viennese fashion, to dispose of his theory of dreams by means of irony or by lightly distorting it to a humorous parlor game. Once a week a faithful group visited the solitary man and at those evening discussions the new science of psychoanalysis was molded into form. Long before I grasped the implications of the intellectual revolution which slowly shaped itself from Freud's first fundamental labors, I had yielded to the moral strength and steadfastness of this extraordinary man. Here, at last, was a man of science, the exemplar of a young man's dreams, prudent of statement until he had positive proof, but unshakable against the opposition of the world once he was satisfied that his hypothesis had become a valid certainty. Here was a man of the most modest personal demands but ready to battle for every tenet of his teaching and faithful unto death to the immanent truth of the theories which he vindicated. A more intellectually intrepid person could not be imagined; Freud always dared to express what he thought even if he knew that his straight, positive declaration might disturb and distress; he never sought an easy way out by making even perfunctory concessions. I am confident that if Freud had only been willing to drape his ideas carefully, to say "eroticism" instead of "sexuality," "eros" instead of "libido" and not always rigidly to insist on his final deductions instead of just indicating them it would have been possible for him to give unhindered utterance to four-fifths of his theories before any academic body. But when the doctrine and the truth were concerned he remained intransigent; the tougher the resistance, the tougher became his determination. When I search for a symbol of moral courage—the only earthly heroism that can be performed solo—I always see before me the handsome, masculine, candid face of Freud with his dark eyes and direct and quiet gaze.

The man who had fled to London from his native land to which he had given worldwide and eternal fame, was old in years besides being very ill. But he was neither weary nor bent. I harbored the secret fear of finding him embittered and distressed after all the hours of torture which he must have endured in Vienna, but I found him more unrestrained and even happier than ever. He led me out into the garden of his house in the outskirts of London. "Did I ever have a nicer home?" he asked with a bright smile

about the once so stern mouth. He showed me his beloved
Egyptian statuettes which Maria Bonaparte had rescued
for him. "Isn't this home again?" And on his desk lay the
large folio pages of his manuscripts which, at eighty-three,
he wrote with the old legible rounded script, every day, as
clear in his mind as in his best period and equally tireless;
his strong will had risen superior to everything, illness, age,
exile and for the first time the kindness of his being which
had been dammed during long years of struggle flowed
freely from him. Age had only made him mellower, the
trials he endured more forbearing. Once so reserved he
would now proffer a familiar gesture; he would lay his arm
around my shoulder and his eyes would glow more warmly
through his shining glasses. Over the years a conversation
with Freud had always constituted one of my greatest
intellectual satisfactions. While one learned one marveled,
it was plain that one's every word was fully comprehended
by this magnificent, unprejudiced person whom no admission startled, no statement excited, and whose impulse to
make others see and feel clearly had long since become an
instinctive life impulse. Never, however, was I more gratefully sensible of the irreplaceable quality of those long
conversations than during that dark year which was to be
his last. At the moment of entering his room it was
as if the madness of the world outside had been shut
off. Whatever was terrible reverted to the abstract, confusion
resolved itself, that which was concerned with our moment
of time clicked into its humble place in the great cyclic
phases. It was my first experience of a true sage, exalted
beyond himself, to whom neither pain nor death longer
counted as a personal experience but as a super-personal
matter of observation and contemplation; his dying was
no less a moral feat than his life. Freud already then suffered
greatly from the illness that was soon to take him from us.

One could see that it was a strain for him to speak with his artificial palate and one was almost apologetic for every word that he granted because articulation cost him exertion. But he would not let one go; it was the pride of his spirit of steel to manifest to his friends that his will remained more potent than vulgar bodily torments. His mouth distorted by pain, he wrote at his desk until the last days, and even when pain tortured his sleep at night—that wonderfully sound, healthy sleep which had been the prime source of his strength for eighty years—he denied himself sleeping potions and any narcotic. He did not wish the lucidity of his mind to be dulled for a single hour by such alleviation; rather suffer and remain alert, rather think under torture than not think at all, hero of the spirit to the very end. It was a terrible struggle and it became more magnificent the longer it lasted. From one day to the next, the shadow of death showed more plainly on his face. It hollowed his cheeks, it chiseled the temples out of his brow, it twisted his mouth, it checked the words on his lips; against the eyes alone the Dark Reaper was impotent, against this unconquerable watch-tower from which the heroic mind gazed into the world: eye and mind remained clear to the last moment. Once, on one of my last visits, I took Salvador Dali with me, in my opinion the most gifted painter of the younger generation, who revered Freud immensely and while I talked with Freud, he worked at a sketch. I dared not show it to Freud, because clairvoyantly Dali had already incorporated death in the picture.

The struggle of this strongest will, this most penetrating mind of our time against destruction became increasingly cruel; only when he himself realized clearly—he, to whom clarity always had been the highest quality of thinking—that he would not be able to continue to write, to function, like a Roman hero he permitted the doctor to end his pain.

It was the noble end of a noble life, a death memorable even among the hecatombs of that murderous time. And when we friends lowered his coffin into English soil, we knew that we had given it the best of our homeland.

In those hours I frequently spoke with Freud about the horror of Hitler's world and the war. The outburst of bestiality deeply shocked him as a humanitarian, but as a thinker he was in no way astonished. He had always been scolded as a pessimist, he said, because he had denied the supremacy of culture over the instincts; but his opinion that the barbaric, the elemental destructive instinct in the human soul was ineradicable, has become confirmed most terribly. Not that he got any satisfaction in being right. Perhaps coming centuries might find a formula to control those instincts, at least as regards the common concerns of people; in everyday life, however, and deep within man they survived ineradicably, perhaps as useful energizing agents. The problem of Judaism and its present tragedy occupied him even more in those days but his science provided no formula and his lucid mind found no solution. Shortly before that he had published his work on Moses in which he presented Moses as a non-Jew, an Egyptian, thus giving offense by this allocation of dubious scientific worth to devout Jews and to those holding the nationalist ideal. He had come to regret having published the book right in the most terrible hour of Jewry, "now that everything is being taken from them, I had to go and take their best man." I could not but agree with him that by now every Jew's sensitiveness had increased sevenfold for even in the midst of the world tragedy they were the real victims, everywhere the victims, because, already dispersed before the blow, they knew that whatever evil was to come would touch them first and with sevenfold force, and that the most hate-maddened man of all times wished to humiliate them especially and to harry them to the end of and under the earth. Every week and every month refugees arrived in growing numbers and each lot was poorer and in greater consternation than the one that came before. The first ones, those who had been prompt to leave Germany and Austria, had still managed to save their clothes, their baggage, their household goods; some even had a little money. But the longer one of them had placed trust in Germany, the greater his reluctance to wrench himself from his beloved home, the more severely he had been punished. First the Jews had been deprived of their professions; they were forbidden the theaters, the movies, the museums, and scholars lost the use of the libraries; they had stayed because of loyalty or of indolence, cowardice or pride. They preferred being humiliated at home to humiliating themselves as beggars abroad. They were not permitted to have servants, radios and telephones were removed from their homes, then the homes themselves were taken; the star of David was forced on them so that they might be recognized, avoided and mocked like lepers expelled and proscribed. Every right was withdrawn from them, every spiritual and physical cruelty was practiced on them with playful sadism and the old Russian proverb had suddenly become cruel truth for every Jew: "No one is safe from the beggar's pack and the jail." Whoever did not leave was thrown into a concentration camp where German discipline crushed even the proudest. Then, robbed of all, he was pushed over the frontier without further concern, with the suit on his back and ten marks in his pocket. They pleaded at the consulates and almost always in vain, for which country wanted newcomers who had been plundered to the skin, beggars? I will never forget the sight which once met me in a London travel bureau; it was filled with refugees, almost all Jews, everyone of them wanting to go—anywhere. Merely to another country, anywhere, into the polar ice or the scorching sands of Sahara, only away, only on because, their transit visa having expired, they had to go on, on with wife and child to new stars, to a new language-world, to folk whom they did not know and who did not want to receive them. There I met a once very wealthy industrialist from Vienna, who had been one of our most intelligent art collectors; he was so old, so gray, so weary that I did not recognize him at first. Weakly with both hands, he clung to the table. I asked him where he was going. "I don't know," he said, "who asks about one's wishes nowadays? One goes wherever one is still admitted. Someone told me that I might be able to get a visa for Haiti or San Domingo here." My heart skipped a beat: an old worn-out man with children and grandchildren atremble with the hope of going to a country which hitherto he would not have been able to find on the map, there only to beg his way through and again be a stranger and purposeless! Someone next to him asked in eager desperation how one could get to Shanghai; he had heard that the Chinese were still admitting refugees. There they crowded, erstwhile university professors, bankers, merchants, landed proprietors, musicians; each ready to drag the miserable ruins of his existence over earth and oceans anywhere, to do and suffer anything, only away, away from Europe, only away! It was a ghostly flock. But my most painful thought was that these fifty tormented people were no more than a skirmish troop preceding an army of five, eight, perhaps ten million Jews who, at the rear, were striking tents and already pressing forward; those millions, first plundered then trampled over by the war, who were waiting for help from charitable institutions, for official permits, and the wherewithal to move on. It was a gigantic mass which, murderously roused and fleeing in panic before the Hitlerite forest fire, besieged the railway stations at every European frontier and filled the jails; the expulsion of a whole people which was denied nationhood but was yet a people which, for two thousand years sought nothing so much as to stop wandering and to rest their feet on quiet, peaceful earth.

What was most tragic in this Jewish tragedy of the twentieth century was that those who suffered it knew that it was pointless and that they were guiltless. Their fore-fathers and ancestors of mediaeval times had at least known what they suffered for; for their belief, for their law. They had still possessed a talisman of the soul which today's gen-eration had long since lost, the inviolable faith in their God. They lived and suffered in the proud delusion that they were selected by the Creator as a people chosen for a special destiny and a special mission and the promise of the Bible was to them commandment and law. Thrown on the pyre they pressed the scripture that was holy to them against their breast and through their inner fire were less sensitive to the murderous flames. Driven from land to land, there still remained for them a last home, their home in God, from which no earthly power, no emperor, no king, no inquisition could expel them. As long as their religion bound them together they still were a community and therefore a power; when they were segregated and expelled, they atoned for the fault of their own doing by having consciously segregated themselves through their religion and their customs from the other nations of the earth. But the Jews of the twentieth century had for long not been a community. They had no common faith, they were conscious of their Judaism rather as a burden than as some-thing to be proud of and were not aware of any mission. They lived apart from the commandments of their once holy books and they were done with the common language of old. To integrate themselves and become articulated

with the people with whom they lived, to dissolve themselves
in the common life, was the purpose for which they strove
impatiently for the sake of peace from persecution, rest on
the eternal flight. Thus the one group no longer understood
the other, melted down into other peoples as they were,
more Frenchmen, Germans, Englishmen, Russians than
they were Jews. Only now, since they were swept up like
dirt in the streets and heaped together, the bankers from
their Berlin palaces and sextons from the synagogues of
orthodox congregations, the philosophy professors from
Paris, and Rumanian cabbies, the undertaker's helpers and
Nobel prize winners, the concert singers, and hired mourn-
ers, the authors and distillers, the haves and the have-nots,
the great and the small, the devout and the liberals, the
usurers and the sages, the Zionists and the assimilated, the
Ashkenasim and the Sephardim, the just and the unjust
besides which the confused horde who thought that they
had long since eluded the curse, the baptized and the semi-
Jews—only now, for the first time in hundreds of years the
Jews were forced into a community of interest to which they
had long ceased to be sensitive, the ever-recurring—since
Egypt—community of expulsion. But why this fate for them
and always for them alone? What was the reason, the sense,
the aim of this senseless persecution? They were driven out
of lands but without a land to go to. They were repulsed
but not told where they might be accepted. They were
held blameful but denied means of expiation. And thus,
with smarting eyes, they stared at each other on their flight:
Why I? Why you? How do you and I who do not know
each other, who speak different languages, whose thinking
takes different forms and who have nothing in common
happen to be here together? Why any of us? And none
could answer. Even Freud, the clearest seeing mind of this
time, with whom I often talked in those days, was baffled

and could make no sense out of the nonsense. Who knows but that Judaism because of its mysterious survival may not, in its ultimate significance, constitute a reiteration of Job's eternal cry to God, so that it may not be quite forgotten on earth.

~~~

No experience in life is more spectral than when that which one has thought long since dead and buried, again advances on one, unannounced, in the same form and shape. The summer of 1939 had come, Munich with its short-lived delusion of "peace in our time" was long past; by this time Hitler had invaded and seized dismembered Czechoslovakia contrary to oath and vow, Memel was occupied, Danzig and the Polish corridor were being demanded by the German press in its artfully created frenzy. A sad awakening from her generous credulity had broken over England. Even the plain uninformed people whose loathing of war was a mere instinct, began to express embittered ill-humor. All of the usually restrained English were moved to utterance, the doorman of our large flat, the lift boy, the chambermaid while tidying up the room. None quite understood what it was all about, but all remembered the one thing, the undeniable fact that Chamberlain, the Prime Minister of England had three times flown to Germany to preserve the peace and that no spirit of concession served to satisfy Hitler. Stern voices in the English Parliament were heard crying "Stop aggression!" On all sides one perceived the preparations for (or really against) the coming war. Again the light barrage balloons, looking innocent enough like gray toy elephants, began to float over London, again air raid shelters were dug and the gas masks were distributed and carefully examined. The suspense equaled that of a year ago and was perhaps even greater because now it was not a naïve and guileless population but an already determined and angered one that stood behind the Government.

During that season I had left London and retired into the country, to Bath. Never in my life had I been so cruelly conscious of man's helplessness against world events. Here one stood, an alert, thinking being, engaged in matters remote from politics, devoted to his work, quietly persevering in the task of transforming one's years into achievement. And off there, somewhere in the invisible, were a dozen other persons whom one had not ever known or seen, a few each in the Wilhelmstrasse in Berlin, in the Quai d'Orsay in Paris, in the Palazzo Venezia in Rome and at 10 Downing Street in London, and those ten or twenty, of whom few had thus far manifested any particular wisdom or cleverness, talked and wrote and telephoned and made treaties about things one knew nothing of. They made decisions in which one had no part and the details of which one never heard and yet made final dispositions about my own life and every other life in Europe. My destiny lay in their hands, no longer in mine. They destroyed or spared us helpless ones, they permitted freedom or compelled slavery, and for millions they determined peace or war. And there in my room I sat like everybody else, defenseless as a fly, helpless as a snail, while life and death, my innermost ego, and my future were at stake, the forming thoughts in my brain, plans born and unborn, my waking and my sleep, my will, my possessions, my whole being. There one sat, waiting and staring into the void like a doomed man in his cell, immured, enmeshed in this senseless, helpless waiting and waiting and one's fellow-prisoners to right and left inquired, guessed and chattered as if any one of us knew or could know how and what was to become of us. The telephone rang and a friend asked my views. There were the newspapers and they confused one only still more. One declaration over the radio

contradicted the other. I would walk out and the first man
I encountered would ask me, equally ignorant, whether
I thought war would come or not. And, in one's own uneasiness, one would put the same kind of question and would
chatter and debate, well knowing that the knowledge, experience, wisdom and foresight that were the accumulation of
years and to which one had educated oneself, were valueless against the verdict of that dozen strange men; that, this
second time within twenty-five years one was exactly as helpless and will-less in the face of fate as the first, and meaning-
less thoughts kept pounding against aching temples. In the
end the capital got to be too much for me, because the
shrill words on the newspaper posters that were present at
every street corner sprang at me like hateful hounds, because
I found myself trying to read the thoughts behind the thousands of faces that swept by me. Those thoughts, theirs and
mine, were identical, they were solely of the Yes or No, of
the Black or Red in the decisive game in which my whole
life was part of the stake, my last hoarded years, my unwrit-
ten books, everything which heretofore had constituted the
meaning and purpose of my life.

But the ball rolled undecidedly hither and thither on the
roulette table of diplomacy with exasperating slowness.
Back and forth, forth and back, black and red, and red and
black, hope and disappointment, good news and bad news
but yet not that which was determinant, final. "Forget!" I
commanded myself. "Flee, take refuge in your innermost
self, in your work, flee to where you are no more than your
own being, not the citizen of a state, not a plaything of this
infernal game, where alone your bit of intellect can still
function rationally in a world gone mad."

I did not want for a task. For years I had been accumulat-
ing material preparatory to a large two-volume study of
Balzac and his work but had never had the courage to start

on so comprehensive a labor that was calculated to occupy
a long period. But it was just my gloom that produced the
courage. I withdrew to Bath, and to Bath in particular
because that city reflects more faithfully and impressively
than any other in England a more peaceful century, the
eighteenth, to the reposed eye; it is the city, too, where
many of the best men of England's glorious literature,
Fielding above all, achieved their best. But how painful the
contrast between this gentle countryside endowed with a
mild beauty and the growing unrest of the world and of my
reflections. Just as July of 1914 was the most beautiful that
I can remember in Austria, so challengingly beautiful was
this August 1939 in England. Again, the soft silken-blue sky
like a heavenly tabernacle, again this benign sunshine over
meadows and woods besides an indescribable splendor of
flowers—the great equable breathing of peace over the
earth while mankind girded itself for war. As unbelievable
as at that former time seemed the madness in the face of this
quiet, persistent exuberant flowering, this rhythmical calm
that seemed to take joy in itself, in the valleys of Bath
which in their loveliness reminded me strangely of that
Baden countryside of 1914.

And again I was reluctant to believe it. This time, too,
I made preparations for a summer trip. The congress of
the P. E. N. Club was planned for Stockholm in the first
week of September 1939 and the Swedish group had invited
me as a guest of honor since, in my amphibian existence,
I no longer represented any nation; my kindly hosts had
already seen to it that every hour of the weeks to come was
fitted into a program. Long since I had booked for the crossing, then came threatening report after report increasing in
intensity of the imminent mobilization. According to the
rules of reason I ought to have quickly packed my books and
manuscripts and left the British Isles, a possible theater of

war, because I was an alien in England and in case of war automatically an enemy alien, menaced by all possible restrictions of personal freedom. But something inexplicable in me opposed the thought of safety by flight. It was half disdain to flee once more since fate dogged me everywhere anyhow, and half fatigue. "Let us meet the time as it seeks us," I said to myself with Shakespeare. If it seeks you, nearing sixty, make no further resistance. Your best, the life you have already lived, remains unaffected. And so I stayed. However, I wished to put my private affairs in the best possible order and as it was my intention to contract a second marriage I did not want to lose a minute, in order not to be separated for long from my future life-partner by internment or other unforeseen measures. Thus I went that morning—it was September 1, a Friday—to the registry office at Bath to secure my marriage license. The official took our papers and was uncommonly friendly and zealous. Like everyone else at this time, he understood our desire for haste. The ceremony was set for the next day; he took his pen and, in a careful script, began to write our names in his book.

Just then—it must have been about eleven o'clock—the door to the next room flew open. A young official burst in, getting into his coat while walking. "The Germans have invaded Poland. This is war!" he shouted into the quiet room. The word fell like a hammer blow upon my heart. But the heart of our generation is already accustomed to all sorts of hard blows. "That doesn't have to mean war," I said in honest conviction. But the man was almost incensed. "No," he cried vehemently, "we've had enough! We can't let them start this sort of thing every six months! We've got to put a stop to it!"

Meanwhile, the clerk who had already begun to fill out our certificate laid his pen down thoughtfully. After all, we were aliens, he reflected, and in case of war would automatically become enemy aliens. He did not know whether marriage in such circumstances was still permissible. He was very sorry but in any event he would have to apply to London for instructions. Then came two more days of waiting, hoping, fearing, two days of the most terrible suspense. Sunday morning the radio gave out the news that England had declared war against Germany.

~

It was a strange morning. Silently we stepped back from the radio that had projected a message into the room which would outlast centuries, a message that was destined to change our world totally and the life of every single one of us. A message which meant death for thousands of those who had silently listened to it, sorrow and unhappiness, desperation and threat for every one of us, and perhaps only after years and years a creative significance. It was war again, a war, more terrible and far-reaching than ever before on earth any war had been. Once more an epoch came to an end, once more a new epoch began. Silently we stood in the room that had suddenly become deathly quiet and avoided looking at each other. From outside came the unconcerned twitter of the birds, frivolous in their love and subject to the gentle breeze, and in golden luster the trees swayed as if their leaves, like lips, wished to touch one another tenderly. It was not for ancient Mother Nature to know the cares of her creatures.

I went to my room and packed a small bag. If the prediction of a friend in high place were fulfilled then we Austrians in England would be counted as Germans and would be subject to the same restrictions; it seemed unlikely that I would be allowed to sleep in my own bed that night. Again I had dropped a rung lower, within an hour I was no longer merely a stranger in the land but an "enemy alien," a hostile foreigner; this decree forcibly banned me to a situation to which my throbbing heart had no relation. For was a more absurd situation imaginable than for a man in a strange land to be compulsorily aligned—solely on the ground of a faded birth certificate—with a Germany that had long ago expelled him because his race and ideas branded him as anti-German and to which, as an Austrian, he had never belonged. By a stroke of a pen the meaning of a whole life had been transformed into a paradox; I wrote, I still thought in the German language, but my every thought and wish belonged to the countries which stood in arms for the freedom of the world. Every other loyalty, all that was past and gone, was torn and destroyed and I knew that after this war everything would have to take a fresh start. For my most cherished aim to which I had devoted all the power of my conviction for forty years, the peaceful union of Europe, had been defiled. What I had feared more than my own death, the war of all against all, now had become unleashed for the second time. And one who had toiled heart and soul all his life for human and spiritual unity found himself, in this hour which like no other demanded inviolable unity, thanks to this precipitate singling out, superfluous and alone as never before in his life.

Once more I wandered down to the town to have a last look at peace. It lay calmly in the noon-day sun and seemed no different to me from other days. People went their accustomed way in their usual manner. There were no signs of hurry, they did not crowd talkatively together. Their behavior had a sabbath-like quality and at a certain moment I asked myself: "Can it be that they don't know it yet?" But they were English, and practiced in restraining their emotions. They needed no flags and drums, clamor and music

to strengthen themselves in their tough, unemotional determination. How different from those days of July 1914 in
Austria, but how different was I, too, from the inexperienced
young man of that time, how heavy with memories!
I knew what war meant, and as I looked at the well-filled,
tidy shops I had an abrupt vision of those of 1918, cleared-
out and empty, seemingly staring at one with wide-open
eyes. As in a waking dream I saw the long queues of care-
worn women before the food shops, the mothers in mourning, the wounded, the cripples, the whole nightmare of
another day returned spectrally in the shining noonday
light. I recalled our old soldiers, weary and in rags, how they
had come back from the battlefield,—my beating heart felt
the whole past war in the one that was beginning today and
which still hid its terror from our eyes. Again I was aware
that the past was done for, work achieved was in ruins,
Europe, our home, to which we had dedicated ourselves
had suffered a destruction that would extend far beyond our
life. Something new, a new world began, but how many
hells, how many purgatories had to be crossed before it
could be reached!

The sun shone full and strong. Homeward bound I suddenly noticed before me my own shadow as I had seen the
shadow of the other war behind the actual one. During all
this time it has never budged from me, that irremovable
shadow, it hovers over every thought of mine by day and by
night; perhaps its dark outline lies on some pages of this
book, too. But, after all, shadows themselves are born of
light. And only he who has experienced dawn and dusk,
war and peace, ascent and decline, only he has truly lived.

STEFAN ZWEIG ON THE S.S. URUGUAY ON HIS LAST JOURNEY TO BRAZIL, AUGUST 1941

PUBLISHER'S POSTSCRIPT

STEFAN ZWEIG and Elizabeth Charlotte Zweig, his wife, died by their own hands at Petropolis, Brazil, on February 23, 1942. This was Mr. Zweig's last message:

Before parting from life of my free will and in my right mind I am impelled to fulfil a last obligation: to give heartfelt thanks to this wonderful land of Brazil which afforded me and my work such kind and hospitable repose. My love for the country increased from day to day, and nowhere else would I have preferred to build up a new existence, the world of my own language having disappeared for me and my spiritual home, Europe, having destroyed itself.

But after one's sixtieth year unusual powers are needed in order to make another wholly new beginning. Those that I possess have been exhausted by long years of homeless wandering. So I think it better to conclude in good time and in erect bearing a life in which intellectual labor meant the purest joy and personal freedom the highest good on earth.

I salute all my friends! May it be granted them yet to see the dawn after the long night! I, all too impatient, go on before.

Stefan Zweig

Petropolis, 22. II. 1942

Mr. Zweig always encouraged his friends to set down their reminiscences, not necessarily for publication but for

Declaração

Ehe ich aus freiem Willen und mit klaren Sinnen aus dem Leben scheide, drängt es mich eine letzte Pflicht zu erfüllen: diesem wundervollen Lande Brasilien innig zu danken, das mir und meiner Arbeit so gute und gastliche Rast gegeben. Mit jedem Tage habe ich dies Land mehr lieben gelernt und nirgends hätte ich mir mein Leben lieber vom Grunde aus neu aufgebaut, nachdem die Welt meiner eigenen Sprache für mich untergegangen ist und meine geistige Heimat Europa sich selber vernichtet.

Aber nach dem sechzigsten Jahre bedürfte es besonderer Kräfte um noch einmal völlig neu zu beginnen. Und die meinen sind durch die langen Jahre heimatlosen Wanderns erschöpft. So halte ich es für besser, rechtzeitig und in aufrechter Haltung ein Leben abzuschließen, dem geistige Arbeit immer die lauterste Freude und persönliche Freiheit das höchste Gut dieser Erde gewesen.

Ich grüße alle meine Freunde! Mögen sie die Morgenröte noch sehen nach der langen Nacht! Ich, allzu Ungeduldiger, gehe ihnen voraus.

Stefan Zweig

Petropolis, 22. II 1942

FACSIMILE OF STEFAN ZWEIG'S
PARTING MESSAGE

the pleasure and benefit of their children, their families. In his opinion every life includes inner or external experiences worthy of record. It may be that the lifelong fascination which manuscript diaries, personal memoirs, and all kinds of handwritten relics held for him, and his adeptness in interpreting such remains, led him to overestimate the importance of the plain man's autobiography. He waited long before putting his own on paper, possibly because of his repugnance to the limelight. Certain it is that Stefan Zweig did not write this book as a farewell message, for it was an old project to which he sometimes adverted in happier days. He undertook it with gusto during his last visit to the United States. Part of the book was sketched during his residence at the Hotel Wyndham, New York City; part at the Taft Hotel, New Haven, where he sojourned for a period while toying with the thought of settling in the shadow of Yale University; and most of the actual writing was done in the early summer of 1941 at Ossining, New York, where he had rented a house. One chapter, "*Eros Matutinos*," he wrote in Brazil. It was by no means an afterthought; the delay was rather because he wanted to ponder over the right form for a delicate but important subject which autobiographers generally skirt or shy away from.

Mr. and Mrs. Zweig sailed for Brazil on the S.S. *Uruguay* on August 15, 1941; he loved that land and was confident that it would restore his peace of mind and offer peace for literary pursuits. His early letters from there indicated that the oppression caused by world events had lifted. He plunged into work; work was his idea of a holiday. Zweig was forever writing or busied in studies preliminary to writing. He liked being engaged on several book manuscripts at the same time.

Fascinated by Montaigne as a subject for these days (he had chanced on a volume of the *Essays* in his Petropolis villa), he immersed himself in the great Frenchman's works and the rich collection of books on Montaigne in a fine private library to which he had been offered access. The resultant manuscript seems not sufficiently complete to publish as a whole. He began a novel, too, but put it aside; his principal desire was to resume the biography of Balzac which had absorbed him at Bath, until he left England in 1940. His last complete work (as yet unpublished) is a story in which a tense contest at chess provides the background for a poignant tale of the present day in the characteristic manner of his shorter fiction. Zweig's letters suggest that this story re-established—for the time being—the mood of those years in which art was his only concern. The finished manuscript, neatly typed by his wife, was enclosed with a last letter to New York, and then, it seems, they were ready for death.

A BIBLIOGRAPHY OF THE ORIGINAL
WORKS OF STEFAN ZWEIG

INDEX

A BIBLIOGRAPHY
OF THE ORIGINAL WORKS
OF STEFAN ZWEIG IN BOOK FORM

*Indicates books published in English. The title of the American edition has been included where it diverges from the German.

SILBERNE SAITEN. *Poems.* 1901.

DIE LIEBE DER ERIKA EWALD. *Novelettes.* 1904.

*VERLAINE. *Critical biography.* 1905.

DIE FRÜHEN KRÄNZE. *Poems.* 1906.

TERSITES. *Play.* 1907.

*ÉMILE VERHAEREN. *Critical Biography.* 1910.

*ERSTES ERLEBNIS. *Four stories of childhood.* 1911.

DAS HAUS AM MEER. *Play.* 1912.

DER VERWANDELTE KOMÖDIANT. *Play.* 1912.

ERINNERUNGEN AN ÉMILE VERHAEREN. *Criticism.* 1917.

*JEREMIAS. *Play.* 1917.

DAS HERZ EUROPAS. *A visit to the Geneva Red Cross.* 1918.

LEGENDE EINES LEBENS. *Play.* 1919.

FAHRTEN. *Travel.* 1919.

*DREI MEISTER: Balzac, Dickens, Dostoefsky. *Biography.* 1920.

*DER ZWANG. *Novelette.* 1920.

MARCELINE DESBORDES-VALMORE. *Biography.* 1920.

*ANGST. *Novelette.* 1920.

*ROMAIN ROLLAND: der Mann und das Werk. *Critical biography.* 1921.

*DIE AUGEN DES EWIGEN BRUDERS. *Legend.* 1922.

*AMOK. *Novelettes.* 1922.

DIE GESAMMELTEN GEDICHTE. *Poems.* 1924.

*DER KAMPF MIT DEM DÄMON: Hölderlin, Kleist, Nietzsche. *Biography.* 1925.

*BEN JONSON'S "VOLPONE." *Play.* 1926.

*DIE UNSICHTBARE SAMMLUNG. *Novelette.* 1926.

*DER FLÜCHTLING. *Novelette.* 1927.

*VERWIRRUNG DER GEFÜHLE. *Three novelettes.* 1927.

ABSCHIED VON RILKE. *An address.* 1927.

*STERNSTUNDEN DER MENSCHHEIT. *Five historical miniatures.* 1927. *(The Tide of Fortune)*

*DREI DICHTER IHRES LEBENS: Casanova, Stendhal, Tolstoi. *Biography.* 1928. *(Adepts at Self-Portraiture)*

*KLEINE CHRONIK. *Four novelettes.* 1929.

DAS LAMM DES ARMEN. *Play.* 1929.

*JOSEPH FOUCHÉ. Bildnis eines politischen Menschen. *Biography.* 1929.

*RAHEL RECHTET MIT GOTT. *Legend.* 1930.

*DIE HEILUNG DURCH DEN GEIST: Mesmer, Mary Baker Eddy, Freud. *Biography.* 1931. *(Mental Healers)*

*MARIE ANTOINETTE: Bildnis eines mittleren Charakters. *Biography.* 1932.

*TRIUMPH UND TRAGIK DES ERASMUS VON ROTTERDAM. *Biography.* 1934.

*MARIA STUART. *Biography.* 1935.

DIE SCHWEIGSAME FRAU (Libretto for R. Strauss opera). 1935.

*BAUMEISTER DER WELT. *Biography.* 1935. *(Master Builders)*

    (Zusammenfassung in einem Band von:
      DER KAMPF MIT DEM DÄMON
      DREI MEISTER
      DREI DICHTER IHRES LEBENS.)

*CASTELLIO GEGEN CALVIN. *Biography.* 1936. *(The Right to Heresy)*

*DER BEGRABENE LEUCHTER. *Legend.* 1936.

*GESAMMELTE ERZÄHLUNGEN. *Fiction.*

    1. Band: DIE KETTE. 1936.

    2. Band: KALEIDOSKOP. 1936.

BEGEGNUNGEN MIT MENSCHEN, BÜCHERN, STÄDTEN. *Essays and lectures.* 1937.

*MAGELLAN. *Biography.* 1938.

*UNGEDULD DES HERZENS. *Novel* 1938. *(Beware of Pity)*

WORTE AM GRABE SIGMUND FREUDS. *Funeral address, privately printed.* 1939.
*BRASILIEN, LAND DER ZUKUNFT. *Travel.* 1941.
*AMERIGO. A Comedy of Errors in History. Biography. 1942.
*DIE WELT VON GESTERN. *Autobiography.* 1942.
*SCHACHNOVELLE. *Novelette.* 1943. *(The Royal Game)*
ZEIT UND WELT. *Essays and lectures, 1904–1940.* 1943.
*BALZAC. *Critical biography.* 1946.
*STEFAN ZWEIG–FRIDERIKE ZWEIG BRIEFWECHSEL 1912–1942. *Letters.* 1951.
RICHARD STRAUSS–STEFAN ZWEIG BRIEFWECHSEL. *Letters.* 1957.
EUROPÄISCHES ERBE. *Essays.* 1960.
UNBEKANNTE BRIEFE AUS DER EMIGRATION AN EINE FREUNDIN. *Letters to G. Selden–Goth.* 1964.

LANGUAGES INTO WHICH BOOKS BY STEFAN ZWEIG HAVE BEEN TRANSLATED:

Armenian	French	Norwegian
Bulgarian	Georgian	Polish
Catalan	Greek	Portuguese
Chinese	Hebrew	Rumanian
Croatian	Hungarian	Russian
Czech	Italian	Serbian
Danish	Japanese	Spanish
Dutch	Lettish	Swedish
English	Lithuanian	Ukrainian
Finnish	Marathi	Yiddish

For Further Reading

Jules Romains. *Stefan Zweig, Great European.* New York, 1941.

Raoul Auernheimer. "Stefan Zweig" in *The Torch of Freedom,* ed. E. Ludwig and H. B. Kranz. New York, 1943.

Friderike Zweig. *Stefan Zweig.* New York, 1946.

Hanns Arens (ed.). *Stefan Zweig. A Tribute to His Life and Work.* London, 1951.

Alfred Werner. "Stefan Zweig, the Last Humanist," *Chicago Jewish Forum,* Oct. 1951.

Harry Zohn. "Stefan Zweig and Modern European Literature," *German Life and Letters,* Apr. 1952.

Stefan and Friderike Zweig: Their Correspondence, 1912–1942. New York, 1954.

Harry Zohn. "Stefan Zweig's Last Years," *Monatshefte,* Feb. 1956.

Joseph Leftwich. "Stefan Zweig and the World of Yesterday" in *Leo Baeck Institute Year Book III.* London, 1958.

D. A. Prater. "Stefan Zweig and England," *German Life and Letters,* Oct. 1962.

W. I. Lucas. "Stefan Zweig" in *German Men of Letters,* vol. 2 ed. A. Natan. London, 1963.

INDEX

ABBAYE, 199
Addams, Jane, 347
Adler, Viktor, Dr., 60, 108
Africa, 192
Agadir, 197
Aksahov, 330
Albania, 197, 205
Altenberg, Peter, 23, 46
America, 108, 182, 187 ff., 192, 279, 280, 327, 333, 344
Amok, 303, 317
Amsterdam, 192
Annonce faite à Marie, L', 163
Anschluss, 282
Anthroposophy, 115, 301
Anzengruber, 404
Appassionata, 301
Arcos, René, 199, 267
Argentina, 398
Aristotle, 134
Artstetten, 217
Asch, Shalom, 347
Ashkenasim, 428
Aube, L', 201
Au-dessus de la Mêlée, 240, 241, 242
Austria, 12, 20, 24, 26, 30, 33, 59, 60, 61, 99, 102, 112, 197, 206, 219, 225, 226, 228, 235, 244, 245, 259, 261, 281, 282, 284, 291, 293, 297, 301, 304, 307, 313, 365, 377, 382, 383, 384, 386, 389, 390, 393, 400, 401, 402, 403, 405, 406, 408, 413, 419, 425, 432, 436
Austrian Schools, 29
Austro-German Offensive, 246

BADEN, 214, 218, 432
Badeni, Count, 65
Bahr, Hermann, 44, 46, 47, 324
Balkan War, 197, 205, 206
Balkans, 198, 401
Baltic provinces, 306
Baltimore, 189

Balzac, Honoré de, 41, 51, 132, 162, 210, 319, 431
Barbusse, Henri, 241, 244, 272, 302
Barcelona, 400
Barnay, Ludwig, 169
Bartok, Bela, 347
Bath, (England), 430, 432, 433
Baudelaire, Charles Pierre, 42, 411
Bavaria, 296, 306, 360
Bazalgette, Leon, 134, 136, ff., 181, 198, 201
Beer-Hoffmann, Richard, 23, 46
Beethoven, Ludwig van, 162, 202, 214, 235, 301
Belgium, 119, 221, 228
Benedikt, Moritz, 99
Berchtesgaden, 347, 359, 377
Berg, Alban, 347, 368
Berger, Alfred Baron, 173
Berlin, 110, 111, 118, 119, 192, 261, 294, 313, 393
Berliner Tageblatt, 238
Bermuda, 190
Bibliothèque Nationale, 133, 202
Bierbaum, Otto Julius, 97
Binyon, Lawrence, 158
Bismarck, Otto, 63, 179, 362
Blake, William, 158, 161, 391
Blätter für die Kunst, 55, 56
Blériot, Louis, 196
Bloch, Jean-Richard, 135, 199, 379
Bohème, La, 113
Bojer, Johan, 125
Bolsheviks, 271
Bonaparte, Princess Maria, 419, 422
Borgese, G. A., 199, 305
Bösendorfer Saal, 16
Bosnia, 197, 215
Boston, 189, 190
Boulogne, 327
Brahm, Otto, 112
Brahms, Johannes, 41, 43
Brandes, Georg, 125, 165, 347
Brazil, 399

Brettauer, (family of author's mother), 9 ff.
Breuning, Stephan, 352, 353
Briand, Aristide, 362
British Museum, 156, 158, 382
Bronx, 189
Brooklyn Bridge, 188
Brothers Karamazov, The, 117
Brünn, 353
Brussels, 120, 326
Buchs, 262, 283
Budapest, 250
Budberg, Baroness Marie, 339
Bulgaria, 197
Bülow, Bernhard, Prince von, 362
Burgtheater, 15, 16, 19, 41, 42, 102, 170, 172, 173
Burlington Magazine, 39
"Burning Secret, The," 367
Burschenschaften, 64, 94
Buschbeck, 45
Busoni, Feruccio, 203, 276
Byron, George Gordon, Lord 140

Café Bellevue, 274
Café Grienstadl, 47
Café Odéon, 274, 275
Café Vachette, 131
Cahiers de la Quinzaine, 201, 202
Caillou qui bique, 212
Calais, 380
Calcutta, 184
Calvin, John, 168
Carlyle, Thomas, 95
Casanova de Seingalt, Giovanni Jacopo, 274
Cassel (Theater), 170
Castellio, Sebastian, 167
Catholic Groups, 198
Catholic, 145
Cavell, Edith, 241
Cena, Giovanni, 124
Century of the Child, 124
Chamber of Writers, 375
Chamberlain, Joseph, 156, 226, 413 ff., 429
Chaplin, Charles, 211
Charcot, Jean Martin, 69
Chartres, 149
Chaux de Fonds, 278
Chicago, 189
Chotek, Countess, 217
Christian Social Party, 62, 63, 95, 297
Civil War, 239

"Clarté," 302
Claudel, Paul, 135, 163
Clemenceau, Georges, 260, 271
Clerambault, 265
Clerical party, 377, 382
Cloister, 125
Collected Poems (of Stefan Zweig), 98
"Coming Ones, The" 113, 115
Communism, 302
Communists, 367, 386
Convent zu den Englischen Fräulein, 234
Cook's Tours, 183
Coopération Intellectuelle, 321
Corps Students, 64
Corriere de la Sera, 305
Council or Culture, 375
Critica, 342
Croce, Benedetto, 245, 342
Crommelynck, 220
Cultural Propaganda, 257
Cyrenaica, 197
Czechoslovakia, 383, 401, 413, 417, 429

Dahn, Felix, 45
Daladier, Edouard, 226, 413, 415
Dali, Salvador, 423
Dannhäuser, 353
Dante, Alighieri, 235, 245
Danzig, 429
Death and Transfiguration, 369
Debussy, Claude, 44
Dehmel, Richard, 97, 98, 111, 119, 204, 229, 243, 255
Demain, 267, 270 ff.
Demelius, Mrs., 164
Desbordes-Valmore, Marceline, 132
Dickens, Charles, 165
Dijon, 327
Doctor Faust, 276
Dollfuss, Engelbert, 382, 383, 384, 390
Doorn, 363
Dostoievsky, Fyodor, 44, 212, 319, 328, 330
Dresden, 178, 376
Dresden Court Theater, 170, 375
Dreyfus, Alfred, 102
Drinkwater, John, 393
Drohobycz, 247
Dublin, 275
Duhamel, Georges, 135, 199, 327, 379

Duncan, Isadora, 75
Durtain, 135, 199

EBERS, Georg Moritz, 45
Eekhoud, Gerbrand van den, 120
Effort libre, L', 199
Egyptian Helena, 370
Ehrlich, Paul, 88
Einstein, Albert, 367
Eisner, Kurt, 269
Elektra, 368
Elizabeth, 167, 218
England, 58, 99, 182, 211, 226, 232,
    275, 362, 380, 382, 390, 392, 393,
    403, 413, 414, 418, 419, 429, 432,
    433
Ensor, James, 220
Erasmus, Desiderius, 167, 229, 254,
    381
Ehrhardt, Captain, 358
Erzberger, 310
Eulenberg Affair, 179
Europe, 192, 401, 405, 413
European National Consciousness,
    196
Evening Standard, 402, 403
Everyman, 346
Exiles, 275

FABIAN Society, 394
Fascism, 308
Fascists, 306, 344
Faesi, Robert, 274
Fall, Leo, 23
Feldkirch, 283
Feu, Le, 241, 244, 302
Feuille, La, 267 ff.
Fey, Major, 384
Flaubert, Gustave, 165
Fliegende Blätter, 79
Florence, 305, 326
Flower Parade, 18
Fouché, 376
France, 51, 194, 196, 198, 199, 209,
    221, 233, 235, 362, 379, 413, 417
France, Anatole, 178
Franco, Francisco, 397
Franco-German Fraternization, 204
Frank, Leonhard, 274
Frankfurter Zeitung, 278
Franz Ferdinand, 215 *ff.*
Franz Josef, Emperor, 8, 21, 63,
    103, 205, 225, 287
Frederick the Great, 243
Freecorps, 358

Freilassing, 294
Freud, Sigmund, 4, 23, 69, 87, 124,
    163, 202, 224, 367, 419, ff.
Fried, Alfred A., 273
Fried, Oscar, 274
Friedenswarte, 273
Furtwängler, Wilhelm, 257, 373

GALICIA, 246, 329
Galsworthy, John 302
Galuppi, Baldassare, 203
Garibaldi, Guiseppe, 362
Garmisch, 372
Geiger, Benno, 305
Geneva, 239 264 267 272
Genoa, 309
George, Stefan, 41, 46, 50, 55, 141
"German-Austrians," 281
"German Christians," 377
German General Staff, 184
German National Party, 63, 64
German Nationalists, 363
German Nationals, 64
Germany, 55, 185, 197, 198, 205,
    226, 231, 232, 233, 241, 244, 257,
    258, 259, 261, 291, 293, 294, 301,
    302, 309, 314, 315, 354, 361, 362,
    364, 365, 367, 374, 375, 382, 389,
    391, 393, 401, 403, 414, 417, 418,
    425, 434, 435
Gesellschaft, 55
Gestapo, 367, 375, 377
Gewandhaus, 372
Gide, André, 133, 379
Giovanezza, 307
Godesburg, 413
Goebbels, Paul Joseph, 366 373
    375, 376, 417
Goering, Hermann Wilhelm, 364,
    373, 375, 376, 407
Goethe, Johann Wolfgang von, 9,
    48, 49, 115, 140, 161, ff., 165, 167,
    171, 201, 245, 274, 361, 371
Goethe, Ottilie von, 163, 164
Goethe Society, 164
Goldmark, Carl, 23
Gorky, Maxim, 163, 321, 328, 330,
    338 ff., 390
Goya, Francisco Lucientes, 44
Graben, 112
Grand Hotel, 176
Graphology, 302
Graz, 373
Greater Germany, 186, 393
Greco, El, 44

Grey, Sir Edward, 232
Grillparzer, Franz, 23, 317, 342
Grünewald, Mathias, 44
Guilbeaux, Henri, 138, 269 ff.
Gymnasium, 28, 33, 34, 35, 37, 41, 43, 46, 47, 49, 52, 53, 59, 94, 95, 97

HABSBURG, 12, 216, 217, 261, 282, 284, 285
Hague, The, 259
Haiti, 190
Halifax, Lord Charles Lindley Wood, 402
Hamburg, 197, 204
Hamlet, 300
Hanslick, Eduard, 44, 100
Harden, Maximilian, 55, 179
Hardy, Thomas, 70
Hartmann, Eduard von, 43
Hauptmann, Gerhart, 38, 41, 44, 45, 229, 243
Haus am Meer, Das, 173
Haushofer, Karl, 184 ff.
Havas Agency, 135
"Heart of Europe, The," 239
Hebbel, Friedrich, 89
Heimwehr, 383, 384
Hellerau, 380
Hermitage, The, 332
Herzen, Alexander, 336
Herzl, Theodor, 101, ff, 115
Hess, Rudolf, 186
Heymel, Alfred Walter, 165
Heyse, Paul, 45
Hille, Peter, 114
Hitler, Adolf, 23, 62, 63, 64, 179, 186, 226, 232, 233, 241, 254, 314, 315, 316, 317, 327, 354, 358, ff., 392, 396, 400, 401, 402, 403, 405, 406, 407, 413, 414, 415, 417, 418, 424, 429
Hofburg, 14
Hofmannsthal, Hugo von, 23, 46, 47, 48, 49, 51, 52, 53, 55, 97, 100, 106, 166, 243, 346, 347, 368, 373
Hölderlin, Johann Christian Friedrich, 49
Holland, 257, 326
Hollywood, 190
Homer, 319
Homosexuality, 299
Hotel de l' Europe, 293
Hotel Schwerdt, 274

Hötzendorf, Konrad von, 207
House of Commons, 414
Huebsch, Benjamin, 321
Hugenberg, 363
Hugo, Victor, 132
Hungary, 296
"Hymn of Hate," 232, 241

IBSEN, Henrik Johan, 43
India, 182, 183, 192
Indo-China, 184
Inflation, 291 ff., 311, 314, 361
Innsbruck, 286
Inselbücherei, 318
Insel-Verlag, 166, 167, 355
"Internationale," 61
"Italian Visits Goethe, An", 245
Italy, 194, 197, 205, 226, 245, 343, 344, 362, 403

JACOBOWSKI, Ludwig, 113
Jammes, Francis, 140
Japan, 184, 185
Jaurès, Jean, 199, 203, 221
Jean Christophe, 163, 203, 242
Jeremiah, 173, 255, 256, 259, 268. 278 282, 317
Jewish Bourgeoisie, 116
Jews, 11, 20, 21, 25, 63, 81, 102, 103, 104, 107, 181, 232, 247, 310, 358, 366, 372, 373, 378, 407, 408, 424, 425, 427, 428
  Galician, 81
  German, 363
  Viennese, 22, 23
Jonson, Ben, 368
Journal des Débats, 100
Jouve, J. P., 267, 268
Joyce, James, 275, 347

KAINZ, Josef, 42, 125, 169 ff.
Kaiserlied, 284
Kalman, Leo, 23
Kapp, General, 358
Kapuzinerberg, 347
Karl, Archduke, 217
Karl, Emperor, 258, 259 ff., 284
Karsavina, Tamara, 178
Keats, John, 46, 49, 119
Keller, Gottfried, 43
Key, Ellen, 124, 181
Keyserling, Count Hermann, 50, 305
Kienthal (Congress of), 271
Kierkegaard, Soren K., 40

King John, 159, 391
Kippenberg, Professor, 167, 352
Knopf, 120
Kolbenheyer, Erwin Guido, 125
Kraus, Karl, 103
Krupps, 197, 205
Kun, Bela, 269, 296

Lamm des Armen, Das, 173
Lammasch, Heinrich, 259, 261
Latin Quarter, 128
Latzko, Andreas, 274
Lay Down Your Arms, 209
League of Nations, 316, 321, 378, 401, 402
Lebensraum, 185 ff.
Le Coq, 219
Leibl, Wilhelm, 43, 62, 63
Leipzig, 372
Lemberg, 247
Lemmonnier, Camille, 119, 120, ff.
Lenbach, Franz von, 45, 134
Lenin, Vladimir Ilich, 138, 267, 271, 272, 333, 340
Leningrad, 321, 378
Leopardi, Giacomo, 49
Lerberghe, Charles van, 119
Lesbianism, 299
Letter from an Unknown Woman, 303, 317
Lilien, E. M., 117
Liliencron, Detlev, Baron von, 97, 98
Linz, 384
Lissauer, Ernst, 231 *ff.,* 241
Lloyd George, David, 362
Loeffler, Charles M., 190
London, 155, ff., 192, 380, 381, 382, 390, 419, 421, 429, 430, 434
"Loris," 46, 47
Loti, Pierre, 183
Ludendorff, Erich, F. W., 278, 280 310, 314
Ludwig, Emil, 347
Lueger, Karl, 25, 62, 63
Lunacharsky, Anatol V., 271, 333
Lunt, Alfred, 318
Lusitania, 241
Luther, Martin, 167

MADAME Bovary, 70
Maeterlinck, Maurice, 120
Magic Mountain, The, 319

Mahler, Gustav, 19, 23, 33, 41, 178
Mainz, 302
Mallarmé, Stephane, 43, 44
Mann, Heinrich, 367
    Thomas, 243, 347, 367
Marie Antoinette, 319, 381
Martin du Gard, Roger, 327, 379
Marx, Karl, 301
"Marxists," 405
Mary Stuart, 167, 382
Masereel, Frans, 267, 279, 327
Master Builders, 303, 317
Matteotti, G., 344
Matkowsky, Adalbert, 169 ff.
Mayerling, 216
Meistersinger, Die, 371
Memel, 429
Mendelssohn, Jakob L. F., 372
Mensch ist gut, Der, 274
Menschen im Kriege, 274
Mercure de France, 136, 245
Merejkovsky, Dmitri, 215, 342, 408
Meunier, Constantin, 120 ff.
Miesbach, 359
Miesbacher Anzeiger, 359
Milan, 192, 305, 306, 377
Ministry of Education, 375
Minne, 120
"Moderns," 55, 99
Moissi, Alexander, 125, 173, ff.
Molotov, Viacheslav M., 376
Mombert, Alfred, 97
Monod, Olga, 165
Morisse, Paul, 274
Morocco, 197
Morris, William, 119
Moscow, 272, 331, 338
Moses, 424
Moussorgsky, Modeste, 44
Mozart, Wolfgang Amadeus, 162 236, 369
Munch, Edward, 44, 118
Münchener Neueste Nachrichten, 386
Munich, 111, 178, 226, 358, 361, 363, 386, 403, 413, 414, 415, 418, 429
Musée Rath, 240
Mussolini, Benito, 175, 226, 305, 306, 308, 342, 343 ff., 362, 377, 378, 383, 402, 413, 414, 415

NAPLES, 340, 342
Napoleon, 51, 52
Narcotics, 301
Nation (London), 395

National Library of Vienna, 354, 386
National Socialist Chamber of Writers, 374
National Socialists, 64, 179, 186, 359, 360, 362, 365, 366, 367, 373, 374, 375, 376, 377, 382, 386, 388, 390, 401, 403
Nationalism, 410
Nazi Chamber of Music, 373
Neue Freie Presse, 99, 101, 103, 106, 107, 109, 246
Neue Rundschau, 39
"New Order," 406
New York, 188
Nietzsche, Elizabeth Förster, 165
Nietzsche, Friedrich Wilhelm, 39, 40, 44
Nightingale, Florence, 209
Nijinsky, Vaslav, 178
1914, 214, 224, 225, 226, 233, 235, 240, 243, 257, 432, 436
1939, 224, 225, 227, 240, 429, 432
"93 German Intellectuals," 241
Nobel, Alfred, 209
  Peace Prize, 273
  Prize, 209
Non si sa mai, 175
Nuremberg Jewish Laws, 186

Oblomovism, 333
Oehler, August (pseudonym), 55
Opera, 37, 42
  Dresden, 111
  Imperial, 19, 33, 35
Orgies, 313
Orient, 185
Ostend, 219

Pacific Ocean, 190
Palais Royal, 132
Palestine, 103
Palm-reading, 301
Pan, 55, 56
Panama, 190
  Canal, 190
Pan-German, 259
Panslavists, 199
Paracelism, 301
Paris, 10, 102, 126, ff., 192, 201, 212, 271, 342, 380
Parliament, 429
Pascoli, Giovanni, 140
Peace Conference, 259
"Peace in our time," 226

Péguy, Charles, 135
P. E. N. Club, 302, 396, 432
Pernambuco, 400
Pervert Balls (of Berlin), 313
Philadelphia, 189, 190, 327
Philharmonic, 19, 25, 54, 257, 296
Pirandello, Luigi, 175, 176
Poerio, Carlo, 245
Poincaré, Henri, 211
Pointillists, 44
Poland, 246, 329, 433
Polish Corridor, 429
Popolo d' Italia, 308
Portrait of the Artist as a Young Man, A, 275
Post-war Period, 299, 302
Prague, 377
Prater, 18, 20, 61
Prostitution in Europe, 83
Proust, Marcel, 200
Prussia, 226
Prussian State Theater, 169
Psychoanalysis, 68
Puberty, 67
Putsch (German), 361
  (Vienna), 297

Ragaz, Leonhard, Pastor, 274
Rapallo, 309, 310
Raskolnikov, 332
Rathenau, Walter, 179 ff., 243, 255, 309, 310, 311
Ravel, Maurice, 347
Red Cross, 239
"Red Guard," 297
Red Square, 331
Redl Affair, 205
Reger, Max, 99, 203, 368
Reich, 112, 179, 205
Reich Chamber of Music, 377
Reichenhall, 294, 359
Reichstag Fire, 364, 365, 367
Reichswehr, 359, 360
Reinhardt, Max, 23, 112, 125, 204, 346
Renan, Ernest, 203
Renoir, Pierre Auguste, 134
Revue de France, 39
Rhenish Separatists, 358
Rhineland, 302, 306
Rilke, Rainer Maria, 38, 46, 52, 53, 97, 98, 132, 139, ff., 158, 163, 166, 236, 243, 266
Rimbaud, Arthur, 44, 46
Ringstrasse, 14, 18

Risorgimento, 245
Rodin, Auguste, 146, ff., 212
Rolland, Romain, 135, 163, 200 ff.,
    211, 237, 239 ff., 255, 264 ff., 271,
    272, 279, 347, 379, 411
Romains, Jules, 135, 199, 212, 327
Rome, 344
Rops, 44, 120
Rosé Quartet, 17
Rosenbach, Dr., 327
Rosenkavalier, 178, 368, 369, 374
Rotterdam, 229
Rouen, 212
Royal Theater (in Berlin), 169
Rudolf, Crown Prince, 216, 218
Rumania, 205
Rüschlikon, 279
Russia, 206, 207, 213, 233, 259, 267,
    283, 302, 328 ff., 333, 336, 337,
    340, 378, 418
Russell, Archibald, G. B., 159

SAAR, 302
Sacco, Nicola, 344
Sacher's, 21, 172, 176
Sadoul, Captain, 271
Sainte-Beuve, Charles Augustin,
    100
St. Petersburg, 211, 332
Saint Sulpice, 132
Salome, 373
Salzburg, 259, 286, 287, 293, 304,
    321, 346, 347, 354, 358, 371, 377,
    378, 379, 380, 384, 387, 388, 403,
    404
Salzburg Festival, 346, 370
Salzkammergut, 194
San Francisco, 190
Sanchschak, 235
Sarajevo, 213
Scala, La, 377
Schickele, René, 199 277 302
Schiller, Johann Christoph Fried-
    rich von, 39
Schlenther, Paul, 170
Schneider, 63
Schneider-Creusot, 197, 205
Schnitzler, Arthur, 23, 46, 47, 48,
    324, 347
Schönberg, Arnold, 23, 44, 45, 301
Schönbrunn, 14
Schönerer, Georg, 64
Schubert, Franz, 42, 353
Schuster & Löffler, 97

Schutzbund, 384, 387
"Secession," 44
Seipel, Ignaz, 259, 383
Sephardim, 428
Serbia, 197, 205, 218, 219, 221
Shadowy Waters, The, 157
Shakespeare, William, 48, 235, 433
Shaw, George Bernard, 380, 393,
    394, 395
Silberne Saiten, 98
Silent Woman, The, 368, 372, 374
Sixtus, Prince of Parma, 260
Social Democrats, 108, 235, 297, 307,
    359, 363, 377, 383, 384, 386
Socialist International, 199
Socialist Party, 60, 198
Socialists, 271, 344, 386
Society, 113
Somnambulism, 301
Sonnenthal, Adolf, 15, 23, 42
Sorrento, 338, 341, 342, 390
Southampton, 197, 397
Spain, 384, 398
Spanish Civil War, 205, 396
Speidel, Ludwig, 100
Spengler, Oswald, 185
Spiritualism, 301
Stalin, Joseph, 336, 376
Starhemberg, Prince, 383, 384
Stein, Baron vom, 362
Steiner, Rudolf, 115, 116
Stefansdom, 14, 102
Stifter, Adalbert, 23
Stinnes, Hugo, 312
Stockholm, 432
Strassburg, 195
Strauss, Oscar, 23
Strauss, Richard, 38, 44, 99, 165,
    347, 368 ff.
Streicher, Julius, 63
Streicher Guard, 375
Strindberg, Johann August, 39, 44
Stringa, Albert, 305
Studio, 39
Sturm-Abteilung, 360, 405, 406
Suarez, 132, 135
Suttner, Berta von, 208, 244
Sweden, 257
Switzerland, 239, 257, 258, 271, 273,
    278, 282, 326, 377
Symons, Arthur, 157

TARNOW, 246 ff.,
Telemann, 203
Teltscher, Josef, 353

Temps Le, 99, 100
Tenth Symphony, 178
Texas, 400
Theater Guild, 318
Théâtre du Peuple, 201
Theosophy, 301
Thersites, 167, 253, 318
Three Masters, 212, 317
Tide of Fortune, The, 322
Till Eulenspiegel, 369
Times, The, 99
Times Square, 188
Tirano, 327
"To Friends Abroad," 238, 245
Tolstoy and Dostoievsky, 215
Tolstoy, Leo, 203, 329, 330, 333, 334, 336
Toscanini, Arturo, 368, 411
Tours, 210
Trotsky, Leon, 271, 333
Tsar, 221, 225
Turkey, 197

Ulysses, 275
United States, 396
Unruh, Fritz von, 273
University, 14, 23, 25, 65, 92

VALÉRY, PAUL, 43, 50, 135, 140, 200, 347, 379
Van der Velde, 120
Van der Stappen, 121, ff.
Van Loon, Hendrik Willem, 347
Vanzetti, Bartolomeo, 344
Vaterländische Front, 403
Vehmic Murderers, 358
Venice, 306
Verdi, Guiseppe, 369
Verhaeren, Emile, 120 ff., 124, 134, 138, 140, 146, 154, 158, 181, 190, 195, 201, 202, 204, 212, 214, 218, 219
Verklärte Nacht, 301
Verlaine, Paul, 44, 119, 131
Versailles, 225, 302
Verwandelte Komediant, Der, 171
Victoria Station, 380, 390
Victoria, Queen, 211
"Victorious Peace," 260
Vienna, 12, 14, 17, 18, 19, 20, 22, 23, 24, 33, 43, 44, 46, 47, 56, 59, 63, 77, 88, 96, 100, 101, 103, 104,

112, 160, 184, 192, 196, 209, 211, 217, 223, 236, 257, 292, 297, 377, 384, 385, 387, 389, 391, 401, 402, 404, 405, 406, 407, 420, 421
University of, 420
Vigo, 397
Viking Press, The, 321
Vildrac, Charles, 135, 199, 379
Vogel, Dr., 164
Völkische Beobachter, 359
Volpone, 173

WAGNER, Cosima, 165, 351
Richard, 165, 203, 235, 369
Wallmann, Margarete, 386
Walpole, Hugh, 393
Walter, Bruno, 203, 347, 368
"Wandervögel," 299
War Archives, 229, 236, 247
War of 1866, 209
Warsaw, 329
Wassermann, Jacob, 243, 347
"Watch on the Rhine," 232
Wedekind, Franz, 45
Weise von Liebe und Tod, 145, 163
Wells, H. G., 347, 380, 393, 394
Weltfreund, 199
Werfel, Franz, 199, 274, 325, 347, 367
Werthers Leiden, 305
West End (Berlin), 112
Westerland, 308, 311
White Russian, 337
Whitman, Walt, 42, 120, 138, 165, 187, 239
Wilbrandt, Adolf, 45
Wilhelm, Emperor, 179, 181, 221, 232, 235, 280, 297, 363, 373
Wilhelmstrasse, 232
Wilson, Woodrow, 280, 298, 401
Wittelsbach, 363
Wolter, Charlotte, 16, 42
Wolves, The, 201
Workers' House, 384
World War, The, 160, 185, 270, 412
World War (First), 192, 257, 399
World War (Second), 224, 227, 257, 396

YASNAYA Polyana, 333, 334
Yeats, W. B., 157, 158
Yoga, 301

ZABERN Affair, 205
Zeppelin, 195
Zimmerwald (Congress of), 271
Zionism, 103, 106
Zionists, 428

Zita, Empress, 284
Zola, Emile, 44, 70
Zukunft, Die, 55, 179
Zurich, 268, 273, 274, 278
Zurich Stadttheater, 256